YOUR LABRADOR RETRIEVER PUPPY

SECOND EDITION

TERRY ALBERT, DEB ELDREDGE, DVM, AND DON AND BARB IRONSIDE

ALPHA

A member of Penguin Random House LLC

Publisher: *Mike Sanders*

Associate Publisher: *Billy Fields*

Managing Editor: *Lori Cates Hand*

Development Editor: *Christy Wagner*

Designer: *William Thomas*

Compositor: *Ayanna Lacey*

Proofreader: *Lisa Starnes*

Indexer: *Brad Herriman*

Second American Edition, 2016
Published in the United States by DK Publishing
6081 E. 82nd Street, Indianapolis, Indiana 46250

Copyright © 2016 Dorling Kindersley Limited
A Penguin Random House Company
20   10 9   8
008-291434-May/2016

ISBN: 9781465451064
Library of Congress Catalog Card Number: 2015951838

Note: This publication contains the opinions and ideas of its author(s). It is intended to provide helpful and informative material on the subject matter covered. It is sold with the understanding that the author(s) and publisher are not engaged in rendering professional services in the book. If the reader requires personal assistance or advice, a competent professional should be consulted. The author(s) and publisher specifically disclaim any responsibility for any liability, loss, or risk, personal or otherwise, which is incurred as a consequence, directly or indirectly, of the use and application of any of the contents of this book.

DK books are available at special discounts when purchased in bulk for sales promotions, premiums, fundraising, or educational use. For details, contact: DK Publishing Special Markets, 1450 Broadway, 8th floor New York, New York 10018 or SpecialSales@dk.com.

Printed and bound in the United States

This book is dedicated to my friend and mentor, Liz Palika. Thank you so much for your friendship and inspiration over the 25 years we've known each other. —Terry

CONTENTS AT A GLANCE

MONTHS 1-2

The Littermate   2

Your puppy grows rapidly these first 2 months. Her mother provides most of her care, and she and the rest of the litter teach your pup the skills she needs to know.

MONTH 3

Your Puppy Comes Home   20

You choose your pup this month and then go home and prepare for his arrival. When you have him home, you begin crate and housetraining, get him his vaccines, and more.

MONTH 4

Finding Her Way   60

Teething begins month 4. You start socializing her to other dogs and people, introduce obedience training, and have fun playing together.

MONTH 5

The Rebel   90

Your puppy becomes more independent this month. His vaccines are finished, socialization continues, and obedience training and household rules are reinforced.

MONTH 6

Full Speed Ahead   124

She starts to look less like a puppy and more like a growing dog this month, and injuries are likely as she romps and runs. Expect some shedding and behavior issues.

MONTH 7

The Silly Tweenager   154

At 7 months, your pup can be spayed or neutered. Exercise is important, and training continues, further cementing the bond between the two of you.

Adolescence

186

Teenagers are a challenge, as you learn this month. Watch for and treat coat problems if they develop, and help her learn concentration and self-control.

In Search of a Leader

214

Your pup begins to develop mature male or female physical characteristics this month. Expect him to test your authority; be sure to react kindly and fairly.

In Transition

248

You can begin comparing your puppy to the breed standard this month. You'll see some teenage behavior regression as you prepare for off-leash control.

Putting Your Lab to Work

278

At 11 months, he's almost an adult. You can more easily travel with him now and get him involved with dog sports. You also can work on obedience and tricks.

Your Lab Grows Up

312

More physical changes occur this month, and she goes in for her annual checkup. Continue training and exercise, and from here out, enjoy your best friend!

A	Glossary	333
B	Body Condition Assessment	337
C	Household and Yard Hazards	341
D	Resources	347
	Index	351

INTRODUCTION

Labrador Retrievers have been the most popular dog breed in America for more than 25 years, and with good reason. Bred to work at a hunter's side and patiently wait long hours for the chance to retrieve a bird, these same qualities make Labs a great family dog. These dogs are trainable, eager to please, and want nothing more than to spend time with you, whether you're throwing a ball or just relaxing by an evening fire. Never much of a watchdog, a Lab loves everyone he meets.

Labrador Retrievers are high-energy dogs who love to work, which makes them excellent competitors in a variety of dog sports. These same traits make them ideal dogs for helping people in many different roles: assistance dogs for the physically disabled, search-and-rescue dogs, therapy dogs, and more.

All this talent and energy bundled up in a small puppy requires loving care, guidance, and discipline so he'll grow up to be a well-behaved member of society. This book helps you reach that goal and have lots of fun with your Labrador Retriever pup along the way.

In This Book

Each chapter in this book covers a month of your Lab puppy's development. You learn what you can expect from your pup and how to deal with each stage of growth. It's easy to be overwhelmed by the challenges of raising a Lab puppy, and we hope this book helps you through the first 12 months of this big adventure!

First you find out what goes on at the breeder's and how her care affects your puppy's future. You get tips on choosing the right breeder and puppy for your family, and you learn how to prepare for his arrival and make him comfortable in his new home.

Then we explain the various aspects, month by month, of your puppy's physical development, health care, nutritional needs, grooming, socialization, behavior, and training. And we end each chapter with a special section dedicated to building your friendship with your new Labrador Retriever puppy—because after all, isn't that one of the most important things?

Although no two Lab puppies mature at exactly the same rate, the process is the same. If your pup grows faster or slower, it doesn't necessarily mean something is wrong. He'll catch up or slow down and turn out wonderfully normal.

The Extras

Throughout the book, we share additional information to help you raise your Labrador Retriever puppy. Here's what to look for:

DOG TALK
These sidebars offer definitions of words you might not know.

HAPPY PUPPY
Look here for ideas on raising a happy and contented puppy.

TIPS AND TAILS
These sidebars share hints and helpful advice on dealing with the challenges of puppy raising.

Acknowledgments

It takes a village to raise a Lab, and it took a village to help me write this book. Special thanks to my advisers, Barb and Don Ironside and Deb Eldredge, DVM, who offered valuable input and carefully reviewed every word. Also thank you to the many breeders, trainers, and other experts who shared their knowledge and experience with me: Susan Eberhardt; Pat Hastings; Pat Schaap; Sarbit Singh, DVM; Heather Luis; Nina Mann; Melanie Montiero; Lorna O'Connor of CCI; Fran Scarinci; Christine Rinaldi; Cary Saunders; and Nancy Shahan-Wall. —Terry

	SOCIAL	BEHAVIOR	TRAINING	PHYSICAL	HEALTH
MONTH 1	Breeder starts socialization		Littermates and mother teach appropriate canine behavior	Rapid growth	
MONTH 2	Breeder starts socialization		Littermates and mother teach appropriate canine behavior	Rapid growth	
MONTH 3	Socialization at home with new owner and other pets	Fear-imprint period	Begin house- and crate training	Rapid growth	1st DHPP vaccine
MONTH 4	Socialization at home with new owner and other pets	Teething begins—heavy chewing period	Enroll in puppy class	Rapid growth	2nd DHPP vaccine
MONTH 5		Teething begins—heavy chewing period	Ready for basic commands	Switch to adult food	3rd DHPP and rabies vaccines
MONTH 6			Ready for basic commands	Switch to adult food	
MONTH 7			Enroll in basic obedience class	Moderate growth	Sexual maturity
MONTH 8	Socialization in public		Enroll in basic obedience class	Moderate growth	Sexual maturity
MONTH 9	Socialization in public	Adult teeth are in—chewing continues	Enroll in basic obedience class	Moderate growth	
MONTH 10		Adult teeth are in—chewing continues	Ready for more advanced training		
MONTH 11			Ready for more advanced training	Slow growth—reaches adult size	
MONTH 12 AND BEYOND			Ready for more advanced training	Slow growth—reaches adult size	Annual vaccinations and checkup

MONTHS
1-2

The Littermate

Welcome to the first 2 months of your Labrador Retriever puppy's life! Even before your puppy is born, hundreds of outside factors influence her future health and happiness.

In this chapter, we follow a litter's physical and mental development from birth through the first 8 weeks. You learn how the mother dog's health care, nutrition, and temperament affect her puppies. You also discover that the breeder plays a crucial role before, during, and after birth. The breeder also starts socializing the puppies before they go to their new homes.

PHYSICAL DEVELOPMENT

A Lab puppy is totally dependent on her mother during the first 2 weeks of life, when she's unaware of anything in her world except food and the warmth of her mom and littermates. But by the time she's 8 weeks old, she'll have gone through several important developmental stages and be independent enough to leave the litter and move on to her new home.

At Birth

Lab puppies average 12 to 20 ounces at birth. Their weight depends on how many puppies are in the litter, with bigger litters producing smaller puppies. Weight can also vary from puppy to puppy within the litter. Size doesn't matter at this point; the smallest puppy can grow up to be the largest adult, and vice versa.

The average litter size for Labs is 8 to 10 puppies, although it can range from a single puppy to as many as 16. With a large litter, the breeder spends more time ensuring each pup gets a turn to nurse. The breeder also may have to supplement the mother's milk with hand-feeding.

As each pup is born, the mother severs the umbilical cord and removes the amniotic sac that surrounds the puppy. At birth, puppies have an incomplete nervous system and don't move spontaneously on their own, so it's up to Mom to get them started. She licks them to make them breathe, stimulate blood circulation, and prompt them to eliminate.

The breeder supervises the birthing process and removes the amniotic sac if Mom is busy with other puppies. She also cleans and ties off the stump where the umbilical cord was attached. She then puts an ID collar of sorts—usually rickrack or ribbon—on each pup. Each collar is a different color so the breeder can keep track of each puppy and his or her development.

For at least the first 2 weeks, the *whelping box* is kept in a quiet, private place. Mom doesn't want other dogs around and won't welcome canine intruders. Too much commotion is stressful for her and her puppies, and she'll burn precious calories fussing and protecting her babies. She'll eventually calm down as she gets used to her duties. After the puppies' eyes open, the whelping box can be moved to a more stimulating environment so the pups can start getting used to household sights and sounds.

When first born, some Lab puppies have ridges in their coat that look like corduroy fabric, or like someone ran a comb though their fur. This is from being squished together in the womb and goes away almost immediately. Some breeders think it's a predictor of a thick, healthy coat later in life.

When the puppies are 3 or 4 days old, their blood is capable of clotting, and some breeders will have their veterinarians remove the front *dewclaws*. This used to be standard procedure for many breeds, but it's not necessary and is now seldom practiced. Some people feel removing the dewclaws is important for hunting dogs because the dewclaws get snagged and torn in the brush while dogs are working. Others feel that dogs use their dewclaws for holding onto things, such as when they're chewing on something, and for climbing.

DOG TALK

The **whelping box** is a large nesting area where the mother gives birth to her puppies. It often has a ledge around the sides so Mom doesn't accidentally crush a puppy against the wall. The **dewclaw** is a vestigial toe and toenail partway up a dog's front legs.

The period between birth and 2 weeks is called the neonatal period. Puppies sleep 90 percent of this time and eat the remaining 10 percent. They're born with a sucking/rooting reflex so they can nurse; this is more pronounced when they're 24 to 48 hours old. But by 4 days old, this reflex disappears and the puppies nurse on their own.

At birth, a puppy has underdeveloped, primitive senses of touch and smell, and orientation to objects. She can't see, hear, or move away from stimuli yet; if something hurts, she'll squeal and wiggle in distress. By 2 days old, she's able to move on her own toward Mom and her littermates and compete for a place to nurse. The breeder places a surface such as fleece in the whelping box so she and the other pups can dig in their feet, which helps them get around.

A newborn's eyes and ears are closed. Her eyes might blink as a reflex, but she can't see yet because her retina isn't fully developed. She sleeps with her head tucked to her chest. During the first week, she and the other puppies move a lot in their sleep—kicking, whimpering, and jerking as they start to exercise their muscles. By 6 to 10 days of age, their sleep is quieter and their waking time is more active.

At 8 to 10 days, she and the other puppies should be double their birth weights. By 7 or 8 days, her front legs can support her weight and she'll start to stand. Within a day or two, her rear limbs are able to support her pelvis. By 10 to 12 days old, she'll be walking.

A Lab pup's eyes and ears open at about the same time as she begins walking. At 10 to 14 days, her eyelids open. She can't see anything but shadows at this point, and blinking is still a reflex rather than a voluntary reaction. At the same time, her ear canals open, she starts to hear, and she'll startle at noise.

Weeks 2 and 3

Days 14 to 21 mark what's called the transitional period. During this time, the puppies' senses and motor skills are still poorly developed, but they are able to explore more of their surroundings. A sure sign of good neurological development at this time is a puppy who, when set down, extends her back legs in anticipation of reaching the ground.

The mother Lab is now producing peak amounts of milk, and the puppies' suckling is strong and well developed. They're growing fast in these last days prior to *weaning* and weigh approximately 2½ to 3 pounds and gain about 1 pound during this week.

DOG TALK

Weaning is the process of gradually changing a puppy's diet from mother's milk to solid food.

Mom continues to clean up after her puppies until they're 3 or 4 weeks old and then the breeder takes over. By keeping their potty area clean, the breeder starts the housetraining process. At about 18 days, the pups move to a corner of the whelping box to relieve themselves. By 21 days, they've established a group elimination area. The breeder enlarges their living area to take advantage of the fact that the puppies don't want to sleep and play in their own waste. She might add a wire pen so the pups can leave the whelping box to play, but they're still too young to have the run of a large room.

Around 19 to 21 days, a pup responds to light by moving her head away or blinking. Her hearing also continues to develop, and she'll startle to loud noises. Her sight improves as well, and she becomes more mobile.

When the puppies are 3 weeks old, the socialization period begins and continues until approximately 12 weeks. Positive and negative experiences during this time will affect her behavior for the rest of her life. So to give her the best start possible, the breeder introduces a variety of household sights and sounds, like the television, dishwasher, vacuum cleaner, and radio. She also handles each puppy so they're used to human contact. The puppies also start interacting with each other. They experience a dramatic increase in motor development as they start to chew and explore their surroundings.

Weeks 4 to 6

Labs grow dramatically during this period, and their puppy coats get longer and thicker. The puppies' central nervous systems continue to mature. Even those cute little wagging tails indicate neuromuscular development.

The puppies start to look less like baby rats and more like dogs. At 4 weeks, a Lab pup is a pudgy little lump that doesn't appear to even have legs and weighs roughly 6 or 7 pounds. By 6 weeks, she's found those legs and is making good use of them.

The pups can now orient to sights and sounds around them. The optic nerves mature by 28 days, so the puppies can see more than just shadows. Shapes begin to have meaning. By 30 days, they start to recognize familiar sounds. The ears are fully open at 35 days (5 weeks), and the pups no longer startle to noise as they did when their ears first opened.

At $3\frac{1}{2}$ to 4 weeks, their teeth start to come in, and the pups are able to chew semisolid food for first time. Mom starts to wean her litter now, and the breeder introduces puppy food.

Often the breeder starts feeding the litter outside. The pups naturally wander away from the eating area after the meal to relieve themselves. This helps them learn a routine of eating, eliminating outside, and coming inside. Because of this seemingly simple action, many litters are well on their way to being housetrained before they go to their new homes.

By 4 weeks, puppies need to start eliminating on different surfaces. If a puppy is encouraged to potty on grass, dirt, concrete, and gravel now, she'll be willing to go on various surfaces throughout her life (for example, if she's boarded in a concrete kennel run). Both males and females now squat when they relieve themselves.

A host of new behaviors start when a Lab puppy discovers she has teeth. She now has the tools she'll use to explore her world, and everything that fits in her mouth is fair game. She'll chew dog beds, towels, chair legs, anything that moves … and anything that doesn't. She'll carry things around and even tug on your pants leg.

Her interactions with her littermates change dramatically, too. Puppies follow each other around play-fighting, guarding their toys, and growling. She'll compete for food and guard it from the others. She'll shake her head while holding a toy. She'll start to understand how her jaw pressure affects others, learning the critical skill of *bite inhibition*. Play-biting leads to discipline from her littermates as well as from her mother, but it teaches her to communicate without injuring. The mother also disciplines her puppies if they bite her too hard while nursing, which speeds up the weaning process.

DOG TALK

Bite inhibition is a skill a puppy's mother and littermates teach her that helps her control how she uses her teeth. She soon learns to bite hard enough to communicate but not so hard as to injure.

At this age, individual puppies can be taken away from their mom and littermates for short breaks so they get used to being separated. This helps a puppy feel less frightened when she leaves her family to go to her new home.

Weeks 6 to 8

By this time, a litter of Labs is a lot of fun. They start to gang up on each other, wrestle, sniff each other's faces and butts, and learn to recognize each other. Puppies begin actively hunting and playing around now, too, and they can be seen pouncing on bugs and butterflies. They also begin play-mounting each other.

At 6 weeks, a Lab puppy weighs 10 or 11 pounds, with males being heavier.

The puppy's vision is not completely developed yet, but as the retina matures, she can follow objects with her eyes and respond to light. She can recognize shapes, so the breeder starts exposing her to other animals, like cats, rabbits, and birds. It's enough for the pup to get acquainted with the sight, sounds, and smells of other animals right now. Too much interaction isn't safe for either species.

Now also is an excellent time to introduce the puppies to people of various sizes and shapes. A hat or umbrella dramatically changes what the puppy sees, even on the same person she just met. Research has shown that a puppy who has met a large variety of people, places, and things when very young accepts new and unusual things much more easily throughout her life. By 8 weeks, a puppy is mature enough to learn and remember new things, and it's time to start some basic training, especially housetraining.

At 10 to 12 pounds, she's also getting a bit hefty to carry around, but until she's had all her inoculations, the breeder carries her whenever she leaves home. You should continue this practice when she arrives at your home. When she's inside, she should happily follow her new friends, but until she's able to walk nicely on a leash, let Mom or Dad carry the pup when you go out. Lab puppies are too heavy for small children to carry, so don't let kids drag Puppy around by her armpits or collar.

HAPPY PUPPY

To carry your Lab puppy, with her facing sideways, scoop under her front legs from the side with one arm and over her rear with the other. Steady her hind end as you lift by holding up her legs while you grasp the front of her body slightly higher. Cradle her against your body so she feels secure and isn't likely to wiggle free.

HEALTH

A diligent breeder does her best to produce healthy Labrador Retrievers. Even before the mother is bred, the breeder takes steps to prevent health problems in future puppies. When the puppies arrive, she monitors both the mother and the litter to ensure they all thrive and remain healthy.

Health Clearances the Parents Should Have

Careful pretesting for inheritable defects helps ensure your puppy lives a long and healthy life. In some cases, an affected dog never shows symptoms but is still a carrier of the genes that can pass along the defect. If two carriers are bred to each other, a percentage of the puppies will develop the disorder.

The breeder should have her veterinarian conduct the following tests before the dogs are bred:

Brucellosis: This is a bacterial disease causing reproductive problems in both male and female dogs. Therefore, both parents should be tested before breeding. Brucellosis causes stillborn puppies or pups who die within a few days of birth. Affected dogs should be spayed or neutered.

Hip dysplasia: Hip dysplasia is a crippling disease that affects many Labs. Symptoms often don't appear until a dog is older, when arthritis begins to affect her movement. At 2 years old, a Lab's hips are mature enough to be x-rayed to identify the condition. The x-rays are sent to the Orthopedic Foundation for Animals (OFA) or PennHIP for grading. OFA rates the hips from excellent to severely dysplastic. The hip grades of Excellent, Good, and Fair are within normal limits. PennHIP uses a percentile rating, comparing a dog's hips against others of the same breed. A rating in the fiftieth percentile and above is considered normal.

Elbow dysplasia: Like hip dysplasia, elbow dysplasia affects many Labs and also can be identified through x-rays when a dog reaches 2 years old. OFA only grades affected dogs, designating Grade I through III, to explain the level of degenerative joint disease associated with elbow dysplasia.

Progressive retinal atrophy (PRA): PRA is an incurable disease that causes blindness in Labs. PRA often has late onset in Labs, at about 5 to 8 years, which is well past the first time a dog is usually bred. Although PRA was once widespread, in recent years, a genetic test has been developed to identify affected dogs. The test can be done at any age, which helps breeders decide which dogs should be bred, and results are registered with OFA. Some breeders state that their puppies are "clear (normal) by parentage." This means two clear parents were bred to each other so the puppies could not have inherited the gene. Therefore, they don't need to be tested.

Retinal dysplasia: Currently, there's no genetic test available to identify this abnormal development in the eye's retina, so breeders have their dogs' eyes tested annually and register the results with OFA. While examining the eyes, the veterinary ophthalmologist also checks for cataracts. Breeders also have each puppy checked at 7 or 8 weeks old for retinal folds, which can be an indicator of retinal dysplasia.

Tricuspid valve dysplasia: This causes congestive heart failure. Dogs are tested at 1 year old by a veterinary cardiologist who listens for a heart murmur or other abnormalities. If the cardiologist has any doubts, he recommends a Doppler reading to confirm the condition. Some breeders automatically have the Doppler reading done for all their breeding dogs to eliminate any doubt. Results are registered with the OFA.

Centronuclear myopathy (CNM): CNM is an inherited condition that results in weak muscles and causes the dog to have difficulty walking. A genetic test identifies the disease and is administered at 1 year old. All breeding dogs should be tested. The testing facility provides a certificate saying whether the dog is clear (normal), a carrier, or affected.

Exercise-induced collapse: This is an inherited condition that appears in some young Labs (at about 1 year old) that causes them to appear rubber-legged, have difficulty walking, or even collapse after a short period of strenuous exercise. A genetic test is available for the disease, and the testing facility provides a certificate saying whether the dog is clear (normal), carrier, or affected.

TIPS AND TAILS

Many Labs don't show symptoms of a genetically inherited problem until they're adults. In Month 12, we go into further detail about these conditions and their effects on an adult dog's long-term health.

The Mother Dog's Care

Well before the puppies are born, the mother dog needs extra food and care because her health directly affects that of her brood. She needs to be in optimum physical condition when her litter is born.

Mom won't want to leave the nest when she's getting ready to whelp and for the first day after giving birth, but she needs to eat because the puppies need nutrition. Producing milk for a large litter of puppies uses a tremendous amount of energy. The breeder feeds her in the whelping box every 4 or 5 hours so she produces enough milk for her litter. The breeder also takes the mother out for a short walk several times a day so she can relieve herself and have a break.

The mother gets most of the breeder's attention during the first few days. A vet examines the *bitch* within 24 hours after whelping to be sure there are no retained placentas or unborn puppies. He also examines her milk to be sure it looks healthy and safe for the pups.

DOG TALK

A female dog is called a **bitch,** and the mother of the litter is referred to as the *dam.* A male is called a *dog,* and the father of the litter is the *sire.*

The breeder cleans the bitch's nipples and mammary glands after each nursing session. This keeps bacteria from causing her pups to get sick and also protects Mom from mastitis (an infection of the mammary glands) and other problems. The breeder takes Mom's temperature daily to be sure she isn't developing any delivery-related complications. One problem that can arise is pyometra, a uterine infection. If it's a small litter, Mom can have too much milk, which is very painful and can cause mastitis. The breeder also watches for signs of metritis, a bacterial uterine infection that can develop immediately after giving birth. Eclampsia, another postwhelping ailment, is caused by a calcium deficiency.

An unhealthy mother can pass an infection to her litter, and the veterinarian can't give her most antibiotics for fear of passing a toxic dose to her puppies through her milk. If an antibiotic is necessary, the puppies have to be removed from their mother and hand-fed.

TIPS AND TAILS

When you visit the litter, the mother might not appear as healthy or pretty as you expected. After her puppies are weaned, the mother dog *blows coat* and for several weeks, sheds so much of her undercoat and outer coat that patches of skin might show. Her tail appears more like a whip than a typical Lab tail. Even if she was in excellent shape when the pups were born, she's undergone extreme physical and hormonal changes during pregnancy, birth, and nursing. As her milk dries up and she finishes nursing, her coat slowly returns to normal, her mammary glands shrink to normal size, her hormones stabilize, and her body gradually returns to its original condition.

Breeder Vigilance

Although individual breeders might handle some of the details differently, they still play a significant role in the care of the mother Lab and her litter. The breeder's first priority during whelping is to assist with delivery. She cleans and stimulates a puppy if Mom is busy with the others. She also ensures the pups start nursing. If there's a lengthy delay between puppies, she might have to transport Mom to the vet for a caesarean (surgical) delivery.

After whelping, the breeder cleans the whelping box and continues to clean it daily while the pups are growing. If bacteria and waste are allowed to accumulate, the health of the puppies and their mother is jeopardized.

The mother goes through tremendous emotional and physical stress during the early weeks after her litter is born, and even the nicest female can get a little testy. To avoid upsetting her, the breeder keeps visitors and commotion to a minimum. Overhandling the puppies also upsets the dam, and an upset mother could kill or injure her brood.

Observing the mother and her litter, the breeder ensures Mom bonds with her puppies and is caring for them. She checks daily to see that everyone—Mom and the puppies—has bright and clear eyes, no runny noses, nor any other signs of disease.

The breeder also weighs each puppy daily so she can verify they're all gaining weight and getting enough food. They should double their weights in the first week. If they aren't growing according to plan, the breeder must figure out if the mother doesn't have enough milk, if she has an infection, or if something else is going on.

One of the biggest health risks for newborns is exposure to parvovirus. The virus lasts in the environment for a year or more, and a person or an animal can pick it up on their feet simply by walking in the grass. To protect the litter, the breeder takes precautions when anyone enters the house. Family and guests are asked to take off their shoes before coming indoors, and visitors are asked to wear clean clothes and wash their hands when they arrive. These measures are continued until the pups have all left for their new homes.

When Puppy Problems Occur

If a puppy is fussy, she's usually cold, hungry, or in pain. The breeder needs to figure out what might be the problem because it could be a life-threatening situation.

Too cold: Newborn puppies have very little fat, and their blood vessels aren't developed enough to retain heat on their own. Therefore, keeping the litter warm is the breeder's highest priority during the first weeks. Nestling with Mother and their littermates keeps the pups warm, and the breeder often provides a heat lamp. If Mom leaves the nest for even a few minutes, the temperature starts to drop, and the puppies' metabolisms slow. If this goes on too long, the pups can become weak and can't nurse or digest food. By 2 weeks old, the puppies can better regulate their temperature and don't have to sleep in a pile to keep warm.

Navel infection: The mother severs the pup's umbilical cord with her teeth, but if she cuts too close, the pup's navel area can get infected. To prevent this, the breeder cleans and disinfects each pup's navel and applies an antibiotic ointment.

Fading puppy syndrome: A seemingly healthy puppy may fail to gain weight and gradually fade, acting listless and losing interest in nursing. If the breeder can identify the cause, she can take steps to save the puppy. Some causes are cold temperatures, not getting enough milk, or birth defects. If the mother was in poor health when the pups were born, she might not be able to produce enough healthy milk, which often contributes to this problem.

Swimmer puppy: A puppy who doesn't stand up by 10 days old and start walking soon after is called a *swimmer*. A swimmer's legs will splay out sideways, and she'll use a pedaling motion to propel herself around on her tummy. The condition is more likely to affect large or overweight Lab puppies and may be caused by delayed development or muscle weakness. If allowed to continue, the puppy's rib cage flattens out and the condition becomes permanent. The breeder must step in and get the puppy up on her feet several times a day. Putting the pup on carpet or other rough surface gives her traction. With help, most puppies make a complete recovery.

Hernia: A small bump in the navel or groin area indicates a hernia. A veterinarian can identify the cause and decide if it needs attention. Many hernias close on their own in a few weeks or months. If not, it can be repaired when the dog is spayed or neutered.

NUTRITION

Before she gives birth and while nursing, the mother dog needs extra food and water to produce adequate milk. As the pups grow, she needs still more calories and fat—up to three times her usual amount by the third week. Some breeders feed the mothers high-performance or puppy food to provide extra nutrition. If the mother's diet is still inadequate, her coat will look poor and she'll lose weight. She also might get uncontrollable diarrhea and become dehydrated.

The mother needs a constant supply of fresh water. The moisture supplied in the mother's milk is just as important to the puppies as its nutritional content. Both the mother and her pups can get dehydrated quickly. If she doesn't get enough water, she can't produce enough milk for the puppies. Young puppies process a lot of water through their systems because they need to maintain blood volume and stay hydrated.

By the fourth week, the puppies are ready to wean. At this time, the mother gradually reduces her food intake and her milk starts to dry up.

Mother's Milk

Mother's milk, especially during the first 24 hours after birth, is critical to protecting her puppies from disease. When born, the puppies' immune systems are not yet fully developed. If the mother has been vaccinated regularly, her first milk, called colostrum, contains *antibodies* that provide *passive immunity* from diseases like parvovirus and distemper.

DOG TALK

Antibodies are large proteins the immune system uses to fight disease-causing bacteria and viruses. Through **passive immunity,** the mother transfers protective antibodies to her puppies via her milk, which protect them from disease even though they haven't been vaccinated.

Breeders sometimes have their female tested to determine the amount of antibodies in her system before she's bred. The more antibodies she has, the more she can pass on to her pups. A healthy mother with a strong immune system passes enough antibodies to her puppies in those first 18 hours to protect them until they can develop their own.

Puppies are only able to absorb maternal antibodies during the first 12 to 18 hours of life, so it's essential that they nurse as soon as possible after birth. After that, the mother's milk cannot provide any further protection.

The mother's milk changes as the puppies grow. It supplies all their nutritional needs up until 4 weeks of age, and the milk's energy content increases steadily as the puppies become more active. The fat level in the milk also increases dramatically and then gradually decreases by weaning time. Calcium content increases until the pups are 4 weeks old.

Supplementation

Supplements like vitamins and minerals aren't necessary if the mother is fed a complete food. In fact, excess nutrients can throw things off balance and actually cause problems.

The veterinarian helps the breeder decide what, if any, supplements are needed for the mother. Some breeders feed the mother dog yogurt or cottage cheese to maintain her calcium levels, especially if she has a large litter. If she's not producing enough milk, the pups must be given a homemade or commercially made milk replacer. The breeder feeds the puppies every 3 hours with an eyedropper or feeding tube, or she uses a baby bottle if they're more than 2 weeks old.

Weaning

Weaning starts naturally, initiated by the mother when the puppies are 3½ to 4 weeks old. If the mother doesn't have enough milk, weaning can start earlier. When the puppies' teeth begin coming in, those sharp little teeth hurt mom when the pups nurse, so she lets them nurse less often. She also begins to spend less time in the nest. She'll stand while they nurse and leave when she's tired.

Weaning takes 1½ to 2 weeks. The process starts gradually, and the puppies continue to nurse during the transition. For the first week, they get one meal a day made of puppy food and water, blended until it's almost liquid. The breeder might have them lick the food off the end of her finger to help them understand what to do. The puppies make a terrific mess, lapping it up and stepping in their gruel. A few days later, the breeder increases their meals to two a day. By 5½ weeks, the pups are fully weaned, although some moms let the pups nurse occasionally until they leave for their new homes.

By 6 weeks, the puppy teeth have fully erupted, and the litter is able to chew dry food for first time. Their food no longer needs to be soft and wet.

GROOMING

Even the tiniest puppies need some grooming to keep them clean and healthy. Their mother starts the process, and the breeder often helps out when the puppies are a few weeks old.

Initial Grooming

Mom grooms the litter during the first weeks. Besides keeping them clean, her licking stimulates them so they'll eliminate. She also keeps the whelping box clean. By the time the pups are 4 weeks old, she no longer needs to lick them; they can eliminate on their own.

During weaning (4 to 6 weeks), the breeder cleans the puppies' faces with a wet rag as they finish each meal because the watery gruel tends to get everywhere and can cause puppy acne. Acne in puppies is a surface skin infection, which, if not treated, can spread to the mother when the pups nurse.

Clipping Toenails

Sharp puppy toenails hurt Mom, and scratches can cause her teats to get infected. To avoid this, the breeder starts clipping the puppies' toenails at 4 or 5 weeks. She only needs to trim the front toenails to protect the mother; the rear nails give the puppies traction for walking. By the time your puppy comes to you, she's already used to the clipping procedure.

SOCIAL SKILLS

It's never too early to start a Lab puppy's social education. These early experiences prepare her for the many new people and things she'll encounter when she leaves the comfort of the whelping box.

Socialization Starts at 3 Weeks

When a pup's eyes and ears are open and she's able to stand and walk, she's a sponge, ready to soak up everything she can in her exciting new world. Her experiences for the next 9 or 10 weeks—both positive and negative—will permanently shape her social and psychological development. Breeders and new owners take advantage of this limited window of opportunity to introduce their puppies to hundreds of people, places, and things—a process called socialization.

Socialization will be well under way by the time you bring home your puppy. Invest time during these pivotal weeks of your Lab's development, and you'll reap the rewards for the rest of her life.

TIPS AND TAILS

Researchers have tried to explain how much of a puppy's personality depends on inherited traits and how much is due to her environment, or her early socialization and training—things you can control to a great extent. The conclusion was that about 35 percent of a pup's personality traits, such as shyness, dominance, and other factors, are inherited. This leaves 65 percent of her adult personality to be shaped by her environment, including you, the breeder, and her experiences.

Inadequate socialization during this period results in an adult dog who is fearful, who is possibly aggressive, and who avoids contact with animals and people. An unsocialized dog will likely be turned out in the backyard to live alone, where she'll become increasingly wild and poorly behaved. It's a sad scenario that happens all too often, and one that can easily be prevented.

Puppies Discover Their World

Before 8 weeks of age, a Lab puppy has no fear—she approaches anything and anyone. Next month, she'll be less confident and feel much more vulnerable and hesitant. But for now, mildly frightening experiences are unlikely to permanently affect her personality.

In the 1980s, Pat Schaap, an expert dog trainer, developed "The Rule of Sevens" for socializing a puppy. With her permission, we offer them here:

By the time a puppy is 7 weeks old, he/she should have ...

○ Been on 7 different types of surfaces: carpet, concrete, wood, vinyl, gravel, dirt, wood chips, etc.

○ Played with 7 different types of objects: big balls, small balls, soft fabric toys, fuzzy toys, squeaky toys, paper or cardboard items, metal items, sticks, hose pieces, etc.

○ Been in 7 different locations: front yard, back yard, basement, kitchen, car, garage, laundry room, bathroom, crate, etc.

○ Met and played with 7 new people: children; older adults; someone with a cane, walking stick, or walker; someone in a wheelchair; etc.

○ Been exposed to 7 challenges: climb on a box, climb off a box, go through a tunnel, climb up steps, go down steps, climb over obstacles, play hide and seek, go in and out of a doorway, run around a fence, etc.

○ Eaten from 7 different containers: metal, plastic, cardboard, glass, china, pie plate, frying pan, etc.

○ Eaten in 7 different locations: crate, yard, kitchen, basement, laundry room, living room, bathroom, etc.

It's essential that you and the breeder repeat and build on these early experiences throughout the socialization period and throughout your Labrador Retriever's life.

HAPPY PUPPY

The socialization period from 3 to 12 weeks of age is the most critical period in a puppy's life. A well-socialized puppy grows up to be a dog who learns faster, adapts to new situations with less stress, is confident, and is less likely to develop behavior problems. Although later training and socialization might improve her behavior, it can't completely erase the effects of this early learning period.

Puppy Testing

By the time the puppies are 7 weeks old, you might have met the litter several times and are wondering how to choose which pup is right for you. Many breeders use puppy testing to help evaluate a litter. The breeder knows the pups well, and testing is a way she can evaluate the differences between puppies. It's not a pass-fail test; she simply observes the puppies' reactions to different situations to get an idea of how each pup will react as he or she grows. Puppy testing is usually done at 7 or 8 weeks, before the pups leave for their new homes, before they have been influenced by training, and before the first fear period.

Over the past several decades, many scientists and behaviorists have developed puppy tests. Clarice Rutherford, a scientist and long-time owner of Labrador Retrievers, and veterinarian Dr. David Neal first published a puppy test in 1981. As far back as the 1950s, scientists John Paul Scott and John L. Fuller were evaluating how the early weeks of a puppy's life affect her lifelong personality.

You could ask the breeder if she does puppy testing and if so, if you could watch a session. She knows her bloodlines, has tested other litters, and can compare them to how previous puppies matured. One test doesn't deliver an ironclad verdict on a puppy's temperament; the troublemaker could be tired today, and the shy one might have just woken up from a nap. The breeder knows this.

The tester looks at how the pup interacts with the tester, how willing she seems to be to please, and how quickly she forgives when the tester does something she doesn't like. The tester puts each puppy through a series of short manipulations. To test her willingness to be handled, the breeder restrains her, holds her up off the ground, and gently pinches between her toes. Other tests check her social attraction to people. The breeder asks her to come from a few feet away and then follow. Sensitivity tests explore how she reacts to loud noises, moving objects, and petting. By looking at the total picture of her responses, an experienced tester can come to some conclusions about the pup's personality at this point in her life.

After observing the test, talk to the breeder about the puppy's overall reactions. Is she over the top, jumping on the tester, always active and hyper? Does she resist handling? Is she enthusiastic, outgoing, and eager to please? Is she quiet and thoughtful but willing to participate? Is she shy and fearful? Is she independent and aloof?

Think about what each of these personality traits mean for you. The breeder can help you look at each puppy's behavior to help you select the puppy who will best fit with your expectations, experience, and lifestyle.

BEHAVIOR

A puppy's mother and littermates begin teaching her how to successfully interact with others in her world. What she learns in the first 8 weeks of her life establishes a foundation you can build on when she comes to live with you.

Mom Is First Teacher

A well-behaved, calm mother raises well-behaved, calm puppies. If she's fearful, stressed, or aggressive, she teaches her puppies to react in the same way. She might be somewhat agitated and protective when her puppies are first born, but she should soon settle down and her temperament should return to normal.

As soon as weaning starts, Mom also starts to wean the puppies from her constant attention. She spends less time with them, and they no longer depend solely on her for food. When they are out in the yard, she watches over them as they start to explore, and they discover they don't need her nearby every second.

She gently but firmly disciplines them when they jump on her or bite her ears—this is their first lesson in dog manners from Mom as she teaches them the doggie version of "No." Her growl and bark when she "yells" at her puppies sound ferocious but are all for show. Often another "auntie" dog goes along with the pups, and they learn that another dog also will discipline them if they get out of line.

A puppy learns to appease Mom if she gets annoyed. The pup rolls on her back and shows her belly in submission. She might even release a little urine. The scent reminds the mother dog, "See, I'm just a baby. I'm sorry." This skill also comes in handy when Puppy tries her antics on older or unknown dogs as she grows.

Learning from Littermates

Puppies practice the skills they'll use as adults by playing with their littermates. They learn to hunt, pounce, chase, and get along peacefully with each other. The pups also teach each other how rough they can play and how hard they're allowed to bite. Bite inhibition is one of the most critical skills a puppy needs to learn, and she needs to learn it from her peers. The other puppies quickly forgive her, and they're soon back to romping together.

A puppy who is in a single-puppy litter or is removed from the litter too soon might never learn her dog manners. Her mother and her human family can help make up the difference, but they're no substitute for learning from her siblings.

	SOCIAL	BEHAVIOR	TRAINING	PHYSICAL	HEALTH
MONTH 1			Littermates and mother teach appropriate canine behavior	Rapid growth	
MONTH 2	Breeder starts socialization				
MONTH 3	Socialization at home with new owner and other pets	Fear-imprint period	Begin house- and crate training		1st DHPP vaccine
MONTH 4		Teething begins—heavy chewing period	Enroll in puppy class		2nd DHPP vaccine
MONTH 5			Ready for basic commands	Switch to adult food	3rd DHPP and rabies vaccines
MONTH 6					
MONTH 7	Socialization in public		Enroll in basic obedience class		
MONTH 8				Moderate growth	Sexual maturity
MONTH 9		Adult teeth are in—chewing continues			
MONTH 10			Ready for more advanced training		
MONTH 11				Slow growth—reaches adult size	
MONTH 12 AND BEYOND					Annual vaccinations and checkup

MONTH

3

Your Puppy Comes Home

Your Lab puppy has gotten a good start in life from his mother, littermates, and breeder. Now, at 8 to 12 weeks old, it's time for him to meet you, his new family.

In this chapter, we share the information you need to select the best puppy for your family, prepare for his arrival, and navigate his first few weeks in your home. You learn the ins and outs of puppy-proofing your home, vaccines, health care, feeding, grooming, socializing, and the first steps of training.

CHOOSING YOUR PUPPY

Before you decide on a breeder or visit a litter of pups, make some decisions about the dog who will be part of your family for the next 10 to 14 years. You might have already given some thought to the type of Lab you want. This section offers information that will expand your knowledge and help you make educated decisions when you visit breeders.

Labrador Characteristics

Labrador Retrievers have distinct characteristics, including color. Labs can be yellow, black, or chocolate, and all three colors can appear in the same litter.

Yellow Labs can vary from almost white to a deep fox red color. Most have black pigment around their eyes, around their mouths, and on their noses. Some have brown pigment, and still others have pink. The pink coloring is called Dudley, and although it disqualifies him from dog shows, it has no effect on his health or ability to be a wonderful pet. As your Lab grows up, his black nose may become what's called a *snow nose*, where small patches fade to pink. Again, this has no health consequences.

DOG TALK

There's no such thing as a "golden Lab." There are Golden Retrievers and Labrador Retrievers, but they are not related. Some service dog breeders purposely breed the two together to get a Golden-Lab—a mixed-breed dog. But a purebred Labrador is referred to as yellow, not gold.

Black Labs have a thick, glossy, solid black coat and usually have black noses, black eye rims, black lips, and dark brown eyes. If you see a Lab with light eyes—brown or yellow—that's just a variation and does not signify blindness or other problems.

Chocolate Labs range from light brown to deep chocolate. Their eyes might be brown, gold, or yellow. The nose, eye rims, and around the mouth should also be chocolate, although you'll often see dogs with pink coloring. When you pick out your puppy, he'll still have his puppy coat, which might be lighter. His feet and face will be his true color, which appears when he sheds his puppy coat in a few months. You may have heard the old wives' tale that chocolate Labs are more hyperactive. In reality, there's no difference in the personality of any particular color.

TIPS AND TAILS

At some point in your search for a puppy, you might come across an ad for a "rare silver Labrador." There's much debate as to whether these dogs are actually purebreds or Labs mixed with Weimaraners. Labs don't carry the gene for silver (also referred to as blue) coloring. When dogs are bred purely to produce a certain rare color, it's likely that closely related dogs were bred to each other, and inherited health problems are more likely to show up. Even if the dog has "papers," don't pay premium prices for what's not accepted as a Labrador by the national club or the American Kennel Club.

Labs are often described as either "English style" or "American style." These descriptions refer to their size and build rather than where they come from. "Show" versus "field" is a better description. The English/show style is a shorter, heavier dog with a blocky head. These are the dogs you see at dog shows. The American/field style is usually taller and finer boned and has a less-dense coat. These dogs are bred primarily as hunting dogs and have more energy. Most Labs fall somewhere in between the two extremes. And *all* Labs are energetic and active.

There's minimal difference between the sexes. Dogs are individuals, and sex has little impact on their personalities. Owners report that males are more affectionate and bond better with you, while females are more aloof and independent. Males also mature more slowly than females sometimes.

If you're looking to get more than one Lab, it's generally not a good idea to get two puppies from the same litter. They'll often bond with each other more than their human family, and one will usually be more shy and reserved, relying on his sibling for cues. Two dogs from the same litter—especially females—might not get along because their personalities are too similar. Get your second dog from a litter with different parents, and wait at least 6 months before doing so. Then your puppy will bond to you, not his playmate.

What's Important to You?

When you've decided on a sex and color for your puppy, your next decision is whether you want show or field type. If you plan to hunt with your Labrador, find breeders whose dogs have proven hunting ability. Ask if they hunt with their dogs, if they've obtained hunting titles, and if they've sold puppies to hunting homes. You can ask for references, too. Many show dogs also hunt, and their breeders compete in hunting tests to ensure their dogs are still able to do what they were bred to do.

If you plan to compete in obedience, agility, or other dog sports, take this into consideration. Field dogs often have an intense drive to work and make excellent competitors, but they might be too high-energy for the average pet home. Again, ask breeders if their dogs have competed successfully in these venues.

Registration Papers and Contracts

When you purchase a puppy, you'll encounter some potentially unfamiliar terms and confusing paperwork. Don't feel overwhelmed; this is typical of what all breeders provide. Here are the meanings of some items you'll be dealing with:

Contract: The contract between the breeder and a puppy buyer states the conditions of purchase. For example, the dog may not be bred, the breeder retains co-ownership, or the dog must be returned to the breeder if the owner can no longer keep him at some later date. Another part of the contract guarantees the puppy's health and states under what conditions you can return the pup for a refund.

AKC: This is the American Kennel Club, the main registry in the United States for purebred dogs. The AKC is a nonprofit organization.

Registration papers: Your puppy's breeder will provide AKC papers naming the sire and dam, date of birth, and other information. To register your puppy, you fill in the name you choose for your dog and submit the papers to the AKC.

Limited registration: Most pet puppies are sold on a limited registration, which means if the dog eventually produces puppies, they cannot be registered. The dog is still eligible to compete in most performance events, though. Some breeders convert the registration to full status when the dog reaches 2 years old and the owner provides records of favorable health checks for hips, elbows, and eyes.

TIPS AND TAILS

Are registration papers important? Papers are no guarantee your puppy is a certain quality or the parents were health-tested. But papers do give you the sire's and dam's names, and you can research their pedigree with the AKC. Without papers, you have no guarantee your dog is a purebred Lab. The breeder also might not be careful to breed healthy, correct-looking dogs; follow any code of ethics; or offer any kind of guarantees.

Letting the Breeder Help

Your breeder can help you pick out the right puppy for your family. After all, she has lived with the litter every day for 2 months, and she knows their personalities. By the time the puppies are 10 days old, individual puppies are more active as they try be the first to nurse, while others hang back and need some help. The pups have been interacting since they were just a few weeks old, and the breeder knows who's the bossiest, who loves everyone, and who is the quietest. She's been watching the puppies' activity level and their dominance during play, and she knows who makes the most eye contact with people.

When you interview breeders, tell them what activities you plan to do with your Lab. When the breeder knows what you have in mind, she can pick out the best matching pup for your family. She'll give the more active puppies to owners who want to hunt or compete in agility, for example. If you plan to do therapy visits with your Lab, she'll pick a more laid-back, people-oriented pup.

TIPS AND TAILS
To find a reputable Labrador Retriever breeder, go to the website for the Labrador Retriever Club of America (thelabradorclub.com), the Labrador Retriever Club of Canada (labradorretrieverclub.ca), or the AKC (akc.org). These sites also have listings of local breed clubs and often include a list of breeders.

When you first talk to a breeder about buying a Lab puppy, know that a responsible breeder might ask you to complete a questionnaire and interview to be sure you'd be a good fit for one of her puppies. You all want the same thing—the right puppy in a home he'll stay in for his entire life and grow up happy and loved.

At the same time, you want to ask some questions and make some observations of your own:

- Are the puppies raised in a clean environment?
- Are they well socialized?
- Are the other dogs in the breeder's house clean and well cared for?
- Do the other dogs seem to have good temperaments?
- Does the breeder offer copies of all health clearances for the sire and dam?
- Does the breeder offer a written contract and/or guarantee?
- What does the breeder do with her dogs besides breed them? Are they performance dogs, show dogs, hunting dogs, etc., or is the breeder just breeding to make money?

The breeder should be happy to answer your questions. If she's not, move on to the next breeder on your list.

Lab Puppy Personalities

Lab puppies, even those from the same litter, exhibit entirely different personalities. You can't label a pup with absolute certainty, but there are some characteristics you might see.

The **tank** bowls over his littermates, eats first, grabs the toy first, and hogs all the attention. His intense drive makes him a good prospect for hunting, drug detection, or performance sports. This same dog can be hard to train for a first-time owner. Teaching self-control from the time he's young helps channel his over-the-top personality.

The **social butterfly** is the life of the party and will keep you laughing. He's happy, enthusiastic, confident, and ready for anything, although he might be a little rambunctious and easily distracted. He's still a really fun dog and perfect for an active family with older children.

Mr. Sensible is also happy and enthusiastic, but he's a little more low-key. Whatever you want to do, he's fine with that. He's affectionate, willing, and eager to please you, but he has a calmer disposition than his social butterfly littermate.

The **aristocrat,** often a female, is also affectionate but can be aloof and independent when she chooses. She might seem to learn slower, but don't let her fool you. She's thoughtful and methodical about everything she does.

The **quiet one** might have been raised outside in a kennel, and he may not have had much socialization. Very few Lab puppies are shy or fearful, but when one is hesitant to join playtime or seems a little skittish, a conscientious breeder steps in and helps the puppy, who soon catches up to his littermates. Patience and confidence-building exercises can make this dog a loving and devoted pet. He might not be a good choice for a family with small children who might overwhelm him, however, or for a first-time dog owner.

ADOPTING A TEENAGE OR ADULT LAB

You might consider adopting an older adult dog who needs a home. Although rescue groups occasionally have puppies available, most of their Labs are teenagers or young adults. Older dogs might have some behavior and health-care issues, but they're far from a lost cause. They could have been neglected for a long time, but most thrive with the attention from their new family, love other dogs, and settle in with few adjustment issues.

Rescue groups report that the majority of Labs they get are between 10 and 18 months old and often untrained. Many haven't been allowed indoors since they got big and unruly. The owners realized it takes a commitment of time and money to care for a dog, and they were overwhelmed. These are the lucky dogs because they'll readily adapt to a new home with some care and education.

When you adopt a Labrador Retriever from a rescue group, you won't know much—good or bad—about your dog's life up to this point. If your new dog has been in a foster home, the foster family can fill you in on what they've learned while he's been staying with them. For example, maybe he's housetrained, friendly toward cats, appears well socialized, and has had some training. Your dog also will have had all his shots and been neutered (or spayed). In addition, the rescue group takes care of any health problems and discusses ongoing issues with you.

Labrador Retrievers in animal shelters are usually strays who have not been claimed by their owners. As a result, you'll have no history of the dog's health or behavior, so getting him off to a good start is especially important.

One thing is for certain: what you do in the first few weeks and months will have a big impact. He'll eagerly soak up everything he sees and hears so he can figure out the rules and routine in his new home. Labs are friendly, adaptable, and anxious to please you. Take advantage of it! Many of the sections in this book, particularly those about behavior and training, will help you as your rescued Lab, no matter what age, joins your family and settles into your home.

PREPARING FOR YOUR LAB PUPPY

It's fun to shop for your new puppy while you're waiting for him to arrive. In this section, we give you a shopping list of the supplies you need to keep your pup healthy and safe.

Bowls: Stainless-steel bowls with nonslip rubber bottoms are easier to sterilize and last longer than other types of bowls. Labs eat fast, and your puppy will push his bowl around the floor in his rush to gulp his dinner. Lab pups are notorious chewers, and plastic bowls get teeth marks that make them harder to clean. Ceramic bowls are pretty, but a bouncing Lab puppy can break even the heaviest crockery.

Collar and leash: Pick a collar that fits around his neck but has enough holes so you can loosen it as he grows. A flat nylon or leather collar is the only type of collar you need. When you put it on, you should be able to fit two fingers between the collar and his neck. Be sure it isn't so loose he can pull out of it. Tighten the collar enough that it rides closer to his ears, not down by his shoulders.

One option is an adjustable martingale collar that slips over his head and tightens only when he pulls on the leash. There's no buckle. If he decides he doesn't want to go where you're going, he can't back out of a martingale collar. Don't leave a martingale collar on an unattended puppy, however; he could get caught in something and strangle.

Select a matching nylon leash, or get something made of leather or cotton rope that's easier on your hands. A 6-foot leash is helpful while your pup is learning how to walk nicely at your side. When he's older and taller, a 4-foot leash is long enough, and you won't get tangled up in the extra length. Stay away from adjustable-length leads for now. That'll just teach your puppy to pull, and you don't want that.

As your puppy gets older and more rambunctious, you may opt to use a head halter while going for walks. This style goes over his nose and behind his ears like a horse's halter, which makes it easier to control a pup who pulls. Some styles have a clip that attaches to his regular collar so if he rubs it off, he's still attached to the leash. Your puppy will still be able to open his mouth to eat and drink while wearing a head halter.

TIPS AND TAILS

Lab puppies can be really destructive. They see everything as toys, and they can quickly demolish the sturdiest things. Choose relatively chew-proof supplies, and be diligent about keeping them out of your inquisitive pup's reach when not in use. Provide him with plenty of other things he's allowed to play with and chew instead.

Crate: From the very beginning, your puppy should spend some time in his crate. It's his safe haven, a place he'll enjoy throughout his life. The crate is also an essential housetraining tool. Choose one that's bigger than your pup, but not so big he can soil in it and sleep at the other end. Some crates come with a divider you can remove as your puppy grows.

Crates come in a variety of styles. Your puppy will feel safe and surrounded in a plastic crate, which simulates a den. Some of the flimsy plastic crates aren't strong enough to hold a rambunctious Lab puppy, so get a heavy-duty one. Many plastic crates are airline approved, so if you're going to travel, this is the one you need. Check with your airline for confirmation that the crate you choose is acceptable.

Wire crates offer different advantages. They allow air to circulate, which is essential in hot weather. Your puppy can see out of a wire crate and feel like he's part of the action, even when he's confined. A wire crate often has a side door and an end door, so you can rearrange it to suit your room. If your pup won't settle down, you can spread a blanket over the crate to block his view. These crates fold down flat and are easy to store. If you opt for a wire crate, choose one made of heavy-gauge wire that will resist the efforts of a strong Lab puppy.

Mesh or fabric crates are best for adult dogs who are already crate trained.

HAPPY PUPPY

Consider buying two crates: a plastic one to keep in the bedroom for sleeping and a wire one for the family room where he can spend time with you without getting underfoot.

Rubber curry: These brushes come in several shapes, including round, oval, and rectangular. The curry fits in the palm of your hand, has rubber bumps on the business side, and loosens your pup's undercoat before you brush him—an essential tool during shedding season.

Slicker brush: A slicker brush has short, metal pins on a rectangular rubber backing. This is the brush you'll use the most. It gets out all that loose undercoat when your Lab starts shedding and is good for quick touch-ups when he rolls in dirt or leaves.

Shedding blade or tool: A shedding blade is a metal piece about 12 inches long that's serrated on one edge with rubber handles at each end. It quickly skims loose hair off your dog's coat. Or use a tool such as the Furminator, which pulls out gobs of loose hair and undercoat during the heavy shedding seasons.

Toenail clippers: The breeder started the toenail-clipping process for you, and 8 weeks old is not too young to trim a puppy's toenails. Choose either guillotine- or scissors-style clippers, and get extra blades because dull blades tear the nails. An alternative tool is a grinder. A grinder uses a sandpaper-covered tip to grind the nail instead of clipping it.

Toothbrush/toothpaste: There's no time like the present to teach your pup to enjoy having his teeth brushed. Get either a toothbrush or a fingertip brush and toothpaste formulated especially for dogs. Don't use human toothpaste; it makes dogs and puppies sick.

Pet gates: When he's not in his crate, you'll still want to confine your puppy so you can prevent housetraining accidents and chewing. Pet gates come in sizes that block doorways or even large spaces between rooms. You can buy inexpensive plastic, fancy metal, or furniture-quality wood gates. Some styles mount permanently with screws, while others are pressure-mounted so you can remove them when your puppy grows up. Deluxe models have a pass-through gate so you don't have to take them down every time you want to walk through the doorway.

Exercise pen/playpen: A folding wire exercise pen (or ex pen) gives your puppy some room to move around while still confined. If he's acclimated to it when he's little, he'll respect the pen when he's bigger. Use the ex pen when you leave him alone and while you're at work. The pens are available in heights from 24 to 48 inches; get a tall one so he's not tempted to climb out.

Cleaning supplies: A pooper-scooper set is made of a long-handled rake and pan you can use to pick up after your puppy. You'll also need to carry plastic bags–grocery sacks, newspaper bags, or poop bags purchased especially for the task–whenever you take your puppy out in public. Nature's Miracle or other enzymatic liquid cleaners eliminate the scent of urine when your puppy has an accident indoors.

Puppy toys: Anything that comes apart is not a good toy for a Labrador because he can swallow pieces, and that could cause a bowel obstruction. Most toys made especially for puppies aren't strong enough for Labs. Get larger toys, even for the youngest pup. Heavy-duty rubber bones are best.

HAPPY PUPPY

If your puppy doesn't seem interested in his chew toys at first, coat them in chicken broth or smear on some peanut butter. That'll get his attention!

Born to retrieve, Labs always have something in their mouths. Yours will constantly bring you his toys, and his favorites are probably stuffed animals. A toy made especially for dogs shouldn't have buttons or pieces that come off easily, but he'll still do his best to pull out the stuffing or squeaky device and eat it. If you get stuffed toys, pick them up when you aren't able to supervise.

Balls awaken your puppy's retrieving instinct, so they're always a hit. Choose sturdy ones that are too big to get stuck in his mouth.

Plastic water bottles—gallon or liter size—are noisy, fun, and disposable. Knotted rope toys are fine until they start to fall apart, so replace them as needed. Rawhide chews soften as your puppy chews and can break apart. They can cause an obstruction or upset tummy, so monitor his activity with them.

Toys that dispense food entertain your pup while you're away. The heavy-duty KONG toy is good for Lab puppies. Stuff it with kibble and peanut butter, and freeze it before presenting it to your pup. Get several, and leave a different one in his ex pen each day.

TIPS AND TAILS

Test all toys while you're home with your pup before you give him something and leave for work. Labradors are chewing maniacs and can destroy almost anything.

If Puppy has the house strewn with toys, he'll have a hard time learning what's okay and what's not okay to chew. Set up a toy box, and let him pick out his favorite of the moment. Switch toys out regularly so they seem new and exciting to him.

Bed: An inexpensive bed is fine until your pup grows up a bit. An old throw rug or beach towel keeps him just as cozy as a $100 plush bed. And just a heads-up: he'll probably destroy several beds between now and the time he's an adult.

Puppy-Proofing Your House

Anything that can hurt a human baby can hurt your puppy, too. Puppies don't have hands, so he is going to explore his new world with his mouth. Anything he can sink his teeth into is fair game, and it's your job to be sure he stays safe. That means puppy-proofing your home.

Start by getting down on the floor for a puppy's-eye view of your home. You might be surprised what you find under the couch. Do the same in your garage and yard. Puppy-proofing is an ongoing project, so remember that within a month, he'll be able to get to things that are out of reach right now.

TIPS AND TAILS

Have your children help you puppy-proof the house and yard. They'll enjoy finding things that might hurt the new puppy and helping put them away.

Remove dangling objects. While you're on the floor checking for stray objects, remove or reposition drapery or window blind cords, tablecloths, and houseplants. It's not unheard of for a pup to strangle on a drapery cord.

Tie up electrical cords out of reach, or encase them in a cord-keeper or PVC pipe. A puppy who chews through a cord can be electrocuted and even killed. Cover electrical outlets, too. Remote controls and telephones have your scent concentrated on them, so your pup will gravitate toward these toy-size items. Don't leave them out on the coffee table. In fact, take everything off the coffee table for the next year.

Move breakable knickknacks out of reach of puppy teeth, and later, Labrador tails. A Lab's tail can wipe out an entire shelf of figurines with one swipe. And paperclips, pens, buttons, jewelry, and other tiny bits that fall out of your pockets or off the dresser are very attractive to puppies—and very dangerous. Be vigilant about picking up anything your pup might find interesting.

Now is also the time to teach your kids to pick up their clothes. If they don't, they'll learn this lesson the hard way the first time Puppy carries their underwear into the living room in front of company! Shoes and socks are heavy with your scent and, therefore, most appealing. Many a Lab puppy has had emergency surgery after swallowing a sock.

Wastebaskets provide an open invitation to a curious Lab. Purchase cans with hard-to-remove lids, or put the trash bin in a latched cabinet.

Take chemicals and cleaners out of bottom cupboards in the kitchen, bathroom, and garage, and use childproof latches to keep Pup out of mischief. Sharp puppy teeth can cause a can of deodorant to explode, for example. Put medications and cosmetics out of reach, too. Close toilet lids so your puppy doesn't drink toxic cleaners or fall in and drown.

Foods such as chocolate, onions, yeast dough, and coffee are dangerous for dogs so be sure to keep these well out of his reach. (See Appendix C for a complete list of foods and other household hazards to keep away from your dog.)

Screen off fireplaces or wood-burning stoves. An exercise pen works well for this purpose. Put the wood somewhere he can't get to it. A Lab of any age *will* chew wood!

TIPS AND TAILS

During the holidays, block his access to the Christmas tree with an ex pen or other fence. Ingested tinsel or ornaments can cut his insides or cause a fatal blockage.

Identify poisonous houseplants and remove them. It only takes a leaf or two of some plants to kill your beloved Lab. (See Appendix C for a list of poisonous plants.)

Puppy-Proofing Your Yard and Garage

Even if your puppy won't be spending a lot of time out in the yard, it still needs to be puppy-proofed in case you ever need to let him out. As with the inside of your house, you need to be sure the outside of your house and yard are safe for your dog.

If your yard is fenced in (and it should be), check your fence for loose boards, holes, or any place you can see daylight through or under. The slightest hint of an escape route will tempt him to dig. Be sure the tension wires at the bottom of chain-link fencing are securely fastened. Don't forget to look behind bushes and sheds, too. Block small spaces where a pup might get stuck, like between the garage or a shed and a fence, and be sure to recheck regularly. You never know what he might do out there.

Your barbecue grill, drip pan, and the accompanying cooking tools are full of wonderful food smells. Put them out of reach after use. Stow away patio chair pads when you're not using them. Build a temporary fence around the pool, hot tub, or pond if you have these water areas. Block access to decks and balconies to prevent your puppy from falling off.

Bulbs and some outdoor plants, like oleander for example, are poisonous. (See Appendix C for a complete list.) Cocoa mulch contains the same deadly ingredient as chocolate—theobromine—and a small amount can quickly kill a puppy. Compost bins should be off-limits to your puppy as well. Fermenting materials produce molds and bacteria that are toxic when eaten.

Don't use snail or rodent bait in your yard. Both are especially attractive to dogs.

Store garden and pool chemicals in a puppy-proof cabinet. Likewise, keep fertilizers, pesticides, and herbicides out of his reach, and consider limiting their use on your yard. These might not seem especially toxic to you or your children, but your puppy is low to the ground and his entire body is exposed to concentrated doses. Keep your pup out of the yard for at least 48 hours after you treat it.

Antifreeze can kill quickly. Dogs are attracted to its sweet taste, and your Lab puppy will have no trouble getting under the car to lap it up. Motor oil and radiator fluid are also hazards. Check under the car often, and wipe drips up immediately.

Ice-melting products contain assorted chloride compounds, and even a small amount can be lethal for dogs. Your puppy may ingest it if he licks his paws after playing outside. When shopping for these products, buy pet-safe versions; they are identified on the label.

HAPPY PUPPY

Watch your Lab puppy extra carefully the first few weeks when he's outside your home. He'll surely show you something you've missed picking up or putting away.

Your Pup's Professional Staff

It's easy to feel overwhelmed when you have a new puppy, especially if you're a first-time dog owner. But you're not alone. You have a staff of helpful professionals available to assist you.

Your first and most important adviser is your veterinarian. If you don't already have one, ask your friends, especially fellow Lab owners, if they have a vet they like. If your breeder lives close, she can suggest someone. Local trainers or kennel staff might recommend a clinic. You can also check with your state's veterinary medical association for a listing of local vets. The American Animal Hospital Association (AAHA) maintains a list of members at healthypet.com.

Schedule a visit to the clinic to meet the veterinarians and staff, and make some observations while you're there:

○ Is the clinic clean and neat?

○ Does the staff seem friendly and willing to answer your questions?

○ Do you like the vet's bedside manner?

○ What are the doctors' specialties and education?

   ○ Do they treat many Labs?

   ○ What kinds of Lab health problems have they treated?

   ○ Are the hours convenient?

   ○ Where are you referred for after-hours emergencies?

A dog trainer should be on your list, too. Although your Lab won't start puppy kindergarten for a few weeks, start asking around now for a good trainer who offers puppy classes. Try to find an instructor who has experience training Labradors. Different breeds learn at different rates, and methods that work on a Sheltie, for example, may not be successful with a Lab.

Ask if you can watch a class, and make some notes on what you see:

   ○ Do the puppies seem happy and safe?

   ○ Do students get enough individual attention?

   ○ Are they having fun?

   ○ Are their questions answered?

   ○ Does the trainer offer more advanced classes for when your puppy is older?

   ○ Does she use positive training methods?

TIPS AND TAILS

Puppies should *not* be wearing chain collars or be trained with any kind of force. If you see this while observing the class, find another trainer.

Ask the trainer what clubs or professional associations, like the Association of Pet Dog Trainers (APDT), she belongs to. Although obedience instructors aren't legally required to be certified in any way, you want to know yours is keeping up with knowledge and advances in the field.

You might plan to have a pet sitter come to your home mid-day while you're at work so your puppy can get his lunch and a potty break. This helps him housetrain much faster. When you interview the pet sitter, ask for references and proof of liability and property damage insurance. Ask about her experience with puppies and if she's a member of any professional organizations.

Don't forget your puppy's breeder. She can answer questions, provide referrals to experts, and help you if any issues arise. She'll also enjoy hearing progress reports as your Lab grows up.

DEVELOPMENT

A Lab puppy goes through dramatic physical and mental changes during the first few months of life. As he grows into his feet and adds pounds to his frame, his brain also develops, so his ability to concentrate and learn improves at the same time.

Physical Development

At 8 weeks old, your Lab puppy starts a growth spurt that will continue until he's about 6 months old, when it slows down dramatically. That roly-poly little butterball you brought home probably weighs between 10 and 12 pounds. By the time he reaches 12 weeks of age, his weight could double. That's an increase of 2 or 3 pounds a week! He'll alternate between being clumsy and sure-footed as his legs start to grow, and the little squirt who can barely keep up with you now will soon be galloping ahead and running circles around you.

His sight and hearing ability are now fully functioning, as is his brain. At this stage, different Labs can vary by a week or more in their growth level, so if yours lags behind, don't worry too much.

Mental Development

Although your puppy is physically advancing, he's still emotionally immature. He's capable of learning, but his attention span is very short. He'll need his lessons broken up into tiny steps and reinforced with plenty of praise. He'll retain anything he learns during this period, good or bad, for the rest of his life.

HEALTH

Start your Lab pup out right with proper health care. Like human babies, puppies need extra attention during their first year.

Your Puppy's Health Records

The initial health records from the breeder will help you set up a schedule with your veterinarian for future exams, vaccines, and parasite prevention. In your puppy's going-home packet, the breeder should provide a complete health history, including the dates the pup was wormed, the brand name of the wormer, the dates of the first vaccines, and the specific vaccines administered.

She also should provide an OFA certificate (see Months 1 and 2) showing when the puppy's eyes were examined and what the results were. If the puppies were treated for giardia or other parasites, that should be noted as well.

A copy of the sire and dam's health clearances, explained in the first chapter, should also be included. You might receive photos of the parents and each of their pedigrees, too.

TIPS AND TAILS

Your breeder might give you a bag of the food your puppy has been eating, a familiar toy, and a piece of the blanket or T-shirt the puppies have been sleeping on. Put the latter in with your puppy the first few nights so he's comforted by the scent of his mother and littermates. Along with your sales contract, receipt, and AKC registration form, the breeder also might give you articles and information on Labradors and puppy-raising. Go over each item with the breeder before you leave so you're comfortable you understand what you're signing and how to use the information she provides.

Diseases, Vaccinations, and Schedule

The breeder will have given your puppy his first in a series of immunizations. It covers distemper, hepatitis, parvovirus, and parainfluenza (DHPP), the basic core vaccines every dog should have. He's too young for the rabies vaccine right now.

You may not hear about these ailments very often, but that's because most dog owners vaccinate their dogs. Ask any shelter worker, and they'll tell you disease occasionally breaks out in their shelter. Unfortunately, they have to euthanize an entire population of shelter dogs to contain an outbreak. Needless to say, these diseases are pretty serious.

Distemper, a viral infection, causes upper-respiratory symptoms such as runny nose and fever. As it progresses, the puppy suffers from vomiting, diarrhea, pneumonia, and neurological problems. Once it causes bleeding in the intestinal tract, it's quickly fatal. Distemper is transmitted through saliva, urine, feces, and airborne droplets such as a sneeze, and your puppy can get it from another dog or a wild animal like a fox, ferret, raccoon, or skunk. It most commonly occurs in puppies 9 to 12 weeks old. Regular cleaning with detergents and disinfectants destroys the virus.

Canine hepatitis, caused by an adenovirus, was originally transmitted to dogs from foxes, and today it's common wherever dogs, foxes, or coyotes exist, spread by direct contact with an infected animal. The puppy will have a fever and enlarged lymph nodes on the head and neck, and he could die within a day or two from internal hemorrhaging, liver disease, and swelling in the brain. Hepatitis comes on very quickly in puppies 6 to 10 weeks old, and there is no cure. It's harder to eradicate from the environment because it's resistant to detergents and disinfectants.

TIPS AND TAILS

You might be confused when you see your puppy's vaccine records. DHPP is sometimes designated DAPP. If *H* stands for hepatitis and *A* stands for adenovirus, what disease was your puppy vaccinated for? Hepatitis is caused by the canine adenovirus type 1 (CAV-1), so the two terms are sometimes used interchangeably. To confuse matters more, there's an adenovirus type 2, which is part of the kennel cough, or bordetella, group of diseases, which are much less serious.

Parvovirus is a relatively recent canine disease, first striking in the late 1970s and now found throughout the world. Parvo also affects coyotes. It's one of the most highly resistant viruses and can survive in the environment for 5 months or longer. The symptoms include bloody, foul-smelling diarrhea; fever; and depression, and your veterinarian will test a stool sample to confirm the diagnosis. Parvo is treated with intravenous fluids and medications to control vomiting and diarrhea. The disease is most severe in puppies 6 to 14 weeks old, and many die even with expensive veterinary care. Chlorine bleach is the only effective disinfectant.

The parainfluenza virus, part of the kennel cough syndrome, is highly contagious. This isn't considered a core vaccine, but it's usually included as part of a puppy's initial set of vaccines. The main symptoms are a dry cough and runny nose. If not treated, it can lead to secondary pneumonia and death.

Many other noncore vaccines are available. Rather than overload your puppy's immune system right now, discuss them with your vet and decide together if and when your puppy should receive them. Some optional vaccines include bordetella (kennel cough), Lyme disease, coronavirus, leptospirosis, and rattlesnake vaccine. We go into more detail about these in later chapters.

TIPS AND TAILS
Wait in your veterinarian's office for half an hour after your puppy receives a vaccination. If he's going to have a reaction to the vaccination, it usually begins in that time period.

Your puppy won't be fully protected until he's had several booster shots. The vaccine he received at 6 to 8 weeks old primed his system to develop antibodies now that the ones provided through his mother's milk longer protect him. Boosters are given at 3- or 4-week intervals up to a total of three—for example 6, 10, and 14 weeks, or 8, 12, and 16 weeks. The last one is administered at about 14 to 16 weeks of age and then a booster is given 1 year later. After the 16-week vaccine, it's safe for him to venture out in public.

TIPS AND TAILS
Protect your puppy from infection by limiting his contact with the outside world until he's fully immunized.

Your Puppy's First Veterinary Appointment

Within a week of bringing your Lab puppy home, take him for his first vet visit. Pack along some treats, and make it a fun experience. What he learns about the vet's office now determines how he views it for the rest of his life.

Carry him into the vet's office, and don't let him explore on the floor. Although the office looks clean, your puppy is especially susceptible to illness at this age.

The doctor will do a complete physical exam and review the health records you provide. She'll listen to your puppy's heart and lungs, look in his ears, examine his mouth for abnormalities, check for a hernia on his belly, and make note of his weight and overall physical condition. She'll also look for signs of any congenital health defect—a defect that was present at birth. If the vet finds your puppy is not healthy, you have the right to return him to the breeder.

Dealing with Parasites

When a puppy moves to his new home, the stress of being in a new and different environment away from his mother and littermates may depress his immune system, allowing parasites like worms, giardia, or coccidia to take hold.

Roundworm, hookworm, and whipworm are intestinal parasites that grow and reproduce in a puppy's body. He might not show any symptoms, or you might see worms in his stool. Weight loss, a dry and dull coat, diarrhea, or potbelly are also indicators he may have worms. All three types of worms can be transmitted when the puppy accidentally eats, licks, or walks on contaminated soil and then licks his feet. Roundworms can be passed from the mother to her puppies.

If your puppy has worms, it doesn't mean the breeder did something wrong. Most vets assume all young pups have worms and recommend a deworming now and again in two weeks. Even though the breeder wormed the pups, it doesn't kill all the worms. The first worming kills adult worms, but it doesn't kill the larvae. The second worming kills the worms that have developed since the last worming. It may take several treatments over a period of weeks to eliminate all of them.

If your puppy is having diarrhea, the vet will test a stool sample to check for giardia and coccidia, two other parasites that sometimes affect puppies (and adult dogs). Your pup can ingest these single-celled parasites from infected water or soil or from contact with an infected puppy's feces. Both also can be transmitted to humans. Medication quickly kills the parasites.

Some topical flea-control products are made specifically for puppies. Ask your veterinarian what to use so your pup doesn't get a toxic dose. Some orally administered flea-control products also prevent heartworm and other types of worm infestations and are available by prescription only.

NUTRITION

Feeding your Lab puppy is more involved than just setting down a bowl of kibble once or twice a day. Choose a food with the nutrients a puppy needs to develop strong muscles, organs, and bones. By feeding him quality food and developing good feeding habits when he's a puppy, you'll help ensure his future good health.

Your Lab Puppy's Nutritional Needs

Dog food manufacturers want you to feed your pup puppy food for a year or more, but Lab puppies don't need excess nutrients to grow and thrive. In fact, many breeders recommend you buy one bag of puppy food and switch to adult food as soon as that's gone. Puppy foods encourage overly fast growth, which can cause orthopedic problems later in life.

Puppy food contains the same basic nutrients as adult food, but in slightly different amounts. A healthy, balanced diet includes protein, carbohydrates, fat, minerals, vitamins, and water. For puppies, manufacturers sometimes add more protein, fat, vitamins, and minerals.

Dog food ingredients are subject to regulation by the Association of American Feed Control Officials (AAFCO). AAFCO establishes the minimum and maximum percentages of each nutrient that must be present to declare the food "healthy and balanced." AAFCO also approves labeling "for puppies" or "for all life stages." However, it doesn't regulate what exact ingredients should make up the foods, and that's where it gets tricky to select a food for your Labrador.

TIPS AND TAILS

You might be interested in feeding your puppy a raw diet. A puppy's immune system needs time to grow and mature, and he's more susceptible to salmonella and E. coli from raw meat when he's little. We cover the pros and cons of a homemade raw diet in Month 12, but in general, we don't recommend it for dogs under 1 year old. Consider feeding a commercially made raw food, like Honest Kitchen (thehonestkitchen.com), so your puppy gets the necessary balance of nutrients without endangering his health. And talk to your veterinarian.

The quality of the ingredients is the most important factor when selecting a brand because low-quality ingredients can affect your dog's digestion and behavior. Read the dog food label, and choose a food that's higher in meat protein and fat and lower in grain carbohydrates. (Ingredients are listed in order according to volume.) Dogs are meat eaters and don't do well on a vegetarian diet.

Your pup needs protein because it contains amino acids that help build his healthy bones, muscles, skin, and hair. The best protein sources are meat, fish, and poultry. Less-expensive sources come from plants, like wheat or corn gluten, and are harder for your puppy to digest.

Puppy and dog food labels should name a specific meat source—beef, lamb, or chicken—as the first ingredient. Meat meal is also a good, concentrated source of protein. Meat by-products are made up of the less-desirable parts of the animal, such as t-he feathers or feet.

Also important, carbohydrates provide sugars (glucose), starches, and dietary fiber. Simple carbohydrates, such as fruit, absorb easily into the body. Complex carbs like whole grains, potatoes, peas, and beans also provide fiber and starches to help your puppy's digestion. Additional starches are sometimes added to dry food during manufacturing to help the kibble retain its shape and texture.

Whole grains are a healthy source of carbohydrates. Refined grains such as white rice and white flour are stripped of their most important nutrients—B vitamins, dietary fiber, and iron—and add calories but not much nutrition. Some "empty" carbohydrates, such as cellulose or peanut hulls, are used as fillers and aid in forming a solid stool, but they have no nutritional benefit. They're harder to digest and sometimes cause excess gas.

Recent scientific studies have suggested that excess cereal carbohydrates cause hyperactivity in dogs, and that's the *last* thing a Labrador Retriever needs. Cereal carbs include all grains, refined or whole, such as wheat, rice, etc. Noncereal carbs include beans, apples, and potatoes.

Fat provides energy and essential fatty acids and helps your pup's body absorb fat-soluble vitamins. The essential fatty acids help lubricate his joints and keep his coat shiny and healthy, while the calories in fat give him energy to grow. Fat also adds flavor and texture to dry food and is sprayed onto the food after cooking.

Your pup needs certain vitamins and minerals, too. Vitamins are crucial to cell functioning, and minute quantities of the fat-soluble vitamins A, D, E, and K are stored in the liver until they're needed. The safest sources are whole foods such as green vegetables, eggs, liver, and fish. Excess water-soluble vitamins (C and assorted B vitamins) are eliminated in the urine. If food becomes rancid, the vitamins are destroyed, so manufacturers add antioxidants to extend the shelf life and prevent spoilage.

Minerals build healthy bones and teeth. Dog food companies used to add a lot of calcium to their puppy formulas to aid growing bones, but this practice has changed because excess calcium can cause your Lab to grow too fast and develop overly large bones with less density, making them brittle and easily broken. Large-breed puppy formulas contain less calcium than small-breed foods for this reason. Calcium is necessary in the right amount because it works with phosphorus to aid functions such as muscle contraction.

Some additional minerals important to your puppy's overall body functioning are zinc, iodine, selenium, and copper.

TIPS AND TAILS

The quality of any dog food can be affected by heat, storage conditions, and age. Be sure to check the expiration date on the bag to ensure the food is fresh, and use within 6 months of purchase.

If you're feeding a "complete and balanced" puppy food made with meat and other high-quality ingredients, you shouldn't have to add any vitamins, minerals, or other supplements to your puppy's diet. In fact, doing so can cause more harm than good. So opt for a good-quality food, and discuss any nutrition concerns you may have with your veterinarian before supplementing.

Making Changes Slowly

The breeder will probably send home a small bag of the brand of kibble your puppy has been eating. If you're going to continue with this brand, that's fine. If you decide to change brands, make the change *gradually* to avoid upsetting his tummy.

Start by mixing 25 percent of the new food with 75 percent of the old food for several days. If your pup seems to tolerate it well, with no diarrhea, you can increase the amount of the new food to 50 percent for a week. During the next week, mix 75 percent of the new food with 25 percent of the old. Eventually, you should be able to eliminate the old food with no problems.

How Much to Feed?

Lab puppies are notorious for being overweight, and fat puppies grow up to be fat adult dogs. Your puppy should be at a healthy weight, and you should be able to feel his ribs, even when he's only 8 weeks old.

There's no hard-and-fast rule about how much to feed your pup this month. Most breeders recommend about 2 cups per day at this age. Whatever you do, don't blindly follow the recommendations on the bag of puppy food, which are usually way too high.

Proper Feeding Practices

This month, feed your puppy three meals a day if at all possible. He'll survive if you're working and he only gets fed twice a day, but he'll get pretty hungry.

When feeding, select a spot where your puppy can eat undisturbed, possibly in his crate. Feed him in the same place every meal. Put his food down and leave it for 10 to 15 minutes. If he hasn't eaten by then, pick it up until the next mealtime. Because you know when he has eaten, you also know when he needs to go out, and that helps with housetraining. He'll also look up to his people as the providers of food—an important motivator when you start training.

Your pup doesn't need any table scraps or other goodies to make his food tasty. In fact, giving him scraps only teaches him to turn up his nose at plain kibble. Practice good feeding habits now to avoid a beggar later on.

Keeping Your Puppy Hydrated

It's especially easy for puppies to get dehydrated, so keep plenty of water available to your puppy, both indoors and out. The lack of other nutrients causes illness, but your puppy cannot survive without water.

TIPS AND TAILS

Keep your puppy's water fresh, and clean the bowl daily because bacteria can build up from bits of food and saliva dropped into the water. Fresh water also encourages him to drink more.

GROOMING

It might seem unnecessary to groom your Lab puppy when he's only 8 weeks old, but if he learns to tolerate grooming when he's young, he'll be easier to groom throughout his life. And you'll be glad you took the time now when you see how much an adult Lab sheds!

Instead of looking at grooming as a chore, make it fun and an opportunity for you and your pup to spend time together. Take advantage of his need to cuddle, and teach him to enjoy handling at the same time. You'll need to clean his ears, trim his toenails, brush his teeth, and investigate injuries throughout his life, so you want him comfortable being touched anywhere on his body.

Massaging Your Puppy

Gentle massage is a loving way for your puppy to get used to handling and grooming. Massage him in short sessions when he's naturally tired and ready for his nap, and you'll soon have a sleeping pup. Always keep it short and fun with lots of treats. He doesn't understand what you're saying yet, so your tone of voice is more important than what you say. Speak to him in a soothing voice, and you'll help him calm down and relax.

Sit down on the floor with your legs out in front of you. He'll probably climb right in your lap. Roll him on his back or side. He'll struggle as you hold him, so reward him when he stops wiggling, even for a second, by giving him a treat and letting him get up. Let him move around a little between tries. If he's not happy to come back to you, you've pushed him too far. Remember that he doesn't have much of an attention span yet. By the third time you put him on his back, he'll start to figure out what you want and calm down faster. After a few sessions, he'll relax quickly.

A firm touch is less likely to tickle, so keep that in mind as you slowly pet his body and legs and rub your fingers between his toes. Work with his paws until you can hold each one in your hand without a struggle. Gently stroke his ears from base to tip, and turn each ear inside out. Stroke his tail from the base to the end and pull your hand off the tip as if the tail was longer than it is. (Suddenly stopping at the end of his tail feels jarring to him.) Massage his mouth, and lift his lips and massage his gums with your fingertip.

Let him fall asleep if he wants to and sleep on your lap or next to you for a bit. If he's awake, take him out for a potty break and then let him play.

Introducing the Brush

When he readily allows you to hold on to a paw without snatching it away, introduce the brush and other grooming tools. At this point, you aren't trying to do a complete grooming job; you just want him to see the tools, feel them on his body, and get lots of praise for allowing you to touch him with them. Let him investigate each tool for a minute or so while you praise him and hand out treats. Next, let him feel the sensation of each tool on his body for a second, and immediately praise him and take it away. Gradually work up to brushing his tummy, chest, neck, and legs. Do this several times a week.

Trimming His Toenails

In another session, reintroduce the toenail clippers. Although the breeder probably trimmed his toenails, he was so young he might not remember it anymore. He needs a refresher course because he's in a new home with new people.

Hold him on your lap, or put him on a table so he can't run away. Stroke his leg with the clippers while you hold his foot, and let him investigate this strange object. Tap lightly on his toenail, and give him a treat when he doesn't pull back. Do this for all four feet and each toenail. Break it into several sessions, or take play breaks between feet or toes. Stop when he's done something right. If you have to, back up a bit in the process. Quitting is his reward for doing the right thing.

Once he accepts tapping on his toenails, trim off a tiny piece of one toenail. Praise him while you cut, and immediately give him a treat and release him. The point is not to actually shorten his nails, but to get him used to the feeling of the pressure from the clippers. If he can't tolerate that, just close the clippers on his nail for a second and release without cutting.

Watch out for the quick, the blood-filled vein that runs down the middle of each nail. If you accidentally cut the quick, it will hurt and bleed, and your pup will *not* want you to go near his feet again! Black and chocolate Lab puppies have dark toenails, and you won't be able to see the quick through the nail. Yellow Labs often have white nails so you can see the quick. The more often you trim his toenails, the farther back the quick will recede and the less likely you are to nick it. Always err on the side of caution and cut back less than $\frac{1}{32}$ inch. If you cut the quick, hold your fingertip tightly over the end of the nail until the pressure stops any bleeding. Then apply a product called Kwik Stop or run a bar of soap across the tip of his nail to help the blood clot.

If you choose to use a nail grinder, you'll be less likely to cut into the quick. Run the grinder about foot away from him so he gets used to the noise, and gradually move it closer. You don't want him to investigate it with his mouth or nose while it's running; it might hurt him. The grinder can get hot, so just touch it to his nail for a second or two at first. Gradually work up to several seconds, and check it often to be sure it's cool to the touch.

Whether you use clippers or a grinder, try to hold a grooming session every 3 or 4 days. That might seem like a lot, but it's much easier to trim off just a little every so often on just a few nails than to try to clip every nail in one session. Plus, it gives you that much more bonding time with your pup.

SOCIAL SKILLS

Labs are naturally happy and outgoing, but they need proper socialization when they're young to ensure they mature into well-adjusted adults. Systematically introduce your puppy to the creatures and experiences he'll encounter throughout his lifetime so he learns the world is a great—and safe—place. By starting when he's young and carefully controlling his interactions, you'll prevent future behavior and temperament problems.

The Labrador Temperament

Originally, the Labrador Retriever was developed as a hunting dog. Why is this important to you? Because the same characteristics that make a Lab a good hunting dog also make him an excellent family dog.

He has to cooperate with the hunter, be ready to obey, and be eager to please. Intense and focused on the job at hand, Labs have a strong work ethic and great perseverance, while at the same time, they're able to wait quietly for hours in a duck blind between retrieves.

For you, he'll be ready to play at a moment's notice or rest quietly at your feet for the evening. He'll work for you at whatever task you send his way for no more payment than the chance to be with you. Not independent like a Bloodhound or a guarding breed, Labs are all about their people. Lousy watchdogs, yours might tell you someone is at the front door, but he'll have no desire to scare anyone away. His sense of humor will keep you entertained, and his happy-go-lucky attitude will last his lifetime.

Fear-Imprint Period

Lab puppies are naturally curious and interested in everything around them. But between 8 and 12 weeks, most puppies go through a *fear-imprint stage* during which they're more likely to be significantly affected by a scary experience. A traumatic encounter during this phase could spoil his attitude toward that thing for the rest of his life.

Most pups won't experience anything overly frightening at this age, but it's worth taking precautions to avoid unnecessary scares. This is a bad time to discipline him severely, yell at him, or force him to approach something he finds scary.

DOG TALK

The **fear-imprint stage** lasts for several weeks and usually starts soon after you bring home your puppy. He might remember overwhelming or frightening incidents that occur during this time for the rest of his life and always react to them with fear.

When something traumatic happens, it's hard to know how your puppy looks at it. For example, an 8-week-old pup, just entering the fear-imprint period, might be badly startled when someone drops a bowl of apples behind him. This could cause a lifetime phobia, but what exactly the puppy might become afraid of is difficult to predict. It could be objects hovering over his head, things coming up behind him, apples, bowls, or some other factor he focused on during the incident.

In spite of the risks, he still needs to be socialized. Allow your worried pup to approach a scary person or thing in his own time. Try not to overwhelm him or accidentally reward his fearful behavior. If you overreact, he might decide there really is something to be frightened about. Or he could conclude he's being praised for acting scared, and he'll act frightened to get attention from you. Sometimes Labs are *too* smart.

If he barks or makes a big fuss when he sees something, try to ignore it and praise him when he calms down. Remember, praise desired behavior, ignore unwanted reactions or frightened behavior, and just keep patiently working with him. Continue to present experiences he was familiar with before this period and introduce him to new things. In about 2 weeks, he'll regain his confidence.

There's a balance between overprotecting and overwhelming your puppy. With that in mind, it's time to start the socialization process in earnest.

Socialization Basics

When your puppy's 8 to 12 weeks old, he learns easily, and what he picks up now, he'll remember for his lifetime—good and bad. Therefore, your goal over the next few weeks is to introduce him to a multitude of positive experiences.

Socialization is not a one-time thing. You need to expose him to new things every day. If you bring your Lab home at 8 weeks of age and he never sees another dog, person, or place until he's 16 weeks old or older, he won't develop into the outgoing, confident dog he has the potential to be. An unsocialized puppy can become excessively fearful or aggressive, not typical for Labradors at all.

The breeder started socialization when your puppy was just a few weeks old (see "Puppies Discover Their World" in the first chapter). Now it's your turn to continue her efforts. Remember, because your pup hasn't yet completed his vaccines, this isn't the time to take him to the park or out in public. But there are still many things you can do to socialize your pup.

Invite assorted people to your home one at a time or in small groups. Your Lab needs to meet people who are tall, short, fat, thin, old, and very young. He should see hats, coats, uniforms, umbrellas, and wheelchairs. When Puppy approaches someone or something new, praise him for being brave.

Keep in mind that people are quite large in relationship to your Lab puppy. If you greet your puppy by bending over him, you block his view of everything else in the world—a terrifying thing to a puppy. Think of how uncomfortable you are when a large person gets in your personal space and hovers over you—you want to move away, don't you? No wonder a puppy is sometimes afraid of new people.

Make introductions easier on your puppy by inviting everyone to get down on the floor at his level. Pet him by scratching his chest rather than patting him on top of the head. A hand looming over him might cause him to shy away, but the palm of your hand, down low and reaching in his direction, isn't so scary.

If your puppy is fearful, start with the new person at a distance so Puppy can get used to him before getting too close. Act like the stranger is no big deal. Talk in a normal tone of voice, and shake hands or touch the person's shoulder so your puppy understands that you think the scary person is just fine. Give your pup the opportunity to interact with everyone while they give him treats and pet him. Do this several times a week until he's at least 16 weeks old.

TIPS AND TAILS

Include your mail carrier in the socialization process. After all, he or she will arrive on your doorstep every day for the rest of your dog's life. Provide a box of biscuits and ask him to offer one to your puppy every time he delivers the mail.

Although your Lab saw many things at the breeder's home, those same things might seem new to him at your house. Continue to expose your puppy to various surfaces: asphalt, gravel, concrete, grass, snow, dirt, and puddles. When he has a chance to interact with his environment, he's more likely to remember it, so play with him on each material.

Accustom him to different locations, too, such as the bathroom, the living room, the garage, the patio, his crate, and your car. You can safely take him to homes that have no pets if you carry him to and from the house. Visit the vet's office for a pet-and-treat session.

Introduce your Lab to assorted sounds, like the lawnmower, the television, the dishwasher, music, thunder, yelling, kids, sirens, motorcycles, gunshots (if you're going to hunt), and other loud noises. Start with the sounds far away, and slowly move closer, or record sounds and play them back while gradually increasing the volume.

Remember that at this age, you want him to have positive experiences, not terrify him to the point where he'll be emotionally scarred for life. If your puppy seems worried, adjust the exposure accordingly.

TIPS AND TAILS

If your rescued Lab seems overly afraid, don't assume he was abused. He probably just didn't get adequate socialization. He might react fearfully or even aggressively to unfamiliar things. Start training and socializing him like he's a young puppy, and don't overwhelm him.

Set up some physical challenges for him, and let him figure out each item for himself. Set up an obstacle course in the back yard, and have him climb steps, go through a tunnel, play in a cardboard box, climb over and under obstacles, and walk up a ramp or small teeter-totter. Lay a board across several bricks, and teach him to walk on it.

By allowing him to figure out new things for himself, you're helping him build confidence and problem-solving skills. When he reacts in a calm and happy manner, praise him and give him a treat. You're there to provide a comfort zone for him, and he needs to know all is going well. You're also there to protect him from overwhelming situations and remove him when something is just too much for him.

Your Lab Puppy and Children

Labs and children were made to be together. Puppies need to learn how to interact with children, and equally as important, children need to learn how to properly interact with puppies. If you don't have kids, borrow some and have a puppy party. Start by inviting over just one well-behaved child at a time. For the initial introductions, keep the sessions short, calm, and controlled so your puppy doesn't get overtired or overwhelmed.

Avoid tug-of-war and teasing games. Teach the child to give the puppy a treat for looking at them when they say his new name. Help them teach the pup to sit or learn a trick like shake. Play "puppy-come" games, where everyone sits in a circle, each one calls the puppy in turn, and everybody rewards him with a treat when he comes. Have the child brush the puppy, hold his leash, pet him, or toss a toy a few feet away.

TIPS AND TAILS
Never leave your puppy alone with children. It's up to you to protect him while you supervise and direct the activities.

As more kids visit, there might be lots of yelling and running around. You want your pup to get used to the commotion, but all this activity encourages him to join in. Children often run and scream, waving their arms and batting at the puppy when he jumps on them. To him, this is an invitation to play.

Teach kids to "be a tree" when Puppy gets too excited and starts nipping or pulling on their clothes. Have the child fold her arms across her chest, stand perfectly still, and not look at the puppy. When your pup quits leaping, quietly praise him and have everyone stay settled for a few minutes. Distract him with a toy or chewy and put him on a leash to prevent him from jumping and nipping again.

Puppies tire quickly, so watch your puppy's reactions as he plays with children and remove him if he seems overwhelmed. After a short play session, he can snuggle while he falls asleep in a child's lap.

Introducing Other Family Pets

If you have other dogs in the house and they're over 6 months old, choose a neutral territory, possibly at a friend's house, for them to meet your puppy so they won't see him as an invader. Introduce each dog one at a time, loosely holding the leashes. A tight leash makes the adult dog feel restrained and like he can't get away, which makes him more likely to lash out at the puppy. If things get tense, pick up your puppy and start with them farther away from each other. Praise the older dog and offer treats, so he'll think the puppy brings good things. Be sure the older dog gets plenty of attention so he doesn't get jealous and take it out on the pup.

Also, don't leave your pup alone with the big dogs. They need supervision for several weeks until everyone is comfortable and the puppy has figured out his place in the hierarchy (see the "Socializing to Calm Adult Dogs" section in Month 4). Use baby gates and ex pens to separate them when you can't supervise.

If you have a cat, know that the cat takes much longer to get used to your pup than the puppy to her. A cat's first instinct is to run, and a puppy's is to chase—what fun! It might take a few weeks for things to settle down. Be sure your cat has a place up high where she can get away from the puppy. Baby gates can block Puppy's access to the cat's territory, for example.

Let them smell each other through a closed door, and take the puppy on a leashed tour of the cat's favorite room. Let the cat leave when she wants to. At night, when the pup is in his crate in your room, Kitty will get used to his smell and learn the pup can't get to her. Whenever the cat is around for the first week or two, leash the pup so he can't chase her. When he gets too close, Kitty will hiss and swat him. They may become great friends eventually, or they may just tolerate each other.

Small pocket pets like birds and hamsters and caged animals like snakes are safest in their cages when a young Lab is on the scene. He can get used to their presence from his crate. Don't try to introduce them nose to nose; you're the one that's likely to come away with wounds.

If you don't make a big deal of it, they won't either, and everyone can peacefully coexist without interacting. Keep doors to the pet rooms shut when you're not able to supervise, so a curious puppy doesn't knock over a cage or aquarium.

TIPS AND TAILS

Prevent your puppy from leaping on or otherwise interacting too much with other animals. A bird can peck or bite, and a cat will scratch and hiss at a overactive puppy. Besides the risk of injury to either animal, you want this to be a positive experience for your pup. His first exposure to other species should be from a distance or otherwise controlled.

Introducing Other Puppies

Contact with other puppies is important. Puppies teach each other acceptable dog manners. If one plays too rough or bites, the other one disciplines him or quits playing. You might be able to set up play dates with your pup's littermates, or your veterinarian might have other puppies in her practice she can refer to you.

Limit your puppy's contact with other dogs, both puppies and adults, unless they're vaccinated and show no signs of illness. The risk of not socializing your puppy during this period is much greater than the risk of illness.

BEHAVIOR

Perfectly normal puppy activities might test your sanity if you're not used to having a puppy in your home. Plan ahead for a few inconveniences and challenges during the first few weeks.

Sleeping Through the Night

At night, put Puppy in his crate by your bed, and expect to get up and take him out once or twice. His little bladder can't hold it more than a couple hours. By 10 to 12 weeks, he should be able to sleep through the night.

Pick up all the water an hour or two before bedtime so he doesn't tank up right before he goes to sleep. And give him one last break outside before you put him in his crate for the night.

Curiosity—Not Just for Cats

Without constant supervision, unwanted behaviors become habits and are much harder to eliminate later. As your Lab pup gains confidence, he'll start to explore his world more and more. If left to his own devices, he'll discover that digging is fun and chewing keeps him entertained. These are normal doggie behaviors but not something you want to encourage! That same curiosity leads Puppy into every nook and cranny, searching for more exciting things to eat and play with, exposing him to things that could hurt him.

Be sure to always supervise your pup when he's out of his crate, and you'll both be better off.

When Your Puppy Starts Biting

As Puppy starts exploring, he uses his teeth like babies use their hands. He tastes everything. He doesn't know his own strength, so he tests to see what happens when he bites hard or tugs.

It's never okay for him to use his mouth on a person, so teach him bite inhibition from the first day you bring him home. His littermates started the job, and you can continue teaching him using the methods his fellow puppies used. When Puppy starts nipping at your arms or clothes, yelp loudly like another puppy would. This tells him you're displeased. Fold your arms, turn away from him, abruptly leave the room, and ignore him. Game over. He'll get the message after a few tries. When you see him consider biting but then think better of it, praise him. Redirect his attention to a toy or acceptable chewy.

If he's too wound up to quit, put him in his crate for a 3-minute time-out. If family and friends are consistent in their reactions, he'll quickly learn to keep his teeth to himself.

TRAINING

At 8 weeks, your puppy is capable of learning specific lessons and connecting his actions with certain words. Teaching good habits now prevents bad habits from developing later. It's much easier to stop problem behaviors early, before they become a habit, than to change them when he's a teenager.

Training Techniques

Positive training methods make learning fun. Your pup's attention span is limited right now, so keep sessions short—no more than 5 minutes. Remember, he doesn't understand what you're saying to him at this point, but your body language and tone of voice communicate your meaning.

Always reward him for doing something right. Lure him with treats, or shape him into position and reward him. Add the command name once he understands what you're asking him to do.

Treating Him Kindly

An 8-week-old puppy needs to feel safe and secure in order to grow up confident and well adjusted. He's had close contact with his littermates and mom, and now he's all alone in the world except for you.

Remember, your pup is making both positive and negative memories and associations during this time, so be sure his lessons are always positive. Never drag your puppy by the collar. If you need to make him go somewhere, pick him up until you've taught him to walk on a leash.

HAPPY PUPPY

There's no need for harsh corrections with a puppy this young. Instead, interrupt him and redirect his energy to something else. And never swat him with a newspaper or rub his nose in an accident. You aren't teaching him anything except to be afraid of you. After all, he doesn't even know the rules yet.

A Family United

Everyone in the household needs to agree on the dog rules. Your puppy must be confident that he not only understands the rules of the house but that everyone reacts the same to his behavior.

Lab puppies are cute and cuddly, but will you want him on the couch when he's an adult? Will he have access to every room? Where will his preferred elimination spot be? Where will he eat? Does everyone agree not to let him jump up on people? If you're inconsistent in enforcing the rules, your puppy will be confused and you'll wonder why he isn't learning anything. Decide on the rules together, and enforce them equally.

Agree on the words you'll use for different commands, too. Does "Down" mean "lie down" or "get off me"? Do you call him by saying "Come" or "Here"? Too many names for the same action confuses him.

Evenly enforce discipline as well. Rather than drag your pup by his collar, hang a few leashes around the house so anyone can easily hook him up to control his behavior. Agree that you all will ignore bad behavior or distract him rather than hit him or yell at him.

Prioritizing Housetraining

Start housetraining the first day you bring your new puppy home. Your Lab needs to go potty as soon as he wakes up, right after eating or drinking, and after a play session. In fact, he needs to go almost hourly that first week. By 12 weeks, he should be able to last an hour and a half.

Keep him close and supervise him during this time, or put him in his crate. Don't allow him to make a mistake. When you take him out, go to the spot you want him to use and he'll probably pee immediately. Don't play or entertain him. Just stand there and wait. When he goes, praise him to the skies and offer a treat. He'll quickly learn that peeing outside produces treats. If he doesn't go immediately, put him back in his crate for 20 minutes and try again. When he performs, give him some supervised freedom indoors before confining him again.

It's worth repeating: you must go outdoors with your puppy and praise him when he eliminates so he'll know he's done the right thing. If you just put him outside, how will you know he's done his business? How will he know why he's outside?

Housetraining often takes longer in winter, when it's cold and snowy outside. You don't want to go out and stand in the cold, and Puppy doesn't want to get his feet and tummy wet. Dig out a snow-free area, or erect a small shelter over his potty spot so you both won't mind so much.

When you leave your pup at home alone, set up his ex pen with his crate (door open or removed), water, and a spot to relieve himself. He'll select a corner of the pen to use. Encourage him with a piece of turf, a piddle pad, or even a doggie litter box in that spot. The best solution is to use the same surface he's expected to use outside. He'll quickly make the connection.

If he has an accident in the house, you have to try to catch him in the act and interrupt him. Make a loud noise, scoop him up, and take him straight outdoors. Wait with him while he finishes going, and praise him. If he's scolded for having an accident in the house, he'll just go to another room next time. In his mind, because you can't see him, he doesn't get in trouble, so it must be okay. He's figured out that peeing in front of you is bad, and out of your sight is fine.

If you don't see the accident happen indoors, clean it up and forget about it. He'll have no idea what you're mad about if you scold him at that point.

Crate Training

The crate is a training tool for you and a safe haven for your puppy. Don't use it as a punishment, and don't confine your pup in it for more than a few hours. If you use it correctly, he'll learn to like his crate and choose to go in it when he's tired.

To introduce the crate, toss in a treat and let him go in and get it. Do this a few times throughout the day, leaving the crate open so he can explore it on his own. At mealtime, place his dinner inside the crate with the door open. After a few meals, close the door while he eats.

He might whine and cry a little the first few times you close the door. If he does, wait until he settles down and then reward him by letting him out. If you let him out because he doesn't like it, he learns that making a fuss gets him what he wants.

At bedtime, place the crate next to your bed. Give him a chewy toy, place the blanket the breeder gave you (with his mother's smell on it) in the crate, put him in, and close the door. You might not get much sleep the first night!

Practice putting your puppy in his crate for a few minutes while you read or watch TV nearby. Give him a chewy filled with treats, and let him see you leave the room and return a few times. He'll soon be comfortable and settle down for a good chew and a nap. Save the best chew toys for crate time, so he looks forward to it.

Limiting His Freedom

For the next few months, your pup is too young to have the responsibility of the entire house and yard. With no one there to instruct him, he learns bad habits like digging in the wastebasket and chewing. He also could get hurt. Housetraining progresses faster if you keep him in the same room with you.

Indoors, use pet gates to block his access to other rooms. For the first few weeks, if you have to leave him outside alone for a while, put him in his ex pen. He'll get to enjoy the great outdoors without the hazards.

TIPS AND TAILS

Your pup will jump up against the wire pen you've set up to confine him, and if he doesn't stop now, he'll learn to knock it over. Never pick him up when he's jumping; ignore him until he puts his feet on the floor. Rattle the pen until he backs down and then praise him. Don't pet him while he's on his hind legs, either. That's just rewarding him for pushing on the pen. This method also works when he's jumping against a pet gate.

Teaching "Come"

As we've mentioned, the "come" command is an easy one to train and lots of fun for you and your Lab. The way to get a lifelong reliable recall is to start training early. Always call him for a positive reason. Take advantage of his willing nature; he'll probably race to you as soon as you call. If good things happen every time he responds, he'll always be happy to come to you. If you're going to do something he won't like, you go get him.

To introduce come, put your puppy on a leash. Get down at your puppy's eye level a few feet away and open your arms wide. In a high, happy voice, say, "Come!" or "Come here!" Reward him with praise, play, and treats when he responds, and cheer him on as soon as he looks your way. If he doesn't come, encourage him with a little tug on the leash and reel him in.

Practice from just a few feet away at first. Later, hook him to a longer lead, like a clothesline rope, so you can enforce the recall. Then start over in a new place from close up again, gradually working farther away.

Have family and friends call your pup, too. Play games where one person calls him and then another. Keep it short, and quit before he gets tired.

TIPS AND TAILS

Here's a helpful training tool: put a few pieces of kibble in a small food storage container, and shake it when you call your puppy. He'll soon learn that the shaker means treats. You can even shake it from another room, and he'll come running. Make several shakers, and set them around the house so you can find and use them easily.

YOU AND YOUR PUPPY

During the first few weeks, you and your puppy are both learning about each other. What's more, he's learning even if you aren't actively teaching. He's figuring out his name, who's who, what makes you happy, what not to do, and what his new routine is. You're starting to recognize when he needs to go out and when he's tired, hungry, frightened, or in the mood to play. You're all settling into your new life together.

Naming Your New Lab Puppy

Your Lab will have two names, a *call name* and a registered name. His call name is the one you use every day. His registered name is the one on his AKC papers. The two don't have to be similar at all.

The best call name for your pup is one he'll easily recognize and has an upbeat, happy sound to it. A name that's one or two syllables is short and snappy. If you make his call name too long, you'll undoubtedly shorten it to a nickname. For instance, Frederico will soon be Freddy, and Francesca will be Franny, etc. Also, don't choose a name like Flo, which sounds too much like "no." Think about what the name will sound like when you call him from across the park. Will you be embarrassed? Will he recognize what you said?

His AKC registered name is limited to 36 characters, including any spaces. (For an extra fee, the name can have up to 50 characters.) With the breeder's permission, the kennel name can precede the puppy's name, as in Shadow Hills Coming Storm, for example. Here, Shadow Hills is the kennel name, and his call name is Stormy. On the other hand, he could have Louie as his call name, or something else totally unrelated to his registered name. Sometimes the sire's or dam's name are first on the registration: Samantha's Chocolate Surprise. In this example, the dam's name is Samantha and his call name is Cocoa. It's up to you.

DOG TALK

Your Labrador Retriever's **call name** is the name you use for him every day. It may or may not have anything to do with his AKC registered name.

What to Expect During the First Week

It's finally time! The breeder has done her job, and now that wonderful ball of fur is delivered into your arms, ready or not. Here's what to expect the first few days.

Your puppy might fall asleep in your arms on the way home. That's okay. Take him outside as soon as you get home so he can relieve himself in his designated spot. Once the smell is there, it'll remind him to go in that place again. Let him explore around outside for a few minutes—supervised, of course. When you're sure he's emptied his bladder and bowels, bring him inside and let him explore the main room where you spend most of your time. If he has an accident, ignore it. He'll be too confused to remember anything you try to teach him at this point.

Let your Lab tell you what he wants to do next. He may approach you for attention. If so, get down on the floor with him for quiet introductions, sniffing, and maybe a few treats. He may fall asleep immediately. Puppies need a lot of sleep and tire quickly. But every puppy is different.

On the first day, let him get to know your family; visitors can meet him later. After a few days, he'll recognize individual family members. It's everyone's job to make him feel welcome and safe. Don't overwhelm him with lots of noise or roughhousing. As he starts to feel safe, he'll watch what you're doing and start to follow you. He'll be excited to see you and begin to learn his name.

Be sure his basic needs for food, water, and sleep are met. Take him out hourly for potty breaks, and be patient with accidents and chewing.

HAPPY PUPPY

Lab puppies are naturally happy and outgoing. Right now, playing is fun *and* instructive. This isn't the time to be serious about anything. Make training a game, and he'll learn fast and remember forever. Even a pup who makes a mistake can be corrected in a positive way by distracting and redirecting him to an acceptable behavior. A full tummy, a soft toy, and a warm bed all make for a *very* happy puppy.

Practicing Patience

A Lab puppy doesn't learn everything on the first try. It takes several repetitions for him to start getting the idea, and you might have to start all over tomorrow. He'll make mistakes, have accidents, chew something, and whine in his crate. Remember, he's just a baby. Forgive him, and keep training. He's learning how to learn, and he wants desperately to please you; he just needs time to figure out right from wrong.

When you run out of patience, let another family member take over for a while or put him in his ex pen or crate. If you lose your temper, he'll be frightened and see you as unpredictable.

Manage your puppy's environment. Even though you've puppy-proofed your house and yard, he still requires direction, supervision, and confinement. Keep temptation out of reach, and prevent trouble before it occurs.

The Importance of a Routine

A puppy starts to feel safe and secure when he knows what's expected of him and when he'll be fed, walked, put to bed, and left alone. Set up a daily schedule with fixed times for every activity, and stick to it as much as possible. Try to keep weekends the same as weekdays. If you get up at 6 A.M. on weekdays, he'll quickly learn to anticipate getting up at that same time on weekends.

TIPS AND TAILS

Write down your puppy's schedule, and post it where the entire family can refer to it. It'll help you remember potty breaks, mid-day feedings, and nap times. Be sure to include times for grooming, socialization, and training, too.

Many people take a few days off from work when they get their new pup. If you do, don't shower him with attention for 4 days and then suddenly go off and leave him on the fifth day. Introduce his schedule immediately. A young puppy sleeps as much as 16 to 18 hours out of every 24, so he needs a lot of rest and quiet time, even when you're home.

	SOCIAL	BEHAVIOR	TRAINING	PHYSICAL	HEALTH
MONTH 1			Littermates and mother teach appropriate canine behavior	Rapid growth	
MONTH 2	Breeder starts socialization				
MONTH 3	Socialization at home with new owner and other pets	Fear-imprint period	Begin house- and crate training		1st DHPP vaccine
MONTH 4		Teething begins—heavy chewing period	Enroll in puppy class		2nd DHPP vaccine
MONTH 5			Ready for basic commands	Switch to adult food	3rd DHPP and rabies vaccines
MONTH 6					
MONTH 7			Enroll in basic obedience class		
MONTH 8	Socialization in public			Moderate growth	Sexual maturity
MONTH 9		Adult teeth are in—chewing continues			
MONTH 10			Ready for more advanced training		
MONTH 11				Slow growth— reaches adult size	
MONTH 12 AND BEYOND					Annual vaccinations and checkup

Finding Her Way

This month, your puppy looks to you for everything. She follows you anywhere and is eager and happy. The period from 12 to 16 weeks, or 3 to 4 months, is a lot of fun for your family and your puppy. You continue socialization and training and take her to puppy class. Her focus is more social than studious, but lessons set the foundation for future learning and good behavior.

This month also is a challenge as your joyful toddler becomes more active. Overenthusiastic about everything, she acts first and thinks later. She starts teething, and her entire world changes as she gnaws on anything that might comfort her sore mouth.

Keep in touch with your breeder, and call her when you have questions about your puppy's development. You may be worrying about something entirely normal, but you won't know unless you can ask an expert. Plus, she'll enjoy hearing about your Lab's progress.

PHYSICAL DEVELOPMENT

You'll notice big changes in your Lab puppy this month. She loses her roly-poly physique as her legs get longer in proportion to her body. She also begins teething, as mentioned earlier, and that means chewing.

Size and Weight

A 12-week-old puppy weighs somewhere between 20 and 25 pounds—roughly double what her weight was at 8 weeks. She'll gain another 10 or more pounds this month. By 16 weeks, she'll be about half of her adult height and weight.

With Labs, it's hard to accurately predict specific heights and weights because there are so many variations within the breed. Assess her body condition (see Appendix B), and work with your vet to estimate what your dog's weight should be.

Teething

By 16 weeks, your puppy is losing her baby teeth, and her adult teeth are pushing through her gums. First her incisors, the small front teeth on her upper and lower jaw, start to come in. Females usually start teething earlier than males.

As with human babies, the process is painful, but instead of fussing and crying like a baby would, she'll chew to relieve the pain. Hide your most precious possessions, shoes, handbags, and the remote control. She doesn't target these items with evil intention. They smell like you, and that comforts her. When you catch her chewing on your golf shoes, trade them for an approved chew toy. You might see some blood on her toys, but that's normal.

Provide a variety of safe chew toys for your pup, and keep them handy because you'll be negotiating plenty of trades. Rotate the toys so she has just a few at a time. Then they'll seem new and exciting when you offer them.

TIPS AND TAILS
Don't yell and chase her when you catch her chewing. She'll think you've suddenly lost your mind, and she'll be afraid of you. Next time, she'll hide with her prize and you'll have trouble getting it away from her.

Frozen bones, cold carrots, ice cubes, or stuffed frozen KONG toys feel good on her sore gums and keep her occupied for longer periods. Frozen treats will make a mess, so confine her when you give her these gum soothers, or give them to her outside. You also can rub her gums with a teething product like Orajel or use a natural remedy like chamomile.

Know that on occasion, she might not feel like eating—that's normal. And she might not want her mouth touched. Remember, her mouth hurts right now. To make mealtime easier for her, soak her food in a few tablespoons of water so it's softer and easier to chew.

Your puppy might get bad breath, have soft stools, or be a bit lethargic during teething. All this is normal. However, if you have any concerns, consult with your veterinarian to rule out infection or other problems.

HEALTH

At this stage of your Lab puppy's life, some new concerns are worthy of your attention. The most important things to watch for this month are signs that your puppy has eaten something she shouldn't. Because she's teething, revisit your puppy-proofing efforts (covered in Month 3) and supervise her carefully. When you can't watch her, confine her.

When to Take Your Lab Puppy to the Vet

As you and your Lab puppy get acquainted, you might wonder when a case of puppy diarrhea or vomiting means it's time to head to the vet. What might be a minor condition in an adult Lab can quickly become critical in a puppy, so watch her, and if signs of illness continue for more than a few hours, contact your veterinarian.

The following warrant a trip to the veterinarian:

Diarrhea or vomiting: A puppy can get an upset tummy from eating too much or too fast. She may have swallowed a piece of stick in the yard or eaten too much grass. Or she might have parasites. If her feces contain blood or mucus, this could be a sign of parvovirus. Vomiting is also a symptom of poisoning. If your puppy is staggering or shaking, *take her to the vet immediately.*

Refusing food or water: A puppy can get dehydrated quickly, so offer your Lab plenty of water. If she doesn't want to drink, offer her ice cubes. They'll provide the moisture she needs but not make her queasy. Gnawing on the ice cubes also gives her something to think about besides how she feels.

TIPS AND TAILS

To check for dehydration, lift your puppy's skin along her back. If she's well hydrated, it should make a tent shape and immediately drop back into place. If the skin remains standing in a ridge, she's dehydrated. Also check her gums; they should be moist, not dry.

Some other breeds might skip a meal, but this is especially unusual for a Lab puppy. If meal skipping is accompanied by lethargy or listlessness, it could indicate something is seriously wrong. When she feels like eating again, start off slowly, feeding her a bland food like cooked plain skinless chicken and steamed rice or cottage cheese. When she feels better, gradually switch her back to her regular food.

If she doesn't feel better within 12 hours, call your vet. Your puppy may have a blockage caused by something she ate, such as socks, gravel, sticks, or bones.

Sudden changes in activity level: Beyond just a tired puppy taking a nap, is your pup lethargic, dull-eyed, and uninterested in her surroundings? Or is she frantic and hyperactive? Sudden changes like this might be a sign of fever, disease, or something as minor as a thorn in her foot.

Signs of pain or injury: Is she limping, whining, or crying when you touch her? Does she bite or snap at you? She might be trying to tell you where it hurts.

Breathing problems: If she's gagging, wheezing, or suddenly appears unable to breathe, this could be an emergency. She may have something stuck in her throat or might have been stung by a bee.

Fever: A puppy's temperature, taken rectally, is usually between 100°F and 102.5°F. Her nose is normally moist and wet, but it may be dry and warm if she has a fever. However, feeling your puppy's nose is not a foolproof way to detect a fever. Use a digital thermometer to get an accurate reading.

TIPS AND TAILS

To take your puppy's temperature, use a rectal thermometer lightly coated with petroleum jelly. Keep her occupied at the front end with treats. Hold up her tail, and gently put the thermometer into her rectum about 1 inch. Hold it there for 2 minutes or until it beeps (if you have a digital model). Call your veterinarian if it reads over 103°F.

Urine or bladder problems: Is an almost-housetrained pup suddenly having frequent accidents? Is there blood in her urine, or is it a dark color? Is she straining to go? This could be a urinary tract or kidney infection.

Constipation: Straining to eliminate could mean your pup isn't drinking enough water. Offer her canned food; it contains more moisture than dry food and helps get things moving. She also may have eaten something that caused a blockage. Sometimes, a puppy appears to be straining when she actually has diarrhea, so try to get an accurate read on what's happening.

Eye or nose discharge: If you see this, it could mean she has inhaled a foxtail or has something in her eye. It could also be a sign of upper-respiratory illness.

Unusual odor from mouth or ears: She could have a broken tooth that's infected or some decayed food stuck in her teeth. She also may have an ear infection or ear mites.

The veterinarian will want to know when the symptoms began and how the puppy has been acting. For digestive issues, you might be asked to bring in a stool sample.

Watching for Labrador Retriever Myopathy

Centronuclear myopathy is an inherited disease in Labradors that may show symptoms this month. A DNA test identifies this degenerative muscle disease, and your puppy's parents should have been tested for it.

Symptoms become apparent at 3 or 4 months. You'll first notice that your puppy's gait is odd and that she bunny-hops with her rear legs instead of running normally. The symptoms are worse when she's cold, stressed, or overexcited. She might start to look bony with muscle wasting around her head and shoulders. She might hold her head down and tucked against her chest.

The disease doesn't progress beyond 6 to 8 months of age, and although your Lab can recover and be a good pet, she won't be as active as most Labs. See your vet for an accurate diagnosis.

Getting Her Booster Vaccines

About 3 or 4 weeks after your Lab's first vaccines, you should visit the veterinarian for her second DHPP vaccine. Each booster continues to build her immunity by stimulating the production of antibodies that protect her from disease.

At 12 weeks, she's not completely protected yet. The final vaccine, at 14 to 16 weeks, completes the series, and she can start visiting the outside world. At 16 weeks, or 4 months, your veterinarian gives your pup her first rabies vaccine, which is effective for 1 year. Your pup needs a booster for both DHPP and rabies 1 year later.

The core vaccines all dogs should have—distemper, hepatitis, parvovirus, and parainfluenza—have a low risk of side effects. But you should be aware of the symptoms in case your dog has a reaction. They can occur minutes, hours, or days later and can last from a few minutes to hours.

At the site of the injection, bad reactions include pain, swelling, hair loss, inflammation, abscess, or intense itching. A reaction to nasal or oral vaccines could include ulceration in the nose or mouth, eye discharge, or coughing. The most severe vaccine reaction in dogs is anaphylactic shock, which is an extreme allergic response. Symptoms include difficulty breathing, swelling, low blood pressure, and weakness.

A mild allergic reaction can be treated with an antihistamine, but consult with your vet before administering any over-the-counter drug so you don't overdose or give your Lab anything toxic.

Dealing with External Parasites

Gone are the days when you had to constantly spray, dip, and bathe your dog in toxic pesticides to get rid of fleas and ticks. For the most part, you can control or eliminate these pests with over-the-counter products. However, some situations do require a visit to the vet.

Here's how to check your pup for these nasty critters:

Fleas: Roll your puppy over on her back, and you may see fleas scrambling across her tummy to hide. Often you'll just see flea "dirt." The black specks are flea droppings, and the white specks are their eggs.

Controlling fleas is also the key to preventing tapeworms, an internal parasite. If you see small bits that look like grains of rice around your pup's rectum, these are tapeworm segments. When a flea bites your puppy, she chews at that spot and ingests the flea. If the flea is carrying tapeworm eggs, they then hatch in your puppy's intestinal tract. Dogs can get these parasites by eating rodents such as mice or voles, too. Tapeworms can cause diarrhea and soft stools.

Ticks: Ticks feed on your dog's blood (as do fleas). A tick embeds its head in your dog's skin and can remain attached for several days, filling up with blood. A full tick looks like a raisin or grape hanging off your puppy's body.

Both fleas and ticks can quickly get out of hand if you don't protect your puppy. Ticks can transmit serious diseases to your dog—and you—such as Rocky Mountain spotted fever, ehrlichia, and Lyme disease. Ticks also have a toxin in their salivary glands that can cause a condition called tick paralysis, which causes a dog's hind legs and ultimately her entire body to become progressively weaker.

A puppy who has been bitten by a flea or tick may become lethargic, have a nasal discharge, or exhibit joint pain and lameness. If these symptoms occur, take her to the vet to test for parasite-borne diseases. Your pup also might have an allergic reaction to flea saliva and develop a skin infection that requires treatment.

Many topical preventives like Advantage II or FRONTLINE are approved for puppies older than 8 weeks. The dose is in proportion to your dog's weight, but read the label carefully. These products are easy to apply between the shoulder blades and partway down the spine so she can't lick or scratch off the medicine. The product distributes through your pup's coat and oil glands in the skin without being absorbed completely into the body. Many brands are even still effective after your Lab swims or has a bath. Most products are effective for 30 days, and fleas or ticks are usually killed within 12 to 48 hours. A bonus: these pests don't have to bite your puppy to be killed, as with some preventives.

Sometimes a dog has an allergic reaction to a topical product, with symptoms including itching, redness, or swelling. To ease these irritations, bathe her with a dish detergent such as Dawn to remove the product without harming her.

TIPS AND TAILS

Oral flea and tick preventives are often combined with heartworm pills in a single dose. Administered once a month, they offer continuous protection for your puppy. Some brands also kill lice and other types of worms like roundworm, hookworm, and whipworm. Plus, they don't leave a greasy residue on your dog's coat or cause skin irritation.

You'll find flea dirt not only on your pup, but also in her bed, in her crate, and anywhere else she's been. Fleas jump off your dog and hide in the carpet until another warm host walks by, so you haven't eliminated all the fleas around you just by treating your puppy. You'll have to treat other dogs, the cats, your yard, and your house as well to completely get rid of fleas. Nontoxic borax-based products and services like Fleabusters that dehydrate and kill fleas are available to treat your house and yard.

Ticks are common in the woods and in fields of tall grass. They like to hide several feet off the ground along hiking paths, waiting for an unsuspecting victim—you or your puppy—to latch onto. The more remote and overgrown an area, the more likely you and your Lab are to come home with a few hitchhikers, so stick to open trails as much as possible.

When you get back to your car, go over your dog thoroughly so you can remove the ticks before they attach to your puppy and start to feed. Rub her hair against the direction it grows so you can see down to her skin. A tick can look like a small black spec no bigger than a pencil point. Ticks look for warm spots, so pay special attention to your dog's "armpits," the folds of her neck, her groin, and her ears.

At home, go over her with a flea comb to remove any hangers-on. Just because you remove a tick doesn't mean it won't hop right back on, and ticks have a hard shell that's difficult to crush. To be sure it's gone for good, douse the tick in alcohol or insecticide.

Once a tick is attached and feeding, it's much harder to remove. Use tweezers or a specially made tick-puller. Grasp the tick as close to your pup's skin as possible, and slowly pull the tick from your dog's body. Be careful; the head breaks off easily, and you don't want to leave it embedded where it can cause an infection. Resist the temptation to crush an engorged tick. It's filled with blood that will explode everywhere. After you've removed and killed the tick, clean your puppy's skin and dab on some antibiotic ointment.

Fleas and ticks are common on rats, mice, rabbits, deer, and coyotes, so there are plenty of opportunities for your puppy to be re-infested. Even if your Lab doesn't currently have fleas or ticks, consistent use of flea and tick control products will protect her.

NUTRITION

A growing puppy needs plenty of food, but what she eats is also important. While you ensure she's getting enough, be careful that she's eating the right kinds of foods, and not learning any bad habits, like begging.

Appetite and Growth Spurts

Your puppy needs more food this month to keep up with her growth—up to about 4 cups a day. She'll probably eat as much as you give her, so don't think she's still hungry just because she's wolfing down her food. Increase her food in small amounts—maybe ¼ cup at a time—to match her growth, not her appetite.

When the growth spurt is over, her appetite may diminish a little, so cut back on her food. Be ready to increase the amount again when her next growth spurt occurs.

Don't forget, you're giving her a lot of treats during training, too, and that adds to her total calorie count. Use part of her daily kibble ration as training treats, and continue to monitor her weight.

Feeding Your Puppy

The eating habits you teach your Lab puppy now are established for life. If she has to compete with other dogs for her food, she'll learn to gulp down her meals. If you feed her from the table while you eat dinner, you'll create a lifelong beggar. Set up a feeding routine now, and stick to it.

Feed your Lab at the same times every day. If she knows when mealtime is, she won't pester you at all hours. If you feed her just before you sit down for your dinner, she'll be full and not so anxious to join you (but then again, it seems Labs are *never* full …). After she's eaten, that's it—no seconds. Don't let those big sad "Oh please, I'm starving!" puppy eyes fool you.

If it's too late, and you already have a beggar on your hands, put her in another room, put her in her crate, or tie her to something until you're finished eating.

Feeding your dog table scraps can be dangerous. "Give the poor dog a bone" is one of the worst things you can do, especially if it's a cooked bone. Cooked bones are dry and brittle, and they can break apart easily and puncture your puppy's esophagus, stomach, or intestines. Poultry bones are smaller and more dangerous than beef, and larger pieces of bone can cause an intestinal blockage. Raw bones are safer, but raw poultry bones are still risky.

TIPS AND TAILS

People who feed their dog a raw diet often grind the raw bones to minimize danger.

Holiday leftovers are especially hazardous for dogs. Greasy turkey (and the bones) tossed in the trash is just too tempting for a curious Lab to resist. Besides the danger bones present, fatty foods can cause pancreatitis, a potentially fatal inflammation. Severe vomiting, diarrhea, dehydration, and lethargy are symptoms of pancreatitis, and your puppy will require several days of hospitalization—if she survives.

GROOMING

Labs are hardy, wash-and-wear dogs who shed dirt easily and require minimal maintenance. But they still need some regular grooming to keep them in good condition and ensure they're healthy. With routine grooming, your puppy will look and feel better, and you'll catch small health problems before they become big issues. Best of all, you'll enjoy time together.

Grooming Your Puppy

A Lab needs a good brushing about once a week, but she rarely needs bathing because her thick, double coat is water- and dirt-repellant. She'll shed heavily twice a year, in the fall and spring, and her coat will need more attention during these times.

A weekly grooming routine should include brushing her coat, clipping her toenails, checking and cleaning her ears as necessary, and brushing her teeth.

In Month 3, you introduced your pup to some grooming tools and started teaching her to enjoy being groomed. This month, you continue grooming … in spite of her protests. An active Lab puppy is in no mood to sit still, and she'll wiggle, bite, and play puppy games to get out of being groomed. Take her for a long walk or vigorous play session just before it's time to groom so she'll be tired and sit still for you. Give her a toy stuffed with peanut butter or biscuits, and let her gnaw on that while you work on her.

Reward her for sitting still, and break grooming into small segments between treats. For example, trim one toenail, give her a treat, and brush her for a minute. Then trim another toenail and give her a treat. Stop after a few minutes, and do some more a half hour later.

Include a health check as part of your routine:

Skin: Check for lumps and bumps, cuts, and scratches. Carefully examine under her legs against her body where ticks and grass seedlings might stick to her.

Feet: Examine her paw pads to be sure they're not raw or cracked. Look for thorns or other foreign objects embedded between her toes or in her paw pads. Check her toenails for any broken or infected nails that need attention.

Mouth: Check to see if her gums are red or sore, especially while she's teething. Look for broken teeth or objects stuck between her teeth, and check for lumps or cuts on the roof of her mouth and under her tongue. Be sure her gums are bright and pink.

Eyes: Her eyes should be clear and bright, not cloudy, and with no mucus in the corners. Be sure no grass or other irritants are in her eyes.

Ears: Wipe out her outer ear with a damp cloth or cotton ball, and look to see if there's discoloration or debris down in the ear. Smell her ears; a bad smell means an ear infection.

If you look over your puppy carefully on a regular basis, you'll recognize immediately when she's injured or ill. And when she's used to being checked over, she'll be more likely to let you examine her when she's not feeling well.

Setting Up a Grooming Schedule

Pick one afternoon or evening once a week, and spend some quality time cuddling and grooming your Lab puppy. Place a beach towel or old sheet in front of the TV, and combine grooming time with your favorite sitcom. Set out your tools: brush, flea comb, toothbrush and toothpaste, toenail clippers, Kwik Stop, and treats. By the time you're ready, Puppy will be ready, too, because she knows what's up.

Once a week might not be enough. If you're an especially tidy housekeeper, you'll soon realize that Labs shed a lot, and the more often you brush her, the less often you'll have to vacuum. Two or even three brushings a week may be necessary. During shedding season, you might want to take the grooming party outside because you'll have more hair to deal with.

Other grooming chores, like trimming her toenails, may only need attention once a week or every other week. You might want to skip toothbrushing if her mouth is too painful from teething. If so, to keep her in the habit, rub a little pet toothpaste on your fingertip and let her lick it off.

SOCIAL SKILLS

Your last opportunity to have a significant impact on your puppy's personality is between 12 and 16 weeks. This month ends the first critical period of socialization. Continue the lessons you started last month by exposing her to more people, sounds, smells, and textures.

Socializing to Calm Adult Dogs

If you have another dog in your household, you've seen her interact with your puppy. But your Lab needs to meet other dogs, too, especially dogs of different breeds and sizes, while she's young. One-on-one encounters are safer.

Choose your puppy's companions carefully. The only adult dogs your puppy should meet now are well-socialized and tolerant dogs of both sexes. A puppy needs older dogs to teach her lessons you and other puppies can't teach. Adult dogs generally forgive a pup or discipline her lightly for her transgressions while she's still very young. It's better that your puppy learns her doggie manners now, when no one is likely to hurt her.

When she meets an adult dog, your puppy will use the same appeasement behaviors she offered her mother back in the litter. She'll approach the adult with a low-slung "I'm-a-little-puppy" wiggle and her tail tucked between her legs. Then she'll roll over and offer her tummy for a sniff. She may release a little urine so the adult dog can tell how old the puppy is. By doing this, your puppy is communicating that she's not challenging the older dog and that she's not sexually mature yet. She may also lick the adult's muzzle or lift one paw toward her, both submissive behaviors she learned when just a few weeks old.

A pup who doesn't offer submission when she approaches an adult may be chastised. Most dogs will tolerate a baby until she steps out of bounds. Leaping on the adult, walking over her, yanking on her tail or ears, chasing, pouncing—all play behaviors—are fine until the grownup has had enough.

Another favorite puppy ploy is to try to steal a bone or toy from the adult dog. You'll see the grownup purposely put the bone just out of reach and watch the puppy approach it. When the puppy attempts to take the item, the adult will come to his feet with a bark and reclaim his rightful ownership.

An adult dog uses varying degrees of discipline. He might growl, give a severe look, air snap, or even give a short and sharp bark—all low-level corrections. After one or two incidents, most puppies understand. Some pups, however, are oblivious to the message, and the adult will ramp up his response. He'll roar like a lion, chase away the pup, or stand over the puppy and plant a paw on her body. All this sounds very ferocious, but no one gets hurt.

TIPS AND TAILS

When introducing your puppy to an adult dog, try to stay out of the action and let nature take its course as long as possible. Don't discipline the older dog; she's just establishing the dog rules, and your puppy needs to learn these valuable lessons.

Monitor the behavior of both dogs to ensure a safe encounter. If your puppy is persistently obnoxious, step in and stop her and give the older dog a break before she loses all patience. If the older dog is standing over the puppy with her hackles up, stiff tail, and ears forward, or if she's chasing your puppy, this might be a sign of an overactive prey drive. Stop it before instinct takes over and your pup gets hurt.

Meanwhile, don't make excuses for your Lab puppy. "She's just a baby. She doesn't know any better," isn't going to teach her a thing. And if you step in and rescue her, she'll learn she can be a brat with no consequences.

Socializing to Many People and Things

Get creative this month. Her fear-imprint period is over, and your Lab pup is more responsive and outgoing. Invite the cheerleading team to come over in uniform, a football player in uniform, kids wearing backpacks, babies in diapers, and other people in unusual clothes.

Let her investigate your wet umbrella when you come in. Then pick it up and hold it over your head and shake the water off onto her. Let her walk over a metal grate or figure out a pile of rocks. Although her vaccines are almost done, she doesn't have full immunity, so limit her exposure to public places.

HAPPY PUPPY

Have a contest to see who in the family can come up with the most interesting new thing to introduce to your puppy.

It might seem obvious, but if you pet a puppy in different ways, you get different reactions. The way you pet her can even cause her to mouth or bite at you. Here's how to properly pet your pup:

○ Stroke her in the same direction her hair grows. Rubbing against the growth may be uncomfortable and make her move away from you.

○ Scratch her chest rather than reach for her head. An incoming hand is the perfect target for an excited, mouthy Lab puppy, and a shy pup will cower at a hand looming over her.

○ Pet her quickly if you want her to get excited (she'll probably start to mouth you); stroke slowly if you want her to calm down.

○ Stop before your puppy decides she's had enough. Always leave her wanting more.

When your puppy meets new people, she may offer her belly and release some urine, just as she did when meeting adult dogs. This is normal canine behavior, and Labs almost always outgrow it. An especially submissive Lab may continue to urinate even when she no longer rolls over on her back to greet someone.

To prevent submissive urination from becoming a habit, avoid situations that cause her to urinate. Let her approach people rather than allowing them to loom over her or corner her. It might seem like no big deal to you, but from your puppy's viewpoint, this new person might as well be King Kong. If someone is too rough with your puppy, move the puppy away.

Also, don't punish your puppy for the submissive urination. This just frightens her more. You want to build her confidence, not punish her for what's a purely physical reaction.

That said, don't comfort her, either. Your sympathy and worried voice may have the opposite effect of what you intended and convince her there was good reason to be afraid.

BEHAVIOR

Your Lab's personality will really start to shine this month. She'll gain confidence as she has successful experiences, and she'll enthusiastically tackle new challenges. She wants to stick close to you, but she also wants to check out the world. She takes her cues from you when she's unsure, and she fearlessly follows you everywhere. Enjoy it now, and take advantage of her devotion because next month she'll be a preteen and ready to take over the world.

Preventing Separation Anxiety

We wish our dogs could be with us all day, every day, but it's not possible, and puppies do need to learn to spend time alone. A dog who can never be left home alone without destroying the house may be suffering from separation anxiety. Teach your Lab to feel safe and comfortable at home alone while she's still a puppy, even if you're home all day. Your life or job situation may change someday, and you're heading off future trauma by teaching this lesson now, when she is young.

Your puppy's not yet mature enough to have the run of an entire house or yard, so confine her in her crate or pen when you're gone. What you might think is separation anxiety might really be simple puppy mischief. When you're not there to supervise, she's free to indulge her curiosity and entertain herself in doggie ways. She knows she can't dump the trash and eat the kitty litter in front of you, but when you're gone, she makes her own rules.

Teach your puppy not to rely on your constant attention every minute you're at home. Set up her crate, pen, or wherever she can stay when you're gone, and practice leaving her in it for short rests during the day. She'll learn to feel safe there, chewing on her toy and listening to household noises. She'll also realize that being in her pen doesn't always mean she's going to be left for long periods.

Deafening quiet could unnerve your puppy, so when you leave, turn on the radio or television so the house still has signs of activities she'd hear when you're home. Background noise also blocks out scary sounds from outdoors, so she won't react to unknown terrors.

HAPPY PUPPY

Exercise your puppy before you leave her alone at home. Take her for a walk, practice obedience, or play a game. Then give her a chance to settle down and relax so she won't still be excited when you put her in her pen.

She'll quickly learn that the rustle of keys followed by you picking up your briefcase or purse, getting your jacket out of the closet, or picking up your books all mean one awful thing: you're going, and she's staying. While you're teaching her to spend time alone, occasionally go through your leaving routine without actually leaving. Pick everything up, fiddle with it so she can see you're doing so, put it all back down, and go back to what you were doing.

Don't make a fuss over your puppy when you come and go. Put her in her pen and do something else for a few minutes before you leave. Then just leave. Big good-byes and lots of farewell petting just rev her up and upset her. When you come home, ignore her while you put down your things and get settled. Then greet her calmly and take her outside for a break.

Minimizing Mouthing and Overexcitement

Puppies learn by playing, and her over-the-top behavior this month includes plenty of chasing, pouncing, biting, and mounting. We talked about puppy biting in Month 3, but now your Lab is constantly grabbing and biting everything she sees.

Labs are an oral breed. They're genetically wired to use their mouths, a behavior that goes back to what they were bred to do: carry a bird back to the hunter. A good hunting dog has a soft mouth, but a Lab should never put her teeth on her people. Don't allow puppy-biting to continue—a 60-pound piranha is not what you signed up for when you got a Lab.

Mouthing and overexcited behavior go hand in hand. Here are some tips to minimize both:

- Pet her body first, not her head. Your hand reaching toward her face is an easy target. Pet slowly, using long strokes on her body and head.

- Don't roughhouse. Your hands darting at her encourage mouthing. Rough handling of her head, even in fun, also invites her to play bite.

- Be sure she's getting enough exercise and sleep. A wound-up or tired puppy is more likely to jump and bite.

- Schedule play dates with other vaccinated puppies. They'll discipline her if she bites too hard.

- Stop the game if she won't quit mouthing. Step in and stop the action when she plays too rough with kids or other puppies.

- When she's really excited, use less body language and a soft voice. Calm her with some quiet massage and petting. Offer a chew toy after she calms down, not before, or she'll think it's a reward for all her frenzied activity.

- If she's too wound up to accept handling, let her drag a leash so you can lead her away from an overactive situation to a place where she can calm down.

- Teach her to bring you a toy when she's overexcited or mouthing you. Make a big deal out of it, and she'll quickly learn to go get her toy whenever she's excited.

- Give her a short time-out in her crate or pen.

Dealing with Vocal Discovery

You'll wake up one morning this month and realize your puppy has discovered she can do things with her voice. Barking at the cat makes the cat run, barking at other puppies makes them play, and barking at the mailman makes him go away. This is about the time many Lab owners throw up their hands and enroll in puppy classes.

It starts when she barks excitedly and you respond. Next thing you know, she's standing in front of you barking for attention. And it works, doesn't it? If only to shut her up, you immediately take action. This rewards the behavior, and before long, you have a chronic barker. Instead, distract her by making a noise or dropping a book. When she stops and looks at you, praise her and give her something else to do.

When she's barking for attention or just getting too wound up, put her in her crate for a time-out and don't let her out until she's quiet. Don't talk to her, either. It might take 5 minutes or a half hour, but if you give in and release her, she learns that if she barks enough, there's a chance you'll let her out. She'll keep trying until she hits the jackpot.

If you don't accidentally reward her for barking, she'll eventually grow out of this stage.

TRAINING

At 12 to 16 weeks, it's time to teach your puppy specific behaviors. She needs to learn vital skills by the time she's 5 months old, but if you don't start until then, she'll be too distracted by adolescence to learn much. The commands you teach her now build a framework for later training and communication.

Your puppy is focused on you right now, and she's an eager student. She's realized that watching and listening to you produces good things. She's able to connect your words to her actions and remember what worked for her yesterday. And whether or not you're teaching, she's certainly learning.

When teaching your puppy something new, work with her in a quiet place with no outside interference: no TV, video games, or other household activities. You want her to focus on you. Once she learns a behavior, you can teach her to respond in spite of distractions.

Enrolling in Puppy Class

You're doing everything right for your Lab puppy. She's meeting new people every week, you've started training, and her housetraining is going well. Even so, puppy class, often called puppy kindergarten, is an essential part of her education and social development, and the window of time when this can benefit her the most is closing fast.

You started searching for a trainer when you first got your puppy. (See Months 1 and 2 for tips on selecting a puppy trainer.) Now it's time to finalize your decision and enroll.

HAPPY PUPPY

Approach training as a game. Your puppy's attention span is still short, and she'll learn faster if she's having fun. If she's really active, train after she's had a short play session, when the edge is off and she can concentrate better. Adjust your methods to her personality and mood.

You might be worried about enrolling in a training class knowing your puppy isn't yet fully immunized. But the risk of inadequate socialization is greater than the risk of disease. If you select the school carefully, her chances of getting sick are less likely. Choose a facility that's clean and well maintained. Check out the health requirements for all dogs entering the premises, including for other classes. (Most trainers require puppies to have two distemper/parvo combination vaccinations prior to starting the class, and by 13 or 14 weeks of age, most puppies have had those shots.) All dogs should be vaccinated, and no unknown dogs should be allowed. Some facilities rent their space on weekends for dog clubs and competitions; does this one? What are the health requirements for dogs who attend these events? Do they clean and disinfect thoroughly afterward?

Expect to see a mix of big and small puppies in class. The instructor separates the pups if the bigger ones overwhelm the littler/younger ones. You don't want a sensitive puppy to be overwhelmed and frightened or a bully rewarded for pushing other puppies around. Puppy class is for developing social skills and confidence, not destroying them.

Don't be offended if your bundle of joy is singled out. Any pup who plays too roughly should be removed and introduced slowly to just one or two puppies at a time. That's a lesson she needs to learn, and that's why you're at class.

Classes are a combination of playtime and lessons. All play, all the time gets the puppies too fired up. Your Lab puppy learns the difference between when she can play and be active, and when she has to settle down or pay attention, and her reward for calming down is to go back and play some more. She's handled, trained, and corrected by new people. Equally important is the opportunity to play and learn her dog manners and bite inhibition with other puppies.

The instructor sets up play equipment that presents new and fun challenges you don't have at home, like agility equipment. While observing you with your pup in class, the instructor is able to identify potential problems and help you explore solutions. The instructor also helps the entire family get involved with the puppy's lessons.

Puppy classes are as much about training you as training your puppy, and everyone in the family needs to be consistent, so bring the whole family along. You learn how to teach your puppy, properly reward her, and introduce her to basic obedience exercises like sit, down, and come. You also learn how to shape her behavior to manage play biting, jumping up, and chewing. You practice social skills like meeting new people and animals and discover how to handle situations when she's afraid. You play games with your puppy that both teach her and build your bond with her. And you can ask your instructor questions when you get stuck.

Many puppy class instructors follow the American Kennel Club S.T.A.R. (Socialization, Training, Activity, and Responsibility) Puppy Program. This 6-week course ends with a quiz for both owners and puppies. Owners also make a Responsible Dog Owner's Pledge to accept responsibility for the care and training of their puppy. For more information, visit akc.org/starpuppy.

Teaching "Sit"

"Sit" is practical and easy to teach your puppy. It's a command you'll use over and over again. For example, you can tell your Lab to sit for many reasons, such as before you put her food down, so you can attach her leash, to greet people, for a vet exam, or before you go through a door. The first thing she'll learn is to sit for a treat. Many people teach their puppy to sit for her dinner as early as 8 weeks.

Let's review the steps for sit. (Your pup doesn't need to be on a leash unless you have trouble keeping her attention.) With your puppy standing, facing you, hold a treat just above and in front of her head—don't hold it so high she tries to jump up and take it. She'll look up to reach for it, and as she does, slowly move your hand backward toward her tail, keeping it just above or in front of her nose. She'll naturally rock back and sit when you lean into her. Immediately feed her the treat and praise her while her rear is still touching the ground. Then say "Okay!" and let her get up. She'll soon learn that "Okay!" means she's finished and can move.

TIPS AND TAILS

If you have trouble getting her to sit, have her stand with her back near a wall or piece of furniture. Then she can't back up because she has nowhere to go.

Repeat this three or four times, and you'll find she starts to sit as soon as you lift your hand. As a bonus, you're teaching her the hand signal for sit before she's even learned the word. When she reliably sits for you, add the word "Sit" just before she actually sits. Don't say "Sit down"; save "Down" for another behavior. Pretty soon she'll associate the word with the action.

When she understands the word "Sit," ask her to sit without the hand signal or lure. Produce the treat and praise as soon as she responds. If it doesn't work, she doesn't understand yet, so back up and work some more on the initial steps.

At first, let her up as soon as she gets her treat. Once she's responding well, wait for a second or two before you release her with "Okay." Don't stare at her; that will make her uncertain and she'll stand up. Work up to a few seconds before you release her. Then alternate with some immediate releases and sometimes letting her sit for a few seconds. You'll see her fidget and think about getting up. Try to release her while it's still *your* idea, not hers.

When her sit is consistent, ask for it in other rooms and outside, with you facing her, and with you at her side. Always praise her warmly, even if you don't have a treat. Pretty soon she'll sit whenever you look at her!

Invite everyone in your household to tell her to sit. Hand out treats, and have your guests tell her to sit before she greets them.

Teaching "Down"

"Down" is an easier position for a puppy to hold when she has to stay in one place for more than a few seconds. Down is useful when you're out in public, standing and talking to someone, waiting at the vet's, when you groom her, and when you need her to settle for a period of time. A dog can hold a sit for a minute or two, but she can be trained to stay in the down position for 30 minutes or more.

Down is a little harder to teach for several reasons. Your little wigglewort will want to play instead of letting you manipulate her into a down. Down is a submissive position, and she may not want to accept your control. If you've been practicing handling her, she'll learn the down much more quickly.

Let's review the steps for down. With your pup sitting (try this on a slippery floor to make the process easier), hold a treat in front of her nose and slowly lower it to the floor, letting her nose follow your hand. When your hand gets to the floor, pull the treat slowly away while pressing gently between her shoulder blades. She should gradually lower herself to the floor. If she does, watch her elbows. As soon as they touch the ground, feed her the treat, praise her, say "Okay," and let her up.

Some dogs will feel the pressure of your hand and immediately push back—a natural opposition reflex. If your puppy does that, you'll need a different approach. Instead of pressing between her shoulder blades, scoop your arm under her front legs and pull them forward, lowering her body to the ground.

TIPS AND TAILS

Training your Lab isn't a one-person job. Take advantage of your family's interest in your new puppy to involve everyone in training and socialization. When you play and train together, you all learn how to work with her, get the results you want, and are consistent in what you teach. As an added bonus, your pup will respond to and bond with everyone in the family.

Another method to teach down is to sit on the floor and bend one knee up with your foot on the floor. Lure your pup under your leg with a treat. She'll have put her front end down to reach under and get the treat. As soon as her elbows touch the floor, give her a treat, praise her, and release her. Lure her farther each time until her entire body is down before you give her the treat. Sometimes she'll get stuck with her rear up in the air, and you might have to scoop under her rear legs to settle her back end. Help her understand that *all* of her needs to be on the floor.

As you did with the sit, practice numerous times over several sessions. Then start practicing in different places and on different surfaces. Your puppy will test you and try to get out of going down by rolling over, wiggling, and biting at your hands. Have patience! Don't give her a treat until her elbows and back legs are on the floor.

When she anticipates what you're asking, she'll lie down as soon as you start to shape her into position, and you'll be able to touch her less and less. Pretty soon, the motion you use—luring her nose down with a treat and pulling it out in front of her—turns into a hand signal, and you can add the command "Down" as she starts to comply. Always follow through and be sure she goes all the way down.

Up until now, you've been on the floor with your puppy, and that's the picture she has in her mind of the exercise. She won't understand what you're asking if you stand up and tell her "Down." Gradually work with her until you can stand on your knees and then stand completely and she'll still comply. Don't bend down toward her when you give the command; stay upright. Bending over her is an invitation to get up and come to you.

HAPPY PUPPY

Once she can do both a sit and a down in response to a verbal command, play a game of push-ups with her. Ask for a sit, a down, a sit, and a down, alternating several times. She'll pop up into a sit and throw herself down. Once she understands it's a game, she'll anticipate your next command, and you can make her wait until you tell her. She's learning to listen and respond quickly—and you're both having a lot of fun.

Talk to your puppy as you train her. Your Lab responds to your body language and tone of voice more than she hears the words you say. Some people, often women, politely ask their dog to comply. "Puppy, sit?" The pup hears you're not sure about it, and she worries. Another approach is baby talk, which tells her it's playtime. Either way, she gets confused. Other people, including many men, take the words *obedience command* seriously. They stand up stiff and straight in an authoritative pose and bark out a gruff "Sit!" Their harsh tone and overpowering body language make the puppy think she's done something wrong. About this time, the owner thinks her dog is a sissy, and the puppy decides her owner is a tyrant.

Tell your dog once, say it firmly, expect her to comply, and reward her with happy body language and warm and loving praise. You're not just teaching an obedience command here; you're building a relationship of mutual respect and trust.

Introducing Leash Walking

Until now, you've been carrying your Lab puppy out in public, and she happily follows you around at home. But she's getting heavy, and it's time for her to learn to walk nicely at your side. In this section, we learn leash walking.

Break the following steps into short sessions. At the beginning of each session, start with something she knows well before you move on to new things.

To begin, take your hungry puppy to a confined area with no distractions. Hook the leash to her flat collar (no chain collars, no harnesses). Let her drag the leash around, get tangled, and figure out how to untangle herself. Let her step on it and get stuck. She'll figure out to move her feet or give to the pressure of the leash to relieve the pull on her neck.

Next, stand, kneel, or sit on the ground. Hold one end of the leash steady, and put just enough pressure on it that she feels it. Every action provokes a reaction, and her first instinct when she feels the pressure is to pull away from it. She may struggle, flip over, bite at the leash, and throw a full-fledged tantrum. Be a statue, don't say anything, and let her figure it out.

Continue to hold firmly, but don't pull her. The instant she gives the tiniest bit to the pressure and the leash slackens, release the leash, praise her, and give her a treat. If you loosen the pressure before she gives to it, she learns that struggling makes it go away. You want her to learn that calmly moving toward you makes the pressure stop.

Pick up the leash again and repeat. After a few tries, she'll realize that if she gives in to the pressure, you'll give her a treat.

TIPS AND TAILS

Although you're teaching her, she's also teaching herself what leash pressure is and how to make it stop. Make it easy for her to learn, and don't move on to the next step too quickly.

Stand up and step backward, keeping light, steady pressure on the leash. Wait quietly until she leans toward you or takes a step in your direction. Don't look directly at her because she might be intimidated by your gaze and afraid to move forward. And don't go to her; she's learning to come to you.

Encourage her with praise when she even thinks about moving forward. You'll be able to tell. If she comes all the way to you, great! That's where you want her. Give her some extra loving every time she comes to you. If she balks, just keep the steady pressure on the leash until she gives in and complies. She's confused, and you may have moved on before she really understood what you wanted. Practice backward steps until you both can move two or three steps without pressure.

Now turn so you're sideways and a step ahead of her. Because you're no longer facing her, it presents a different picture, and she'll be confused at first. Repeat the previous steps in this position. Pay careful attention to the feel of the pressure on the leash. Without looking, you can tell if she's giving to the slight pull.

Stand with your puppy at your left side with the leash in your hands. The clip should hang loosely from her neck. Take one step forward with your left foot and tighten the leash slightly as you do so. If your puppy moves with you, give her a treat, praise her, and have a party! She did just what she was supposed to do! If she balks, stop and wait until she gives in to the pressure and then quietly treat, praise, and take another step.

TIPS AND TAILS

When you want your dog to walk with you at your left side, always start out with your left foot. That's a visual signal down at her eye level that it's time to move. When you want her to stay in place, step off with your right foot.

Work up to taking several steps before you stop and praise her. If she pulls against the leash, stop briefly and try again. This trial-and-error method keeps her thinking. As she understands what works and what doesn't, she'll catch on.

At this point, just before you take your first step, add your command word, such as "Let's go" or "Walk." Don't use "Heel." That's a precise position used in obedience competition where a dog is at your left side, her ear lines up with the seam on your pants, and she's looking at you. You might want to teach a variation of heel later to use when you take her out in public or if you plan to compete with your dog. For now, you're just teaching her to walk nicely at your side with no pressure on the leash, a much looser position.

Don't add steps too quickly; remember, you want her to be successful. When she starts getting pretty good at leash walking, you can add variations to make it fun for both of you. Take several steps, turn in the opposite direction, and invite her to catch up. Go fast, go slow, turn left, turn right, and walk in a circle. Always encourage her, praise her, and give her treats when she's by your side or catches up. She needs lots of feedback.

By now, she's walking well in the living room, but that's not the real world. Practice in the backyard, on the driveway, and in other places so she *generalizes* the concept of walking on a leash.

 DOG TALK

A puppy **generalizes** a lesson when she learns that a particular command means the same thing in many different places and situations. For example, "Sit" means "rear end on the floor" in the living room, on the driveway, in the garage, in the yard, and at puppy class. She also learns "Sit" means sit when someone else uses the word, even when the person is standing, sitting, or across the room.

When she's walking nicely in a few places, add a mild distraction, like a family member walking at a distance. Remember to keep this practice short—just a few minutes.

If you begin to lose her attention, try to get it back quickly. As soon as her attention wanders, make noise, change directions, skip, or pull a squeaky toy from your pocket. She'll hurry to catch up and find out what she missed. Be more interesting than the distraction, and always praise and reward her when her attention is back on you. Gradually add other distractions as she gets the hang of the game, such as a ball, a cat, a child on a bike, or a car going by.

Natural distractions, like a good smell or a leaf, will always tempt your canine buddy. If you stop and wait while she sniffs, *she's* teaching *you* the rules of the walk. If you decide to let her sniff, give her permission before she gets to the item. Give it a name, like "Go sniff." Practice calling her back to continue walking, and praise her when she responds. She'll soon learn.

Housetraining Progress

By the end of this month, your Lab puppy should be almost, if not completely, housetrained. She should easily sleep through the night in her crate without needing to go out. If this isn't happening, first be sure she doesn't have a urinary tract infection. Have your vet check a urine sample.

If she's healthy and still having accidents, review the housetraining process outlined in Month 3, and tighten up your supervision. Labs are relatively easy to housetrain compared to other breeds.

The main cause of delayed housetraining is that owners stop going outside with their puppy each time she needs a break, and she hasn't really learned why she's out there. They let her out and give her a treat when she comes back in. They don't know if she's eliminated or not, and the puppy thinks she's being rewarded for coming in so she doesn't take her time and get the job done.

If she's having accidents in the house, keep her in the same room, next to you, on a leash. Do you recognize the signals that she needs to go out? If you're busy and can't watch her, put her in her crate. Every time she pees in the house, she's essentially being rewarded for her behavior. The smell remains, and it becomes harder for her to understand why she can't go there again.

So plan ahead. Keep track of when she eliminates, and a pattern will emerge. Anticipate those times, and take her out before she asks. If she doesn't go, confine her in her crate for 30 minutes and try again. These methods should help you catch up on her housetraining and quickly make a difference.

Handling Your Puppy's Collar

When your Lab gets too heavy to pick up, you may be tempted—especially when she's been into some aggravating mischief—to take her by the collar and drag her outside or to her crate. Think again. It only takes once or twice for this action to create a hand-shy dog who plays keep-away—or worse, snaps at you to get away from punishment.

The alternative? Keep leashes hanging on every doorknob so you can hook her up and escort her. A puppy who hangs back and resists being dragged will usually happily follow you on a leash. Or grab a few treats and show them to your pup. She'll quickly stop and follow you. If she doesn't want to go out, let her see you put the treats just outside the door and close it. The same method works with her crate. Put the treat in her crate, and shut the door with her outside. Pretty soon she'll want to go where the treats are, and she'll be happy to comply with your wishes. You have just successfully distracted her from her misbehavior and turned it into a learning opportunity.

Still, your puppy needs to allow you to take her by the collar without protesting. Someday, your 60-pound Lab will crash out the gate or front door, and you need to know you can grab her in an emergency. By that time, she'll be much stronger than you, and you might not win.

You've been working on handling your pup. Now it's time to focus on this specific lesson. Take hold of her collar, and offer her a piece of kibble. If she shies away, start by reaching for other parts of her body where she enjoys being touched. Do this many times. When she's comfortable with you touching her collar, wrap your hand around it for a few seconds and release. Every once in a while—not often and not more than once per session—grab the collar quickly. You don't want this to turn into a hand-biting game. She'll learn you aren't coming at her to hit her.

Everyone in the family should practice this skill with your puppy so she trusts all of you.

YOU AND YOUR PUPPY

You love your new puppy and want to keep her safe, so select safe toys and supervise her while she plays with them. Even though she's still just a baby, try not to overprotect her. As you play and get to know each other, you'll learn to read her canine body language and communicate better with her.

Choosing Safe Toys

Your Lab will destroy toys no other puppy could dismantle. Remember, Labs are mouth-oriented, and chewing is an important part of their play. If you don't provide chew toys, she'll make her own—usually something you'd prefer she not chew, like your designer shoes or the coffee table leg.

Toys fall into several categories:

- **Toys she can tear apart:** Many toys are fine as long as you're there to take them away when they start to fall apart.

- **Toys she can have when you leave her alone:** Super-tough indestructible toys (you'll soon learn which ones these are) will last several months before they break.

- **Real bones and chewies:** These are made of natural substances, and you can offer them to her while she's young if you supervise carefully.

Stuffed animals with squeakers inside could be shredded in minutes, or they may last days. Knotted ropes, tough fabric toys, Planet Dog Orbee-Tuff toys, tennis balls, and other items may be safe now, but as she grows and her mouth gets stronger and bigger, she'll easily shred or swallow them. There's no magical list of safe toys. The best way to know for sure is to test them on your pup.

TIPS AND TAILS

For a Lab, choose heavy-duty chewies that are larger than you might think a puppy needs. Never give her a toy she can get completely in her mouth, especially a round ball. If she swallows it, it can block her airway or lodge in her stomach and cause an obstruction.

Galileo Bones are a super-tough version of the Nylabone and almost indestructible. These are usually safe to leave with your pup when you're not home. Hard rubber toys like a KONG, which you can stuff with treats and freeze, last for several months. A frozen, stuffed KONG also eases her teething pain. As with other toys, check her KONG for cracks or missing chips of rubber. When she's started to break it up, throw it away.

Real bones and chewies made from real animal parts (as opposed to rubber or nylon versions) are fine for a puppy, but most of these products are unsafe for an adult Lab. Many varieties are available, including marrowbones, stuffed bones, smoked or filet mignon–flavored bones. Watch carefully to be sure they don't cause her diarrhea and there are no bits and pieces in her stool. Be vigilant. A Lab puppy's strong jaws can break off sharp chunks that she'll then swallow. Pieces can lodge in her intestines and cause a life-threatening blockage that requires surgery. A small chunk could lodge in her windpipe. A sharp sliver might perforate her intestine.

Here are some examples of real chews:

Rawhide bones, made of cowhide (leather) are not digestible, which means a puppy's body cannot break down the material and pass it through her system and eliminate it. Rawhides soften as your puppy chews, and she can tear off a large piece and swallow it.

Bully sticks are made of beef muscle and are digestible. Your puppy will get hours of entertainment from a bully stick, but take it away when it gets small enough to lodge in her mouth or swallow.

Stuffed bones are made from femur bones and are cut, cleaned, sterilized, and filled with peanut butter or meat-flavored mixture (not necessarily real meat). The stuffing could contain additives and chemicals. The outside will splinter after a certain amount of chewing, so take them away when they reach this point.

Cooked bones, as mentioned earlier, are never safe for any dog. Cooking dries out the bones, making them splinter easily. Your puppy could swallow chips or sharp pieces, and those could hurt her insides.

Pig snouts are made of flesh, not bone, and are easier for your puppy to digest.

TIPS AND TAILS

Choose products made in America whenever possible. Many imported chew bones are processed with chemicals that are dangerous to your puppy.

Overprotecting Your Puppy

There's a fine line between protecting your puppy and *overprotecting* her. Allow your pup to figure out new things for herself as much as possible. She doesn't have much experience yet, so she'll try things and get stuck. If she's cautious, let her take her time.

For example, if she climbs into a cardboard box tipped on its side and it falls over, there's no door for her to exit. Resist the temptation to rescue her. Let her poke around and try different things. Unless she collapses in blind panic, she'll eventually climb out or knock the box over. Then you can throw toys in the box to encourage her to continue exploring what the box will do. Will the flaps hit her as she crawls out? Does the bottom break out if she paws at it?

A puppy who's allowed to experiment grows up self-confident and eager to try new things. She develops problem-solving abilities and learns to think for herself. If you're too overprotective, she grows up shy and fearful, expecting you to step in and save her from every situation. This learned helplessness is hard to undo once she grows up. Her dependence on you will lead to separation anxiety and other unwanted behaviors.

Of course, you'll want to protect her from a charging dog or a horde of unruly children. But whenever possible, let her learn about her world in her own way.

Understanding Canine Communication

Dogs have three primary ways of communicating with each other: body language, voice, and smell. They'll try to communicate with you the same way, so learn how to read your puppy and what she's telling you. Look at the total dog, her posture and her arousal level, and try to figure out what might be triggering her response.

Some behaviors are obvious, and it won't take you long to recognize them. A play bow and bouncing around, for example, are signs of a happy puppy who is ready to interact with you.

A wagging tail is pretty obvious, too … or is it? It actually can mean many things. If she holds her tail high and stiff, she's excited or curious. She may be wagging her tail furiously while she barks at a stranger. A slowly wagging tail may mean she's uncertain. A tucked tail indicates fear or submission.

Her ears also tell a story. If they're forward and alert, she's interested, happy, or paying attention. If she folds her ears back and down, she may be worried, frightened, or submissive.

Even her mouth helps indicate her state of mind. A drooling puppy or one licking her lips might be stressed. If she's trying to lick your face, that's a submissive gesture she used with her mother. What might sometimes look like a snarl could actually be a smile.

The hair along her spine may stand up (known as piloerection) when she's overly excited or meeting a new dog.

You'll quickly learn the different tones of your Lab puppy's bark, from her "someone's-here-and-I'm-upset" bark to her "I'm-happy-you're-home" bark. Other variations include "I want something," "I need to go out," and "Ouch." A whimpering puppy could mean she wants something or is in pain. She might also yelp in pain or because she wants your attention. A growling pup might be playing with a buddy or threatening a tennis ball. Most growly Lab puppies are just trying out their vocabulary during play.

TIPS AND TAILS

If you have a truly aggressive puppy who growls as a threat and follows it up with a warning snap or bite, get help from a qualified behaviorist *now*.

Our noses don't give us even a fraction of the information a puppy picks up when she smells something. Puppies smell another dog's urine, feces, anal glands, tail glands, and more. All this gives them information about the other dog's identity, age, and sexual status. They can tell if their friend Rover peed on this bush yesterday or if a rabbit was in the backyard overnight. We can't compete, but we can realize that dogs need to sniff to get vital information about what's going on around them.

The Importance of Play

When you brought your puppy home, you removed her from her entire social group: her mom and her littermates. She needs you to be her playmate now. She needs to run, chase, wrestle, bark, and explore. Because she's spending hours alone while you're at work, she'll be raring to go when you walk through the door at night. Fifteen minutes of play here and there is hardly adequate in her eyes.

Now you know why she endlessly drops a toy at your feet, chases and nips at your pant legs, pesters your other pets, and just generally gets into mischief. She needs to play!

Toys and chewies help occupy her time, but she needs time with people and other animals—not just to teach her social skills, but because, like any living being, she gets lonely.

HAPPY PUPPY
If you work full-time, consider hiring a pet sitter to come in for a midday play session to keep your puppy company.

Balancing Teaching, Guidance, and Play

Right about now, you might be thinking that owning a Lab puppy is a lot of work. In some ways it is because you're adding another family member who needs education, discipline, and love to grow into a socially acceptable adult.

But don't lose sight of why you got your puppy. While you teach her new things, play with her, and redirect her misbehavior, remember she's just a baby and she's not purposely trying to get into trouble. She's trying to figure out the world around her, and she can only do that by trial and error. She'll learn faster through fun and play; punishment and isolation won't teach her what you want her to know.

While you navigate these first memorable months together, you'll both have a lot of fun.

	SOCIAL	BEHAVIOR	TRAINING	PHYSICAL	HEALTH
MONTH 1			Littermates and mother teach appropriate canine behavior	Rapid growth	
MONTH 2	Breeder starts socialization				
MONTH 3	Socialization at home with new owner and other pets	Fear-imprint period	Begin house- and crate training		1st DHPP vaccine
MONTH 4		Teething begins—heavy chewing period	Enroll in puppy class		2nd DHPP vaccine
MONTH 5	Socialization in public		Ready for basic commands	Switch to adult food	3rd DHPP and rabies vaccines
MONTH 6					
MONTH 7			Enroll in basic obedience class		
MONTH 8				Moderate growth	Sexual maturity
MONTH 9		Adult teeth are in—chewing continues			
MONTH 10			Ready for more advanced training		
MONTH 11				Slow growth—reaches adult size	
MONTH 12 AND BEYOND					Annual vaccinations and checkup

MONTH
5

The Rebel

A Lab puppy goes through dramatic growth and changes between 4 and 5 months of age (weeks 16 through 20). He's not quite a teenager yet, but he's not a baby, either.

In this month, we talk about physical changes like teething and growth and ways to monitor your puppy's health. By now, he has completed his vaccines so you can take him out in public to continue and expand his socialization.

His behavior is rapidly changing as he grows and gains confidence. You'll see him exert his independence, and he'll test your limits to see what the rules are and what he can get away with. You have a good foundation in place to guide you both through this headstrong month, and your consistent training and guidance will prevent behavioral problems before they become entrenched habits. Your priorities right now are exercise, teaching, and plenty of chew toys.

Your Lab is ready for a license, microchip, and ID tags now, too. And of course, your active puppy will give your entire family hours of laughs and fun.

PHYSICAL DEVELOPMENT

Think of your puppy as a preteen right now. Some physical characteristics are permanent, but his awkward proportions and teething pain are, thankfully, temporary.

Paws and Legs

During this month, your Lab pup's body grows rapidly. He'll reach approximately 60 percent of his adult height this month and about half of his adult weight. He'll look out of proportion and clumsy because he's growing from the outside in. His paws, nose, ears, and tail will be too big, almost adult size. Eventually his torso will start to lengthen and his legs will gradually catch up.

A male who will eventually weigh 65 to 80 pounds weighs about 32 to 36 pounds at 4 months. A 24-inch-tall adult male is about 14 inches at the shoulders during month 5. A female who will weigh 55 to 70 pounds at adulthood weighs roughly 26 to 35 pounds and is about 11 or 12 inches tall at the shoulders. These are estimates based on a dog who will fall within the breed standard when mature. Your dog may be larger; most Labs aren't smaller than the standard.

His brain is developing, too, and by 5 months old, he'll have a maturity level similar to what you'd expect in a 10-year-old child. He's still very much a puppy but approaching puberty. He'll be very active and always a step ahead of you this month, much to his delight.

Teething Continues

The adult molars along the sides of his mouth start to come in this month, and his canine teeth—his two upper and two lower fangs in the front—follow. His teeth won't finish emerging to their maximum height until he's 10 to 12 months old. That means he'll continue to chew voraciously during the next few months to ease his teething pain.

Except for the canines, the adult teeth come in behind the puppy teeth. If his puppy teeth aren't loose and falling out by 6 months, have your vet examine his mouth. If the puppy teeth don't fall out soon enough, the emerging adult teeth can come in crooked and cause bite problems.

Twizzles, Zippers, and Other Characteristics

Many Labs have identifying characteristics that set them apart from their fellow pups. For example, according to the AKC Labrador *breed standard*, a Lab might have a small white spot, no bigger than a quarter, on the chest.

DOG TALK

The **breed standard** is a description of the ideal Labrador Retriever as developed by the Labrador Retriever Club, the parent club of the breed in the American Kennel Club (AKC). The standard specifies guidelines for size, color, structure, and temperament.

In Newfoundland, where the Labrador originated in the 1700s, there were two types of water dogs, a Lesser Newfoundland and Greater Newfoundland, and both had some white on their bodies. The Lesser Newfoundland became the Labrador, and the other became the large Newfoundland breed we know today. Both breeds occasionally still have a small white spot on the chest.

Many Labs develop a "twizzle" at the end of their tails at around 4 or 5 months. A Lab's thick coat wraps itself around the tail, and an inch or so continues off the end in a twist of hair. Breeders often consider this a sign he'll have a healthy "correct" coat when he matures. The twizzle stays with the Lab all his life.

Does your Lab puppy have a "zipper" between his eyes? This is a little ridge of standing-up hair that runs down his forehead between his eyes. It's easier to see in a black or chocolate dog. There's nothing wrong with this little quirk, and many owners point to their dog's zipper with pride.

Some Labs have what's called a "Bolo mark" on their feet. Named after the famous black Lab Dual Ch. Banchory Bolo (1915–1927), a Bolo mark is a small white patch on the bottom of a dog's feet behind the pads. This peculiar marking has survived through generations of Labs descended from this one dog.

A "splash" Labrador puppy is a rare surprise in an otherwise normal litter. Picture a yellow dog with a black spot on his side, or a black lab with a yellow patch somewhere. This genetic mix-up can range from the tiniest speck to large splashes of color.

Another variation occurs when a puppy is born with tan "points"—markings over the eyes, chest, and legs. This is a throwback to Gordon Setters who were bred to Labs in England during the early years of the breed. Brindle markings (black, broken stripes on a brown background) appear very rarely on the legs and chest of a black dog, and you might not notice them until he's several months old.

Whatever your Lab puppy looks like—black, yellow, chocolate, or totally mismarked—he'll still be a great pet or hunting dog.

TIPS AND TAILS

A white spot on the chest and Bolo marks are acceptable under the breed standard; other markings are disqualifications for a show dog.

HEALTH

Vaccines and heartworm prevention are priorities for your puppy during his fifth month. Once vaccines are completed, he can safely venture out in public. As you travel with your pup, you might find he gets carsick, so spend some time acclimating him to the car to prevent tummy upsets.

Finishing Puppy Vaccines

If you didn't finish your Lab's vaccines last month, be sure to schedule a vet visit this month to get his last DHPP booster. The series should be complete by 16 weeks of age. He also gets his first rabies vaccine this month.

Considering Additional Vaccines

After your pup has completed his core vaccines, discuss additional vaccines with your veterinarian so you can decide together when and if your puppy needs them. Noncore vaccines should be administered based on your geographic location, lifestyle, and risk of the disease. Consider the environment your Lab will be exposed to—outdoors, hunting, contact with other animals, tick-infested areas, etc. Regional considerations come into play, too—for example, if you live in an area with rattlesnakes.

Here are some other vaccines to discuss with your Lab's vet:

Bordetella: Bordetella, or kennel cough, is a group of upper-respiratory bacteria that causes coughing, sneezing, and other symptoms similar to the common cold in humans. Kennel cough is highly contagious and spreads from dog to dog quickly. Healthy adult dogs recover quickly, but in puppies, it can progress to pneumonia. There are several strains of kennel cough, and the vaccine doesn't protect against all of them.

The vaccine is given either intranasally or by injection and is required by boarding kennels and dog day cares. To be effective, a booster should be administered a week before exposure to other dogs. If you're going to board your puppy, he should receive the vaccine at least a week before going to the kennel and then get a booster every 6 to 12 months.

Coronavirus: This disease can be quite severe in puppies, especially if he has other infections as well. The virus is transmitted by contact with infected oral and fecal secretions. Once a dog is infected, the disease is shed in his stool for several months. The puppy may have no symptoms at all or have diarrhea, which can cause dehydration. Coronavirus is rarely fatal and responds well to treatment, so vaccination is not usually recommended.

Giardia: If you camp, hike, or hunt with your Lab, you might consider this vaccine. Giardia is a single-celled protozoa the dog ingests through infected water or soil. Puppies are especially susceptible, even if they aren't outdoors much. Adult dogs who hunt or spend a lot of time in the woods or near water may be reinfected over and over. The main symptom is watery or mucousy diarrhea. The vaccine doesn't protect against infection, but it does prevent the dog from shedding the protozoa.

Giardia is a *zoonotic disease,* which means humans also can be affected. It's inexpensive and easy to treat, so most people do not choose to vaccinate for it.

DOG TALK

A **zoonotic disease** is transmissible from one species to another, for example, from dogs to humans.

Lyme disease: Transmitted by a tick bite, Lyme disease is one of several tick-borne diseases. If your dog spends time in the woods or if ticks are common in your area, discuss this vaccine with your veterinarian. It doesn't protect against other tick-borne diseases, though. The initial vaccine is two doses, 2 to 4 weeks apart, followed by an annual booster at the start of tick season, which may vary depending on where you live.

Leptospirosis: Leptospirosis is a bacterial disease transmitted by skin contact with the urine of infected animals, primarily rats and mice. It also can contaminate streams, rivers, and lakes, where a dog might ingest it. Vaccinate your dog only if you live in an area where there have been known cases of the disease. Two doses are recommended, 2 to 4 weeks apart, along with an annual booster. Leptospirosis is also a zoonotic disease and is transmissible to humans.

Rattlesnake venom: This vaccine protects against western diamondback rattlesnake venom. It also provides some protection against the eastern diamondback rattlesnake. If you live in an area where these snakes are common, the recommendation is two doses, 1 month apart, and a yearly booster. The vaccine doesn't provide complete protection, but it does give you more time to take your dog to the vet before the most severe symptoms begin.

Tetanus: Tetanus is commonly found in soil contaminated by horse and cow manure, and it enters the body through an open wound. This vaccine is not often recommended because dogs have a natural resistance to infection from the bacteria.

Heartworms and Preventatives

Heartworm is caused by a parasitic worm and is transmitted to your dog by mosquitoes. Formerly confined to the Southeast, today it affects dogs throughout the United States.

The mosquito bites an infected dog and ingests the heartworm larvae in that dog's blood. The mosquito moves on to your dog and injects the larvae into him, where they migrate to the bloodstream. There they grow into mature heartworms that attack the pulmonary arteries, which lead from the lungs to the heart. As the worms reproduce, the dog's body tries to fight them off and sometimes has an allergic reaction to the worms.

You can prevent heartworm infestation in your puppy by administering a monthly prescription preventive that kills the immature larvae before they have a chance to grow or reproduce. The preventative medication can be started anytime after 8 weeks of age and well before mosquito season begins in your region.

Once a puppy reaches 6 months old, your veterinarian will need to do a heartworm blood test before beginning the medication. Your Lab will require an annual retest. Some people discontinue the preventative during the winter months, so a retest is required before you restart in the spring.

Symptoms of heartworm include coughing, weight loss, vomiting blood, and ultimately heart failure and death. Treatment of heartworm is long and hard on your dog. Arsenic is used to kill the worms, and the dog must be strictly confined. Too much exercise will cause a large mass of worms to go into the lungs and cause serious complications. The worms die slowly over a period of 4 to 6 weeks and are passed into the lungs where the dog's immune system destroys them. Once that step is complete, the dog is treated with another medication to kill the surviving larvae. A heartworm test at the end of treatment confirms that the parasites are completely gone.

As you see, prevention is the best choice for dealing with the threat of heartworm.

Giving Your Puppy a Pill

Labs, especially puppies, eat anything, so you might never have a problem giving yours a pill. Hide it in a dab of peanut butter, liver sausage, cheese, or canned food, and you're done … you hope.

Some Labs are masters at eating around the pill and spitting it out. In this case, you'll need to be more assertive. If you've been practicing handling exercises with your puppy, he's used to you looking at his teeth and touching his face, so you're halfway there. From behind, put your hand over his muzzle and your thumb and middle fingers behind his large canine teeth on either side. Squeeze in his lips. Pry open his mouth with your other hand, push the pill to the back of his tongue and down his throat, and close his mouth. Hold his mouth closed, and stroke his throat with your finger until he swallows. Give him a spoonful of canned food, cheese, or other special treat so he'll keep swallowing and you can be sure the pill is down.

If that doesn't work, you can purchase an inexpensive pill gun from your vet. This is basically a long syringe that holds a pill on the end. Coat the pill with butter so it goes down easily, stick the plunger in the back of your pup's mouth, and inject the pill. Hold his mouth closed and stroke his throat until you feel him swallow the pill.

Dealing with Carsickness

Labs love nothing better than a car ride, but all that excitement can be too much, and suddenly … he's carsick. A puppy's ears and sense of balance aren't mature yet, so he's more likely to get sick than an adult dog. Once he's gotten carsick, he dreads riding in the car and it's likely to happen again. Typical signs he's getting sick include yawning, panting, whining, drooling, and eventually retching and vomiting.

To help prevent carsickness, crate him so he can't wander around the car or look out the windows, which contributes to nausea. Cover the crate so he can't see out, and anchor it so it doesn't tip when you go around corners. Or put him on a harness and attach it to a seatbelt so he faces forward.

TIPS AND TAILS

An airbag is dangerous to puppies, so disable it if you put him in the front seat. Or better yet, put him in the back seat.

Lower a couple windows about 1 inch to equalize the air pressure in the car. Give your Lab a toy he loves when you put him in the car—call it his special "car-ride" toy, so he makes positive associations with car rides.

Ginger is a natural treatment for nausea, so a gingersnap cookie may help settle his stomach. Or open a capsule of ginger and pour the granules onto some food or a bit of yogurt. Limit his food and water an hour before travel.

If nothing seems to work, talk to your veterinarian about motion sickness medication for your Lab.

If your puppy has developed a phobia against riding in the car, retrain him to think of it as a fun experience. Stop taking him on long car rides for a couple weeks. Instead, take him on short trips to fun places. If every car ride takes him to the vet or boarding kennel, no wonder he doesn't want to go.

You also can feed him treats or meals in the car. If he won't get in, start by feeding him next to the car, and work up to a treat on the running board, one on the car floor, and one on the seat. Don't start the engine or go anywhere; just let him get used to the idea that the car isn't a bad thing. Then start the car and turn it off immediately while he's in the crate or backseat. Sit in the car with the engine running for a minute or two while he eats, and shut it off and quit.

Gradually progress to where you drive to the end of the driveway, down to the corner, and around the block. Your goal is a series of short, pleasant trips without your puppy getting sick.

NUTRITION

Your Lab puppy's appetite may fluctuate this month because his growth is uneven—one day his legs are longer, the next his feet are growing, and then nothing may change for a week. Teething pain also contributes to his occasional lack of appetite. This is nothing to worry about, unless you see symptoms of illness.

Monitoring Your Puppy's Weight

There is no hard-and-fast rule about how much a Lab should weigh at any given age because their size varies so much within the breed. A shorter, stocky Lab looks heavier even if he's the right weight. A taller, lanky Lab puppy has finer bones and looks lighter overall.

A taller puppy does not necessarily need more food. If you hear or read that his weight should fall somewhere between 26 and 35 pounds, that's not very specific, so you really need look at your dog's body and condition to assess his weight (see Appendix B).

Even though a young puppy gets a lot of exercise, he can still eat too much and get fat. An overweight puppy has a higher risk of injury because his bones aren't strong enough yet to carry the extra pounds. If you can't feel his ribs or see that his tummy has a little tuckup behind his rib cage, cut back on his food. Give him a little more in the morning and less at night so he'll have extra calories to get him through the day.

If his coat is shiny, his eyes are clear, and his body feels and looks good, you're feeding him the right amount. If his coat is dingy, his eyes are runny, or his tummy looks bloated all the time (not just after he's eaten), he might have worms and need another round of deworming treatment.

Switching to Adult Food

If you haven't switched to adult food yet, do it now. As you did when you brought him home and changed brands of food, make the switch gradually. Mix 25 percent of the adult food in with his puppy food for several days. Then go to 50 percent of each for a few days. Complete the switch after a week or so. A pet Lab doesn't necessarily need food designated specifically for Labrador Retrievers. A quality adult dog food is perfectly adequate.

Now is also the time to switch your Lab puppy to two meals a day. Start by gradually cutting back the amount of his midday meal and adding it to his other two meals. Right now he's eating more than he will as an adult, about 4 cups a day.

Paying Attention to the Feces

A puppy's bowel movements provide important clues about his health. Feces should be formed and solid, not runny or extremely dry. Blood or mucus may be a sign of illness, a sudden change of food, or a result of eating something he shouldn't. A very black stool may have blood in it. Look for foreign objects such as grass, gravel, fabric, or bits of plastic from a toy or bone. Freshly deposited feces could contain live worms if he's infested.

While you're changing your pup to adult food, check his feces for loose stools or diarrhea. Cut back on the new food, or slow down the transition if he has loose stools. You also can add 1 tablespoon yogurt to his meals to help his digestion.

Keep an eye on your puppy's stool volume, too. A large amount of stool could mean he isn't absorbing his food well. Or you might be feeding him too much. Decrease his food a little, or change to a higher-quality food. Dogs who have a small stool volume are using their food to its maximum potential.

GROOMING

Your Lab puppy doesn't need endless grooming, but he does require light brushing year round and regular grooming sessions during shedding season. His ears also need regular attention so you can catch problems before they become chronic.

A Labrador's Coat

Labs are born with a short, thick double coat. The harsh outer coat has natural oils that repel dirt and water—perfect for a hunting retriever and an added bonus for the pet owner. (However, his coat should never feel oily or greasy to the touch. If it does, he either needs a bath or may need a change in diet; ask your breeder or have him checked by your vet.) The soft undercoat protects your puppy from extreme cold and heat.

Labs shed lightly year-round and heavily twice a year—spring and fall. (Females also shed heavily about 10 to 12 weeks after their heat cycles, about the same time they would be blowing coat, or shedding, if they were weaning a litter of puppies.) The undercoat starts to shed first, followed by the outer coat. You might have to brush your pup daily during shedding season. Frequent brushing speeds up the shedding process, and the sooner the old coat comes out, the sooner the new coat grows in.

TIPS AND TAILS

Although it's tempting when he's in full shedding mode, you should never shave your Lab. He'll continue to shed anyway as the new hair grows in, and by shaving him, you've taken away his protection from hot sun and winter cold.

Lab hair is not like other breeds, whose shedding fur gathers into fluffy puffs and wafts across your floor. A Lab's hair is short and straight, and it weaves into carpet fibers, blankets, and woven furniture fabrics. It's hard to remove, even with a vacuum cleaner. It helps to brush your Lab regularly to cut down on your household cleaning chores.

Brushing Your Lab

Frequent brushing distributes the natural oils in your Lab's coat and keeps it healthy and shiny (not as obvious in a yellow Lab). Brushing also removes a lot of dirt that gets down in the undercoat. If brushed often and thoroughly, your Lab may never need a bath. If the weather is nice, you'll save yourself a lot of housework if you brush him outside. In spring, the birds will thank you because they'll use the fur for soft nesting material.

You've been teaching your puppy to tolerate and even enjoy grooming, so getting him used to brushing shouldn't be much of a problem. Start with the rubber curry, and massage his skin in circles. This brings the loose hair to the surface. Follow with the slicker brush. Start at his rear end, and work your way forward, brushing in the same direction the coat grows, away from your pup's head. A slicker can scratch his skin, so don't use too much pressure. And don't forget the feathers on his rear legs. Even his tail needs attention.

Then use the slicker to brush *against* the direction the coat grows to loosen more undercoat. (This is the one time you brush against the grain.) His coat is heaviest under his throat and along his shoulders, so pay extra attention to these areas. When you're finished, use a shedding blade on his outer coat to rake off loose hair that's still embedded in the coat.

By now you're covered in dog hair, but you haven't gotten it all yet. An undercoat rake or a medium-tooth metal comb pulls out mountains of undercoat. Start again at his rear, and work your way forward. By taking this extra step, you may be able to brush less often.

Use a damp cloth on his face and outer ears rather than a brush. When you're completely finished brushing, run the wet cloth over his entire body to pick up stray hairs and remove static electricity or dandruff. A fabric softener sheet also removes static in dry weather.

Labs shouldn't have doggy odor. If yours does, check his ears for a problem. If his coat is dry and he has dandruff, he could have a skin condition or allergies. If you've left soap in his coat after a bath, it could also cause irritation, so be sure to rinse well.

Cleaning His Ears

Labs are notorious for getting ear infections. Because your puppy's ears lie flat against his head, they limit airflow and trap moisture and debris inside. Labs are also prone to allergies, which cause redness and inflammation in the ear area.

Wipe out his ears every week so he's used to the procedure and will be more tolerant if he needs treatment. And after he swims, hunts, or runs outdoors in tall grass, check his ears for dirt, grass seeds, ticks, and moisture, and dry and wipe out his ears thoroughly.

Using a barely damp soft cloth or paper towel wrapped around the end of your finger, hold the ear leather (flap) up and away, and wipe his ear from the inside to the outer edge. Clean out the nooks and crannies with a cloth covering your little finger. This is all he should need on a regular basis. Cleaning too often removes the protective layer of wax that protects his inner ear, so don't overdo it.

If his ears are especially dirty, use a cotton swab to gently clean his ear canal. If your puppy doesn't cooperate, this might take two people—one to hold him still, and one to clean his ear. Again, hold up the ear leather. Turn the swab in one direction as you put it in, and hold it in the same direction as you reverse out of his ear so you don't redeposit the dirt. Don't go too deeply because you don't want to damage his eardrum. Also, if your puppy thrashes around, you don't want to poke into his inner ear.

If something gets down in the ear canal, it can cause an infection. If you see reddish-brown gunk or his ears smell bad, it could be a yeast infection caused by water, an infection caused by a foreign object, or even ear mites.

A Lab with an ear problem will shake his head, hold his head at an odd angle, scratch at his ears, and even whimper as he tries to ease his discomfort. He may be unwilling to let you touch his ears. Visit the vet for an accurate diagnosis and treatment plan.

TIPS AND TAILS

If your Lab has chronic ear problems, your vet might recommend medication or regular cleaning with an ear-wash product. Squirt the ointment into your Lab's ear, and massage the base of his ear where it meets his jaw line to push the medication deeper into his ear canal. Your Lab will immediately shake his head, which distributes the ointment in his outer ear. If you use an ear wash, thoroughly dry his ears after cleaning. A diet change might also help with chronic ear problems.

SOCIAL SKILLS

Finally your Lab is able to go out and meet the world. He can accompany you on walks, to the park, to family activities, and other outings. As bold and confident as he is at home, he's now on unfamiliar turf, so he may be uncertain at first. But that'll change as you meet new friends. And do introduce him to new friends. That's part of his necessary socialization. By teaching him to like and respect people now, you're preventing future problems.

The Jolly Routine

Actions speak louder than words. When your puppy is uncertain or frightened, show him by your behavior that there's nothing to be afraid of.

Select an item that makes your puppy wag his tail when he sees it—a ball, a squeaky toy, a stuffed animal, or another small toy. When you notice something you know will worry him, like a large truck driving by, pull out the toy. If possible, before he can even react to the scary thing, act happy, play with the toy, and pretend you're having a wonderful time. Expect your puppy to be confused, but keep going. After a minute or two, put away the toy and ignore him. In about 5 minutes, pull out the toy again and repeat your excitement. You'll know your routine has started to ease his fears when he wags his tail as soon you produce the toy.

You might not have time to head off his fear, but this is a good starting point to distract him from what frightens him. It might take a number of repetitions to change his attitude about whatever scares him.

Socializing to Strangers

When you're out in public with your puppy, you are his protector. Well-meaning strangers will charge up to him with their hands out to say hello. Children will crash toward him with a toy and throw their arms around his neck. As you try to keep people from overwhelming him, they'll respond, "It's okay, I *love* dogs!"

But this isn't about them; it's about your puppy, and after a few of these bulldozer encounters, your pup will hide in fear or take off in the opposite direction when someone approaches him. Worse, he might feel cornered and snap. Don't let that happen. Turn into a linebacker, and bodyblock all comers from your puppy. Don't be afraid of being rude. After all, you wouldn't let them charge at your children, would you? If you do your job, your puppy won't feel he has to defend himself from others.

TIPS AND TAILS

A dog who grows up fearful of strangers will think he has to take matters into his own jaws when danger approaches. He'll bark aggressively and even bite to protect himself—or you—when someone approaches.

Hold your hand up to stop the person. If your puppy seems happy and ready to interact, let him approach the person first. Have the person stop, stand sideways to him (which is less imposing), and even crouch down so he'll feel safe. Use your jolly routine so your puppy understands everything is safe.

Let him watch the person and decide for himself if he wants to say hi. If your Lab isn't comfortable, respect his wishes and don't force him. Put a serious look on your face and explain he's "in training." Hand the person a treat and invite them to toss it in his direction and move on.

Socializing to Children

At home or in public, your Lab will meet children of all ages and, you hope, love them immediately. Tell children you meet to "ask the puppy" if he would like to meet them.

If your puppy says no, ask them to respect his feelings today because he may be tired. How do you know if your puppy isn't in the mood to play? He'll hide behind you, crouch down, avoid looking at the kids, or move away.

If he's ready to say hi, put two fingers through his collar to keep him from jumping on the child. Have the child stand quietly and speak nicely to the puppy, not in a high, squeaky, excited voice. Let your pup choose to approach the child. Have her pet him on his chest or his back where he won't dive for her fingers. Let her put a treat on the ground for him to eat.

Going for Walks

Enjoy daily walks together so your pup can experience new sights, sounds, and smells. But remember, he's still a puppy and will tire easily. Plan to walk about 10 minutes per month of age. So if he's 4 months old, a 40-minute walk will tire him out. Don't worry about how far you get on your walks. There's so much to experience, you might not get very far while he meets people, sniffs, and explores.

Walk your Lab on a 4- or 6-foot leash. A long line or retractable leash won't give you enough control, and he could easily pull it out of your hands if he gets frightened and runs. Don't let him off leash in parks, on trails, or at the beach unless you're in a fully fenced enclosure.

TIPS AND TAILS

A walk is the perfect time for your puppy to practice sit, down, walking politely, and paying attention to you. Don't let him pull ahead, or he'll learn to drag you all his life.

He might balk at new things like a mailbox, parking lot flags, or a motorcycle zooming by. He might bark at cars or kids on skateboards. If he sees a street vendor dressed like a pizza and tossing around an advertising sign, don't be surprised if he spooks. He'll think he's encountered an alien. Wouldn't you?

The world is full of exciting new smells and sounds. He'll encounter trash in the gutter and gum on the sidewalk. He'll know where the nearest restaurant is and quickly recognize the scent of other dogs. Busy traffic will smell like burning rubber, and honking horns and police sirens will startle him. Let him investigate for himself without comforting him, and use the jolly routine to help him gain confidence.

There are a few places you shouldn't take him yet. Street fairs and festivals have hundreds of people jammed together, loud music, food smells, and traffic. Remember, his eye level is around your knees, so all these unfamiliar things coming at him from above his head can be terrifying. Work up to crowded situations slowly. And don't take him to Fourth of July celebrations or anywhere fireworks are being used.

Having Fun at Dog Parks

Visits to the dog park can do more harm than good. You have no way of knowing if the dogs there are vaccinated or trained. Many owners chat with each other and ignore their dogs, allowing them to bully other dogs unmonitored. Dogs squabble over toys, and fights break out. There's no "lifeguard" on duty enforcing rules or asking owners to remove rude or aggressive dogs. You alone are your dog's protector.

And you never know—your own puppy might play too rough at this age, too. Labs can be rowdy, like they don't know their own strength. Yours might easily overwhelm smaller dogs.

Puppies mimic other dogs' behavior. Any kind of aggression from others could teach your puppy that this type of behavior is appropriate. You don't want your Labrador Retriever to grow up to be a bully, so if you see other dogs playing rough or acting aggressively at the dog park, leave.

At peak periods, usually early evenings and weekends, the dog park is crowded and play can easily get out of control as the dogs become overstimulated. A normal dog will quickly be overwhelmed, much less a quiet or shy puppy. Decide if your puppy is ready for this kind of interaction. Consider taking him on quiet weekday mornings instead, when the park isn't so busy, especially when he's young and it's new to him.

TIPS AND TAILS

Wherever you are, be a responsible dog owner and clean up after your puppy. Carry pickup bags, and either deposit them in nearby trash cans or take them home with you.

BEHAVIOR

Your young Lab's behavior changes dramatically this month as he asserts his independence and explodes with endless puppy energy. Prepare yourself with consistent puppy management techniques and a sense of humor so you'll get through this fun and challenging period with your sanity intact.

Your Shadow Disappears

While your puppy is busy physically growing this month, his mind is equally busy absorbing everything it can. He'll have endless energy and very little self-control. He's easily distracted and will use any excuse to ignore you. During this period of creative obedience, he'll tease you by coming close and taking off or grabbing toys and playing keep-away. Busy, busy, busy! However will you get him under control?

Be sure your Lab puppy gets plenty of exercise, training, and mental stimulation this month. It might seem harder to get his attention, but keep working on handling and control exercises. You can demand more from him now, too, because he's not an infant anymore.

If he's not listening to you, let him drag a leash when you're there to supervise. You'll be able to pick up the leash and get his attention to enforce your instructions.

Keeping Him on Leash

When the two of you are away from the house—whether you're taking a walk down the sidewalk in your neighborhood, hiking in the woods, or romping in open fields—*never* let your Lab puppy off leash. At this age, he's impulsive, distracted, and prone to developing selective hearing—in other words, he ignores you. Make liberal use of the sit command to get his attention back on you while you're on walks.

HAPPY PUPPY
Suddenly your calm, well-behaved Lab will cut loose and take off around the yard or house for no apparent reason. Lab lovers have named it "butt-tucking" because he goes so fast his rear looks like it's in front of his chest. This zooming is pure puppy exuberance, so let him run and burn off some steam. Zooming is a better activity for outdoors, where items in his path—like furniture and children—won't interrupt his fun. Labs never seem to grow up, so be prepared for lifelong zoomies!

Chewing

At 5 months, your Labrador Retriever puppy is still teething, and he's certainly still chewing. Continue to provide him with sturdy chew toys. As he gets bigger, some of the old toys and bones may no longer be safe, so monitor what he has in his mouth and remove the unsafe toys. When his adult teeth are in, he'll continue to chew to ease his gum and mouth discomfort. And because he's a Lab, it's safe to assume he'll chew like a puppy for the rest of his life.

With that in mind, watch his behavior and redirect him to appropriate chewies. Don't give him household items like old shoes. He'll have trouble telling which ones are his to chew and which ones he should leave alone.

Take steps to ensure he can't chew certain things, too. For example, don't put a bed in his crate if he's a chewer. Keep clothes picked up and shoes put away. Close bedroom doors. Use a bitter spray product (available at pet supply stores) on items you don't want him to chew; the bitter spray makes it taste bad. If you don't have bitter spray, you could use mouthwash or red pepper sauce mixed with water instead. Be careful not to spray your homemade mixture on surfaces that will stain or fade.

If you find he's chewed something, put him in another room so he doesn't see you clean up the mess. If he watches you, he'll be fascinated that you're paying so much attention to what he's done, and he'll do it again for you.

Making Corrections

By now, your puppy has an idea of right versus wrong in many situations, but during this rebellious phase, you'll have more trouble getting his attention. Commonsense discipline has its place while you're raising your Lab. It's not necessary to yell or hit your puppy. Instead, use a sharp phrase like "Ack" or "Pssst" to interrupt what he's doing, immediately praise him for stopping, and redirect him to something else like a sit or walking away.

TIPS AND TAILS

Don't use his name when disciplining your puppy. If he hears "*[Name]*, no!" he'll eventually think his name is a correction, and you don't want that.

You might wonder why we didn't suggest you use "No" to interrupt your Lab. "No" often turns into "No, no, *no, no, NO!*" and when you get excited, your puppy just hears you making a bunch of noise. You don't sound calm or in charge, and your puppy will ignore you until you get to the last angry "*NO!*"

He Won't Outgrow Bad Behavior

"He's just a puppy" is an excuse that isn't going to work much longer. If there are no consequences when he misbehaves, he doesn't know his behavior is unacceptable.

Any bad habits he's forming now will be much harder to deal with when adolescence is in full swing. A habit takes much longer to *break* than to *make*.

Sure, you're tempted to let him get away with unacceptable behavior like jumping on you once in a while because it's tiring to supervise him constantly. But by doing this, you're inadvertently rewarding the behavior. When he gets away with it sometimes, he'll try it again and again. On the other hand, if he *never* gets rewarded for jumping, he'll eventually quit trying.

HAPPY PUPPY

Don't forget to praise your puppy when he's doing something right. Once he's learned a behavior, it's easy to take it for granted. But if you don't reinforce it, the behavior begins to deteriorate, and suddenly you have a puppy who acts like he never learned it in the first place.

The entire family needs to be consistent with discipline and training. When one person in the family allows your Lab on the couch and someone else doesn't, he soon figures it out and jumps on the couch when the enforcer isn't around.

Stick to your guns, and enforce all the rules, all the time. Make liberal use of the crate for short time-outs when you can't watch him. Loving discipline, plenty of exercise, and readily available chew toys help you both through this stage.

TRAINING

Scientists call this age the "avoidance period." Your Lab puppy is no longer hanging on your every word, and there's so much to see and do in the world, he wants to do all of it *right now*.

This month, break his lessons into small steps so you can keep his attention and better his chances for success. Train thoroughly, and practice a lot this month—a few 1-minute training sessions throughout the day have a bigger impact on him than one 10-minute session, and he'll learn to incorporate these short lessons into everyday life. Labs aren't an overly emotional or sensitive breed, so you can be patient but firm. And keep training fun, or he'll lose interest.

Using His Name

Your dog's name should be a wonderful word he happily responds to. Think about whether he knows or responds to his name already. If he doesn't, here's an exercise you can teach him.

Load up your pocket with treats, and take him out in the backyard or for a walk. Let him get distracted, sniffing at the grass or another mildly interesting scent. Say his name once in a normal voice without a loud or urgent tone. Does he turn and look at you? Or does he ignore you? If he looks at you, give him a treat and have a happy dance.

Usually, when you say a person's name, you expect him to look at you, and you then tell him what's on your mind. You wouldn't say his name and then ignore him. Often that's exactly what we do to our dogs. Or when he doesn't respond immediately, we say his name several times. He may think his name is Rover … *Rover* … *ROVER!* The more we chatter, the less he listens.

TIPS AND TAILS

Your puppy's name is not a command. If you mean "Come," say, "Rover, come," not just "Rover." And never use his name as punishment. That's a surefire way to get him to ignore you when you call.

How many names does your puppy have? Is he "Roverdoofusgoofus" when he's being a darling little puppy, and "Rover-roller-over" when he's into mischief? Or a firm "Rover-Johnson-come-here-right-now" when he misbehaves? All these names could further confuse him.

Don't waste the power of your puppy's name. If you say his name, have a reason for doing so and give him something to do. You need to be worth leaving that luscious scent behind.

Reinforcing Household Rules

As adolescence approaches, your preteen Lab will test the rules again and again, and you'll wonder where all his training went. The more consistent you are in enforcing household rules now, the more control you'll have in the coming months. In fact, if he hasn't mastered some basic obedience by the end of this month, he'll only get more difficult to train.

Sit, down, and walking on a leash should be your priorities, and you should use them often. Have him sit before you feed him, or have him lie down by your chair when you're watching TV. Your puppy might be pushy now, poking you to be petted, but have him earn your attention by asking him to sit first.

If your Lab is misbehaving, let him drag a 6-foot leash in the house. When he's misbehaving, pick up the leash and lead him away from trouble; don't reward him with playtime. If you grab him when he has something in his mouth, you've rewarded him by touching him and interacting with him. He'll think it's a great game, and to him, negative attention is better than no attention at all.

If he's not allowed on the couch, he'll try it this month. Rather than pull him off, pick up the leash and hold it with steady pressure, like you did when you were teaching him to walk on leash. He should respond to the pressure of the leash and get off the couch. Reward him with praise when he does.

Your puppy needs to learn "inside rules," and especially that he needs to settle down in the house. You can use his ex pen to confine him temporarily, or if he's really rambunctious, he could benefit from a tie-down—a leash looped over a doorknob, affixed to a large or heavy piece of furniture, or attached to a large eye screw fastened to the wall. (A chain leash is excellent for this because he can't chew it. Otherwise, spray the leash with bitter spray or mouthwash to prevent chewing.) Either way, he can be in view of his family while still enjoying some freedom. Give him a chew toy to occupy him. He now has limited mobility and should settle down and relax. Be sure he can move around a little but isn't able to eat the wall.

HAPPY PUPPY

Children in your house need to follow inside rules, too. Don't let them play wild chase games with the puppy indoors. Unless everyone is consistent in his training, he won't understand he has to settle down.

Cutting Back on Treats

When you first teach your puppy a new command, you reward him with a treat every time he does the right thing. But you don't want to carry food in your pocket for the rest of your life. So how do you make your Lab comply?

Switch his reward from food to praise. Every time he complies, praise him with a word, like "Good!" along with the treat. Gradually he'll associate the word with the treat and recognize you're pleased. Always use an upbeat and happy tone of voice when saying "Good!" He reads your tone and body language more than what you say.

As he gets used to being rewarded with "Good!" gradually cut back on treats. First, hide the treats in your pocket and don't pull one out until he sits or whatever you're asking him to do. A treat is not a bribe; it's a reward. Always praise him, but occasionally skip the treat so he never knows when he'll get one. Don't use a pattern because he'll quickly figure it out. If you give a treat every third time, he'll pick up on that, and the other two times, he won't respond nearly as enthusiastically. Mix it up so he doesn't know what to expect, occasionally giving him a jackpot handful of extra tasty treats he doesn't usually get. This motivates him to keep playing the obedience game so he can get the jackpot again. Labs *love* this.

If you fade the use of treats too fast, he could lose interest. Labs are so food-motivated that he might hold out for a goodie. If that happens, back up a little and give him treats more often for a while.

HAPPY PUPPY

You don't always have to use treats as his reward. Interrupt a training session with a game of fetch, or pull a squeaky toy out of your pocket. Releasing him from "working" might be enough. Mix up his rewards with tricks and fun time, and you'll always have a reward handy when you need it, even if you don't have a pocket full of cookies.

Remember that when you're a teaching a new skill, give your puppy a treat and praise every time he does something right. Don't reduce the frequency until you're sure he understands the exercise.

Teaching "Stay"

Before you teach him to stay, your Lab puppy should always sit promptly when you give the "Sit" command (which you taught him in Month 4). Stay has two components: time and distance. You can't work on both at the same time because he'll get confused. So start by first lengthening the time he stays and then work on distance, cutting back the time to almost nothing. Once he stays when you walk away from him, you can start building time back into the exercise.

Teaching "Sit-Stay"

As always with a puppy, your body language helps him stay. Have him sit at your left side on a loose leash. Step off with your right foot, and pivot in front of him, several inches away. (If you crowd him, he's more likely to stand up.) If he stays sitting, great!

Praise him, give him a treat, pivot back into position at his right side, and release him by touching him and saying "Okay." Practice pivoting into position and back without letting him stand. Do this a few times until he's used to it, and take a short break.

If he has trouble staying as you pivot, put your finger against his muzzle as you turn. It should be just enough to stop him.

When you taught him to sit, you gave him a treat as soon as he sat. Now, as you teach him to stay, pivot in front of him and wait a few beats. He might look confused. If he makes eye contact, smile at him and say nothing. (Too much eye contact will intimidate him and make him stand up.) Gradually increase the time he sits to about 15 seconds. This takes a lot of concentration, and he's probably sitting there worried he's supposed to be doing something. Intersperse a few instant releases to vary the length of time he's sitting.

If he stands up before you can release him, put him back in the original position and try another, shorter stay. Don't restart where he came to you; go back to the beginning. And don't say anything while you move him. Just put him back in the sit. Keep practicing until you can get a 30-second stay. Then incorporate a short "stay" into your walks and at other times of the day to reinforce his training.

Next, add the hand signal and command word. Before you pivot in front of him, put the palm of your hand in front of his nose and say "Stay."

When he's consistently holding his stay, it's time to throw in some variations. This time when you pivot, step farther away, about 1 foot. He might try to get up and move closer to you, and he'll be watching you intently, waiting for a signal that it's okay to move. As soon as you so much as twitch, he'll try to stand up. Before he's all the way up, lean into him, and he should sit back down. He'll read your body language and know to go back into the sit.

Don't repeat the word "Stay" over and over, and don't stare into his eyes. Relax your posture, as if to tell him, "We aren't going anywhere," and quietly praise him during the stay.

TIPS AND TAILS

To release your Lab from the stay, always go back to him and touch him. You want him to relax and wait patiently. Otherwise, as soon as you step toward him, he'll think he's finished and stand up. Praise him quietly as he stays, walk back to him, praise him again, and touch him as you say "Okay" to release him. Don't ever call him to you from a stay, or he'll be anxiously watching for a command.

Practice variations on the stay where you're up close and farther away and for various lengths of time. When working well at 1 foot away for 30 seconds, try standing farther back, about 18 inches. As you step backward, he might think you want him to come with you, so be sure to keep the leash slack. Say "Ack" and lean toward him if he starts to get up. Go back to him and release him immediately if he stays in the sit. If he doesn't, put him back in position and don't step so far next time. Mix it up with some stays where you're right in front of him again. Each time he's successful, touch and release him. Quit when you're ahead, when he's just done something right.

It'll probably take you a full month to get a steady 1-minute sit-stay from 4 feet away. Doing something, like sit or down, is an action concept. Not doing anything, like stay, is a little harder for him to understand.

Teaching "Down-Stay"

Once he grasps the idea of "sit-stay," "down-stay" is much easier for him to learn. Teach him the down-stay in small increments, as you did the sit-stay. First add time and then reduce the time and add distance. When he stays better with you at a distance, rebuild the time.

Teach him to relax while he's down. If he's lying in a sphinx position, up on both haunches, he's ready to spring into action, so teach him to roll on one hip. Watch him when he's resting, and figure out which hip he usually chooses.

Assume you're facing him and he usually rolls to his right hip. Put him in a down, hold a treat in your right hand, and push the treat back toward his left hip. As he follows your hand, he'll roll onto his right hip. If he doesn't get it, you can put pressure on his left hip with one hand to help him. When he gets the idea, have him roll onto his hip every time he does the down. Making this an automatic part of the down command helps you both be more successful with the stay.

The hand signal for the down-stay is the same as for the sit-stay. Put your open palm in front of his face as you give the command "Stay." Stand up straight, and pivot in front of him. If you bend over him or look him in the eyes, he'll get right up. Stand relaxed with your weight on one hip. He needs to see that nothing is going to happen so he can relax. If he fidgets, say "Ack" but don't go back to him unless he gets up. When he's still, go back and release him. If he gets up, put him back in place and start over a little closer to him.

Your puppy will try to creep toward you. When he moves forward, correct him with your voice. He'll stop, and a few seconds later, he'll creep forward again. He's inching his way to you—Labs love this game. When he creeps, go back to him without a word, stand him up, take him back to the starting point, and put him back in his down-stay. If you have to, put a piece of tape on the floor to remind yourself where you started.

When his stay is solid for about 30 seconds and 2 feet away, add a small variation. Fidget a little, and shift your weight slightly. This teaches him to stay even if you move. He's not to get up, no matter what you do, until you release him.

Introducing Stairs

Your puppy needs to learn to climb and descend stairs. If he doesn't learn this skill as a puppy, he'll probably be afraid to try stairs when he's an adult. It'll be less stressful for you both if you start teaching him about stairs at home or someplace quiet without outside distractions. If you don't have stairs, introduce him to them where he's already comfortable, like a friend's home or a quiet corner at the park.

TIPS AND TAILS
Before you've taught him to be comfortable with stairs, use baby gates at the top and bottom of any stairways in your home to keep your puppy safe.

One or two stairs isn't nearly as frightening as a full staircase, so start by teaching your pup to go up and down one or two steps, preferably carpeted stairs, which are easier for him to negotiate without slipping. Once he's mastered a few carpeted stairs, you can work on a full-length staircase or take him out in public to try it.

Your goal is to keep your Lab from racing up and down the stairs. As a small puppy, he could be badly hurt or even killed if he tumbles head over heels. When he's an adult, you both could take a dangerous spill. Visualize the stairs as a place of calmness and serenity, where he climbs and descends one step at a time at a leisurely pace.

Start with a hungry puppy on his leash and a pocket full of really tasty treats, like cheese or chicken. You might want to do this at mealtime and use his kibble. Kneel on the floor next to the foot of the stairs. Lift up both of his front paws, place them on the bottom stair, give him a treat, and let him go. After a few tries, he'll put his feet up on his own when you lure him with the treat.

After a few repetitions, place the treat farther up and back toward the second stair so he has to lift his rear feet onto the stair to get to the treat. When he gets one foot up, praise him and feed him. When he gets completely on a stair, praise him quietly and have him stand or sit there for a second. This is not a game of speed.

As you gradually add more stairs, have him stop on a stair and sit or lie down for a treat. This keeps it from becoming a race to the top. To make it more fun, set a treat on each stair and let him sniff his way up. As he goes down, have him stop and sit often for a treat.

When he's familiar with one set of stairs, introduce him to new locations. The first few times in a new place, you might have to start over until he discovers that most stairs are alike.

If you have open stairs with no vertical backs, have him practice climbing and descending those stairs, too, because they'll look entirely different to him and seem much scarier. They're also more dangerous for your pup. If he gets in a hurry, he could slip, his leg could slide through the opening, and he could break a leg or tear a muscle. Practice these stairs as if he's never seen a staircase before so he understands how to go up and down safely.

Teaching a Flawless Recall

Remembering how you started his training, calling your puppy should always result in a reward for him. Up until this month, he probably joyously came when you called and followed you everywhere. Now you're seeing a suddenly independent puppy, and he may ignore you completely, or at least until it suits him.

Someday there will be an emergency when he needs to stop what he's doing and come to you rather than race into traffic after the neighbor's cat. To be ready for this, practice the recall when lots of distractions, like other dogs, cars, people, rabbits, and good smells, are around to compete for his attention. He needs to learn that despite anything and everything around him, when you tell him to come to you, he must drop everything and come to you.

TIPS AND TAILS

In your Lab's mind, "Come" from 20 feet away is very different from "Come" from 6 feet away. Don't call him to you if you can't enforce the command. He'll learn that he doesn't have to respond, and you'll just be background noise.

Start teaching him the recall at home. When he understands the command, you can move outside. Keep a treat shaker with you to get his attention if you need it.

Attach a long line to his collar—30 feet of lightweight string or clothesline works well. These materials are light enough that he doesn't have the weight of a leash to remind him he's under your control. Take him to an enclosed area, and let him wander.

When he's 10 to 15 feet away, call him to you. Use your best happy voice. As soon as he looks at you, jump up and down excitedly and encourage him to come to you to see what you're going on about. Reel him in with the line if he doesn't come immediately. Praise him (even if you had to pull him to you), play with him, and give him treats, but then let him go back to what he was doing. He'll learn that coming to you doesn't necessarily end his fun. Don't be a pest; just call him once or twice each 5-minute session. If you have trouble getting his attention, rattle your treat shaker.

Next, add distractions. This is when the kids can have some fun, playing catch or dancing around to get him interested. Be sure they understand that as soon as you call, they should freeze and not look at the puppy. As he gets good at the game, they can continue distracting him while you call. Take turns holding the line and calling so he'll come to everyone in the family.

Practice with the long line at parks and other places you regularly take him so he'll learn that the rules are the same everywhere you go. Have him check in occasionally, reward him, and let him return to play. Teaching him to come when called is not a one-day project. Practice often and in many places.

Catching Your Pup

There will come a day when your Lab gets away from you and refuses to come—he's just having too much fun. Picture the recall as he might see it. You're at the park, and he's running and playing. He sees you take out the leash, a sure signal the party's over. Behind you, he sees the car, another sign it's time to go home. Forget it, he's not coming.

You're bound to be angry and frustrated, but don't let it show. Who wants to come to someone who's yelling and screaming at them? He'll tuck his tail and take off in the opposite direction.

Here are some methods to help you catch him; these also work while you're training him on the long line:

○ As he approaches you, stand sideways to him. A full frontal greeting is intimidating and might cause him to back away from you.

○ Crouch down to his eye level, open your arms wide, and happily call him. When your body language is saying happy things, he's more likely to respond.

○ Change the picture he sees. Don't get the leash out until you have your hands on him. Or never put it away, but keep it hanging around your neck or from your back pocket.

○ Don't call him with your car or the exit gate right behind you in his line of sight. Stand where it looks like this is just another "checking-in" recall.

○ Carry a squeaky toy or ball, and let him see you playing with it. Toss it in the air, juggle it, and dance around like you're having a great time. All that fun is hard to resist, and he'll soon come over.

○ Fall down on the ground face first. Make a big drama of it, and he'll wonder what's up and come running. He'll be licking your ears and climbing on you in no time.

○ Turn around, yell to him, and run away from him. He's likely to give chase.

You've finally got him leashed up, and you want tell him what a bad dog he is for not obeying. Don't. The last thing he did was come to you, and he thinks any punishment or reward is for coming. You can't punish him for something he did 5 minutes ago because he won't make the connection. Praise him, tell him he's a wonderful dog, and take him home for more recall practice.

YOU AND YOUR PUPPY

You'll be having a lot of fun with your puppy this month, especially as he goes out in public with you more, so he needs to wear identification in case he gets lost. He also needs some attention and guidance to keep your friendship on the right track.

His busy antics might frustrate you at times, so prepare yourself with items like food-dispensing toys that can occupy him when you need a break. The kids also need guidance to develop a good relationship with their new puppy.

IDing Your Lab

Identification is your puppy's ticket home if he gets lost. When your Lab reaches 4 months, he's had his rabies vaccine, and most communities require that he be licensed. An ID tag includes your personal contact information, and a license has the animal control jurisdiction's info—an important way of getting in touch with you if your pup is found. And if you haven't already, now's the time to microchip your puppy and register the number.

The well-dressed Labrador should always wear his ID tag, which should include your name and phone number, including the area code. Consider putting both your cell and home phone numbers on the tag so if someone finds your puppy, they can contact you even if you're out of town. If the sound of jingling tags bothers you, order a collar with your phone number printed on it, use a pouch that holds all the tags quietly and attaches to the collar, or purchase tags that slip onto the collar and lie flat against it. A bonus: flat tags are less likely to catch on something and get lost.

TIPS AND TAILS

The lettering on plastic ID tags wears down quickly, and as the plastic ages, it also breaks easily. Engraved metal lasts much longer. Be sure the tag has a heavy ring or S-hook. Put each tag on a separate ring so if one is lost, the others are still attached.

There are many good reasons to license your dog. Anyone who finds your dog will be more willing to handle him if they know his rabies status. If your dog bites someone, his vaccine record is on file. Animal Control will notify you and hold your dog longer than they will an unlicensed dog. Some jurisdictions also give your dog a free ride home. Penalties for having an unlicensed dog are much higher than the cost of the original license, so take time to get your pup licensed.

All 50 states have dog-licensing laws, and either city or county agencies issue the license. You'll submit his rabies vaccine certificate with the license application. Your vet might even send it in for you.

If your Lab loses his collar, a microchip provides lifetime identification he can't lose. Many breeders microchip their puppies before they leave for their new homes. The chip—the size of a piece of rice—is encased in biocompatible glass to prevent infection and is injected between your pup's shoulder blades. The chip operates on a radio frequency. It's not a tracking device, and it doesn't require a power source to be activated. When someone runs a scanner over your dog, it reads the chip like a UPC code on an item at the grocery store.

Once the chip is implanted, you pay a one-time fee for lifetime registration with a national registry, such as the American Kennel Club Reunite (akcreunite.org), American Veterinary Identification Devices (avidid.com), or HomeAgain (public. homeagain.com). The chip number is registered with a national database where it can be traced back to you. Most registries provide a collar tag so whoever finds your dog knows to have the dog scanned. Shelters, veterinarians, and rescue groups usually have their own scanners. If your dog is lost, contact the registry immediately. Most have a 24/7 telephone hotline.

TIPS AND TAILS

A microchip does *not* include your personal information, just a number. If you don't register your Lab's microchip, the shelter can't find you and the chip is useless. Before you register the chip, find out what registry your local shelter uses. Many people designate their veterinarian or breeder as the secondary contact. Be sure to update your contact information with the registry if you move or get a new phone number.

Numerous manufacturers make microchips, and in recent years, universal scanners have been developed that can read most brands and frequencies. These scanners are labeled "ISO compliant" by the International Organization for Standardization. Be sure the chip you purchase is compatible with ISO scanners. More than 160 countries follow these standards, and dogs have been reunited with their owners from around the world. Some countries even require a microchip before you can import a dog.

Shelters usually scan the dog all over because some microchips migrate elsewhere in the body, like down his shoulder or leg, for example. Newer chips have a small hook that anchors the chip so layers of connective tissue can grow over it and hold it in place. Ask your vet to scan the microchip during your dog's yearly health checkup to be sure it's still in place and active.

Global positioning systems (GPSs) for dogs are becoming quite popular. A small tracking device is attached to the dog's collar and interacts with satellite and cell phone towers to follow his movements. You'll receive an email or text message if your dog leaves the designated safe area you've set up. The prices for these devices have fallen dramatically in the past few years, so it might be something worth considering.

Frustrated Owner = Confused Puppy

A new Lab puppy can be a shock to the household, especially if your last dog was very old and you've forgotten what it's like to have a puppy. Or maybe this is your first dog, and you had no idea he was going to be this active or destructive. When the cute factor wears thin—usually right after he chews up the couch pillow or committed some similar crime—what can you do?

Remember, he's a puppy, and Lab puppies are especially active. What he's doing—barking, chewing, biting, digging—are all normal puppy behaviors, and he hasn't developed much, if any, self-control yet.

A tired puppy is a good puppy. Playtime, especially with you, solves a lot of puppy problems. Mental as well as physical exercise wears out your puppy.

Puppies learn by doing, and this month he's testing his limits. If he doesn't try things, he doesn't learn. If you never have to say no, how will he know the rules?

Remember that one correction doesn't mean lesson learned. He's a baby, and he'll forget. Be patient and consistent, and keep teaching.

When you get angry, your puppy gets confused and sees you as unpredictable. He might not understand why you're so upset; he just knows to get out of your way. When his behavior is too much, put him in his crate with a chew toy, hand him off to someone else, or go for a walk by yourself.

Don't give up—get help. Before you get completely frustrated, talk to your veterinarian, puppy class instructor, or someone who can see what your puppy is doing and offer constructive suggestions. Your breeder also can offer suggestions based on her years of experience. What works for one puppy might not work for yours, and there's more than one way to approach any problem.

HAPPY PUPPY

It's bedtime and you're tired, but your puppy won't settle down. What to do? Consider soft music with a low pulsing beat that simulates his mother's heartbeat. You can buy CDs and videos specially made to comfort and quiet your dog.

Food-Dispensing Toys

The way to a Lab puppy's heart is through his stomach. Food-dispensing toys entertain your puppy and keep him from wolfing down his food. (If other dogs are in the house, separate him from them while he plays. Bigger dogs might take away his toy—sometimes aggressively—because food is involved.) Many kinds are available, but hard plastic is best for Labs. The dispensers come in various shapes—balls, cubes, etc. Look for one he can't chew up.

Put his kibble in the toy. Add one piece at the opening so it falls out right away and he's rewarded, and soon he'll be batting and rolling the toy all over to make more food come out. This is a noisy toy if he's on a hard floor.

Another type of food-dispensing toy is an interactive puzzle. The best-known puzzles are made by Nina Ottenson. They're graded by difficulty, and some are made specifically for puppies. Your puppy has to manipulate the puzzle by stepping on a piece, picking it up, rocking it, or pushing it to get to the food prize.

You can make your own version of a food puzzle at home. Put kibble or treats in each cup of a cupcake tin, place a tennis ball over each cup, and let your puppy figure out how to remove the ball and get to the treat. Don't be surprised if he figures out pretty quickly that he can dump the entire tin by stepping on it!

Puppy and Kids: Building the Friendship

The bloom is off the rose, and your puppy isn't brand new anymore. How do you keep the kids involved and build their relationship with the puppy?

When other children come over, tell your kids your puppy is a baby and can't speak for himself, so it's their job to recognize signals the puppy is tired or doesn't want to play. Explain to them that when your puppy turns his back, avoids eye contact, won't come to them, or tries to leave, he's tired and ready for his nap. A child will proudly assume the role of protector.

It's important for you to teach your puppy to respect your kids. A toddler or elementary school–age child won't like a puppy who jumps up or knocks them down. The child might try to tell the pup what to do, and your puppy doesn't listen.

These little people aren't much bigger than the pup, and your Lab might see them as littermates. Help your children use their own body language to stop the pup from jumping on them. Put your puppy on leash, and have the kids practice getting him to calm down by standing up straight and still, not looking at him, folding their arms, and ending the game.

Ensure that your puppy responds when the kids say "Sit" or "Down." Let your child reward the puppy while you hold the leash and enforce commands if necessary.

TIPS AND TAILS

Snap a second leash on your puppy so both you and your child are attached to him. Then, when he doesn't listen, you can help your child get him to respond.

Teach your kids to respect your puppy, too. Establish rules for the children's interactions with the puppy. He'll match his energy level to theirs, and everyone will stay safe. Point out that they wouldn't like it if the puppy did these things to them, and that they need to respect the puppy's feelings, too.

Here are some rules to establish with your kids and your puppy:

- No jumping on or falling on the dog.
- No kicking, hitting, or throwing things at the puppy. (When toys become weapons, take them away.)
- No teasing the puppy or enticing him to chase.

- Don't sit on the puppy or wrap your arms tightly around his neck or head.
- Leave the puppy alone when he's in his crate; no poking fingers in the crate and no teasing.
- Leave the puppy alone when he's eating.

A child might become jealous of the attention your puppy gets when guests visit your home. Children also might get jealous of each other if the puppy spends more time with their siblings or with Mom and Dad.

To avoid this, involve the children in the puppy's training. They can take turns giving commands, praising, holding the leash, and providing distractions. Help them teach the puppy tricks, like shake, they can demonstrate when people visit. Move the puppy's crate into different rooms every few nights so he spends time with everyone. You also could have your child prepare the puppy's meal and give it to him. Your child should have the puppy sit before setting down the food bowl.

You can't expect an elementary school–age child to take complete responsibility for the care of a puppy. In fact, if it becomes a required chore, she might resent the puppy. But one very important job, like putting down his food dish, helps her bond with the puppy and also feel a sense of accomplishment.

You can also encourage harmony between kids and puppy by encouraging your kids to play games with your puppy. Hide and seek is one option. Have one child restrain your Lab while another child hides. Have the hidden child call the puppy. When he finds him, switch sides.

Find the treat is another fun game for both kids and puppies. Let your puppy watch the child hide a treat in plain sight. Release him and praise him for finding it. Gradually hide treats in harder places or out of the room so he has to look harder. You don't want him digging up the couch while looking for a treat, however, so establish some guidelines with the kids about good hiding places.

	SOCIAL	BEHAVIOR	TRAINING	PHYSICAL	HEALTH
MONTH 1			Littermates and mother teach appropriate canine behavior	Rapid growth	
MONTH 2	Breeder starts socialization				
MONTH 3	Socialization at home with new owner and other pets	Fear-imprint period	Begin house- and crate training		1st DHPP vaccine
MONTH 4		Teething begins—heavy chewing period	Enroll in puppy class		2nd DHPP vaccine
MONTH 5	Socialization in public		Ready for basic commands	Switch to adult food	3rd DHPP and rabies vaccines
MONTH 6			Enroll in basic obedience class		
MONTH 7					
MONTH 8		Adult teeth are in—chewing continues		Moderate growth	Sexual maturity
MONTH 9					
MONTH 10			Ready for more advanced training		
MONTH 11				Slow growth—reaches adult size	
MONTH 12 AND BEYOND					Annual vaccinations and checkup

Full Speed Ahead

During months 5 and 6, your Lab puppy finishes another growth spurt, and her body starts to balance out. She has endless energy but not much common sense, so you'll spend time this month reviewing her training. Consider this a keep-her-busy month. Socialization is an ongoing process, so continue to introduce her to more places, people, and things.

Your Lab puppy is prone to injuries at this age—some of which lead to physical problems later in life—so we help you prepare your canine first-aid kit and get ready for emergencies. If it's fall or springtime, you might be experiencing her first major shedding season, so we also share some methods to cope with all that dog hair.

PHYSICAL DEVELOPMENT

Although your Labrador Retriever puppy is looking more like an adult, she's still very much a puppy at heart, as you'll see in her behaviors this month. You'll also notice that the amount of sleep she needs is changing as she matures.

Looking Less Like a Puppy

A puppy grows rapidly during her first 6 months. At this point, she can look mature and well balanced, or she can still be all legs and tail. She's reached about 75 percent of her adult height but only about 60 percent of her adult weight. A female who will mature to $21\frac{1}{2}$ to $23\frac{1}{2}$ inches will be 16 to 18 inches tall and 33 to 42 pounds now. At $5\frac{1}{2}$ months, a male puppy who will be within the standard at adulthood—$22\frac{1}{2}$ to $24\frac{1}{2}$ inches tall at the shoulder—will be 17 to 19 inches and 39 to 48 pounds. These are just estimates, and some puppies will be taller but may not weigh much more yet.

Her adult teeth are in, too, and they're starting to set permanently in her jaws, so the chewing continues.

All About Sleep

A newborn puppy sleeps 90 percent of the time. She sleeps less as she grows up, but she still sleeps as much as 13 hours a day when she's an adult. An adolescent dog, just like a teenage human, sleeps more, especially during growth spurts, when she's using energy to build bone and muscles. And considering her high activity level all day, no wonder she's tired at the end of it.

An adult dog's sleep is different. She wakes up more often, and about 25 percent of her sleep can be characterized as "active," where she seems to be dreaming. She also might twitch and whimper or paddle her legs likes she's running after that last ball you threw for her. In fact, scientists theorize that because a dog's brain is similar to a human's in some structural aspects, dogs do dream. Stanley Coren, PhD, FRSC, noted that a dog enters the dream phase about 20 minutes after falling asleep, and evidence has shown that she dreams about daily activities. Her breathing becomes shallow and irregular, and her eyes move behind her eyelids, just like the dream phase in human sleep.

If your Lab lives indoors and doesn't get much activity, she might sleep more than an active dog. She'll adjust her sleep time so she can be active when you're home and rest while you're at work or sleeping yourself. Some dogs also cope with extreme stress by sleeping more.

TIPS AND TAILS
Yawning doesn't necessarily mean your Lab is tired; it's also a stress response.

Your dog has an internal clock, and a Lab *never* sleeps through breakfast. In fact, you can be sure she'll wake you up at precisely the same time every morning. This quickly becomes a habit when you respond positively by getting up and feeding her. So much for sleeping in on Saturdays!

HEALTH

An active young Lab is more likely to be injured than be ill at this stage in her life. Reckless and uncoordinated, and blasting into adventure with no thought to her own safety, your Lab puppy is her own worst enemy. She's also getting taller, and she may be able to reach objects on high shelves now that were previously out of her reach.

It's essential that you learn to recognize and react to accidents, illnesses, and especially emergencies. Assemble a canine first-aid kit, or combine it with your family's kit because many of the items are the same (more on this in the later "Assembling Your Doggie First-Aid Kit" section). Being prepared gives you peace of mind and the capability to act when the unthinkable happens.

Getting to Know Your Puppy's Vitals

During an emergency, you'll need to assess your Labrador Retriever's vital signs. For reference, you need to know what her normal heart and breathing rates are, and what her gums normally look like, so you can make a comparison during an emergency.

To check your puppy's breathing rate, lay her on her right side and let her rest quietly. As you watch her chest rise and fall, count the number of breaths she takes in a 15-second period. Multiply that by 4 to get the number of breaths per minute. The normal rate is 10 to 30 breaths per minute for an adult and 15 to 40 breaths for a young puppy. At 6 months, her breathing rate will be about the same as an adult's. Her breathing rate is influenced by the temperature of her surroundings and her activity level, too, so keep that in mind when measuring or comparing.

To check her heart rate, again lay her on her right side. Bend her left leg until her elbow touches her chest, and put your right hand on her body where her left elbow meets her chest. You should feel her heart beating. Count the beats for 15 seconds, and multiply that number by 4. The normal resting heart rate for a puppy up to 1 year old is 120 to 160 beats per minute.

Next, look at her gums (mucous membranes). When she's healthy, her gums are pink and wet. Dark red, blue, brown, or very pale gums indicate she's not getting enough oxygen into her blood.

Check her capillary refill time, too. Firmly touch her outer gum with your finger and release. The gum should be white where you touched it. Watch the white fingerprint turn back to pink; it should take no more than 2 seconds. If it returns to pink too quickly or too slowly, she could have a problem with her blood circulation.

Your puppy's normal temperature is between 100.2°F and 102.8°F. (You learned how to take her temperature in Month 4.)

Knowing What's an Emergency

An emergency is any situation in which you must take immediate action to prevent further injury or death. In some situations, you can treat a problem or observe your Lab for a while before contacting the vet. For example, if your puppy has stopped eating, you have some time to look at options. If your puppy can't breathe or seems to be choking, there's no time to lose, and you must respond without delay.

Potential emergencies include the following:

Trauma: If your pup has been hit by a car or fallen from a high place.

Difficulty breathing or choking: She's gasping for air, pawing at her mouth, panicked, or her gums are turning blue or white.

Seizures: Long or short duration or multiple seizures.

Excessive bleeding: Spurting blood or prolonged bleeding you can't stop by applying direct pressure.

Deep cuts: Especially if bones or organs are exposed.

Snake bite: Look for bite marks on your puppy's skin, swelling, bleeding from the bite, trembling or drooling, difficulty breathing, or signs of shock.

Burns: Blisters, swollen reddened skin, or loss of skin and hair.

Suspected poisoning: Symptoms may include vomiting or diarrhea; trembling or twitching; seizure; abnormal gum color; heavy drooling or foaming from the mouth; burns on the lips, tongue, or mouth; or bleeding from the mouth, nose, ears, or anus.

Broken bones: Look for pain, swelling, lameness, bones protruding from her skin, or limbs held in an abnormal position.

Heat stroke: Heavy panting, bright red gum color (may turn blue or gray in later stages), body temperature above 104°F, difficulty walking, or collapse.

Bloat (mostly adult dogs): Can present as drooling, retching, attempting to vomit, unable to defecate, pacing and restless, distended abdomen, or signs of shock.

Staying Calm, Assessing, Calling, and Performing CPR

When you've identified an emergency, you need to stay calm, assess the situation, call the vet if necessary, and administer CPR (cardiopulmonary resuscitation) if required.

It's worth repeating: *stay calm.* Panic can make people do crazy things, and you can't help your dog if you get hurt, too. If she's been hit by a car, for example, don't run out into the road unless it's safe to do so. First, stop and take a deep breath.

Be sure you can approach your puppy safely. A frightened, injured dog, even your own, might bite. Speak calmly and reassuringly to her. Don't make any sudden movements that might cause her to bolt in fear. Use submissive body language: stand or crouch sideways to her, and don't look her directly in the eye.

To restrain your puppy, put the snap end of a leash through the loop for your hand and make a noose. Drop the noose over your puppy's head, and tighten it without touching her. Muzzle your dog by taking a long piece of gauze from your first-aid kit and wrapping it around her muzzle, crisscrossing it under her lower jaw, and tying it behind her neck. You also can use a belt or piece of fabric to do this.

TIPS AND TAILS

Common after serious injuries, especially if there's been major blood loss, shock occurs when internal organs don't get enough blood and oxygen flow. Symptoms of early shock include increased heart rate, pounding pulse, and red gums. Middle stages of shock are indicated by low body temperature, weak and rapid pulse, pale gums, and a woozy and weakened animal. Slow breathing and heart rate, weak or no pulse, depression, unconsciousness, and cardiac arrest can indicate late stages of shock, which lead to death.

Next, assess the situation. Do a visual survey of the scene. Observe your dog's posture, look for blood or vomit, listen to her breathing, and check for any obvious signs of what caused the injury, such as poison or a snake.

Then check her airway, breathing, and circulation—the ABCs of first aid. Assuming you can touch her, does your puppy have an open airway? Check her mouth and throat for obstructions, and clear any if you can using tweezers or forceps from your emergency kit.

Is she breathing? Look at the rise and fall of her chest. If you aren't sure, put your cheek against the front of her nose to feel or listen for her breathing. If she is, move on to the next step. A dog can be unconscious and still be breathing.

If she's not breathing, start rescue breathing immediately.

Does she have circulation, meaning a pulse or heartbeat? As discussed earlier, lay your dog on her right side, slightly bend her left leg until her elbow touches her chest, and put your right hand on her body where her left elbow meets her chest. Can you feel her heart beating?

To check for a pulse, use two fingers on one of three places:

○ High inside either rear leg about halfway between the front and back of her leg where you feel a slight recess

○ On the underside of either front paw just above the middle pad

○ On the underside of either hind paw just above the middle pad

If you can't find a heartbeat or pulse, start chest compressions immediately.

If you're alone, call for help or call the veterinary hospital before you start rescue breathing or CPR. If it's after hours, call the emergency animal hospital nearest you. If you have someone with you, let them call while you start CPR. The veterinarian will want to know a few things:

- Is the puppy breathing? Describe her breath. Is it slow or labored? Is she panting?
- Has she vomited or passed any stool or foreign objects?
- What's her pulse?
- What color are her gums?
- Is the puppy bleeding? How much? Where is the blood coming from?
- What's her temperature?
- Has anyone administered CPR?

The veterinarian might ask additional questions and give you instructions to help you care for your dog until you can get her to the clinic.

Next, administer CPR rescue breathing or chest compressions if your puppy has no pulse and isn't breathing. This life-saving procedure keeps oxygen in her system until help arrives. Continue CPR until she regains consciousness or you arrive at the vet's office.

It's essential that you first ensure your dog is actually unconscious. Never perform CPR on a dog who has a heartbeat or is breathing. Try to rouse her by gently shaking her body and talking to her. If that doesn't work, continue with CPR.

First, check her airway: Tilt her head back to align with her neck to open her airway. Pull her tongue forward, and remove any foreign objects that might be in her mouth.

Administer rescue breathing: Close her mouth tightly, and wrap one hand around her muzzle to keep it closed. Take a deep breath, and put your mouth over her nose, sealing her nostrils. Exhale firmly while watching for her chest to expand, or place a hand on her chest to feel if it rises. If the air does not go in, or if you detect some resistance, reposition her neck and try another two breaths.

Remove your mouth, take another deep breath, and repeat four or five times, allowing her chest to return to normal after each breath. Give her about 20 rescue breaths per minute, and continue until she revives or you arrive at the vet.

TIPS AND TAILS

If you can't get rescue breaths into your puppy or you couldn't remove an object from her airway, you'll have to perform the canine version of the Heimlich maneuver. If she's standing, put your arms around her belly, join your hands, and make a fist. Firmly push up and forward, just behind her rib cage. If she's lying down, place one hand on her back for support and use your other hand to squeeze her abdomen upward and forward. Either way, give five sharp thrusts to her abdomen. Then check her mouth and remove any objects that may have been dislodged.

Perform chest compressions: If your dog still isn't breathing after the first four or five rescue breaths, check again for a pulse or heartbeat. If she has none, her heart has stopped and you need to begin compressions immediately.

With your dog still lying on her right side, position yourself so you face her. Locate her heart (explained earlier). Straighten your arms; cup one hand over the other; and begin rapid, firm compressions, strong enough that your puppy's chest moves about 1 inch. For an adult dog, the chest should move 1 to 3 inches. After five compressions, give one rescue breath and check for a pulse. If she still has no pulse, continue the series of five compressions and one rescue breath until she revives or you get to the vet.

When your puppy is breathing and has a heartbeat, transport her to the veterinary as soon as possible. Ideally, have someone else drive while you concentrate on your puppy.

Assembling Your Doggie First-Aid Kit

A canine first-aid kit enables you to respond quickly when your dog needs help. You can buy premade kits for pets or humans and add additional items you might need. Label your kit clearly, and keep it where you can get to it quickly, possibly in your car. Or keep several first-aid kits in strategic places.

A basic pet first-aid kit should include the following:

- Your veterinarian's contact info and the address and phone number of the nearest emergency vet hospital

- A copy of your dog's health records

- A muzzle to fit your dog or a long strip of gauze (30 to 36 inches long)

- Antihistamine (Benadryl or equivalent) to treat an allergic reaction (Discuss the correct dose with your vet based on your Lab's weight. Remember that the dosage will change as she grows.)
- Tweezers, needle-nose pliers, forceps, or hemostat for removing foreign objects from her mouth or throat
- Saline eye wash for flushing irritants from her eye
- Mild grease-cutting dish soap (like Dawn) for removing sticky or caustic substances from her coat
- Rubber or latex gloves
- A rectal thermometer and petroleum jelly
- Hand sanitizer
- Antiseptic solution
- Antibiotic ointment
- Elastic bandages
- Veterinary wrap (such as VetRap) to hold bandages in place
- Blunt-nose and pointed scissors
- Sanitary pads to bandage a bleeding wound
- Nonstick bandages
- Various sizes and shapes of gauze pads to clean and protect wounds
- A flashlight
- A first-aid book or app

You also might want to keep a leash, several towels, and a blanket in your car or with your first-aid kit. You can use the leash to restrain your puppy or as a muzzle. Use the towels to clean up blood or vomit, and use the blanket as a stretcher or to keep your puppy warm.

TIPS AND TAILS

Keep the number for the ASPCA Animal Poison Control Hotline, 888-426-4435, in your canine first-aid kit. Veterinarians are on call 24 hours a day, 7 days a week, and you're charged a small consultation fee. Be sure to gather as much information as possible about the poison before you call.

Taking Pet First-Aid Classes

The Red Cross and many private trainers offer pet first-aid courses that cover both dogs and cats. Classes last around 4 hours and provide training that prepares you to effectively care for your pet in an emergency situation, including learning how to handle an injured dog, assessing her condition, and safely transporting her to the vet. You also learn what to do in specific situations like a broken bone, heat stroke, snakebite, or excessive bleeding. The course trains you to do a modified Heimlich maneuver on a choking animal as well.

One of the key benefits of pet first-aid classes is that you get hands-on practice bandaging, splinting, and performing CPR using CPR mannequins. The Red Cross program also includes a book and DVD you keep with your first-aid kit for reference. The book covers common injuries and emergency illnesses and reviews all the instruction you received in the class.

Check with the Red Cross, your veterinarian, or local dog trainers for pet first-aid courses in your area.

NUTRITION

Speed eating and food guarding cause ongoing health and behavior issues if not prevented, so it's important you learn to address those now. Also in this section, we look at how to choose healthy treats for your Lab puppy.

Dealing with Speed Eaters

At 6 months, your Labrador Retriever puppy undoubtedly eats like she hasn't seen a bowl of food for weeks. It starts when she's with her littermates and has to compete for a spot to nurse, and the behavior continues at the puppy bowl when she begins to eat solid food. Labs, more than any other breed, elevate speed eating to a fine art. But it can cause problems.

A dog who rushes through her dinner inhales too much air, which causes gas and discomfort. She finishes eating long before her stomach has a chance to tell her she's full, so she still wants more. Then she gulps down a bowl of water. This all adds up to a tummy ache, and as she ages, this puts her at risk for bloat, a potentially fatal condition.

Here are some suggestions to slow down your speed eater:

- ○ Don't make her compete for her food. If other dogs are in the house, feed everyone in separate rooms so they don't feel their food is threatened.

- Add water to her food, and let it soak for a few minutes. The food expands in the bowl and not in her stomach, so she'll feel full faster.

- Don't use a bowl. Instead, toss her food on the floor and let her scavenge and eat one kibble at a time. Be sure to do this on a clean, hard surface like a concrete patio or kitchen floor, because a typical Lab will eat gravel, dirt, seeds, and anything else in her path.

- Put a large rock in her dish before adding her food. She has to eat around it, which slows her down. Be sure to use a rock that's too big for her to put in her mouth.

- Break her meal into small portions, giving her just ¼ cup at a time.

- Put her meal in a food-dispensing puzzle so she has to figure out how it works to get her kibble out. This slows her down and entertains her.

TIPS AND TAILS

Gas and diarrhea are usually temporary problems, sometimes caused by a sudden diet change or by eating something in the yard that didn't agree with her. Gas alone doesn't usually indicate a serious health problem, but if you're worried, talk to your vet. If the problem continues and there's no medical cause, examine her dog food ingredients list for soy, beans, or cellulose that might cause excessive flatulence. Switching to a different food might solve the problem. Remember to switch foods gradually because that in itself can cause gas.

Preventing Food Guarding

Your Lab puppy should feel comfortable when anyone in the family reaches into her food bowl, touches her while she's eating, or takes away her bowl. At the same time, you want to be sure she won't bite you if you need to pick up the bowl. It's always easier to prevent a problem rather than fix one, so it's important to teach your Lab to welcome your presence while she's eating.

Do this exercise once or twice a week, or once every couple days. Don't make a pest of yourself, or she won't be happy to see you coming.

Divide her meal into four or five portions. Give her one portion in her bowl and then sit nearby on the floor, ignoring her. When she's done, pick up the bowl, put more food in it, and again ignore her until she's finished. She'll learn that having you near her food is a good thing because more food is on the way.

Each time you add more food, also add one special goodie, like a bite of cheese or a bit of cooked chicken. Or reach into the bowl while she's eating and add a treat. Touch the bowl while you add treats, or pick up the bowl, add a treat, and give it back to her. Not only does she get more food, but that food is *great!* She'll start to enjoy this game.

Also touch your puppy's collar while you put a treat in her bowl or pick it up. Hold her collar for a second or two, put the bowl back down, and add the treats.

Be sure you teach your kids the feeding game. Once they understand what you're teaching your puppy, they'll enjoy helping.

HAPPY PUPPY
Be sure everyone in the family leaves her reasonably alone when she eats. You want to be able to approach her and her bowl, but you don't want the entire family bugging her to a point that she feels the need to protect herself or her food.

Choosing Treats

Just as you would check the ingredients in a dog food before giving it to your pup, look at what's in the treats you purchase for your Labrador Retriever.

Most treats aren't intended as a complete, nutritionally balanced food, and this will be noted on the package. A junk-food dog treat can upset your puppy's nutritional balance, especially if she gets too many. Treats might be high in fat, salt, and sugar to add flavor, and the added salt will make your dog drink more. Select treats that are the same brand and contain the same ingredients as your dog food—or better yet, use part of her daily food ration for treats.

Soft or semisoft treats often contain added dyes and fillers. Just because something looks like a piece of bacon or beef doesn't mean that's actually what it is. Binding agents are also often added to make the treat stick together and look like a chunk of meat. And some "bones" are made with vegetables and cornstarch and could break apart quickly in a Lab's iron jaws.

HAPPY PUPPY
As an alternative to a constant barrage of commercially made treats, use bits of raw carrot or cooked plain chicken—your puppy will love them. Cheese cubes are also good in small amounts, but too much of a dairy product can cause diarrhea.

Just because you have a big dog (or will soon have) doesn't mean she needs a 4-inch-long dog biscuit every time she gets a treat. Break them up, or buy small biscuits.

Treats should account for no more than 5 to 10 percent of her total daily intake of food. If she's getting a lot of goodies, cut back on her kibble some for balance.

GROOMING

Labrador Retrievers are usually very clean … when they stay out of mischief. She'll need an occasional bath, so you learn how to go about it in this section. And because Labs do shed, it's important that you learn to take some preventive measures to deal with all that dog hair.

Bathing Your Lab Puppy

You can probably get by with only bathing your Lab once a year, during the summer, if that often. Too many baths strip her coat of protective oils and make it dry and dull. In hot weather, you can bathe her outside—an added plus.

That said, if her shedding really bothers you, a bath will reduce the hair she loses around the house. Brush her thoroughly before the bath, massage her coat while you bathe her, blow-dry her coat to remove more loose hair, and then brush her thoroughly again.

Confine your Lab in a big tub (a horse water trough or kiddie pool works great) or on a leash so she'll stay in one place. Ask a helper to restrain her while you bathe her. If the tub is slippery, put a bath mat in the bottom. Use cool to room temperature water to wash your pup because hot water will dry out her skin, and although cold water won't bother her, you shouldn't use ice-cold water.

You don't have to give her a complete bath the first time you introduce her to the tub. The idea is for her to enjoy a short, fun experience, not necessarily get her clean. Have your helper offer her treats throughout the process.

Let your pup sniff the hose and running water and maybe even taste it. Place her in the tub, and add water until it barely covers her feet. If this is too much, just splash a little on her feet and quit this time. Let her out when she's calm. She might try to jump out, but restrain her until she calms down and then let her out. Work with her over several sessions until she enjoys the water and looks forward to it.

Try to separate bath time from play-in-the-water time. You don't want your puppy chasing the hose and biting at the water while you're trying to shampoo her.

HAPPY PUPPY

Labrador Retrievers probably don't need a full bath, just a good rinsing, especially at this age. If that's the case, quit while you're ahead and introduce shampoo another time. It'll be easier on both of you.

When it's time for an actual bath, put cotton balls in her ears, but don't wet her face or head until later because she'll want to shake. Wet her coat, starting at her tail end and gradually moving forward. Hold the nozzle close to her skin so it penetrates her thick coat and she gets thoroughly wet.

Use a shampoo specifically made for dogs, and dilute it before you apply it so you don't have all the soap concentrated in one place. Massage it into her coat, taking care to get her belly and armpits, too. The hair on her neck and throat is especially thick, so add water as you wash. If she's really dirty or shedding heavily, massage her soapy coat with a rubber curry, which will bring soil and loose hair to the surface.

Lastly, put some diluted shampoo in your hand or on a washcloth and wash her face. You might want to put eye lubricant around her eyes to help keep out the soap. Rinse her face with a wet cloth or a gentle stream of water. Wipe out her ears, too, but avoid getting water in them.

Rinse her thoroughly, including between her toes, under her belly, and between her legs, until all the dirt and bubbles disappear. This will probably take longer than the washing step.

To rinse her face, hold up her nose while you rinse the back of her head so the water flows away from her eyes and ears. Her earflaps should prevent water from getting in her ears. Then, using a gentle stream of water, tip her head forward to rinse the front of her head. To rinse her muzzle, hold the hose level and run a gentle stream of water back and forth over her face. When all the shampoo is washed out, the water will run clear. If you leave any soap residue in her coat, it will irritate her skin, so rinse, rinse, rinse. And then stand back and let her shake!

Labs don't generally need a coat conditioner unless they have skin issues. If you like, you can add white vinegar to the final rinse to make her coat shiny. Rinse well so she won't smell like vinegar when you're done.

Now that everyone is soaked, move her someplace dry and towel off the excess moisture. Remove the cotton balls, and thoroughly dry her ears. If you want to keep her clean for a while, put her in her crate with some dry towels and a chew toy until her coat dries. Otherwise, she'll head straight for the backyard and roll in the dirt. If she got water in her ears, she'll rub her head along the ground. If you let her loose in the house, she'll rub along the walls and against the couch.

You might want to use a hair dryer to speed up the drying process, especially during winter or shedding season. The dryer also helps blow out any remaining loose coat. Turn the dryer on the lowest possible setting because a dog's skin burns easily. Your puppy might bite at the air or be afraid of the dryer noise, so start by holding it at arm's length away from her. Never blow the dryer directly in her face, and never put her in her crate with a dryer blowing on her. She can't move away from the heat if it gets too hot.

Shedding: Dealing with Lab Hair

For short-coated dogs, Labs sure shed a lot. A deep, thorough brushing at least once a week makes for a healthy dog and a cleaner house, but it's not enough to totally prevent shedding and the accompanying mess. Some preventive measures make your housecleaning chores less time-consuming.

You'll probably get used to the dog hair and barely notice it after a while. But you'll cringe when Aunt Charlotte comes to visit, sits on the couch, and gets a backside covered in dog fur. Invest in washable furniture covers to protect your furniture. When company comes, uncover the sofa and pretend it always looks that good.

You could teach your Lab puppy never to get on the furniture, but that wouldn't be any fun. Besides, when she lies on the floor in her favorite spot up against the couch, it'll still get dirty and hairy. If you really have to keep a room pristine, limit her access with pet gates. For example, let her nap on the sofa in the family room, but teach her that the living room sofa is off limits.

TIPS AND TAILS

A healthy coat doesn't shed as much. If you're feeding a discount or grocery store brand of dog food, you might see a marked difference in your dog's coat when you switch to a premium food.

A clean dog who sleeps on a dirty bed won't stay clean and sweet-smelling for long, so be sure to wash your Lab's bedding regularly, too. Besides getting rid of excess hair, your house also will smell fresher.

SOCIAL SKILLS

A well-socialized Labrador Retriever is friendly, confident, and well behaved everywhere she goes. This is no small achievement, and it doesn't happen by accident. It takes ongoing training, and this month is no exception.

Teaching "Off" and "Sit-to-Greet"

Puppies jump up because they want to be near your face and smell your breath to identify you. A cute little 20-pound Lab puppy might not be such a bother when she jumps, but a 60-pound jumping Lab quickly becomes a nuisance. You might let her jump on you sometimes, but she can't tell the difference between your Sunday best suit and your Saturday sweats, so she needs to learn not to jump up unless she's invited.

TIPS AND TAILS

"Off" is the command for four on the floor. Don't use "Down" because you've already taught her that "Down" means something else—"Lie down on the floor." You want your Lab puppy to learn that "Off" means "Get off me." It's not a punishment; it's an instruction.

To teach off, you'll first teach her to jump up on command. Pat your chest with both hands and say "Up" just as she starts to jump. Praise her, and as she backs off, say "Off" and add a hand signal: your flat palm toward her with spread fingers.

Meanwhile, as she's learning up and off, don't give her any attention when she's jumping—no eye contact, no touching, no talking. Look away, stand up straight, fold your arms, and turn your back to her. Stand still and wait her out. As soon as she stops jumping, even for a second, praise her and say "Good off." If she immediately jumps back up, ignore her again. When she's got all four feet down, stand quietly and praise her calmly.

Jumping up is a sign of overarousal, so you want her to lower her energy level. If you bend over her or make eye contact, this invites her back up into your face. Ask her to sit when she hits the floor so she has an alternative behavior to keep her busy. When she's first learning and you do pet her, loop two fingers through her collar to help her keep her feet on the ground. Look away and pet her chest so she's more likely to stay in position.

If she doesn't back off when you ignore her, attach a leash to her collar. When you give the "Off" command, give the leash a quick snap to remind her. You also can stand on the leash so she corrects herself when she jumps. If you drag her off you with the leash or use your hands to push her to the floor, she's not learning anything except that you'll do the work for her. Your hands reward her for jumping up, and even though you think it's a correction, she thinks it's a game.

Off is a command you'll use often with your excited Lab. When she can alternate up and off on command, she understands the exercise. Practice often around the house and outdoors, and have every family member teach her to respond.

Your puppy is tall enough to begin playing a Labrador's favorite sport, counter surfing, and off is useful for objects as well as people. Hook a leash to her collar, and let her drag it in the house. When her paws hit the counter, grab the leash and tell her "Off." A quick tug will get her attention. As soon as she looks at you, praise her and call her to you. Remember, don't drag her off the counter; she must decide to remove her paws on her own.

TIPS AND TAILS

To help prevent counter surfing, clean off your counters. Anything that remotely smells like food should be in a cupboard or on top of the refrigerator, and be sure to scrape your dishes and fill the dishwasher as soon as you're done eating. One successful scavenging operation rewards her for counter surfing, and she'll try again and again.

Your puppy will happily claim the couch or king-size bed as her own, and the family will soon be left sleeping on the floor if you allow this behavior. To fix it, use the same method you used for the counters. Let her drag a leash, give the command "Off," and lure her off the couch with a treat. Praise her as soon as she starts to get off. After some practice, hide the treat and don't produce it until she gets off the couch completely.

Invite her up on the bed or couch if you want to. Some dogs get possessive of their favorite spot (usually at about 1 or 1½ years old) and won't want to move, so be sure she willingly gets down when you tell her.

Once she learns off, put it to good use. When your puppy charges full speed at you, hold up your palm in the off position and rush at her. Spread your fingers, put your palm right in her face, and immediately ask for a sit. As she gets the idea, use a less-dramatic hand signal and just lean toward her to remind her to stay off and sit. Eventually, she'll decide off is a two-part command—off and sit—and she'll sit every time.

Sometimes a rambunctious puppy doesn't listen, so you need to use stronger measures. Fill a squirt bottle with water, and keep it handy. When she starts to jump up or is charging at you, squirt her in the face or chest. She'll quickly learn to veer off or refrain from jumping as soon as she sees you holding the bottle. Or because she's a Lab, she'll decide the water bottle is a lot of fun, and you'll have to come up with another method.

TIPS AND TAILS

You might read somewhere to knee your puppy in the chest when she jumps on you. *Don't do this.* It could injure her, either breaking her breastbone or hurting her when she falls. Another recommendation you might hear is to grab her paws and hold on until she struggles to get down. Again, *don't do this.* It could teach her to bite at your hands or be unwilling to let you handle her feet in other situations, like when you want to trim her toenails. Neither method builds a good relationship with your puppy.

A polite puppy greets people she meets with a sit. Once she understands how not to jump on you, expand her lesson and teach her not to jump on anyone else with a sit-to-greet. This is an entirely different exercise in your puppy's mind. In this situation, she's looking away from you rather than approaching you.

Enlist the help of family or friends when teaching this command. Have them ignore your puppy and make no eye contact. Don't let them greet or pet her until she sits quietly. Once she does this consistently, use this same method when she meets people out in public. People will be amazed at your training skills!

Add sit-to-greet to front-door greetings at home. Hang a leash on the doorknob, and hook her up as soon as the doorbell rings. Ask her to sit and stay before you open the door. If she starts to get up, shut the door and have her return to the sit. This might take several tries before she remains sitting.

When someone comes in the door, you'll have to start all over, asking your Lab to sit and stay. Remember to touch her and say "Okay" when she's allowed to stand up.

When the visitor moves away from the door, walk your puppy quietly to the person to say hello and sit for petting. If she just can't settle down at the door, put her in her crate and let her out on leash after your guest has entered and everything is calmer.

If you see your Lab think about jumping but then think better of it, praise her to the skies because she's definitely the smartest puppy on the planet. She'll remember how happy you are and try to do as well the next time she's tempted.

Going Many Different Places

Continue to take your Lab to new places this month. Also return to places you've previously visited so she'll remember them.

In preparation for the adolescent crazies, practice her obedience skills everywhere you go. Bring along a chew bone and have her lie quietly at your feet while you relax on a park bench. For a new sensation under her feet, take her to a harbor if you have one nearby, and let her walk on the floating docks. Walk her across a bridge or over a freeway.

If you have a beach nearby, take her there, too. Although you've introduced your Lab to water at home, and she probably loves it, the family pool and garden hose are a far cry from a lake or beach. Waves crashing on the shore, birds running along the water's edge, the smell of the ocean and seaweed—these all are new, exciting, and potentially scary to your Lab puppy. Bring fresh water with you for her to drink; you don't want her gulping salty seawater, which will quickly dehydrate her.

Consider bringing another dog along for your puppy's first beach expedition, preferably one who has beach experience. Start by allowing your pup to drag a long line. Many dogs are afraid of the approaching water and spook when a wave splashes on their feet. When she sees the other dog having fun, she'll be more likely to try it. Start by walking her along the water's edge and letting her get used to the feel of the wet sand. Don't force her into deep water, and *never* throw her in.

Bring a ball she can fetch on the beach, but don't throw it out in the water until she's happily playing in the shallow waves. Then just toss it in 1 or 2 feet, and let her chase it out on a receding wave. When she's comfortable in the water, she might want to swim farther out, so keep her close enough that you can grab the long line.

When you bring her home, you'll be glad you've been practicing her grooming skills as you hose her down to get the sand and saltwater out of her coat.

TIPS AND TAILS

Teenage Labs and retractable leashes are a dangerous combination. The farther away from you she goes, the less control you have. When she's so far away from you, she might ignore your call because she isn't used to responding from a distance yet. And one good, hard jerk when she sees another dog a few hundred yards away and she's gone, the leash ripped from your hand. If the handle retracts quickly, it could hit your pup and possibly break a bone. Wait until your Lab is at least 3 or 4 years old before trying retractable leashes, if you use them at all.

BEHAVIOR

The training and socialization you've worked so hard on up to this point won't completely prevent your puppy from her madcap adolescent activities, but they have given her an excellent head start and might help her avoid some typical teenage behavior problems. But just in case, here are some areas to work on this month.

The Age of Distraction

At 6 months, your Labrador puppy is ready to take on the world, and sometimes she considers that human being at the other end of her leash (you!) a hindrance to her plans. Expect a lot of overenthusiasm and pulling in every direction when she's out in public, and be ready with calm and consistent training and rule enforcement. This month, you might have to stop what you're doing and invest a few minutes to get her attention so she'll listen to you. She's strong and determined, and you must be equally so. Your Lab isn't mad at you; she's a preteen.

She'll use as many tricks as she can to get out of obeying you. You ask for a sit, and she paws at your leg. When she lies down, she rolls on her back like she has a tremendous itch that just won't wait. When you ask her to stay, she whimpers, snorts, and wraps herself around your legs. She creeps forward as soon as your attention wanders. Patiently use the leash to put her back in position, and release her when you're ready. Repeat the exercise until she does it correctly, but set her up for success by asking for a shorter stay next time. If you give up and quit when she's goofing around, she wins and will try to distract you every time you ask her to do something.

Use your body language to keep your dog calm and focused. Speak softly, stand up straight, and use the leash instead of your hands to correct her or put her back in position.

Digging in the Yard

Labs dig for many reasons, but the most common is because it's fun! Digging rewards her with interesting smells, chewy roots, and other garden delights. You can't train your dog *not* to dig, so the solution includes management and prevention. Conduct a regular perimeter patrol to find and fix any loose boards in wood fencing or broken tension wires at the bottom of chain-link fencing. A determined Lab can and will tear apart a chain-link fence.

Boredom and separation anxiety cause many dogs to take up recreational digging. A young dog left out in the yard all day gets restless and needs something to do, so she makes her own entertainment. She may have seen you working in the garden, so she digs up a spot that still has your scent. If you use bone meal or blood meal when you plant, she could be attracted to that smell. She might dig to bury a bone or toy or to make a cool resting place under a large bush.

HAPPY PUPPY

A young Lab needs lots of physical and mental exercise. Tire her out before you leave her in the yard alone, and also leave food-dispensing toys that will occupy her for an hour or more.

Consider providing your Lab with her own digging pit. Set aside a small area of your yard; fill it with sand (which is easier to rinse off your puppy than dirt); and bury treat-filled toys, bones, balls, and other prizes in the sand for her to find. When you first introduce her to the pit, leave a few goodies sticking out of the sand so she gets the idea.

Of course, some dogs refuse to use your chosen spot. To make it more alluring, make the other holes less attractive. For example, fill holes with dog feces and cover them. Put a balloon in a hole so it pops when she digs and scares her. Place a piece of chicken wire about 4 inches down in the hole and bury it. She won't like snagging her toenails on the wire.

If you have gophers, moles, or other underground pests, your Lab will do some serious excavating to try to find them. The easiest solution to this problem is to get rid of the critters. Rodent poisons usually contain molasses or bran, so they'll also attract your dog and could kill her if she ingests any. Even if the bait is placed underground, your Lab might get to it. Check with your local garden center for dog-friendly methods to eliminate pests.

Your dog might dig because she sees other people and dogs walking past your house, wants to join them, and digs under the fence in frustration. To solve this problem, you could put up a solid fence. Or line the bottom of the fence with concrete blocks or large rocks. You also could attach a 2-foot-wide strip of chicken wire or hardware cloth along the bottom of the fence. Place it so the top 12 inches attach to the fence and the bottom 12 inches bend out into the yard. Cover the part on the ground with rocks and dirt.

When all else fails, keep your Lab indoors or build a dog run for her to stay in when you can't supervise her activities.

Iron Jaws, Soft Mouth

A Labrador Retriever is supposed to gently pick up a fallen bird and deliver it to the hunter in pristine condition—she's not supposed to eat it. She should hold the bird gingerly so she doesn't tear it up, crush it, or otherwise render it inedible. Keep in mind that this is the same dog who can turn a tree branch into toothpicks.

Sometimes people accidentally train their dogs to grab and bite down hard. They worry that she'll bite their fingers as she takes a treat or toy, so they snatch their hands away as the puppy reaches for it. Or they toss the treat on the ground, which encourages the dog to lunge for it. Dogs who are excited grab in the heat of a game. Competition from other dogs also causes a puppy to grab.

Retrievers aren't usually born with a soft bite, so it's important to teach your Lab to take a treat nicely. Introduce this treat-taking lesson separately from other exercises you're teaching your puppy. If you're asking her to sit or down and then correct her for snatching at the treat, she'll get confused.

First, choose a word to use to remind her to be gentle. "Nicely," "Gently," "Easy," or "Softly" are all good choices because they're soft, two-syllable words, which are easier for you to say in a calming way.

If your puppy is a real shark, wear garden gloves. Put a tiny dab of peanut butter on the palm of your hand, and offer it to your puppy. If she grabs, simply close your hand over the goodie. She needs to lick this treat, not bite at it.

Try again. If she lunges at your hand, quickly push your hand at her about an inch to slow her down. As she licks the treat, use your word, "Nicely," and praise her quietly. Say "Nicely" in a calm and friendly voice while she's eating the treat. This isn't a command or a warning.

When she's taking the peanut butter off your palm politely, try it with a piece of her kibble. Hold your thumb over the treat and let her chew it out of your grasp. Correct her with "Ack" if she bites your fingers, but don't snatch away your hand.

Next, switch to holding treats between your fingertips. As she reaches in for the treat, push the treat into her mouth about 1 inch. She'll feel your hand coming at her and back off slightly. Also hand-feed your puppy her meals (or even a portion of her meals) for a few days, practicing her new manners. Then incorporate "Nicely" into your daily routine and training sessions.

TIPS AND TAILS

A puppy who grabs treats probably also grabs toys and holds them in an iron grip. As she grows up and gets stronger, you won't be able to out-muscle her. Avoid teaching your dog to bite hard. Don't play tug-of-war games in which you encourage her to hang on and not let go. And don't pull toys from her mouth; her natural reflex is to bite down. Trade her for a treat or another toy instead.

The "Give" command comes in handy around the house. You'll have a much easier time wrestling items from her mouth using this command than trying to pry something from her grip.

Attach a leash and present your pup with a toy you know she'll want. Be sure to use something you can take without sticking your fingers in her mouth. A tennis ball, for example, may be too small, so choose a stick or retrieving *bumper* instead. Use "Nicely" to encourage her to take it gently, just like she did with food. When she has it in her mouth, show her a treat or another highly desirable toy, and say "Give" as she lets go of the first toy. Your puppy might drop the toy or release it into your hand. Either way, praise her and repeat the lesson several times. Once she gets the idea, introduce the command "Take it" as you present the toy.

Labs love to retrieve, and they love games. To get a fast release when you say "Give," throw the other toy for her to retrieve as a reward for giving up what she has in her mouth.

DOG TALK

A **bumper** is a long, narrow rubber or canvas retrieving toy used for training hunting dogs. Due to their length, they stick out of either side of a dog's mouth so you can take them easily. Rubber bumpers are covered with raised knobs that prevent the bumper from sliding around in your Lab's mouth, which would encourage her to chomp down and hold it even more tightly. Canvas bumpers are usually filled with hard foam and sometimes contain weights. Take bumpers away from your Lab when you aren't using them because she'll shred them easily.

TRAINING

Diligent training is your goal for this month. Your pup will be easily distracted, so give her plenty of reminders as you train, and keep your training lessons interesting and fun by teaching her new skills and polishing old ones. With practice, she should be able to do a 1-minute sit stay and a 1- or 2-minute down-stay by the end of this month.

Basic Obedience Review and Hand Signals

Your puppy should have learned the following commands so far:

Sit: Put your rear end on the floor and don't move. Hand signal: scoop one hand upward, palm up.

Down: Lie down, roll on one hip, and don't move. Hand signal: sweep your flat hand, palm down, toward the ground.

Okay: You're finished; relax. This command releases your dog from whatever she's doing. Hand signal: toss your hands upward happily, palms up.

Come: Stop what you're doing and come here. Signal: wide open, welcoming arms.

Let's go or **Walk:** Pay attention, we're going for a walk. Signal: step off on your left foot when she's at your left side.

Stay: Don't move until I come back and touch you. Hand signal: flat palm in front of her nose as you step off on the foot farthest away from her. For example, if she's on your left side, step off with your right foot.

Off: Put all four feet on the floor. Hand signal: flat palm, fingers spread, pushing toward her.

Take it: Take an item, such as a toy, that I present to you. No hand signal.

Give: Open your mouth and release an item. Hand signal: flat open hand (like a plate) in front of her mouth.

TIPS AND TAILS

Because dogs are so visually oriented, they read your body language before they pay attention to what you say. A hand signal or other cue from you helps your dog understand what you want. You can use the ones mentioned here or make up your own.

Training Problems

She was doing so well with her training, and now she seems to have fallen completely apart. Who is this disobedient puppy? When you lose mental control of your distracted preteen puppy, retain physical control by keeping her on a leash. Insist that she comply with every instruction, even when she gives you a "What? You talkin' to me?" attitude. Training problems might actually be attention problems rather than willful disobedience.

If you slack off and let her respond slowly or get away with not responding at all, you'll slowly lose control over your dog, just when you need it most. That should be enough to motivate you to work through any training issues you're encountering. Don't reward your puppy if you have to ask twice or physically force her to do what you've asked. Show her the treat but then put it away.

Do, however, reward every sincere try. Remember as you train together that you're not angry at your puppy; you're teaching her. Her behavior right now is part of the learning process.

HAPPY PUPPY
It takes at least three repetitions before your dog starts to understand what you're teaching her. Stick to numerous 2-minute practice sessions over several days instead of one 30-minute session every day. A puppy gets tired and loses interest after a few minutes. She's most likely to remember the last thing you worked on and nothing else.

Dole out your praise and treat rewards according to her response. When she's done especially well, give her several treats and big, happy praise. When she responds slowly or late, give her mild praise and no treat. She'll soon learn by your reaction which responses earn treats and exuberant praise, and her performance will improve.

Why is your Lab testing your patience this month? Several reasons might be to blame. For example, she has reached a *learning plateau*. It takes about 6 weeks before a dog's brain converts a behavior from short-term to long-term memory and it becomes a habit. As she's processing the change, she might act like she's forgotten a simple command. Just keep reviewing, and she'll catch up.

DOG TALK
A **learning plateau** occurs when your puppy suddenly seems to have forgotten everything you've taught her. It's common in adolescent dogs and often happens around week 5 in obedience class. This phase may last 2 days or 2 weeks, but it does pass, and you'll see a surge in her progress once she's through it.

She might also be confused. Take a step back in her training and treat her like she's learning it for the first time. Remember, she'll get mixed up if you ask her to do something in a new place or if someone new asks her to do it. Even a simple sit might befuddle her. What's more, if her uncertainty and makes you uncertain, she senses your confusion and delays her response. When you're sure she understands what you're asking, act like you expect her to respond.

Or she might be testing you. She could be bored with lessons or just distracted by adolescent energy. If this is the case, you'll see her offer avoidance behaviors—refusing to look at you, barking at you, or bouncing around. Call her bluff, persevere, and reward her when she gives in. For example, if she sits but pops right back up, wait a second, and if she doesn't settle back into the sit, walk her around you and ask again. Take a few steps and command "Sit" again. Don't give her a treat until she sits promptly the first time you ask her.

If she rolls around and paws at your feet when you tell her "Down," don't touch her, and don't offer any praise, treats, or comments. Remain calm and firm, and repeat "Down" until she responds. Praise her and then quit.

If she won't come when called, attach a long line and reel her in. Be sure she complies every time, and don't call her if you can't enforce it. Always praise her when she gets to you.

Enrolling in More Obedience Classes

Your Lab graduated with honors from puppy kindergarten. She's learning all these things you've been teaching her, and she's growing into a beautiful, well-behaved young dog. Why invest time and money in another obedience class? Beginning obedience might appear to be a review of the things she already knows, but it offers other benefits as well.

You could be ahead of the curve this month, but adolescence approaches, and your puppy still has a lot to learn about self-control and good behavior. Obedience classes give her the opportunity to socialize and hone her skills in a controlled environment with new dogs and people of all ages.

As a bonus, the structure of a class motivates you and the rest of your family to continue practicing with your puppy. You'll have the opportunity to ask questions and try different methods if something you're doing isn't working. There's probably going to be at least one other Lab in your class, so you'll be able to watch how other owners deal with the same challenges you've encountered. Watching other sporting breeds, who also mature late and are very active, will give you insight to your own dog's personality.

Plus, your puppy gets the opportunity to practice things she knows in a new place, and you'll discover if she really understands what you've taught her so far. The instructor can offer new and different distractions to challenge her, too.

Once basic class is completed, you can move up to the next level, where you prepare your Lab for off-leash control.

Teaching the Automatic Sit

While walking your Lab, tell her to sit every time you come to a stop. Pretty soon, she'll automatically sit for you. As always, when she's first learning this skill, give her a treat and praise as soon as she sits. As she gets the hang of it, you can continue to praise and *fade* the treats. Ultimately, you won't have to say "Sit" when you stop walking, but she'll still take a seat.

DOG TALK

When teaching a new behavior, you reward with a treat every time your puppy complies. When she knows a skill, you can wean her off, or **fade,** the treats by skipping an occasional treat reward while still using verbal praise. As you produce a treat even less often, she'll get one only once in a while for her best effort. If her response isn't reliable, you might be reducing the number of treats too quickly.

Teaching "Leave It"

The "Leave it" command is different from the "Off" command. With leave it, you want your puppy to turn her attention to you and away from whatever she's interested in. The idea is to prevent her from doing something before she gets too involved with it. You'll use this command in many situations, such as when you drop a cupcake on the floor, when she focuses on the cat across the street, or when she thinks about rolling in horse manure.

To teach leave it, put her on a leash and walk her past a treat or toy on the floor. As soon as she notices the item, say "Leave it," turn sharply, and walk away while making happy talk and luring her attention back to you. If she gets the item before you can say "Leave it," you're too close, so walk by the item farther away next time.

When she focuses on you instead of the item, praise her and give her a treat from your hand. Don't let her have the treat or toy on the floor. Practice several times, and she'll soon look at you for a treat as soon as you say "Leave it." She'll be more motivated if the treat in your hand is one she likes better than the one on the floor.

Practice several times a day and with many different items. When she's reliably looking to you, try the same exercise without turning away. Just keep on walking while saying "Leave it." When she responds, give her something else to do, like come or sit. If you release her, she'll just dive for the toy.

YOU AND YOUR PUPPY

Raising a Lab puppy shouldn't be all work and no play. Teach her to enjoy fun sports like swimming, but remember to also enjoy some quiet time together. Your Lab is ready and willing to do whatever you have in mind.

Having Fun in the Pool

Labrador Retrievers are born water dogs. Their webbed feet and water-resistant coat makes them naturals at a pool party. But wait! There's one detail you might not be aware of: puppies, even Labs, are not born knowing how to swim. You have to teach your dog how. Once she gets the hang of swimming, you'll have hours of fun together splashing and fetching.

TIPS AND TAILS
Never give your puppy access to a pool until she can swim the length of it and knows how to get out on her own. Even then, you should always be present. If you have a pool cover, don't let your puppy play on or under it. And never throw your puppy in the pool. It won't force her to swim, and instead, she could drown. At the very least, your puppy might never enjoy the water again, which is a tragedy for a Lab.

Start by letting your Lab play in water up to her chest in the bathtub or a kiddie pool. If she's been to the lake or ocean, this will speed up the process. Keep lessons short—maybe only 5 to 10 minutes the first day. Swimming is tiring, and it'll likely frighten her at first.

First and most importantly, teach your Lab pup how to get out of the pool. Have her on a leash if you need to, and if you have a puppy life jacket, put it on her. Get in the pool with her, and hold her while letting her stand on the step. Pat the edge of the patio or the deck outside the pool, and use a few treats to encourage her to jump out of the water. Repeat until she starts to understand how to get in and out of the pool.

Now take her 1 or 2 feet away from the edge and hold her up in the water with your arms under her belly. Most pups start paddling with their front feet immediately, like they're trying to walk. If you don't hold her up, she'll be vertical, rear feet and tail deep in the water, pawing with her front feet as she tries to get out of the pool. She can't swim until she learns to level herself and get her rear up as high as her front.

Continue to hold up her stomach and let her paddle to the steps and get out. If she's willing, take her back in the water and do it again. Always turn her so she's swimming toward the steps. You want her to think that's the only direction to swim.

After a few tries, give her front end less support as she paddles. Pretty soon, you'll notice she's holding up her front end and her rear feet are paddling, too. You'll gradually be able to give her stomach less and less support as she learns to hold herself up. The process might take a day, or it might take a week. Work with her as long as it takes to ensure swimming stays fun and isn't frightening.

Wait until she's completely comfortable swimming and getting in and out of the pool on her own before you let her jump off the edge into the water. Practice with other people in the pool and a lot of commotion around her, too.

Enjoying Quiet Time Together

You probably have fantasies of spending a cold winter's night in front of a roaring fireplace, reading a good book while your devoted Lab sleeps curled up on the rug at your feet.

It's probably hard to reconcile that picture with the active Lab puppy you have today. But even a puppy needs some down time, and so do you. Evenings are also a perfect time for her to quietly keep the kids company while they do homework or watch television. She needs to learn that life goes on around her and she doesn't need to be in the middle of everything that happens. If you respond every time your little tornado asks for attention, she'll just pester you more and more.

Your puppy should be able to lie at your feet without being crated or tethered all the time. As with everything else, practice makes perfect. The first few tries might be more training than relaxation, but she can learn. If she's restless, be patient. It might take her a few minutes to settle down. You can start by having her on leash at your feet for just 5 or 10 minutes each night. Give her something to chew on to help keep her occupied. It might take her a few minutes to settle down, but once she understands the nightly routine, she'll happily comply.

A balance of training, play, and quiet companionship marks the beginning of the partnership you and your Labrador buddy will enjoy for years to come.

	SOCIAL	BEHAVIOR	TRAINING	PHYSICAL	HEALTH
MONTH 1			Littermates and mother teach appropriate canine behavior	Rapid growth	
MONTH 2	Breeder starts socialization				
MONTH 3	Socialization at home with new owner and other pets	Fear-imprint period	Begin house- and crate training		1st DHPP vaccine
MONTH 4		Teething begins—heavy chewing period	Enroll in puppy class		2nd DHPP vaccine
MONTH 5			Ready for basic commands	Switch to adult food	3rd DHPP and rabies vaccines
MONTH 6	Socialization in public		Enroll in basic obedience class	Moderate growth	
MONTH 7		Adult teeth are in—chewing continues			Sexual maturity
MONTH 8					
MONTH 9					
MONTH 10			Ready for more advanced training		
MONTH 11				Slow growth—reaches adult size	
MONTH 12 AND BEYOND					Annual vaccinations and checkup

The Silly Tweenager

Do you remember middle school? Every day was full of drama and excitement. You weren't quite a teenager, but you weren't a little kid anymore either. Your body was changing, and you practiced acting like an adult, unsure about this new role.

Think of your Labrador Retriever puppy going through this same experience. At 6 or 7 months old, he has the emotional maturity of a 12-year-old child, but his physical maturity is dawning. He'll be reckless and uninhibited while he's also insecure and clingy. Most of all, he'll be a whole lot of fun.

PHYSICAL DEVELOPMENT

Although your puppy might not be fully sexually mature this month, the related hormones are developing. Soon you'll recognize changes in your Lab's appearance and behavior.

Understanding Female Sexual Maturity

Female Labs can mature anywhere from 6 to 18 months of age, but most have their first *heat* between 10 and 14 months. The heat cycle is a clear signal of sexual maturity. (In males, the onset of puberty is much less obvious.) A female dog goes into heat twice a year until she's spayed. During this time, you must keep her away from *intact* males to prevent pregnancy.

DOG TALK

Heat is the period when a female dog is receptive to breeding and capable of getting pregnant. Also referred to as "in season," the cycle lasts 18 to 21 days. **Intact** refers an unneutered male or unspayed female dog.

But before you start thinking you'll breed your Lab puppy now, know that a teenage dog is too young to breed. She's not yet emotionally mature enough to deal with a litter, and she could harm or abandon her puppies if she has them this young. In addition, the health testing she should have before being bred doesn't provide accurate results until she's at least 2 years old.

Now, back to her heat cycle. The first stage is called proestrus and lasts about 9 days. During this time, she'll emit an odor that attracts males but reject any who come near her. Her vulva swells, and there's a slight bloody discharge. The first hint you might have that she's in heat is the gang of male dogs hanging out in your front yard. An unneutered male will travel several miles to get to a female in season.

The second stage is estrus, when the discharge increases and is pink in color. This period lasts about 7 days, and during this time, she'll accept a male for breeding. This is when she can get pregnant, so keeping her confined is critical. A chain-link fence isn't enough. A determined dog will breed *through* a fence. Keep her safely indoors.

Diestrus is the final stage of active heat, and it starts about day 14 but could be as late as day 20. The discharge is redder, the vulva returns to normal size, and she no longer accepts a male's advances. Diestrus lasts 60 to 90 days or until she gives birth, approximately 63 days after conception. When the discharge and swelling have ended, the heat cycle is complete.

A Lab's heat cycle gets messy. Doggie diapers and pads are available to protect your house, but you also should wipe away the discharge regularly. During the height of her heat, you might want to clean her twice a day. Besides keeping your house cleaner, it will prevent skin irritation from excess moisture. She might also get cranky, mount other dogs, or try to escape and breed.

Estrogen is the primary female sex hormone. It maintains the female's sex organs and contributes to the development of a feminine appearance. Because of her estrogen, she'll have finer bone structure, be shorter, and weigh less than most males.

Understanding Male Sexual Maturity

Over the past several months, your male Lab's testicles have developed and begun to produce sperm, and soon he'll be capable of siring puppies. Male dogs have an increase in testosterone levels at 4 or 5 months, reaching a peak at 8 to 10 months. His testosterone levels taper off to normal adult levels at around 18 months.

Males don't have heat cycles like female dogs do. Once they reach maturity, they're always fertile. However, like a 6-month-old female, he's too young to be bred now. He doesn't have to raise a litter, but he's not old enough to have health clearances that ensure he won't pass on genetic defects to his offspring.

A sure sign of puberty in the male dog is when he starts lifting his leg while urinating. He also might be more aggressive with other dogs and mount them during play.

An intact male develops distinctly male physical characteristics as he matures. He has heavier bones than a female; a bigger, blockier head; and more muscle.

TIPS AND TAILS

To calm down an intact male dog when an in-heat female is near, dab a bit of pure vanilla extract (natural, not synthetic) or Vicks VapoRub around his nose to interfere with his ability to smell. To help mask the smell of a female in heat, put some Vicks on the fur around her tail. You also can give her a chlorophyll tablet twice a day during her heat cycle. These actions decrease her attractive scent but won't totally remove it.

HEALTH

Pet Labradors should be spayed (females) or neutered (males). Like any issue regarding your dog's health, you should understand why and when it should be done so you can make an educated decision.

In this section, we also take a look at some more external and internal parasites that might plague your Lab. You also risk contracting these pests from your dog, so learn to recognize the signs of infestation so you can treat these conditions.

Spaying and Neutering

The reasons to spay or neuter your dog are many, and the reasons to keep him or her intact are very few. The main reason to spay or neuter is to prevent contributing to pet overpopulation. Shelters and Labrador Retriever rescue groups have hundreds of wonderful Labs available for adoption, sometimes even puppies. Even if you don't purposely breed your Lab, mixed-breed puppies from an accidental breeding have a slim chance of successfully remaining in the same home throughout their lives.

As you learned in previous chapters, being a responsible breeder is expensive and time-consuming. A breeder must ensure both parents have health exams and genetic tests and then spends weeks caring for the mother and her puppies. If something goes wrong, the costs can be huge. The breeder also keeps in touch with the new owners, answers their questions, and takes back a puppy any time during his life if the owner can no longer keep him.

Your breeder probably sold you your puppy on a limited registration, which means any puppies your Lab produces cannot be registered. Labs are the most popular breed in the United States and have been for more than 20 years. The AKC reports more than 100,000 Labs per year—and that just counts the ones who are registered. A lot of study goes into breeding dogs, and only the best of the best should be bred.

Besides the social issues, a spayed or neutered (altered) dog is simply much easier to live with. Your Lab will be more focused on you and less on other dogs. On the practical side, most dog day cares and many kennels don't accept unaltered dogs.

Male Labrador Retrievers

As sex hormones develop in your male Lab, they affect his behavior. He'll be easily distracted, less focused on you, harder to handle out in public, more likely to *mark* indiscriminately, and might not get along as well with other dogs. He'll try to escape and roam when he senses a female in heat, even if she's miles away. An unneutered male is also more susceptible to several kinds of canine cancer.

DOG TALK
A mature dog **marks,** or deposits urine, so other dogs can identify him and determine his age or readiness to breed. Marking also establishes territorial boundaries.

Although a neutered male might still mark, he won't do it as often or in as many inappropriate places as an intact dog. Neutered males are less of a threat to other male dogs and, therefore, aren't challenged as often as they would be if they were intact.

Neutering a male dog consists of surgical removal of both testicles. Unless the testicles have been retained in the abdomen, it's a simple procedure and your Lab will go home the same day. The vet uses surgical glue or sutures to close the incision, and your Lab will have to wear an Elizabethan collar (head cone) for a few days to prevent him from chewing at and ripping open the incision. The testicular pouch usually remains and shrinks up into the abdomen over time.

Most dogs are able to resume normal activity the next day, but don't allow him to exercise too hard. Watch the incision for swelling, discharge, discoloration, or odors, which could indicate an infection. It'll take several weeks for the testosterone level in his system to decrease.

TIPS AND TAILS

Spaying/neutering affects your Lab's sexual behavior, not his ability to learn. He can still hunt, compete in obedience, or participate in any other activities you choose. In fact, he'll perform *better* because his raging hormones won't distract him.

Female Labrador Retrievers

Female dogs also behave differently when they're intact. They're more likely to be aggressive toward other dogs, especially females. When in heat, a female is easily distracted, will try to escape, and will mark more to advertise her availability, bringing intact male dogs from miles around to your house. As her heat ends, she'll be aggressive to males. Her housetraining could lapse during this time, too.

When a female is in heat, she undergoes physical and emotional stress and a complete upset of her usual personality and health. She might not be able to participate in her regular activities like hunting, service, or therapy work.

Intact females are susceptible to more health problems than spayed females. They're prone to mammary cancer, pyometra (uterine infection), and other maladies caused by excess amounts of estrogen in their systems.

A spayed female's personality doesn't fluctuate wildly when she doesn't have the seasonal upset of heat cycles. One health issue that does occur in a few spayed females is urinary incontinence, and she might leak a little urine while she sleeps. This condition is easily managed by inexpensive medication.

Spaying a female dog involves an abdominal incision to remove the ovaries and uterus, so it's more invasive than neutering a male. She'll probably have sutures, which need to be removed after 10 to 14 days. She also will need an Elizabethan collar to prevent her from tearing out her stitches while they heal. Her activity should be restricted for the first few days.

Some vets advocate removing just the ovaries. This is a relatively new method of spaying, and some feel it leaves the dog in a more natural state. The surgery is also less physically traumatic. The risk of pyometra should be very low in a dog spayed this way.

The lack of estrogen after spaying does increase some dogs' appetites, so the old wives' tale about altered dogs getting fat is partially true. Ensuring she gets regular exercise and monitoring her weight should keep her as trim as she needs to be with no problem.

When to Spay/Neuter?

For the past 20 years, animal shelter veterinarians have performed spay/neuter surgeries on dogs as young as 8 weeks old. Their motivation is clear: to prevent pet overpopulation. You shouldn't alter your Lab at such a young age though. When considering when to alter your dog, long-term health effects of the surgery play an important role.

For years, veterinarians recommended that dogs be altered before puberty, meaning before a female's first heat or before a male starts lifting his leg. Today it's believed there are some benefits to waiting. Weigh these against your Lab's behavior and the inconvenience of having an unaltered dog before you make your decision, and discuss the risks and benefits with your veterinarian.

In both sexes, early spay/neuter surgery could cause a dog to grow taller than if he or she was allowed to mature. During puberty, the *growth plates* of your dog's limb bones grow quickly, and he gets taller. After puberty, the cartilage in the growth plates turns to bone, no new cartilage forms, and your dog stops growing. After the bones reach their full adult length, they expand and become wider, denser, and better able to support the weight of the adult dog. A Lab is usually full height by 8 or 9 months old, but the growth plates don't close until 10 to 14 months.

DOG TALK

Growth plates are discs at the end of each limb composed of soft cartilage. Growth plates are located in the hips, knees, elbows, and wrist bones. Older cartilage is eventually replaced by bone as your Lab grows.

Spay/neuter surgery removes the source of hormones that cause the growth plates in your dog's long bones to stop growing. If these hormones are removed, his bones continue to grow. So a dog neutered early will grow taller and lankier than he would if he was neutered later. In most dogs, this doesn't matter. But the growth plates in a dog's body close at different rates. If some close before your dog is altered and some afterward, he might develop odd proportions that impact the long-term functioning of his joints.

In males, early neutering prevents some of the male sex characteristics from developing. A mature, unneutered male Lab has heavier bones and shoulders and a blockier head than a neutered male. Females aren't going to develop these characteristics anyway, so it isn't a consideration. Early spaying in females slightly increases the risk of genital problems like vaginitis due to the incomplete development of their external sex organs.

Other concerns regarding spay/neuter surgery before sexual maturity include the risk of bone cancer, the effect on the development of hip dysplasia, and reduced bone mass in the spine. All these risks are very small, and some have no effect on your dog's long-term health. If you're having behavioral issues with your intact Lab, spay or neuter now.

Dealing with External Parasites

During month 7, your puppy might have some pests you have to deal with. Although your Lab can be affected by some of them at any time during his life, this is the age when you might encounter these parasites for the first time.

Demodectic mange (demodicosis): The *Demodex canis* mite is present on all dogs. It doesn't cause problems unless the dog has a weak or compromised immune system, and it's not all that common to Labrador Retrievers. When it occurs, the mother passes the mites on to her puppies during their first few days of life. An active case is caused by abnormally large numbers of mites or by stress, which weakens the immune system. It most often shows up in puppies, who go through a tremendous number of changes in their early months: teething, vaccines, moving to a new home, hormonal changes, neutering, spaying, worming, and more.

Localized demodex is concentrated on the face and forelegs and is characterized by scaly reddened skin, hair loss, pustules, and plugged hair follicles. Symptoms often resolve and disappear on their own by 6 or 7 months of age.

Generalized demodex is much rarer in dogs, but it's much more serious. It develops from localized demodex and usually appears before 18 months of age. Dogs rescued from hoarding situations or shelters often suffer from demodectic mange because of stress and crowding. Symptoms include patchy hair loss, inflamed skin, enlarged lymph nodes, and severe itching, especially on the feet. Infected dogs are at risk of developing secondary bacterial infections.

Your vet diagnoses demodex by taking a skin scraping and examining it under a microscope. Sometimes the mites are difficult to find, and a skin biopsy is necessary for diagnosis. Treatment of generalized demodicosis includes miticidal dips and oral medication. Your vet will prescribe antibiotics for secondary skin infections.

Canine scabies (*Sarcoptes scabiei*): Also called sarcoptic mange, these mites burrow under your dog's skin and cause intense itching. This highly contagious parasite affects young dogs more often than mature canines. Direct contact with an infected dog or infected wildlife transmits the mite to your puppy, where it immediately burrows into the outer layer of skin and lays eggs.

In addition to constant, intense itching, your dog will develop crusty pustules and hair loss, particularly on his elbows, tummy, edges of his ears, and front legs. Severe scratching and biting also cause infection.

Sarcoptic mites are much harder to see under a microscope, so diagnosis often is based on symptoms. Some oral flea and heartworm medications kill mites on your dog before an active infestation can occur. Treatment includes medicated shampoos, miticidal dips, and a course of ivermectin. Your vet might prescribe anti-inflammatories as well to make your Lab more comfortable.

Sarcoptic mange is a zoonotic disease humans can get from their dogs. In people, the mites die out on their own and no treatment is necessary.

TIPS AND TAILS

Unlike other types of parasites, sarcoptic mange is highly contagious. An infected dog must be isolated from other dogs and cats until he's cleared of the mites.

Cheyletiellosis (*Cheyletiella yasguri*): These mites are most often seen on young and adolescent puppies. Infection is easy to prevent because the same insecticides that kill fleas work on these pests. The mites live on the skin's surface, and the main symptom is dandruff (scaling and crusting) along the dog's back. They also can cause itching and enlargement of the lymph nodes.

Cheyletiellosis mites are diagnosed by examining a skin scraping. Your vet will prescribe shampoos and miticidal dips. Other dogs and cats in the family should also be treated.

Ear mites (*Otodectes cynotis*): Ear mites cause a buildup of a reddish, waxy-looking substance in the ear. It can become so severe that the ear is blocked with debris. Symptoms of ear mites are similar to those of an ear infection: head shaking, scratching, and tilting of his head. Even a small number of mites can set the stage for yeast or bacterial infections.

Once your veterinarian diagnoses ear mites, your dog needs a miticide to kill the mites and a prescription antibiotic or anti-inflammatory ointment to cure any resulting infections. The vet also might prescribe an ear wash. Your Lab's ears could be painful, and he'll resist letting you touch them. Some dogs are in so much pain, muzzling is necessary so you can administer the medication.

Dealing with Internal Parasites

You'll spend a lot of time out in nature with your Lab, swimming and retrieving in lakes, tromping through the woods, and enjoying other fun activities. Your Lab will be exposed to internal parasites that could make him ill—and could infect you, too.

Giardia: A single-celled protozoa, giardia is most often found in contaminated water like streams, lakes, and rivers, but your Lab can pick it up anywhere. Wild animals such as coyotes, rabbits, raccoons, and beavers carry giardia. In fact, it was originally called "beaver fever." An infected animal carries the cysts in his digestive tract and sheds them in his feces. If your dog ingests the stool, drinks infected water, or steps in it and then licks his paws, he can pick up the parasite. Once giardia is in your dog's system, it attaches to the walls of the intestine and reproduces, forming cysts he then sheds in his stool.

The main symptom of giardia is loose stools or diarrhea. This often goes away in a few days, and it's easy to assume your dog just "ate something." A dog can carry the parasite for years with no symptoms.

Long-term effects of giardia include weight loss, damage to the lining of the intestine, and *malabsorption*. Repetitive bouts of diarrhea are the most obvious sign of a problem. You won't see any signs of giardia in your dog's feces because it's a microscopic organism.

DOG TALK

Malabsorption is the inability to process and use nutrients in food.

Your veterinarian will perform a fecal flotation test to check for giardia. The giardia cysts aren't shed in every stool sample, so it might take more than one test to diagnose. Also, before your veterinarian rules out giardia completely, she might send out a stool sample to a medical laboratory for more extensive testing. Treatment consists of a simple round of medication, but reinfection is a risk every time you take your Lab out into nature.

Giardia is also a zoonotic disease. To protect yourself, take care not to touch your face, and thoroughly wash your hands after every outing. Carry drinking water for you and your Lab with you on hikes so he doesn't drink from a contaminated source.

Coccidia: Another single-celled parasite, coccidia most often affects young dogs. It's sometimes found in raw meat, dirty kennel situations, or animal shelters. Livestock are often infected, and a dog can ingest coccidia from manure and grass in pastures. Cockroaches, mice, and flies also can transport and spread coccidia.

As an adult, your dog might carry coccidia in his intestines and shed the cysts in his feces, but if he has a healthy immune system, he can fight off severe symptoms. Stress can trigger symptoms if a dog has coccidia present in his digestive tract. A major infestation can cause damage to the intestines.

The primary symptom of coccidiosis is diarrhea. It could be minor or severe, and it could contain blood or mucus. The symptoms for coccidia are similar to those of giardia and parvo infection. A fecal flotation test identifies the parasite. Medication stops reproduction of the organisms but does not kill them, so a complete cure takes several weeks.

The biggest challenge is protecting your Lab from reinfection. To prevent this parasite from taking hold, practice diligent sanitation, including cleaning with ammonia disinfectants and picking up feces.

Coccidiosis is not a zoonotic disease, so you're not in danger of becoming infected.

TIPS AND TAILS

You can help prevent infestation of giardia and coccidia. Don't allow your dog to eat or lick other animals' feces, and don't let your dog drink from unfiltered sources of water.

NUTRITION

As you look at the myriad choices available in the pet food aisle, choosing the right food for your Lab can seem confusing and even overwhelming. How do you possibly figure out the differences between brands or decipher the tiny type on the labels? With a little education, you can make an informed decision and choose what's best for your pup.

All dogs have the same basic nutritional needs: protein, fiber, moisture, vitamins, minerals, carbohydrates, and fats (see Month 2). Dog foods contain these essentials, but that's where the similarity in dog foods ends. Any one food on the market won't meet the nutritional needs of every dog. The following sections outline some basic facts to help guide you through your options.

Who's in Charge of Pet Foods?

Pet food companies are required to list ingredients and meet manufacturing standards regulated by several federal organizations. Individual states get in on the act, too.

The Food and Drug Administration (FDA), through its Center for Veterinary Medicine (CVM), regulates which ingredients are allowed in pet food, the manufacturing process, and what health claims a manufacturer can legally make. The FDA, working with the U.S. Department of Agriculture (USDA), defines the exact requirements for terminology used on labels. (The USDA is involved in establishing regulations for identification and approval of pet food ingredients as well.) In addition, the FDA, along with state and local agencies, inspects manufacturing plants to ensure compliance with labeling laws. The actual food itself does not have to be approved by the FDA.

The American Association of Feed Control Officials (AAFCO) is comprised of officials from local, state, and federal agencies who enforce laws regarding production, labeling, distribution, and/or sale of pet foods. AAFCO specifies the minimum and maximum percentages of nutrients that must appear in a food for it to be considered "complete and balanced." It also designates requirements regarding product names, flavor designations, and ingredient names that appear on the label. AAFCO publishes the testing requirements manufacturers must follow to meet safety and nutritional standards.

The FDA, USDA, and AAFCO are the heavy hitters, but a few other groups are involved as well. The Federal Trade Commission (FTC) works to prevent misleading advertising by requiring manufacturers to conform to truth-in-advertising standards. The lobbying group Pet Food Institute (PFI) represents pet food manufacturers.

What's on a Label?

With so many regulators involved, the information that appears on a pet food label can be hard to understand at first glance. Just remember that pet food packaging is primarily a marketing tool, with a secondary function of accurately disclosing any information required by law.

When you see pretty pictures of raw beef, colorful carrots, peas, and corn in an attractive arrangement on the bag, the graphics are designed to convince you to buy that brand. The wording, however, is strictly regulated.

The product name: Several rules exist regarding the name:

○ A product can only be named *chicken* if it contains at least 95 percent chicken.

○ A product labeled *beef dinner for dogs* must contain at least 25 percent beef (excluding water sufficient for processing).

○ If the name is *beef formula* (or *recipe, platter, entrée*), the product is only required to contain 3 percent of the named ingredient.

○ If the label states *with beef,* it's required to have at least 3 percent beef.

○ A product labeled *beef flavor* must have enough beef to make it taste beefy. Manufacturers are allowed to use artificial flavoring or a small quantity of extract from beef tissues. There could be no beef at all.

Guaranteed analysis: This list states the minimum percentages of protein and fat and the maximum percentages of fiber and moisture in the food. These aren't exact numbers, so you're getting only a rough idea of the percentages. Companies aren't required to list the percentage of carbohydrates, and the guarantee says nothing about the quality or digestibility of the ingredients that make up the food.

Compete and balanced: In addition to percentages, to declare a food complete and balanced, manufacturers must show their food meets the nutrient requirements in one of three ways:

○ Through actual feeding trials. This might sound like the best method, but there's debate over how realistic this testing is. Dogs eat the tested food for a period of time, and their health is then measured.

○ By formulating the food to meet AAFCO's minimum and maximum standards, confirmed by laboratory testing.

○ By stating the food is a "family member" of another of the company's foods that has passed feeding trials or met formulation standards.

TIPS AND TAILS

Some foods aren't meant to be fed as a complete diet but instead are suggested for supplemental feeding. The label will state *complete and balanced* if the food is formulated for complete nutrition.

Life stages: A dog food is labeled either complete and balanced *for all life stages, for growth,* or *for maintenance.* There's no designation for senior foods.

Miscellaneous: The company's name and address are required. Many also include a phone number, email address, and website so consumers can contact them with questions. The bag is printed with the disclaimer that it contains dog food, not food meant for people, along with the net weight of the contents.

Expiration date: The "best by" date is a stamped or printed code that tells you the latest date food should be used. Some companies include the manufacture date so you can estimate the food's shelf life. Naturally preserved foods don't last as long as those that contain artificial preservatives, but most foods are safe if used within 1 year of manufacture. If a food is close to its best by date, you know it's been sitting somewhere for a while.

Ingredients list: This is the most important part of a pet food label. Like human food, pet food ingredients are listed in order by volume, from the most included in the food to the least. It can be tricky to decipher what you're actually reading here. The first six ingredients are by far the most meaningful, but there are some other key things you should look for, too.

Deciphering Pet Food Ingredients

The first ingredient listed on your dog's food should be an animal protein source. *Meat* could mean cows, pigs, goats, or sheep. You could also find poultry, venison, bison, and fish listed. Ideally, you want to know what kind of animal the protein source is from.

If a pure meat is listed first, it includes natural moisture. On the other hand, meat meal (or chicken meal, etc.) is made of meat, bone, skin, fat, and connective tissue from which the water has been removed, so it contains more protein per pound than just meat. If meat meal isn't listed first, look for it as a second or third ingredient. Meat makes the food taste good; meat meal boosts the animal protein content. Animal by-products are less desirable and can include things like heads, feet, hooves, hide trimmings, and more.

Another source of protein is plant proteins, which are less expensive. When you see corn or wheat *gluten* on a label, that's a plant protein source. These could be harder for your dog to digest.

DOG TALK

Gluten is a mixture of two proteins found in processed grains like wheat or barley. Derived from the Latin term for "glue," gluten literally helps dog food stick together and adds a chewy texture.

When you look at the first three or four ingredients on a dog food label, you might see chicken, corn gluten, wheat gluten, etc. Although chicken is listed first, the combination of the second and third ingredients could contribute a larger percentage of protein than the chicken.

Also look for whole vegetables, fruits, and grains, which contain vitamins, enzymes, and antioxidants that haven't been stripped by processing. Dogs are carnivores primarily, but they eat both plants and animals. They've been eating grains for as long as commercial dog food has been around, and grains are a source of carbohydrates as well as protein. Cereal grain–based carbohydrates are fine for many dogs, but others might have trouble digesting them. Whole grains are more digestible than processed grains like wheat flour or rice flour. Additional healthy carbohydrate sources include beans, sweet potatoes, and apples.

Farther down the ingredients list, you'll find the preservatives. Preservatives extend a food's shelf life, preventing vitamin loss and rancidity from the fats. Natural preservatives like vitamin C and mixed tocopherols are more desirable than synthetic preservatives like BHA, BHT, and ethoxyquin.

When you see little green things that look like peas and orange bits of so-called carrots in your dog's food, don't be fooled. They aren't necessarily peas or carrots. Manufacturers add dyes and binders to make some pieces look like vegetables to attract *you,* not your dog. If vegetables are included, they're either part of the mixture that makes up the kibble, or mixed in to the food after the kibble is made.

GROOMING

Continue your Lab puppy's education this month by teaching him to allow you to brush his teeth—a critical chore that has major health consequences if neglected. You want your puppy to enjoy, or at least tolerate, having his teeth brushed because you're going to be doing it every week (or more often) for the rest of his life.

In this section, we also look at an often-neglected grooming (and health-care) chore: caring for your dog's paws.

Brushing Those Pearly Whites

Now that your puppy's adult teeth are in, they need regular attention, just like your own teeth do. Many dogs have gum disease by the time they're 3 years old, so early care is essential. Although some wear and tear is inevitable as your puppy ages, you can help ward off gum disease by practicing good brushing habits early.

Although Labs chew a lot and that removes some *dental plaque,* it's not enough. Chewing on hard surfaces like bones only cleans the exposed areas of his teeth. Chewing also is the main cause of broken teeth, which can get infected. A Lab who chews throughout his life can completely wear down his teeth to the gum line and expose the nerves. Even chewing tennis balls is bad. Even though they're soft, constant chewing can still wear down his teeth.

DOG TALK

Dental plaque is a buildup of bacteria on your dog's teeth that, if allowed to remain and harden, discolors and turns into tartar.

Gum disease causes severe pain and infection, which can spread through your Lab's body, resulting in kidney or heart disease. If his gums aren't healthy, they recede, causing pockets to form at the base of his teeth where bacteria collect and cause infection. If he has gum disease, you'll notice that his gums are red, inflamed, and bleed easily. Bad breath can be a sign of infection or gum disease, too. To keep his gums healthy, massage them with the toothbrush while you brush his teeth.

Besides cleaning his teeth and massaging his gums, regular brushing gives you the opportunity to inspect your Lab's mouth for broken teeth and tumors. He also might have a bit of bone, a sliver of a stick, or dog food stuck between his teeth you can locate and remove as you clean. If he seems to have trouble eating, suspect a broken tooth or gum problems. Dogs don't usually get cavities like humans do because they don't eat as many sugary treats.

Although your Lab will need a professional teeth cleaning at some point, it'll take much less time and be less painful for him if you practice regular dental care at home. The doctor will anesthetize your dog, remove the tartar, and polish his teeth while cleaning thoroughly beneath the gum line. The doctor also will remove cracked or loose teeth and check for abnormalities.

Your Lab won't automatically allow you to mess with his mouth, especially in this new, unfamiliar way. But you can get him used to it with some muzzle-touching lessons. If you've been practicing handling him since he was a baby, you're way ahead of the game. But still, he'll probably try to turn it into a play session.

Put your hand gently over his muzzle from the top. Just touch it for a moment and release so he won't have a chance to struggle. Don't clamp your hand on his muzzle at first. It's normal for him to resist; this is a move his mother used to discipline him. Feed him a treat with your other hand while you're lightly touching him.

As you work up to more pressure and longer time, he might flip his head around. If he does, don't let go. Just follow his head and reward him by releasing when he stops. Ultimately, you want to put your fingers behind his upper canines and open his mouth. This lesson also makes it easier for your vet when he needs to examine your Lab's mouth. And you'll use it later if he has a run-in with a porcupine or gets something stuck in his mouth.

To brush your Lab's teeth, you can use a toothbrush made for humans, a fingertip brush, or even a piece of gauze wrapped around your finger. Human toothpaste can cause a serious stomach upset if your Lab swallows it, so use meat-flavored doggie toothpaste instead. Or make a paste of baking soda mixed with water.

Begin by massaging your puppy's mouth with your finger so he'll get used to the sensation. Next, add some doggie toothpaste so he learns to enjoy the taste. Gradually transition to using a toothbrush instead of your finger. Brush along his front gum line using small circles, covering both his teeth and gums. Hold the bristles at a slight angle so it isn't abrasive on his gums.

Brush his back teeth, holding the brush at an angle while using back-and-forth strokes. Concentrate on the molars in the back, where food gets stuck between his teeth and cheek. (The inside of his molars won't have as much plaque buildup because his tongue washes away excess food.) Do a portion of his mouth each session until he's used to the routine and accepts it.

HAPPY PUPPY
Let your Lab hold a ball or big chew toy in his mouth while you brush his back teeth.

Caring for Your Pup's Paws

Your Lab puppy's feet are exposed to extreme heat, pesticides, fertilizers, and uneven surfaces that could bruise his paw pads. His feet are constantly getting wet as he runs through mud, streams, grass, and leaves, and mud can accumulate between his toes and dry into clumps. In the summer, he sweats through his paws, which creates the perfect environment for bacteria to grow. If he's licking his paws constantly, something is irritating them. The best way to prevent problems is to keep his paws clean and dry.

Hot asphalt or newly blacktopped streets can burn your pup's delicate paw pads. He also can get road-burn when the bottoms of his feet are rubbed raw from running on hard surfaces. Treat raw feet with a foot soak (more on soaks later in this section) and antibiotic ointment or aloe vera gel. You'll need to bandage his feet to keep him from licking off the ointment. Place a gauze pad on the bottom of his foot, and tape it in place. Put an old cotton sock over his foot, and tape the top to his fur.

Labs can get dry, cracked skin and calluses on their paw pads, too. After a foot soak, apply a small amount of vitamin E oil to help heal his skin. To keep him from licking it off, put it on his feet just before mealtime, so he'll be occupied long enough for it to soak in. Don't apply too much because it will stain your carpet if he walks on it. You also don't want his feet getting too soft because that will make it easier for them to be reinjured.

If you need to wash chemicals, antifreeze, road salt, or cleaners off your puppy's feet, use liquid dish detergent or vegetable oil to completely remove it. Then rinse and dry thoroughly.

TIPS AND TAILS
Be careful when removing goo from between your Lab puppy's toes, and don't use scissors to trim the goo from his fur. Labs have webbed feet, and you could accidentally cut him.

Do your Lab puppy's paws smell like corn chips? You read that right—corn chips. If so, that means he has yeast growing between his toes. Wash his feet in Betadine solution. Betadine is a 10 percent iodine-povidone antiseptic that kills bacteria and prevents skin infections. You can purchase it at a pharmacy or tack and feed store.

For general paw relief or for a Betadine treatment, teach your Lab to love a foot soak. Soaking penetrates all the nooks and crannies of his feet better than washing with a cloth. To prepare a soak, add 1 or 2 inches of water to a kiddie pool or plastic tub and then add the solution. Have him stand in the tub for a minute or two and then rinse his paws and dry them with a towel.

Consider adding green tea, either bags or brewed tea, to his foot soak. The antioxidants in the tea soothe his skin. Chamomile tea also has soothing properties, and apple cider vinegar is another topical disinfectant. Between foot soaks, rinse his feet with cool water to remove the irritants, and be sure to thoroughly dry them afterward.

SOCIAL SKILLS

As your Lab speeds toward sexual maturity, he needs to continue meeting and interacting with other dogs. He's changing as he grows, and other dogs sense that difference and treat him differently. He'll need to adjust his behavior accordingly. A dog who stays in the backyard for the next few months will be in for a rude awakening when he finally ventures out in public.

Enrolling in Doggie Day Care

Doggie day care is a great place for your Lab to have supervised interaction with other friendly dogs. If you select a facility staffed by conscientious professionals, he'll have fun, burn off endless energy, and polish his dog manners. Regular attendance 2 or 3 days a week is easier on your dog and less disruptive for the facility because the dogs all know each other and don't have to get reacquainted each time they visit.

There's no legal requirement that dog day care facilities be certified in any way or that employees demonstrate dog-handling skills. No national oversight organization exists either. Anyone can hang out a sign and offer doggie day care. The local health department usually monitors cleanliness and hazardous materials compliance, and sometimes local animal control requires a kennel license, which specifies standards for the facility, not the staff.

When you contact a prospective dog day care, expect to fill out an application and attend a get-acquainted visit with your dog. The facility will require up-to-date shot records for DHPP, rabies, and bordetella (kennel cough). They also might require proof of a clear fecal test from your vet, showing your dog is free of internal parasites. Your Lab also should be on a regular flea and tick preventative. Most dog day cares require your dog be spayed or neutered after a designated age as well.

While the manager is busy checking out you and your Lab, ask some questions of your own. You might not be allowed to enter the doggie playroom. Don't take that as a red flag; a stranger walking into a room full of dogs can cause an uproar, and scuffles or fights could break out. Instead, many day cares have a doggie webcam or a one-way mirror so you can see the playroom.

Here are some points to consider when checking out doggie day cares:

- How many dogs does the facility allow per day?
- Are there separate groups for high-energy and low-energy dogs?
- Are small dogs separated?
- What's the staff-to-dog ratio?
- What training have employees had regarding dog handling and behavior?
- What are the hours? Are there limited drop-off and pickup times? What about Saturdays?
- Are there special pricing packages? Are ½-day rates offered?
- Do the dogs play all day, or is there a specified nap time?

If you can, watch the employees, too. Are they paying attention to the dogs and what's going on, or are they ignoring the dogs?

No facility, and no dog, is perfect. Accidents can happen, and occasionally a dog is injured by an inadvertent bite during play or a scuffle. Who is responsible for the vet bill when an accident happens? How do they decide if the offending dog will be allowed to come back? Be sure to ask these questions while you're there.

If you choose carefully, dog day care can be a rewarding experience for you and your Lab.

Teaching "Wait"

The "Wait" command helps your Lab puppy refine his manners. Ask him to wait before he goes through a doorway, before he eats dinner, and before he jumps out of the car. Wait means he's not allowed to move forward until he gets an okay from you. He doesn't have to sit; he doesn't have to lie down. Different from stay, with wait, he doesn't have to remain in place until you touch him. This is a temporary pause, not a stay.

Teach this skill with your Lab on a leash, and start in a doorway. As the two of you start through, your Lab will undoubtedly try to rush ahead. Say "Wait," and give him the hand signal you use for stay—an open palm in front of his nose. Walk through the door, and if doesn't try to follow, tell him "Okay," and let him walk through after you. If he does try to follow you, body block him with your hip and turn to face him. Continue to block his way through the door until he stops trying and is still, whether standing or sitting. He'll probably look at you, which is what you want. Now tell him "Okay," give him a treat while he's still on the other side of the doorway, and let him walk through.

Practice this many times in many different doorways. Practice in the car, both getting in and getting out. He'll try to read your body language for a signal he can move. Practice moving around a little without letting him through so he learns he has to wait for your "Okay" release word.

It's tempting to say "Wait … wait … no … stay … *WAIT!*" while you're teaching this command, but don't. That will just confuse him—is he staying or waiting? Dogs really do learn the difference. When you give the command multiple times, he anxiously watches you instead of relaxing and waiting for the release word.

The learning curve might be long and trying for this lesson. It's an advanced concept, but he's old enough now to understand it.

Introducing New Animals

When your Lab was just a pup, you introduced him to the cat, rabbit, and any other animals in the house. He should continue to meet different species so he remembers and is able to deal with any new animals he encounters throughout his life.

If you have the opportunity, visit a place where he can meet some really big "dogs." Donkeys, sheep, goats, cows, horses and ponies, peacocks, and geese are all critters he can get to know. (Terry's own Lab grew up with horses but was fascinated the first time he met a miniature horse. It was an entirely new creature to him!) Be sure to have someone restrain the other animal so he can't run away or attack.

Use your jolly routine, treats, and patience while your puppy checks out the animal from a short distance. Don't approach until your pup is calm. Barking, lunging, and raised hackles will only scare the other animal. Have the owner move the other animal around a little so your Lab sees it walking and realizes it's a living being.

When he's ready to approach, keep the leash loose so he doesn't feel trapped. If he lunges, turn away and start farther back until he can restrain himself. This might be all you can do on the first encounter. If so, practice with a number of animals so he learns this is the proper way to respond to a new animal.

A friendly horse will put her nose down and say hi to your Lab. They'll probably sniff each other's breath. Don't let your puppy jump up against the fence or the horse, though. When you're done, praise your pup and walk away.

TIPS AND TAILS
If the horse (or other animal) is frightened, keep your distance. A scared horse will strike out with her front feet.

Playing Too Rough

Your preteen Lab loves to play, and you love to play with him. But even though you're just playing games, he's learning which behaviors are allowed and which aren't, so be careful what you teach him. Between 6 and 7 months, your puppy is figuring out how strong he is, and he'll naturally try to use his body in his dealings with others.

In his childish enthusiasm, your Lab forgets himself, bowling over smaller or weaker dogs and body blocking his way across the playing field. His newly raging hormones encourage him to try a new behavior: mounting. Play that was fine in a 12-week-old puppy is now too much for many of his peers. If he's allowed to roughhouse, he'll decide it's okay.

His playmates will tell him when he's played too roughly. They'll growl, snap at him, and chase him away. This helps him learn to mind his manners. Watch these interactions closely, and intervene if your puppy isn't getting the message. You want other dogs to discipline him, but you don't want an all-out fight.

It's one thing to roughhouse with his buddies, but he also needs limits when he plays with you and your family. At this age, he'll jump on you, crash into you while he runs around the yard, slam into your legs, and grab your arms. You might enjoy the game, but when he crashes into someone else, it won't be so cute. He could injure someone, or he could be injured. He could land wrong and tear a ligament, crack immature bones, or tear muscles.

TIPS AND TAILS

Once a 6-month-old Lab clipped the back of Terry's knees in the driveway, popped her up in the air, and dropped her down on her head. She spent 5 days in the hospital with a fractured skull and another month recovering. It can happen to you, too.

Interrupt active games with some control exercises. Have him sit before he retrieves the ball, and practice off when he returns it. When kids are playing, slow everyone down, introduce some structured games, or quit when things get overly rough.

Before we leave this section, we want to say a word about tug-of-war. Playing tug-of-war teaches your Lab all the wrong things: he learns to growl aggressively at you, and he's rewarded for holding on and refusing to let go. Tug-of-war makes a pushy dog pushier and encourages grabbing, biting hard, and jumping. Labs are blissfully happy when they can retrieve all day; they don't need over-the-top aggressive games.

BEHAVIOR

Be patient. This month your Lab puppy will have moments when he seems to have forgotten everything you've so diligently taught him. He might not come when he's called, or he might not want to fetch because his teeth hurt. Just remember that this, too, will pass.

Dealing with Teenage Behavior Regression

What looks like a regression in behavior to you is more like a new awakening on your puppy's part. Seemingly overnight, your previously well-behaved and adoring pup has deteriorated into a wild child. His interactions with other dogs may have deteriorated, too, as he has practiced new ways of dealing with others.

Problem aggression and anxieties may develop during this time, but they also recede as your puppy finds his way. Spaying or neutering makes a huge difference in his behavior, lessening fighting, marking, and bullying among dogs.

Because he's distracted by his adolescence, your puppy's obedience skills may falter, and you'll need to use a stronger hand to control and redirect his behavior. This is the age when many Labs are relegated to the backyard because of their overly boisterous behavior.

Adolescence could last until your Lab is 2 or 3 years old. It might be small comfort to know he'll get over it, but if you continue to work with him, he'll get through this period, and so will you.

Here are some of the behaviors you might see:

○ Shyness or fearfulness

○ Destructive, acting-out behavior to satisfy his endless energy

○ Housetraining relapse, marking

○ Aggression

○ Overexuberance

○ Bossiness, rudeness, constant testing of the rules

○ Ignoring commands, distracted

○ No self-control or ability to resist temptation

○ Overprotective

We help you deal with all these issues in this and upcoming chapters.

Working Through a Second Fear Period

The fear-imprint period that was so important during your puppy's first 2 or 3 months may come back to haunt him this month. If your Lab had a bad experience when he was 8 weeks old, he may seem to suddenly remember that event now, months later.

The adolescent fear period starts between 6 and 14 months and can last anywhere from a few days to several weeks. He's going through major physiological and psychological changes now. The fear period seems to correspond to growth spurts, and his anxiety may vary from day to day. He could spook or bark aggressively at something he's seen a thousand times, like the mailbox at the curb. Don't overreact.

In most cases, you can ignore the behavior. As you did when he was a baby, let him approach scary things when he's ready, and don't force him into a situation in which he feels overwhelmed.

TIPS AND TAILS

If you've adopted a rescued Labrador, or if you got your puppy when he was a little older, don't assume he was abused when he reaches his second fear period. If he didn't get adequate training and socialization, this period might be harder on him, and he might react fearfully or even aggressively to unfamiliar things. Honor his fear, and back off until he's comfortable.

Introduce him gradually to unfamiliar things so he's comfortable in new situations, and reward him with treats when he's brave. If you punish him or force him to confront something scary, he'll end up even more afraid. As he learns to trust your judgment and understand that you won't force him, he'll look to you for guidance. Your happy voice and unconcerned body language will reassure him.

A well-socialized dog will get through this period much quicker than a dog who's been kept at home and isolated. Your normal, happy, friendly Lab will grow out of it with less trouble than some other hypersensitive breeds. Be sure to keep him on leash in public in case something frightens him.

Still Chewing

By 6½ months, your Lab's adult teeth are in, but they won't completely set in his jawbones until 8 or 9 months. So until then, he'll continue to be a chewing machine. And because he's bigger and stronger now, he'll be more destructive.

Labs especially enjoy chewing on wood. Stair rails, 2×4s, fence posts, shingles, and other things you'd never imagine he'd eat are all fair game. Invest in some chew-repellent products at your local pet supply store, or make some of your own with red pepper sauce in a bottle of water. (Watch out for potential staining if you use the latter.)

Chew toys are as important now as they've ever been, and diligent supervision on your part will protect your more vulnerable household treasures. Provide a variety of chewables: stuffed frozen KONGs, tire toys, and heavy nylon bones. You'll have to keep an eye on him and remove toys that don't withstand his chain saw molars. He might lose interest in a certain toy, too. If he does, put it away for a week or two, and it will be exciting when you bring it out again.

When you give your Labrador Retriever something new to chew on, supervise him to be sure he isn't going to immediately destroy it and swallow pieces. You can offer him some softer toys, like retrieving bumpers, and then put them away when you can't watch him.

Marking

You know your Lab has reached adolescence when he starts lifting his leg. Testosterone levels start to rise as young as 4 or 5 months old. But it isn't just the boys; females mark, too, just not as often or as obviously.

A male Lab hikes up his rear leg so his hip is perpendicular to the ground, while a female usually lifts one rear leg forward while still squatting. When finished, both may kick the ground with their rear legs to spread the scent of their urine. By doing this, your dog is announcing his sexual maturity and laying claim to that territory, whether at home or away.

When your puppy starts marking, the scent of his urine has changed, and any other dog who smells it will know there's a new sexually mature dog in town. No longer can he roll over on his back and leak a little urine to get the big boys to back off. Other adult males will know he's an adolescent, and his permission to misbehave is immediately revoked. Many male adults will put a teenage dog in his place before he gets too full of himself and tries to challenge the older dogs.

On walks, your male dog will mark repeatedly and often in unacceptable places, like on the neighbor's car. You'll catch him marking over where another dog has just urinated, too. His motives aren't just territorial. Dogs read each other's urine like we read the daily newspaper—comedian Dave Barry called it "yellow journalism." They learn who's been to that spot, when, and the other dog's age and sexual maturity. Then your Lab leaves his own calling card. A dog often releases just a tiny bit of urine, like he's conserving so he has enough for the entire excursion.

There's no reason to let him get away with impolite marking behavior. Don't just stop and wait while he has a good sniff and lines up to pee; correct him and move on. Once excessive marking becomes a habit, it's hard to break. Most dogs continue marking after they're neutered, although not as often.

Sexual maturity can mean a sudden lapse in housetraining, too. It's not really a housetraining issue; it's marking. Males will lift their leg indoors and out, on any vertical surface they can reach. Females will mark indoors, too.

Treat marking like any other accident. Interrupt your dog with a loud "No!" or "Ack!" and take him out to his assigned potty spot you created when he first came to live with you. Go back to supervising him indoors and crating him when you can't. Deal with the problem like he's on his first day of housetraining as an 8-week-old puppy. You can't stop a dog from lifting his leg or marking, but you can teach him where and when he's allowed to go.

TIPS AND TAILS

Labrador Retrievers usually aren't a difficult breed to housetrain. If your pup is marking indoors often, he might have a bladder infection, or your spayed female might be suffering from urinary incontinence. Rule out health problems before you decide your dog just refuses to be housetrained.

TRAINING

Training is a lifelong process, but it doesn't have to be misery. You're investing time raising a well-behaved puppy so you can enjoy years of companionship and fun together. Once you lay the foundation, he'll only need an occasional brush-up to keep his skills sharp and his responses eager.

As he reaches adolescence, a Lab will put your patience to the test. Two or three months of diligent effort now are worth the payoff. And don't forget to keep it fun!

Practice Makes Perfect

Your Lab could be an obedience champion when you're in the backyard practicing, but does he really understand the commands? And can he perform out in public when you're under stress and really need him to behave? What's more, dogs depend on body language for much of their communication. What happens if your arms are full of groceries and you can't give him a hand signal along with a command?

Test your dog to see if he really understands sit. Face your Lab, ask him to sit, and use your hand signal. If he sits, good. Praise and release him. Now look away, ask him to sit, and stand perfectly still with no body language, eye contact, or hand signal. Did he do it? If not, he still needs some guidance. When he can perform all the commands you've taught him without any visual cues, you know he gets it.

When your dog is doing a solid sit-stay and down-stay, it's time to add some distractions. He'll make mistakes and get up when he's not supposed to; that's how he learns exactly what stay means. Here's a progression of increasing distractions to help your Lab understand stay:

1. Put him in a sit-stay.

2. While you're still holding the leash, start to walk around him. His head will follow you, and his natural response will be to stand up as you leave his field of vision. Touch his muzzle with your hand to remind him to stay in place as you move.

3. Once he can stay with you circling him while he's on leash, drop the leash and try it.

4. Circle in the other direction.

5. Circle farther away.

6. Turn your back on him, and walk away several steps before turning to face him.

7. Crouch down without saying anything. Don't look at him. You're not trying to lure him out of place; you want to help him succeed.

Every time he stays in place, verbally praise him from a distance. You don't want him to get excited and get up, but you do want him to know he's done it correctly. He also has to learn that praise doesn't mean he's finished. Always end up at his side, touch him, and say "Okay" to release him. Then have a party! When he makes a mistake, just put him back and continue. No scolding. Take plenty of breaks between tries, and quit when he's done something especially well.

The ultimate practice is to make obedience commands part of everyday life, at home and in public. Practice on walks, at the park, and wherever else you take him. At home, he should sit for his dinner, while you brush his teeth or clip his nails, and when you put a leash on him. He should do a down-stay while you do dishes, brush him, or eat dinner.

Your Lab should walk nicely on a leash wherever you take him. He should wait politely at doorways and wait for permission to jump out of the car. Take time to train throughout the day, and pretty soon it won't be training anymore and you'll have a well-behaved Labrador.

HAPPY PUPPY

Many behavioral problems evaporate once a Lab has had basic obedience training. Issues like barking, digging, and chewing might cure themselves when your dog is comfortable with his position in the household, knows the daily routine, and understands what's expected of him.

Teaching Cooperation, Not Confrontation

A puppy who misbehaves isn't engaging in mutiny; he's just being a teenager. And the only way to respond is with consistent guidance and training. Your dog adores you, but the Lab is a strong-minded breed, and he'll actually behave better with discipline and structure. As he challenges you, look for opportunities to build your relationship.

Reward your dog throughout the day, not just during training sessions. You might not have noticed that perfect sit he offered while you were fixing his dinner, or the way he went to his crate at bedtime without being told. Make a deposit in the bank of goodwill, and praise him when you see he's on his best behavior.

If you correct him or interrupt an unwanted behavior, always give him a chance to do something right and earn rewards. Say "Good boy!" when he stops whatever he was doing that you didn't like. Then ask for sit or down, just so you can praise him. No one, even a dog, likes to be yelled at all the time.

Be fair to your dog, too. Be sure he understands what you want him to do before you tear out your hair in frustration because he didn't do it. Help and reward him, and always set him up for success. Don't expect him to do something perfectly—like a down-stay—the first time company comes over. Put him in his crate, tether him, or hold on to the leash so he can't make a mistake. He'll try harder for you next time.

Teaching the Retrieve

One day you'll look at down at your Lab pup and find he's dropped a big stick at your feet. His wagging tail gives away the game. "Throw it!" he's saying, his body quivering with excitement. And so it begins; you have a retriever.

For 200 years, Labs have been hard-wired to retrieve. If you've ever watched a hunting dog at work, you can see he loves it: he's happy and intense, tail wagging, nose to the ground. You don't have to teach a Lab to retrieve; you just have to teach him to bring it back to you.

It's important that you control the game—when it starts, when it ends, and who keeps the toy at the end (you). If your Lab gets tired and quits, pick up the ball and put it away until next time. He needs to know it's your toy. This is a subtle message that you're in charge, not him. Although it's a game, you're teaching your dog to cooperate with you and respect your leadership. If you let him decide when to quit and take the ball under a bush for a good chew, he's in charge.

For this example, we'll assume he's retrieving a ball. Labs have endless variations on returning the ball, none of which include giving it to you. Why would he bring it back when you're just going to take it away from him? This makes perfect sense to him. He'll invite you to chase him, he'll stop just out of your reach, or he'll drop the ball and grab it as soon as you reach for it.

Attach a long line—about 20 feet of clothesline or other light rope—to his collar. When he's running around the yard after picking up the ball, reel him in, take the ball, and throw it again immediately. You don't need treats as a reward; throwing the ball is what he wants. The longer you hang on to the ball, the less of a reward it is for him, and the less likely he'll be to return it next time. Occasionally, when he gets to you, wait a few seconds before you take the ball from him.

Never go to him to get the ball—if you do, he just taught you to chase him. If he drops the ball before he gets to you or stops just out of reach, take a few steps backward or turn and run away from him. And don't keep throwing until he's bored; always leave him wanting more. Keep track of how many throws he retrieves before he gets tired, and quit before you get to that point next time.

You taught your Lab the "Give" command in Month 6, and fetching is a good time to use that skill. If you're going to hunt with your Lab or compete in formal obedience, you'll want him to release the ball directly into your hand rather than drop it. If you don't care, it's fine if he drops it instead.

When he won't give up the ball, show him another ball. He'll usually give up the one he has and take off after the new one. Don't throw it until he drops the first ball, or he'll take it with him.

YOU AND YOUR PUPPY

Don't expect a lot of downtime this month. He's still very young, and he'll play hard until he collapses and falls asleep. You also can play brain games to wear him out if he won't run himself tired or if it's raining outside.

Continuing to Play

The games you played with your Lab puppy—hide and seek, find it, and others—will still entertain you both, and you can make them tougher now to challenge him. For example, teach him to find a person by name. Have the person hide, and while you restrain your pup, tell him, "Find Joe." Then have Joe call your puppy. He'll quickly learn to find multiple people, one after the other.

Your Lab is probably great at retrieving by now, so this is the perfect time to teach him to retrieve multiple objects, not just a single tennis ball or bumper. As you throw the item, name it for him, and soon he'll learn to identify which item you want him to retrieve by name.

Hit a ball with a tennis racket to send it farther, and make him hunt to find it. Toss a stick in a creek, and watch him search and bring back the right one. Swimming is excellent and tiring exercise for him.

Learning Easy Tricks

When training seems like a chore, switch to teaching him tricks and bring the fun back into your time with your puppy. The whole family can participate.

"Shake" and "Roll over" are two easy tricks you or anyone else in your family can teach your puppy.

For shake, get down on the floor with your pup and have him sit. Don't say anything; just reach out and tickle the back of your puppy's front foot just above the floor. He'll lift the foot off the ground. Say "Good," and reward him with a treat. After a few tries (always reaching toward the same foot), he'll lift his foot when he sees your hand coming. Now give it a name—"Shake," "High five," "Go team," or whatever you want to call it. As he lifts his paw, say your word and take hold of his paw. Give him a treat from your other hand while you're still touching him, and release. Work up to where he'll let you shake his paw.

When he's really good at shake, you can work on variations. You can teach him to put his paw in your open hand or lift his other paw to shake. Give these new behaviors a different name and hand signal. For instance, use a different hand when you want to him to shake with the other foot, and use an open hand when you want a high five. Teach just one behavior at a time until he understands it completely. Later, you can alternate which behavior you ask for.

For roll over, have your puppy lie down and roll on one hip, like he's going to do a down-stay. Put a treat in front of his nose, and move it back and toward his spine so he twists his head as he follows the treat. Pull the treat far enough back that he has to put his head on the ground to follow it. As he lies flat on the ground, roll his legs up and over with your other hand and then give him the treat. He'll quickly get the idea after a few repetitions. Add the word you choose for the command.

Both of these tricks are easy for your Lab to learn in just a few days. Alternate tricks with obedience commands to keep training time fun and interesting for both of you.

	SOCIAL	BEHAVIOR	TRAINING	PHYSICAL	HEALTH
MONTH 1			Littermates and mother teach appropriate canine behavior	Rapid growth	
MONTH 2	Breeder starts socialization				
MONTH 3	Socialization at home with new owner and other pets	Fear-imprint period	Begin house- and crate training		1st DHPP vaccine
MONTH 4		Teething begins—heavy chewing period	Enroll in puppy class		2nd DHPP vaccine
MONTH 5	Socialization in public		Ready for basic commands	Switch to adult food	3rd DHPP and rabies vaccines
MONTH 6			Enroll in basic obedience class		
MONTH 7		Adult teeth are in—chewing continues		Moderate growth	Sexual maturity
MONTH 8					
MONTH 9					
MONTH 10			Ready for more advanced training		
MONTH 11				Slow growth—reaches adult size	
MONTH 12 AND BEYOND					Annual vaccinations and checkup

Adolescence

The race is on. Your Lab puppy is anxious to grow up, and you're scrambling to keep up with her. Between 7 and 8 months, you'll have moments when you feel like you've got a new dog, one you've never seen before. Her personality changes as she inches toward adulthood and finds she has to deal with other dogs differently from when she was a puppy. She'll temporarily forget a lot of what you've taught her, too.

All is not lost, however. Most of her behavior is typical teenage mischief and not a cause for major concern—as long as you deal with it and don't let it become a habit. The training you've done up to this point gives you the tools to handle her behavior. Basic obedience practice solves many seemingly unrelated difficulties, and you'll spend a lot of time reinforcing her training and teaching her self-control and manners. Her teenage exuberance will provide hours of fun and laughs for you and your family, and you'll enjoy even the most challenging times with your Lab puppy.

PHYSICAL DEVELOPMENT

Her body is ahead of itself this month, and she can't figure out where those long legs came from. Her behavior strays into uncharted territory, and she often leaps before she looks. Be prepared for lots of action!

Understanding Dog Adolescence

In Labs, adolescence lasts from about 7 months until 2 to 2½ years of age. With that kind of time span, it's not a phase you can just wait out. But if you're prepared to deal with it, you'll emerge at the other end with a well-behaved adult dog. Enjoy her youthful enthusiasm and energy now, though. She loves to do things and will thrive on the attention you give her.

Hormones play a big role in your Lab's adolescent behavior. This is the time when her sexual maturity is way ahead of her mental and emotional maturity. If your dog's already been spayed or neutered, you're not completely off the hook because brain development also plays a role. Like human teenagers, she doesn't have enough experience yet to make mature choices, and she doesn't understand the consequences of her changing body. But of course, she wants to be all grown up and do what the big dogs do, so she plays the role of an adult and learns from her mistakes.

The first thing you may notice is she'll assert her independence. She "forgets" her name, takes off, ignores you at the park, and refuses to obey obedience commands. She grabs your shoe and plays keep-away to get out of doing what you've told her to do. Treats don't always work anymore, and her appetite fluctuates from day to day.

Your Lab has had 7 months to learn to read your body language and facial expressions. She knows if you mean it when you say something to her, and she's at the stage where she'll call your bluff. To deal with this, use authoritative posture—stand tall and straight when you're dealing with her. That will help her understand you mean it.

You'll find your dog bossy-barking at you when she wants something or urine-marking your belongings (yes, even females mark). She's trying out new behaviors—bullying, marking, mounting, and maybe some aggression. She'll take teenage rebellion to new extremes, becoming possessive of her toys or growling at you when you tell her to get off the couch. She's suddenly overprotective of her territory and barks at every car driving by or person coming to the door.

Your Lab is conflicted. She's trying to balance teenage insecurity with her endless energy. She still depends on you, but she needs to rebel. She remembers what you've taught her, but she needs to be reminded that there are consequences when she misbehaves. Purely positive training might not be enough to keep her attention. Firm but kind discipline has its place this month. What works today might not work tomorrow, so keep trying different things.

Helping Your Puppy Gain Coordination

An adolescent Lab doesn't know she has hind legs, and when she remembers, she trips over them. She runs with her front legs, and her back end just kind of follows. To improve her overall coordination, put together some activities that require her to concentrate on her feet and legs when she moves. You'll be surprised how hard it is for her.

The ladder walk: For this exercise, place a ladder flat on the ground. Put your Lab on a leash, and have her walk through the ladder to the other end. She'll be impatient and want to leave, so you might need someone on her other side to keep her from jumping out of the ladder and walking beside it. Encourage her with treats in front of her nose. She'll practice lifting up her feet to go over the rungs, and after a few tries, she'll be pretty good at it.

Cavalettis: Place some pieces of 4×4 lumber on the ground about as far apart as her stride, and walk her over the boards. She'll stumble at first, unaware that the boards are even there. Adjust the distance apart so she can comfortably trot over the boards. When she's mastered the task at ground level, put them up on bricks, about 3 inches off the ground, and try again.

The platform: Place a 2×2-foot piece of plywood up on blocks. Have her jump up, and guide her with a treat to turn around in a circle once and sit.

Fast and Fearless

Teenage Labradors are big, strong puppies, and they know how to use their strength. Rather than dig under a fence, they'll chew through it. They're pushy and impulsive at this age, and they have no maturity to hold them back. Your little bull in the china shop isn't intentionally torturing you; she's just testing her limits. When you're frustrated, she'll do her best to make you laugh.

The same adolescent Lab who reacts fearfully to fireworks is strangely oblivious when plunging through brush and brambles, icy water, and other physical challenges. Her common sense is on vacation for the next few months, and you need to protect her from herself so she doesn't learn the hard way that some things, like ice-covered lakes, are actually dangerous.

HEALTH

From dangerous weather conditions to holiday safety hazards, your Lab puppy needs to be protected from an assortment of seasonal mishaps. By educating yourself and taking precautions each season, you'll keep your canine buddy safe.

Spring Safety Hazards

It's the season to begin hiking, camping, and enjoying outdoor activities. Do some shorter conditioning hikes to get your and your Lab's muscles in shape before you head out for long expeditions. Even then, remember she's a still a puppy so don't overdo it. If she'll be carrying a backpack, build up the weight gradually, and check with your vet to determine the maximum weight she can carry safely at this age.

Your dog's paw pads are soft and susceptible to cuts and scrapes at the beginning of the season. Walking on asphalt or concrete can cause road-burn, so toughen up her feet slowly.

As the weather warms up, fleas, ticks, and poisonous snakes become active. Be prepared for these pests by using preventatives on your Lab puppy. Consider rattlesnake avoidance training and a rattlesnake vaccine for your dog if you live where these snakes are common.

TIPS AND TAILS

Snake avoidance training has become popular in many areas of the United States where people and rattlesnakes live in close proximity. Training methods vary but have the same general goals. Dogs are exposed to live snakes whose mouths have been taped shut or are otherwise disabled so they can't bite. The dog is introduced to the sight, sound, and smell of a snake so she learns to recognize a snake and alert you even if she can't see it. Most trainers use electronic collars during this training.

Mosquitoes are at their worst during humid summer months, and that increases your puppy's risk of contracting heartworm. If she's not already on a preventative, you'll need to have her tested for the parasite before you can safely put her on a heartworm prevention program. Take care of this chore by mid- to late spring, or keep her on a preventative year-round.

At Easter time, keep wrapped candy, Easter baskets, fake grass, and chocolate bunnies out of your dog's reach. Most varieties of lily, Easter or otherwise, are toxic to your dog. If she eats a petal, leaf, or even just the pollen, it can cause an upset stomach, and if she eats enough, kidney damage could result. Make generous use of your puppy's crate during the holidays throughout the year to keep her safe and out of trouble.

Springtime means gardening season, when people fertilize their lawns and spray their gardens with pesticides. Anything from weed control to garden mulch can be toxic to your pup. Cocoa mulch, for example, which contains the same poisonous ingredients as chocolate, is particularly deadly. If you fertilize or spray, follow the manufacturer's guidelines carefully, let the grass dry completely before letting your puppy walk on it, and wash her feet if you think she's been exposed. And don't let her eat plants or mulch.

Although you take these precautions to protect your dog at home, public parks and neighborhood homes might have these hazards—sometimes invisible—so always be aware when you're out and about, too. (Also see Appendix C for a complete list of household and yard hazards.)

Summer Health and Safety Hazards

Heat exhaustion is the single-most dangerous summer hazard for your dog, and a dog's body temperature can quickly rise to dangerous levels and result in organ failure. Humidity increases the risk of heat exhaustion.

Lightly exercise with your dog in the early morning or evening, and keep her indoors during the heat of the day. A black or chocolate Lab's dark coat absorbs heat even faster than a yellow Lab's. Dogs have a limited number of sweat glands and perspire mainly through the pads on their feet. They pant to cool themselves.

Owners innocently assume their dog can jog or hike with them on a hot day without consequence, and your Lab will do her best to keep up with you. But remember that she's still too young for hard running on solid surfaces. And watch out for hot surfaces that could seriously burn her paws. Place your hand on the sidewalk, sand, or road where you'll be walking with your Lab. If it's too hot for your hand, it's too hot for her paws.

When you're out and about, *never* leave your pup in a hot car. Any temperature over 70°F is too hot to leave your dog in the car, even if you've parked in the shade with the windows open. The car can heat up to 100°F in as little as 15 minutes. Being left in a hot car is the most common cause of heat stroke in dogs.

HAPPY PUPPY

Always keep cool, fresh water available for your Lab. Consider putting out two water bowls in case she dumps one during the day, or tie a full bucket to a fence so she can't dump it, drag it around, and play with it. Many puppies love an ice cube treat on a hot day, so add crushed ice or ice cubes to her bowl. And leave a faucet dripping into her bowl so she can get water even if she runs out. Be sure she has access to cool shade if she's outdoors and it's too hot in the garage or doghouse. It doesn't have to be fancy; a beach umbrella is sufficient. A kiddie pool filled with a couple inches of water gives her a cool spot to beat the heat.

Learn to recognize and treat heat stroke. A tired and overheated dog usually tries to stop and rest. Don't force her to keep going. Find some shade, give her a drink of water, and wet her paw pads to bring down her body temperature. A dog in serious distress will pant heavily, drool thick saliva, have bright red gums and tongue, have an increased heart rate, and may stagger drunkenly or appear disoriented. As symptoms progress, she may vomit or have diarrhea (with or without blood in it), collapse, go into shock, and fall unconscious. In advanced stages, her gums will turn pale gray or blue.

Your first priority is to safely cool your puppy. Lay her on a cool floor, and turn on a fan if possible. Wet her body with cool water from a garden hose. Or place cool (not cold) wet towels on her head, neck, tummy, and feet. Let her drink if she's able. If you can take her temperature, do so. Anything over 104°F is an emergency, so take her to the vet immediately, even if she appears to recover. This is a life-threatening situation. Dogs who have previously suffered from heat stroke are at increased risk for a second occurrence.

More dogs are lost, killed, or injured on the Fourth of July than any other day of the year. And it's not just one day. People shoot off fireworks for a week or more before and after the holiday. Many dogs don't react until something blows up right in front of them, and a panic-stricken dog will do things she'd never consider any other time: rip the leash out of your hands, jump a fence, or run into the street. Protect your Lab puppy by keeping her at home and indoors on the holiday.

TIPS AND TAILS

Fireworks shows aren't just limited to the Fourth of July. If you live near a football stadium, fireworks are part of many halftime shows and homecoming games. New Year's Eve is another noisy, terrifying night for many dogs.

If your Lab is frightened by the noise, take steps to relieve her anxiety. Some dogs are happiest in their crates in a quiet place. You might need to outfit her with a body wrap product like ThunderShirt, which soothes her by putting pressure on key acupressure points. Or turn on the stereo or television to mask the sounds from outdoors. An exceptionally terrified dog might need medication. Plan ahead, and visit your vet for a prescription or to find out about the use of essential oils or aromatherapies. Don't use over-the-counter sedatives on your dog though.

You can desensitize your Lab to the sound of fireworks or thunderstorms. Play a tape of the sounds at low volume, and entertain your Lab with a game or otherwise distract her while it plays in the background so she learns to associate the sound with fun or a chew toy. You might have to start at some distance away from the sounds. When she reaches a point where she recognizes the tape and looks to you for her reward, you can increase the volume slightly and move closer to it.

TIPS AND TAILS

Don't comfort your puppy or try to soothe her when she's frightened of fireworks or thunderstorms. Your anxious tone and body language tell her she really does need to worry. Act happy and confident so your dog will realize nothing is wrong.

Fall Safety Hazards

As cold weather approaches and drivers winterize their cars, beware of antifreeze in driveways and on roadways. This greenish liquid's sweet taste is especially attractive to dogs, and your Lab can lick enough off her paws to cause kidney failure and even death. Wash your Lab's feet with Dawn dish detergent or olive oil if you think she's stepped in antifreeze, and call your veterinarian if you think she's ingested some.

Halloween can be a challenge to your pup. Remember when you were socializing your puppy and invited your guests to wear big hats and raincoats? For your dog, Halloween is all those scary-looking people—times 10. Trick-or-treaters wear wigs and masks and carry large, flapping bags. If your pup barks when the doorbell rings, this is either a great time to practice her obedience or a better time to put her in her crate in the back bedroom.

Burning candles, jack-o'-lanterns, and other flammable decorations tempt your Lab to investigate. Costumes, for pets or people, can include choking hazards like string and ribbons. Wooden sticks from caramel apples, candy wrappers, and gum can cause serious injuries, too. And poisonous chocolate lurks in those goodie bags.

Winter Safety Hazards

If your puppy must be outside for a few hours in extremely cold weather, be sure she has access to a doghouse or other protection from the cold and dampness. Remember, she's still a puppy, and even if she does have the typical Labrador double coat, she doesn't have enough fat yet to stay warm.

Even a Lab can get hypothermia if she gets wet to the skin. The first sign is shivering, a physical reaction that helps her retain heat by elevating her metabolism. Take your puppy indoors immediately if you see her shivering, and warm her body by drying her and wrapping her in blankets. Take her to the vet immediately.

When a dog is hypothermic, her blood retreats to the main trunk of her body to protect and heat her internal organs. That means her paws, tail, the tips of her ears, and other extremities are susceptible to frostbite. A dog with frostbite might limp, and the affected area will be pale and hard to the touch. Dry and warm the area with warm (not hot) compresses.

When you exercise with your Lab puppy outside in cold weather, don't overdo it. Cold air and high altitude cause your puppy to burn more calories and get tired faster. Also beware of frozen water and thin ice. Know where rivers and streams are located, and keep your puppy away from those areas. Don't go in after your dog if she falls in. Send for help instead. Adult dogs can survive in freezing water longer than humans can. Puppies are more vulnerable.

Monitor your pup when she's outside in cold and snowy weather. Snow hides familiar landmarks, and your Lab might not realize she's left her own yard if you're not there to show her the way. She can't distinguish the curb or driveway, and she could wander into the street. Snowplows have a hard time spotting dogs when they're plowing, and yellow Labs are particularly hard to see in the snow. Also, put your Lab inside when you use the snow blower. She'll want to be where you are, and the hard-thrown snow could injure her.

TIPS AND TAILS

After winter outings, wash your dog's feet to prevent irritation from road salt. Salt dries out your Lab's paws pads and leads to painful, cracked skin. If her feet are really dry and irritated, apply vitamin E oil or a lotion with lanolin.

It might not look pretty, but during her first few winter holidays, it might be a good idea to deck the halls with exercise pens and pet gates. Don't be shocked if your adolescent male pees on the Christmas tree; after all, it's okay to urinate on trees when he's outdoors. Decorations make fun, crunchy noises when they break in your pup's mouth, and crinkling cellophane sounds like a package of dog treats. But ribbons can tangle in your puppy's gut and cut off her circulation. As she makes her way to her favorite spot at the window, she could get tangled in extension cords and crush the gifts. Decorations look like toys to her, and candles can light her fur on fire when she stands too close.

Food is equally hazardous this time of year. Cakes and candies wrapped under the tree don't fool her; she knows which box contains something she can eat. Chocolate is especially dangerous. When food is set out for guests, block your Lab's access.

Leftover turkey is also tempting. You might want to feed your Lab table scraps, but don't. Fatty meat, skin, and gravy can cause pancreatitis, a potentially fatal disease, so dispose of the carcass where she can't get to it. Remember, poultry bones are brittle and can break in your dog's mouth, throat, or stomach, causing life-threatening injuries. Freeze leftovers until trash pickup day.

NUTRITION

You go to a lot of trouble selecting the right food for your Lab puppy, and what does she do? She eats kitty litter! As frustrating as that might be, continue to adjust her food according to her growth, and be prepared for her to make some unusual diet choices of her own.

Determining How Much Food Your Lab Needs

Although her growth is slowing down, your Lab is still eating more than she will when she's an adult. When she reaches 75 to 80 percent of her adult weight, she still needs up to $1\frac{1}{4}$ times the calories she needs when she's mature.

How much she needs to eat varies by her size and activity level. In spring and summer, when she's most active, she burns more calories. In the fall, a working hunting dog might need more food than at any other time of year. In the winter, dogs burn more calories outside because of the cold; however, they spend more time indoors and aren't as active overall.

Labs vary so much in size that it's hard to recommend an absolute amount of food for every dog. Labs aren't meant to be large dogs, and they don't need 5 or 6 cups of food a day as an adult. Unless you have a 100-pound dog (which some Labs are), she's going to need between 2 and 3 cups of food a day. The type of food you feed is another factor to consider. Premium foods offer more condensed nutrition, so you don't have to feed as much.

The best way to decide how much food is enough for your puppy is to keep track of her condition and weight. (See Appendix B for instructions on how to determine if your Lab is overweight, underweight, or just right.) When in doubt, consult with your veterinarian.

Dealing with the Icky Things Labs Eat

Although dogs eat things we think are absolutely disgusting, to them, they're delicious. Dogs have been natural scavengers since before they were domesticated, eating waste left behind by the nomadic tribes they followed. Today, when your pup eats cat litter or horse manure—or even her own feces—she's just repeating behavior that's been part of a dog's nature for tens of thousands of years. She considers it completely normal, so punishment doesn't usually eliminate the problem.

There are nutritional as well as behavioral reasons for why they eat feces. If your Lab isn't digesting all the nutrients in her food, they're passed through her body and out into her stool. The stool then becomes a source of additional nutrition. (Dogs have fewer taste buds than humans and aren't as discriminating about what they eat.) Feces also are a natural source of digestive enzymes and B vitamins. A mother dog eats her puppies' feces to clean the den, hide their scent, and protect them from predators. Puppies often eat the stool of older dogs and their littermates. It's a natural way to establish their intestinal *microflora*.

Stool-eating is self-rewarding and may become a habit. When dogs don't get enough exercise and live in a relatively boring environment, they might start eating feces. The best defense is to pick up feces as soon as your pup deposits it.

DOG TALK

Microflora are microorganisms that live in the digestive tract and perform various functions, such as building the immune system, producing vitamins, and preventing growth of harmful bacteria.

Cat feces have a high protein content that's attractive to dogs. But if a dog ingests clumping kitty litter, it could cause an intestinal blockage. The easiest way to avoid this problem is to use pet gates to block your puppy's access to the litter box.

If you want to use aversion training and make her avoid the feces, use a foul-tasting liquid like bitter apple or pepper sauce. Spray some in your puppy's mouth so she'll recognize the taste and smell and want to avoid it and then spray it on the feces. If you don't introduce her to the taste beforehand, this method doesn't work very well.

Dogs who eat horse and cattle manure are searching for another type of nutrition. Manure is full of digested vegetable matter, like hay and grass. Alfalfa hay is also a source of protein. Dogs are carnivores, but they do include plants in their diet, so dogs might eat manure if they aren't getting enough plant matter in their diets. Or it could just be because it's a natural instinct, like stool-eating.

Whatever kind of poop your Lab chooses to eat, she runs the risk of picking up intestinal parasites—just one more reason to prevent this nasty activity.

When Your Pup Eats Grass

All dogs eat grass; it's a perfectly normal behavior. Grass provides nutritional value in your dog's diet, and it's a source of fiber and roughage that's high in potassium and digestive enzymes. Your only concern should be if your lawn is chemically treated with fertilizers, herbicides, or pesticides that could make her ill.

You might notice that your dog vomits after eating grass. If this happens a few times a year, it isn't anything to worry about. A dog with a tummy ache occasionally eats grass to make herself throw up whatever's irritating her. This could prevent her from getting seriously ill from something she ate.

If your dog eats grass and vomits every week, there might be a more serious reason. It could mean gastric upset, parasites, nutritional deficit, or food sensitivity. She might be trying to compensate for something that's missing in her diet, so try switching brands or flavors of food. A different protein or carbohydrate source might work better for her. You also could add some lightly steamed vegetables such as carrots, kale, or zucchini to her diet.

GROOMING

Many Labs suffer from occasional coat problems, and a hundred different causes could be to blame. Besides adolescent hormonal fluctuations, let's look at some other possible reasons for coat problems and ways to treat hot spots.

Addressing Skin and Coat Problems

A healthy coat is a sign of a healthy dog. Your Lab's coat should be shiny, and her skin should be clear, with no dandruff, red spots, or scaling.

Most people don't notice when their Lab sheds out her puppy coat and the adult coat comes in, but during the transition, she'll shed quite a bit and her coat might look scruffy. This is more obvious in chocolate Labs. The loose coat appears lighter because it's dry, and the new coat coming in underneath seems darker. In a Lab of any color, the adult outer coat feels a little harsher than her puppy coat.

A dull, dry coat along with dandruff or inflamed skin indicates that more than just the semiannual shedding is taking place. A health problem like hypothyroidism or liver disease, or poor nutrition, could be the issue. Once your veterinarian rules out health concerns, you can look for other problems that could be the cause.

The Lab is a wash-and-wear breed. Too-frequent baths can remove natural oils and cause a dry coat, so if you need to bathe her often, just rinse her well with water. Be sure to use a dog shampoo when you do use one. Human shampoos dry out her coat more than those made especially made for dogs. Frequent brushing distributes oils, removes dirt, and makes her coat shine. That might be all she needs on a regular basis.

If your dog swims in your pool, chlorine can dry out her coat. Salty seawater dries it as well. Be sure to rinse her thoroughly after she swims.

Some skin problems, like allergies, can be inherited. See Month 12 for more information about allergies and treatments.

Your Lab's food might not have enough of the nutrients she needs to keep her coat healthy, and a protein deficiency can cause dryness, excessive shedding, and ear infections. The deficiency could be caused by grain rather than meat as the primary protein source in the diet. Fat or fatty acid deficiency also can cause a dull coat, dry skin, and itching.

External parasites like fleas or sarcoptic mange make your Lab scratch constantly, leaving patches of bare skin. It only takes saliva from one flea to cause an intense reaction in some dogs. Another parasite, demodectic mange, is passed down from the mother to her puppies during the first few days of life and is aggravated by a depressed immune system. It doesn't necessarily cause itching, but it does affect the coat dramatically, causing patches of hair loss and red, crusty skin.

TIPS AND TAILS

Cool water relieves itchy skin, while warm or hot water aggravates the itching. Antihistamines like Benadryl can provide some relief, too. Your veterinarian can tell you the appropriate dose for your Lab. For more serious itching, the vet might temporarily prescribe corticosteroids or prescription antihistamines.

Internal parasites (worms) also can affect a coat's condition, making it feel wiry and dry. Your vet can analyze a stool sample to identify and treat worms.

Treating Hot Spots

A hot spot is a moist, inflamed circle of skin your dog licks until it's raw. A hot spot could have one of many causes, such as flea allergy or vaccine reaction. They usually develop in warm weather, and rarely in winter. Common hot spot locations on Labs are under the ears, around the ruff on the neck, or on her legs. A hot spot gets bigger and more irritated as your dog continues to bite at it, and you might have to put an Elizabethan collar on her to prevent licking. Chewing and licking the hot spot can cause a secondary infection that must be treated with antibiotics.

To treat the hot spot, apply cool, wet compresses to loosen the crusty outer layer and soothe her skin. If it's not too painful for your pup, trim the hair around the spot and clean twice daily with mild, nonperfumed soap or antiseptic solution.

Here are some more suggestions to relieve hot spots:

○ Wash with cool brewed green or black tea. The tannic acid in the tea helps dry out the spot so it can heal.

- Apply aluminum acetate solution (available from your pharmacy) three times a day using a spray bottle or compresses. This helps dry out the spot and speeds healing.
- Apply hydrocortisone cream to relieve itching. Use just enough to rub in completely. Don't use too much, or your Lab will lick it off.
- Use aloe vera cream or gel to ease pain and help hot spots heal.

If the hot spot doesn't respond in a day or two, a visit to your veterinarian is in order.

SOCIAL SKILLS

Socializing your Lab is an ongoing process, and when she reaches adolescence, she goes through some major changes. This is a critical time for your dog's development, and she needs to continue her socialization.

Preventing Desocialization

Socialization was an easily acquired skill when she was a puppy, and most Labs are naturally friendly throughout their lives. But during adolescence, she undergoes so many hormonal, physical, and emotional changes, sometimes it's just too much trouble to take her out in public much. Continue taking her out, though, because the consequences of not socializing her now are hard to overcome.

If your Lab puppy is isolated during adolescence, she quickly becomes desocialized. She's no longer positively reinforced for friendly encounters with other dogs and people, she has no way of working through her lack of confidence, and she can't develop the social skills an adult dog needs to get along in the world.

Your Labrador is developing a healthy sense of caution at this age that will serve her well in adulthood, when she's learned there are consequences to leaping without thought into every situation. You might think your dog is overly cautious, but she's just practicing the art of self-preservation and will grow more confident as she settles into her new role as an adult dog.

Handling Dog-to-Dog Aggression

Your Lab's relationship with other dogs changes dramatically as she reaches adolescence. No longer on her "puppy pass," she can't just roar up to other dogs and expect them to love her. She has to learn new methods for interacting with her fellow canines.

Other dogs will treat her differently once she reaches puberty. Your dog will be more assertive as she tries to establish herself as an equal and no longer a puppy in the group, and she'll be challenged by older dogs and put in her place. These are natural behaviors, and your dog needs to experience them. If she goes unchallenged, it reinforces any aggressive or pushy tendencies—she never learns she has to restrain herself around other dogs or mind her manners.

For males, it starts with competition for females. He's interested in them in a different way now, and play behavior turns into courtship behavior. She won't put up with it, and the other males aren't going to let him take over their turf. Intact females are the least likely to get along with each other. They also compete, and rather than flirt with males, they argue with each other.

Altering prevents some conflicts between dogs. Once a male Lab is neutered, he no longer competes with other males so they don't challenge him. Spayed females don't usually provoke competition among themselves, either. You'll still observe marking, mounting, and pushy behavior, even in altered dogs of both sexes. If you start seeing aggressive behavior in your Lab, male or female, consider altering now.

HAPPY PUPPY

Play is important during adolescence and allows your Lab to develop her canine instincts. Stalking, chasing, mounting, and other natural doggie behaviors all are part of puppy play sessions. These activities take on new meaning in adult play. Dogs trade roles as they play and relearn how to interact, but adolescent dogs don't always know when to stop, and they might not read their playmate's body language correctly in the heat of the moment. Be sure to supervise so play doesn't get too rough.

Even the best-socialized dogs can lose their temper and get into a spat. Dogs' personalities vary, and not everyone is meant to be best friends. Puppies who formerly played well together might have an occasional dustup. It's almost inevitable that your Lab will get in a few tussles during adolescence. The question is, how serious are these encounters?

Many dogfights are simply arguments, not real fights. Everyone makes lots of noise, but when all is said and done, no one has a mark on them. You'll also see some competitive growling and snapping over preferred sleeping spots or a favorite toy. One dog usually gives in, and it's over. These are puppies who learned effective bite inhibition from other puppies when they were little.

That doesn't mean fighting is okay. When two dogs clearly don't like each other, there's not much you can do about it, and they should be separated. It's important to continue socializing your dog to other friendly dogs, though, so don't give up.

You can help prevent dog aggression when your pup meets new dogs. New introductions can be high-stress situations, filled with excitement, anticipation, and frustration. The worst thing you can do is hold the leash taut while the dogs sniff each other. If you do, your puppy thinks she's restrained and can't escape. She feels the tension in the leash and assumes you're tense, too, which could trigger a fight. It's hard to make yourself do it, but relax your hold and let the leash hang loose from her neck. If both people are holding their dogs back, once you let go, the dogs will explode at each other.

Introduce unfamiliar dogs on neutral territory, not at home. Practice getting your Lab's attention while you're still some distance away from each other and then go for a walk with the person and their dog. As everyone calms down, walk closer together.

Don't reward an aggressive reaction, and don't comfort your dog, either. Use your jolly routine and treats, and reward her for good behavior and for paying attention to you.

If you feel your Lab is developing a real aggression problem, work with a trainer or behaviorist. Someone who is experienced in evaluating dog behavior can give you a realistic picture of what's going on, and together you can craft a plan to prevent dog aggression from becoming a habit.

TIPS AND TAILS

Life on a chain is a miserable life for a dog and can cause chronic aggression in an otherwise nice animal. A dog who spends the day tied up outside gets frustrated. She can see things, but she can't get to them. She can't escape if another animal or a person comes in the yard, and she feels she has to defend herself. A lonely, bored Lab barks all day. She also can get tangled in the chain and strangle herself, get wrapped around a tree, or otherwise get injured. Find another way to confine your Lab.

Hopefully, you'll never encounter an aggressive dog, but if you do, you need to know how to handle the situation. When you're out with your Lab, carry treats to toss away from you and distract the aggressor should you encounter one. Speak in a high, happy tone, and yell "Treats!" "Cookies!" or some other term you hope he'll recognize. You might want to carry pepper or citronella spray, too. Be careful when you aim at an oncoming dog, though, because you don't want it blowing back in your or your dog's face.

Pay attention to the dogs in your neighborhood, so you know if any are a threat. Some dogs are territorial and will bark every time you walk past their house. If they're in the front yard, they might consider the sidewalk and street part of their territory, too. They might be all bluff and bluster, but they might not be. Either way, try to avoid aggressive dogs. Cross the street or turn around.

When you encounter a strange dog, speak firmly and tell him to sit. He might stop in his tracks and obey. If he's really agitated, don't run. This encourages him to chase you and triggers his prey drive. Remember how you caught your runaway Lab in Month 5? You ran so she'd chase you. In this case, that ploy works against you.

Stand sideways and don't look the aggressor in the eyes. You'll be much less threatening, and he might decide you mean no harm and go on his way. If your puppy is still small, pick her up. For bigger dogs, drop the leash. This might diffuse the situation because your dog isn't getting signals from tension on the leash. If they're going to fight, you don't want to be tangled up in the middle of it. If a dog does attack you, curl up in a ball and protect your face and neck.

If the worst happens and your dog gets in a fight, think twice before jumping into the fray. Most fights are over in a few seconds, and you don't have to intervene. If the dogs are really fighting, you're risking your own safety if you try to stop it. In the midst of a fight, instinct takes over, and a dog will bite anything that gets in his way. The worst thing you can do is grab a dog by her collar during a fight. She won't realize it's you and could turn and bite you, thinking another predator is attacking her from behind. Keep your hands and body out of the action.

If you do decide to try to stop a fight, here are a few tips that could help you stay safe:

○ Bang together two metal dog dishes or cooking pots. By startling the dogs, they might separate long enough for you to intervene and safely remove your dog.

○ Avoid screaming or hitting the dogs. They don't hear you or feel the blows. And if they do, it just adds to their arousal.

○ Spray water from a garden hose at the face of the attacking dog.

○ If you're indoors, wedge a chair or broomstick between the dogs to pull them apart.

○ Lift the aggressor by his hind legs to throw him off balance, which might force him to let go. If someone is there to help you, have her do the same with the other dog.

When the dogs are separated, leash your dog and take her out of the other dog's sight. It might not be safe to touch her by the collar yet, so put the end of the leash through the loop at the end, make a noose to slip over her neck, and tighten.

When everyone has calmed down, inspect each dog for injuries. You might be surprised to realize no one has any large bite wounds. Still, look carefully around the neck and face. Small puncture wounds are hard to find in dark fur and might not bleed. If you do find a bite wound, treat it immediately. A dog's mouth contains a lot of bacteria, and bite wounds usually get infected. Puncture wounds can close and trap the bacteria in the wound. Clip the hair around the wound, and wash and rinse the wound thoroughly with water or antiseptic solution. Take your dog to the vet immediately because she'll need antibiotics.

Larger bite wounds, even just 1 inch long, could need stitches to safely heal. Your vet might put a drain in the wound for a few days to allow the bacteria to escape.

BEHAVIOR

One day your Lab is a cyclone whirling through the house. The next, she sleeps all day. One day she's the perfect obedience student. The next day she's forgotten everything you've ever taught her. All this is typical for her age. She hasn't forgotten her lessons, but they're submerged under a wave of adolescent distraction. Although she's testing her limits—and your patience—your Lab needs her family to fall back on when adolescence overwhelms her. The rules and structure in her life are her safety net, and you're there to remind her.

Being Proactive (Rather Than Reactive)

A teenager in the house means something's always happening, and it's a challenge to stay one step ahead of your Lab this month. By taking a few preventive measures, you'll prevent her from getting into mischief—and save yourself a lot of angst. Limit her freedom to keep her safe and you sane.

Just because she's a teenager doesn't mean it's time to give her the car keys; you have to assume she'll get into mischief. Your Lab is still a puppy, so continue to crate her at night and when you can't supervise her. Look at things from her perspective, and set her up for success. She can't chew up your clothes if you shut the bedroom door, for example. And she can't get into the trash if you keep the wastebasket in a closet.

Continue to reinforce her training because what she knows will deteriorate if it's not reinforced during this turbulent period. Enforce household rules, and remind her when she forgets. You've probably relaxed a little because you know she knows what she's supposed to do, but keep in mind that she's testing the waters right now, and if you slack off, she'll take advantage of every opportunity. If she discovers she can get away with jumping on you occasionally, for example, she'll keep trying.

HAPPY PUPPY

If you've adopted a young Lab, congratulations! Labs are adaptable and can love their new family with incredible devotion. This is the age when many Labs change homes because of behavior problems. An untrained teenage Lab can be a handful, but she's not a lost cause. Enroll in an obedience class, and read through this book from the beginning like you just adopted a small puppy. Take advantage of this honeymoon period when she's soaking up information about her new surroundings, and teach her house rules from the first day. Your new Lab will be a treasured family pet in no time.

Mounting

Adolescent dogs, both male and female, begin mounting other dogs when they reach sexual maturity. Mounting is normal canine behavior, just like barking, digging, or chewing. It's less acceptable because it embarrasses you when your dog mounts a guest's leg or humps her stuffed animal in the middle of the living room. Owners often assume the reason is sexual, but there are other reasons, too, so you need to look at the context of each incident to understand what's really happening.

Anxiety and arousal (excitement, not sexual) contribute to a dog's actions. Mounting is a form of *displacement behavior,* a way of acting out to relieve her energy or stress. If she's uncertain of how to react to a situation, or if she's overly excited about the arrival of guests, mounting relieves her tension.

DOG TALK

Displacement behavior is a behavior that occurs out of context in response to an internal emotional conflict such as stress or anxiety.

Sometimes a dog engages in mounting hours after the exciting event, particularly if she's still anxious after being punished for misbehavior she doesn't understand. For example, you might come home and find she's been emptying the wastebaskets. You're angry, and whether you punish her or not (you shouldn't), she senses your anger and is worried. She needs an outlet to release that anxiety.

She also might learn that mounting works as an attention-getting device. You immediately react and try to stop her, and she learns to use it as means to get you to interact with her.

Try to anticipate when she'll mount someone or something, and step in to prevent the behavior. If she's mounting people, attach a leash to her collar, and direct her to a toy or pillow instead. Spaying or neutering your dog decreases mounting behavior but won't eliminate it completely.

The Importance of Exercise

Labradors were bred to be workers, but dogs today spend long hours at home alone. They rarely get enough stimulation, either mental or physical, and they have few outlets for their energy. Your canine athlete needs daily exercise to develop her muscles and her mind.

If you can find a large, fenced field with plenty of interesting smells, she'll entertain herself tracking rabbits, birds, and other scents. Free-ranging exercise like this isn't as stressful on young bones and joints.

Don't forget to give her short breaks during exercise. She'll run until she collapses just to please you, so quit while she still wants more. Take it easy during hot, humid weather because she'll get tired quickly. Also remember that repetitive pounding on hard pavement or jumping on hard surfaces could injure her.

Too much exercise can come back to haunt you. As your Lab puppy builds stamina, she'll need even more exercise to tire her out. If she doesn't get what she needs, you might suddenly have an obsessive retriever, for example, who just can't seem to get enough. For a dog like this, a 15-minute aerobic session followed by calmer problem-solving games works best.

TRAINING

While you train your Labrador during the coming months, you'll develop the fine skill of infinite patience. She'll challenge your skills and creativity as you endure her endless puppy antics. Have a good laugh, and keep training because she's learning even when she's not listening very carefully.

Working with a Hyper Lab

Owners of adolescent Labs often decide their dog is abnormally hyperactive. An adolescent male fidgets, can't relax, and is *always* moving. It seems like he can't concentrate, has trouble learning, and doesn't remember what you taught him from one day to the next. Females aren't exempt from hyperactive behavior.

Labs don't completely mature until they're 2 or 3 years old. Within the breed, there's a huge variation in energy level, so you can't predict how your Lab will behave. Other factors also contribute to a hyperactive personality. Her environment, health, socialization, training, and the amount of exercise she gets all play a part in her activity level.

TIPS AND TAILS

Someone, someday will tell you chocolate Labs are hyper and harder to train than black or yellow Labs. Don't believe it. All three colors can be born into the same litter, and no research exists to prove behavior is a color-linked genetic characteristic.

Spaying or neutering your Lab helps reduce frenzied behavior. Once the sex organs and the accompanying hormones are removed, she's not as distracted or constantly on the lookout for intact dogs.

If your Lab is counter surfing and raiding the trash, lunging at everyone and everything while on walks, and too excited to even notice you're giving her commands, ask yourself some questions: are you accidentally rewarding her with attention when she misbehaves? Even yelling is attention. Did you encourage exuberant greetings and wild play when she was little? If so, she's just doing what she was taught. And is she getting adequate exercise every day?

The absence of bad behavior is hard to recognize sometimes, so pay attention and praise her when you catch her doing something right. She'll learn what behaviors get attention when you consistently reward her for good behavior.

Teaching Self-Control

When the adolescent crazies hit, some owners give up on their puppies. What was previously cute is no fun anymore—the dog is wild in the house, dragging you on walks, and rudely jumping on everyone she meets. She's too much trouble to deal with. The less you take her out in public or allow her indoors, the more her behavior declines. She ends up in the backyard or, worse, a shelter.

Self-control is a developed skill, similar to building muscle memory by practicing a sport. Your Lab is in "react-first, think-later" mode, and she needs to learn to think first, even when she's excited. Help her make correct decisions rather than trying to control her behavior by manhandling her. An excited dog needs calm handling. Many owners instinctively react by yelling and grabbing their dog, which just fires her up more. She learns that you'll stop her; she doesn't learn to stop herself. By moving slowly and speaking quietly, you communicate there's no reason to act wild. That advice is easy to give, but it's hard for almost everyone to do. Rather than try to defuse a situation in the heat of the moment, practice when you're not in the midst of a crisis.

TIPS AND TAILS

At home, practice sit and down dozens of times a day with food treats. It doesn't have to be a stay; you just want her to respond and have enough self-control to stay put for a few seconds. Down is harder, but she'll get better as you practice. Put her dinner kibble in your pockets, and spend the evening doling it out while you work together. You'll hold her attention and keep her occupied, and soon she'll be following you around, offering sits and downs when you didn't ask for them!

Practice sit and down while on your walks so she starts to expect you'll occasionally ask her to do something. When you take her out—which you should do every day no matter how hard it is—watch for opportunities to practice her self-control. You might not go more than a block the first few times, but that doesn't matter. For example, when you see someone walking toward you, focus your Lab's attention on you by asking for a sit and rewarding her before she notices the oncoming person. Start your routine far enough away that she can be successful. Once she gets the idea, start closer on future walks. With enough repetitions, she'll see an oncoming person and look to you, an occasion you should mark with a huge jackpot of treats and praise.

TIPS AND TAILS

In the midst of a hyperactive frenzy is not the time to teach your dog a settle-down cue. Instead, practice with her in a quieter setting so she can learn it without distractions.

Teach your puppy to settle down on command. It's probably easy to get your Lab mildly riled up with a tennis ball or toy, but then stop. Hide the toy in your pocket, don't look at her, ignore her, and cross your arms. At some point, she'll be puzzled and stop jumping around. She might even offer a behavior to get a reaction from you. Ignore her until she sits, praise her quietly when she does sit, and bring out the toy again. Repeat this sequence several times, and you'll soon discover she sits faster and faster because that makes you produce the toy.

Give both the active and the quiet phase a name, like "Whoopee!" and "Cool it." Gradually extend the settle period to a few seconds, and work up to a minute or more. Always praise her for settling, even when you don't have a toy. You now can transfer this behavior to a situation where you need it. She won't be perfect the first time, but with practice, she'll learn.

It's easy to ignore your Lab when she's quietly sitting or lying at your feet, but this is the behavior you want, so watch for it and reward her when you see it.

Clicker Training

In recent years, positive reinforcement training methods have gained favor over punishment methods, and with good reason. It's much more fun for you and your puppy if you're rewarding her for doing something right rather than punishing her all the time for doing something wrong.

Clicker training, in which the handler (you) uses a handheld clicker as a signal to the dog that she's done the right thing, is an example of positive reinforcement training. Besides being fun, clicker training is based on scientific principles and research developed decades ago with dolphin training, similar to Ivan Pavlov's famous operant-conditioning research. Pavlov rang a bell before feeding a group of dogs, and the dogs associated the bell with food and salivated in anticipation.

The idea behind clicker training is simple: you can't force a dolphin to do something. You can't lure her or shape her into position to show her what you want. So instead, trainers "marked" the correct behavior with a click, followed immediately by a food reward. (Sound familiar? That's what you're doing when you praise your dog while she's sitting and then give her a treat. The click, or your praise, marks the sit and tells her food will follow.) The trainers took a sound that had no meaning to the dolphins and gave it meaning. The dolphins knew a treat was coming when they heard the conditioned reinforcer, the click.

Timing is critical in clicker training. It's impossible to deliver the praise and food reward at the exact second the correct behavior occurs. You must click as your dog performs the correct behavior so she understands what brought her the food reward.

When your pup understands that the click means a treat will follow, she'll love figuring out what will make you deliver a click and the ensuing treat. She'll run through her entire repertoire of behaviors until she finally does the one thing you were waiting for.

To use the method effectively, we recommend you find a good book and a trainer to get you started. Any lesson can be broken down into small steps and taught with clicker training, and many owners find it a lot of fun and much easier for teaching their puppy.

Using Equipment to Control Your Dog

Ideally, you should be able to control your dog with training, rewards, and discipline. But Labs are strong, and if she's out of control to the point that you can't handle her, you might decide to look into some equipment to help manage her.

Some of these items, like head halters and no-pull harnesses, might provide a much-needed breakthrough in dealing with your dog. Work with a professional trainer, and use these items while you're teaching your teenager to listen to you. Just remember, these are tools, not solutions. You can't stop training because you have a new collar. You don't want to have to use special devices throughout her life.

Head halters: These work on the same principle as a horse's halter. By controlling your dog's head, you control her movement. You can't out-muscle a horse, but a halter gives you the control you need. The same is true for your dog. With the halter, you can steer her gently, but she can't drag you. The halter's straps go over her muzzle and behind her ears, join with a ring in the throat area where you attach the leash, and the straps tighten over her muzzle when she pulls. There's often another strap you can hook to your pup's regular collar so she can't escape if she rubs and removes the head halter. Add a second leash attached to her regular collar to give you more control.

Most dogs resist head halters at first. She'll pull away, dance around, and paw at it. Expect to spend several short sessions working with it before she's accustomed to it. Once she accepts the halter, it works well. The halter requires some finesse on your part to use it correctly. If you yank on it or drag your dog, you can twist and injure her neck. Never leave a head halter on your puppy.

There's a downside to using head halters. When you meet a stranger, they'll assume your dog is muzzled. Their next assumption is that she's dangerous and will bite. You might have to educate the people you encounter.

No-pull harnesses: A dog who pulls on the leash will cough and gag from the pressure on her trachea. That leads some owners to try a harness, which relieves neck pressure because the straps lie across her chest and rib cage instead. A traditional harness like you see on toy poodles triggers an opposition reflex in a large dog like a Labrador Retriever, and your dog will instinctively resist the pressure. That's why a sled dog wears a harness—it makes her pull. It actually triggers the same reflex in a small dog, but because the owner is stronger than the dog, it doesn't matter as much.

No-pull harnesses were developed so an owner with less strength or with an untrained dog could still walk her dog. Several styles are available. Some attach the leash to a ring on the chest band. Others have straps that go under the legs and fasten behind the shoulders, where the leash attaches. They tighten when the dog pulls and give the owner more control.

Equipment to Avoid

The following sections cover a few devices you *should not* use without a trainer or behaviorist's guidance because they can damage your relationship and actually injure your dog: chain collars, prong collars, and shock collars.

TIPS AND TAILS

In the hands of an inexperienced person, any tool can hurt a dog. If you feel you need special equipment to control your Lab, work with a trainer or behaviorist to evaluate the situation. Then learn how to use equipment safely and without ruining your relationship with your Lab.

Chain collars: The chain collar has fallen out of favor over the past two decades. The training method of choice since the 1950s was what trainers now refer to as the "jerk-and-pull" method. Owners spent their time in obedience classes learning how to give their dogs a "proper" correction, which entailed a quick, hard jerk on the chain and an equally quick release. The method worked, but owners didn't like hurting their dogs, and today, more positive training approaches have taken its place. Unfortunately, many dog owners still use these collars.

Also called choke collars, for good reason, the collar tightens when your dog pulls, which can choke her or injure her trachea. If you put it on incorrectly, the collar doesn't loosen when she stops pulling, so it continues to choke her. This collar should *never* be left on a dog for any reason. Your Lab could get hung up on a branch or fence and choke to death.

Prong collars: A prong collar is a corrective device, not a training tool. The prongs go entirely around the dog's neck, which evens out the pressure applied when the dog pulls or the handler makes a correction. Thus, there isn't as much risk of injuring the trachea as with a chain collar. But if the prong collar is too tight or the owner uses too much force, the prongs can puncture the dog's neck. People without enough strength to control their dog often use a prong collar to give themselves some leverage.

Ideally, a dog self-corrects with a prong collar—you don't have to do anything. The effect when a handler makes a correction is instant and extreme, and it really hurts. A sensitive dog might react aggressively in self-defense or fear. Other dogs become increasingly stressed while wearing one. A prong collar can destroy your relationship or save it. Never use one without expert help.

Shock collars: The manufacturer of electronic or "shock" collars calls it a "stimulation" collar to sidestep the negative image of you giving an electric shock to your dog. But that's exactly what it does, and it has its place in certain types of training.

Hunters who train their dogs to take commands from a distance make use of these collars. When a person understands the scientific principles of negative reinforcement and uses the collar correctly, the dog can learn. But if you hit the button at the wrong time, all you've accomplished is confusing, hurting, and frightening your dog. For pet owners, there's no practical purpose in using these collars. And they should *never* be used on a puppy.

When You Need Professional Help

Pet owners are not professional dog trainers and shouldn't have to be. A frustrated owner with a frustrated dog won't make much progress. If you just can't handle your wild Labrador yourself, get help from a trainer or behaviorist. Many options are available.

More obedience classes: You might want to sign up for a beyond-the-basics class and repeat it if you need to. You'll absorb more information now that you've had more real-life experience with your puppy. Agility classes will burn off some of your Lab's energy, although she's too young to do any jumping on hard surfaces. If you're looking for a professional dog trainer, check with the Certification Council for Professional Dog Trainers (ccpdt.org) or the Association of Professional Dog Trainers (apdt.com).

Private lessons: Sometimes it helps to have a trainer come to your home where the problems actually are occurring. You spend time working together on the particular issues you're having with your Lab, and the entire family can get individual attention and try different solutions.

Professional training: Sending your young Lab to boot camp—a board-and-train program—might seem extreme, but professional trainers will get quicker results from her. If you're an inexperienced dog owner, it'll be easier for you to learn to handle your Lab if she's already had some training. Then you both aren't beginners. If you decide to go this route, be sure you'll get instruction as well. Ask about training methods and what types of equipment are used. A puppy doesn't need to be trained with electronic collars or other harsh devices. Get references from other clients, too.

Behavior consultations: If you're dealing with aggression or other potentially serious behavior in your Labrador, consult an animal behaviorist or other professional with advanced training in behavior modification. A qualified consultant can evaluate your situation and help you work through your dog's specific issues.

Several types of consultants are available, and each has an advanced level of education and experience. Specific organizations train and certify these experts, and they often maintain a database of professionals you can contact for help. Here are some of the organizations and associations you might hear about:

International Association of Animal Behavior Consultants (IAABC; iaabc.org): An IAABC member has been tested and certified in the areas of assessment, counseling skills, and behavioral science. Members also must submit references and case studies demonstrating their skills.

Certified Applied Animal Behaviorists (CAAB; certifiedanimalbehaviorist.com): A CAAB has an advanced degree (MS/MA or PhD) in the science of applied animal behavior and has demonstrated expertise and experience in diagnosing and treating behavior problems.

Veterinary behaviorist: This is a board-certified veterinarian who has a specialty in animal behavior and has completed a 1- to 3-year residency program in veterinary behavior. He has conducted research, published his findings in academic journals, and passed a 2-day exam. These are the only behavior specialists who can prescribe medication for your dog. The American College of Veterinary Behaviorists (dacvb .org) maintains a database of behaviorists in the United States. You'll need a referral from your veterinarian.

TIPS AND TAILS

Before you spend a lot of money on professional advice, commit to working with your dog until her issues have improved to an acceptable level.

YOU AND YOUR PUPPY

When your teenage Lab slows down enough to notice you, seize the opportunity to enjoy her company. Stock up on chew toys, and settle in for the long haul. Adolescence is just beginning!

Time for a Belly Rub!

Teenagers need a lot of rest, and after a frantic day of running and playing, your Lab puppy needs some quiet time—although she might not think so. As long as you'll play, she'll be up for a game, so quit before she exhausts herself.

If you cut off the activity cold turkey and expect her to settle down, she won't. She's still wound up and ready to go. Instead, after an active play session, take her for a quiet walk, or better yet, give her a belly rub or a massage. It will relax you both at the end of a long, active day.

Living with a Lab Teenager

Attitude is everything when you have an adolescent Labrador, so don't take it personally.

Remember when you were a teenager? You stayed out late, didn't listen to your parents, had to be doing something with your friends every minute, and thought you were invincible. Well, that's what your puppy is going through now. She's full of life and having a blast, so you might as well sit back and enjoy it. When she rips up the couch, take a photo so you can laugh about it later. (By the way, who left her alone with access to the couch? Oops!)

TIPS AND TAILS

Write down the stories of your pup's crazier moments. For example, one day Terry looked out the window and saw the shingles from the doghouse roof flying across the backyard. Her 8-month-old Lab was diligently pulling them off one by one and slinging them around the garden. Remember, you're not alone.

	SOCIAL	**BEHAVIOR**	**TRAINING**	**PHYSICAL**	**HEALTH**
MONTH 1			Littermates and mother teach appropriate canine behavior	Rapid growth	
MONTH 2	Breeder starts socialization				
MONTH 3	Socialization at home with new owner and other pets	Fear-imprint period	Begin house- and crate training		1st DHPP vaccine
MONTH 4		Teething begins—heavy chewing period	Enroll in puppy class		2nd DHPP vaccine
MONTH 5	Socialization in public		Ready for basic commands	Switch to adult food	3rd DHPP and rabies vaccines
MONTH 6					
MONTH 7		Adult teeth are in—chewing continues	Enroll in basic obedience class	Moderate growth	Sexual maturity
MONTH 8					
MONTH 9			Ready for more advanced training		
MONTH 10					
MONTH 11				Slow growth—reaches adult size	
MONTH 12 AND BEYOND					Annual vaccinations and checkup

In Search of a Leader

Your adolescent Lab is physically maturing, but mentally he's still very much a teenager. You'll see his attention span improve, he'll be pushy but not as aggressively as some breeds, and he'll be more watchful and protective of you. Yet he still needs your leadership to maintain his good behavior. Enjoy his company and the challenges he presents. He's a lot of fun and joyfully delights in his time with you.

PHYSICAL DEVELOPMENT

You'll see subtle differences in your Labrador's physical appearance between 8 and 9 months. His growth has slowed dramatically, even though he's not yet his full adult height. He might grow 1 inch in a week and then stop altogether for the next 2 weeks. His coordination also improves.

Internally, his bones are developing and hardening, although he might still look light-boned and slightly out of proportion until he's 13 to 18 months old. His teeth have all broken through the gums, and by next month, most of his teething pain will end as his teeth will have set in his jaws.

Males Looking More Masculine

If your Lab is neutered, he'll mature differently from an intact male. A dog of either sex stops growing at some point, and his bones begin to harden and thicken. It's the sex hormones that put the brakes on the height, and if a dog is altered, he'll continue to grow a bit taller and lankier than he would have if left intact. This appears to be more obvious in neutered males because females have naturally lighter bone structure.

Last month, your male dog still looked a little gangly, and his body might have seemed longer than it should be. He might have appeared as if his back legs were higher than his front legs, too. He starts developing more muscle in his rear this month, and as he does, his body starts to look more in proportion. His rib cage fills out and broadens, his head becomes larger as it grows in width and breadth, his neck thickens, and the coat around his neck gets heavier. Again, if your dog is neutered, these changes aren't as dramatic.

Females Looking More Feminine

Males look obviously male, but females are harder to define based on looks because they don't change dramatically like an intact male does as he reaches maturity. Most of the female characteristics stay the same whether or not they're spayed because it's the absence of testosterone that makes them female.

There are coat differences between males and females. These aren't as obvious as on a long-coated breed, but they're still there. The ruff over the shoulders and on the neck isn't quite as thick in females. Also, females have a more feminine head when compared to a male, as well as overall lighter bone structure. If spayed early, they may get taller like neutered males.

HEALTH

There's a lot going on inside your puppy's body this month as he continues to grow and develop. His energy level might differ wildly from day to day, and you'll need to watch for signs of injury or other limb problems that sometimes develop in teenage Labs.

Occasional Lack of Energy

Glucose is the type of sugar found within the bloodstream. It's formed from carbohydrates during the digestion of foods and is then used as energy. Puppies digest their food faster than adults, and this sometimes prevents absorption of all the nutrients in their food. A puppy who overexercises uses the nutrients in his body faster. The combination of the two can cause low blood sugar (hypoglycemia), which makes him tired.

If your puppy is eating a poor-quality food, the carbohydrates in his diet might not be as easily digestible as they should be. This can affect his ability to produce enough energy to keep up with his needs. If your Lab seems to have a frequent problem with low energy, it's worth a look at his food to see if it might be contributing to the problem.

There are other reasons your young Lab might be tired. During growth spurts, he uses a lot of energy to build muscles and bone, and he might need more food as fuel. Don't let him get fat, though. If he looks like he's getting heavy, cut back on the amount you're feeding him. His caloric and energy needs could vary from week to week this month, so pay attention and make changes accordingly.

Parasites like intestinal worms or heartworm can contribute to a puppy's lack of energy, too. Also look for other symptoms, like a dull coat or watery eyes.

TIPS AND TAILS

If your puppy seems overly tired all the time, take him to the vet for a checkup to rule out a serious disease and to treat parasites.

When Your Puppy's Limping

A puppy might limp for several reasons. He could have slipped and twisted a leg while playing, and the limping might go away in a few hours. Or it could be something more serious. Several conditions can occur in adolescent Labradors, so pay close attention to your dog's symptoms and take notes about what you see so your veterinarian can make an accurate diagnosis.

Most bones start off as cartilage, a flexible connective tissue that gradually hardens and is replaced by bone. The longest bones in your puppy's body are his legs. These long bones must grow longer, so your puppy can get taller, and wider, to physically support his adult weight.

We talked about growth plates in Month 7 and the effect spay/neuter surgery has on the timing of when they close. Here, we want to look at this and other problems that might cause lameness in a young Lab. Some scientists believe that feeding a food too high in calcium or one that promotes fast growth could be a contributing factor in any or all of these conditions—a good reason to switch from puppy food to an adult formula, if you haven't already.

TIPS AND TAILS

A dog shouldn't run or jump on hard ground like asphalt until he's at least 18 months old and his growth plates have closed. Because their bones are still soft, teenage dogs are especially prone to leg and growth plate fractures. Such fractures could affect the final length and angle of the bone when he matures, and he could permanently move with an uneven gait. He'll also be more susceptible to arthritis in the joint where the fracture occurred and in other joints affected by his off-balance movement. A fractured growth plate must be surgically repaired.

Osteochondritis dissecans (OCD): Your Lab puppy also might face osteochondritis dissecans. OCD often is caused by excess trauma to one or both of a dog's shoulders, and immature cartilage is fractured from the bone and sometimes floats loose in the joint fluid. Young, rapidly growing Labs 4 to 8 months old are especially susceptible. Hard-pounding exercise contributes to the risk, so if you have slick floors, put down runners to reduce the risk of your Lab slipping and injuring his fragile bones. Other causes include genetics, rapid growth, hormone imbalances, and nutrition.

The first symptoms of OCD might show as your dog being stiff and sore or limping after exercise. If untreated, the lameness will become permanent as arthritis sets in. X-rays are used to diagnose the condition, and treatment consists of 4 to 8 weeks of complete crate rest and anti-inflammatory medications. Surgery to remove the loose cartilage also is an option.

Panosteitis: Also referred to as "growing pains" or wandering lameness, panosteitis affects the humerus in the front legs and the femur in the rear. Common in young, rapidly growing breeds like Labrador Retrievers, it causes lameness that often switches from one leg to the other every few days. It's sometimes misdiagnosed as elbow dysplasia, an inherited condition (see Month 7). At the first stages of panosteitis, your Lab's legs are sore, and he might be unwilling to play or appear depressed. He also might not feel like eating and could have a fever. X-rays can show changes in bone density.

Treatment includes restricting your dog's activity, plenty of crate rest, and analgesic drugs. The condition isn't hereditary or caused by injury, and it usually resolves itself in 4 to 6 weeks. There are no long-term consequences if the dog receives treatment and injuries are prevented.

Torn anterior cruciate ligament (ACL): A torn ACL is a soft tissue injury rather than a bone problem like the previously mentioned conditions. A hard-playing Lab can leap up to catch a ball or flying disc and land wrong, tearing this knee ligament. Other causes include making a sudden turn while running, slipping on a hard surface, or being hit by a car. Overweight dogs are at higher risk because their knee joints are weaker from carrying too much weight. With a torn ACL, your puppy will be in intense pain and limp because the tear allows the tibia and femur to grind against each other.

A partially torn ACL might heal with treatment, including limiting his activity for 8 to 12 weeks, with low-impact exercise like swimming or walking when he's ready to start moving again. Your vet will prescribe anti-inflammatory medications.

At this time, the only treatment for a completely torn ACL is surgery, which involves a recovery time of 6 to 8 weeks. Your pup will be restricted to leash walking with very limited exercise. If the injured ACL isn't treated, the dog usually develops arthritis. Also, because the one leg is injured, the opposite leg bears more weight, which often causes the ACL to rupture on that side, too.

The Nose Knows

Hunting for a fallen bird in heavy cover or water, trailing the scent of a lost person, finding traces of arson after a fire—you'll find Labs, and their keen sense of smell, in each of these situations and more.

Scientists estimate that a dog's scenting ability is millions of times more advanced than that of his human companions, and up to one third of his brain is devoted to scenting and analyzing what he smells. And that's something Labs have at birth, so your puppy can already smell thousands of things you can't.

The canine nose is divided into two cavities with a vertical wall of tissue, called the nasal septum, dividing them. The nasal cavity contains a maze of bony structures that, along with the sinuses and nasal septum, communicates with the olfactory nerve, which sends scent information to the brain.

If you see a dog "licking" the air with his tongue, he's bringing the scent to his nose to absorb it. When a scent reaches his brain, it goes to areas that process memory, pleasure, and emotions, making associations between them. As your Lab puppy encounters new smells, he builds a memory bank of scents and what they mean to him. Just like you might remember the smell of Thanksgiving dinner and all the fond memories you associate with that holiday, your puppy learns that some smells mean good food, some mean a thing tastes bad, and others signify a memorable experience. But with the ability to process thousands or even millions of scents, by the time he's an adult, he's a virtual encyclopedia of scents!

Your Lab puppy's nose is ideally constructed for poking around in the dirt. When he sniffs, his nostrils dilate, and mucus in his nose filters out bacteria, dirt particles, and other matter, which he then exhales. The length of your Lab's nose also has an effect on his scenting ability. Breeds with longer noses, like Labs, have more scent-reception cells.

As if that wasn't amazing enough, in his nasal cavity is a structure called Jacobson's organ (vomeronasal organ). This organ communicates with different parts of his brain and can process "smells" that aren't actually odors but rather chemical messages passed from one animal to another. It's Jacobson's organ that makes a newborn puppy able to recognize his mother's milk and allows her to recognize her own puppies. It also enables a dog to recognize the "scent" of fear in humans.

Pheromones play a big part in communication between dogs, and Jacobson's organ is able to detect and interpret quite a bit of this information. For example, one dog can recognize if another is an adult or puppy, male or female, altered or intact, or ready to breed.

DOG TALK
A **pheromone** is a chemical secreted by animals (including humans) that other animals, usually of the same species, can interpret.

Alternative Health Care

Dog owners who want to treat their pets with natural remedies, or who find conventional medicine isn't working for their dogs, might look to alternative or complementary medicine for treatment. Although your puppy is probably years away from serious illness or age-related disease, some forms of alternative treatment can be used to heal injuries or help behavior-related problems.

Most veterinarians practice Western medicine, and some incorporate complementary therapies into their treatment plans. There also are purely *holistic veterinarians* and *practitioners* who treat patients solely with herbal or other remedies, such as those listed here.

DOG TALK
A **holistic veterinarian** or **practitioner** addresses the whole dog, including mental and social factors, instead of limiting treatment to the symptoms of disease.

Acupuncture: Acupuncture is an ancient Chinese practice that's been successfully used on animals and people for thousands of years to correct energy imbalances in the body and promote healing. Acupuncture addresses pain and inflammation from injuries, arthritis, hip or elbow dysplasia, neurological disorders, and digestive disorders as the practitioner inserts fine needles into the skin or muscles that stimulate predefined acupuncture points. These points lie along meridians, or energy lines, that travel through the body. The meridians contain nerve endings, connective tissue, and blood vessels that release endorphins and other mechanisms to relieve pain and trigger healing. Some acupuncturists add electrical stimulation to the needles.

Your veterinarian might recommend acupuncture in addition to physical therapy or conventional medicine. The treatment usually takes 20 to 30 minutes per visit, and most dogs accept it with minimal discomfort. In fact, they tend to relax noticeably during a session. To find a veterinarian who provides acupuncture for dogs, visit the website of the American Academy of Veterinary Acupuncture at aava.org.

TIPS AND TAILS

Veterinarians have advanced degrees and are licensed and regulated by law. No similar system exists for credentialing alternative practitioners. It's up to you to investigate treatments and the people who supply them to be sure you're getting safe and appropriate care for your dog. Do your research, ask for recommendations, and check references. Also visit the American Holistic Veterinary Medical Association at ahvma.org for more information.

Acupressure: Similar to acupuncture, acupressure works the same energy meridians on the body, but instead of needles, the practitioner uses pressure on the acupuncture points, similar to massage, to treat allergies, diarrhea, digestive problems, ear infections, respiratory problems, and more. Your veterinarian might teach you how to use acupressure at home on a daily basis to treat your dog. Most practitioners recommend 5- to 10-minute sessions. If you find your dog resists the pressure, winces in pain, or otherwise tries to avoid the session, stop and consult with your vet.

Chiropractic: Chiropractic therapy can relieve pain and improve a dog's movement. During a session, the practitioner adjusts the dog's vertebral joints, extremity joints, or head. It's used to treat injuries, arthritis, and hip and elbow dysplasia. The American Veterinary Medical Association recommends you have a vet examine your dog before you pursue chiropractic treatment. X-rays and other tests will help you and your Lab's doctors choose an appropriate treatment plan. Opt for a chiropractor who specializes in animals and is a member of the American Veterinary Chiropractic Association (avcadoctors.com).

Massage: Massage and other body manipulation techniques are helpful for some dogs. Traditional massage helps improve circulation, relieves pain and stiffness, increases flexibility and range of motion, and helps proper functioning of joints and limbs. TTouch is particularly beneficial. Linda Tellington-Jones originally developed this therapy for horses, but it has been used on all species of animals. Moving his or her fingers in circular motions, the practitioner works different parts of the animal's body to promote healing and behavior modification by opening the body's awareness and releasing tension. You can learn to use the technique to relax your Lab puppy and help improve problem behaviors by incorporating TTouch into your training. Find out more at ttouch.com.

Homeopathy: *Homeopathy* is based on the law of similars and the concept of "like produces like." Practitioners use a substance that, in undiluted form, causes a particular symptom; in a highly diluted homeopathic formula, the same substance relieves the symptom. Homeopathic remedies are usually diluted with alcohol or distilled water, and most are administered to your dog in the form of drops you put directly in his mouth.

Homeopathic remedies are used to treat a variety of health problems, including these, to name a few:

○ Pain

○ Inflammation

○ Fluid in the lungs

○ Bruises and wounds

○ Bleeding

○ Skin problems

○ Respiratory illness

○ Allergies

Some remedies address several health problems at once. Practitioners do not claim to cure diseases like cancer or arthritis, but they do strive to help your dog attain the best possible overall health so his immune system can fight these diseases.

DOG TALK

Homeopathy is the practice of using herbs, minerals, and natural compounds to strengthen the body's natural defenses and cure disease.

The Food and Drug Administration (FDA) classifies homeopathic remedies as drugs but does not evaluate them for safety or effectiveness. Do careful research, buy only from a homeopathic practitioner, or use a well-known brand name. To find a veterinarian who uses homeopathic techniques, visit the Academy of Veterinary Homeopathy at theavh.org.

Natural Remedies

Natural remedies make use of plants and other natural substances for healing health and behavioral issues. Although they've been successfully used for centuries, they shouldn't be considered a substitute for veterinary care. They're generally regarded as safe and effective, but always consult with your vet and research potential side effects before giving anything to your dog. The quality and concentration of ingredients varies dramatically from brand to brand, and a remedy might not have the same effect on every dog.

TIPS AND TAILS

Neither the FDA nor any other government authority regulates natural remedies, and manufacturers' claims about their effects have not been scientifically proven.

Supplements: Glucosamine and chondroitin are compounds found in cartilage that are added to dog food, especially senior formula dog foods, to improve joint health. Dogs with arthritis due to hip dysplasia, injuries, or aging can experience increased mobility due to decreased inflammation and pain when given these supplements. For example, if a young dog is diagnosed with hip dysplasia, glucosamine can help prevent cartilage breakdown, while chondroitin contributes to the creation of new cartilage.

These supplements can cause stomach problems like nausea and diarrhea, so be sure to consult with your vet before giving them to your Lab.

Herbal remedies: Humans have used the healing properties of herbal remedies for centuries, making use of roots, flowers, stems, and leaves. Many remedies are made using a number of herbs used dry or made into teas, juices, or tinctures. In a tincture, the herbs are combined with alcohol, soaked, and the liquid drained off. You can make your own remedies or purchase them in tablets or capsules to help with healing in your dog. They sometimes work much more slowly than traditional medicine, and it's not unusual for one to take several months before you see any effects. Some remedies target a specific illness or emotional state; others boost the immune system and overall health.

Thousands of plants contain medicinal properties. Here are some commonly used herbs:

○ Chamomile, for its calming effect

○ Alfalfa, as an anti-inflammatory

○ Ginger, for carsickness

○ Echinacea, to boost the immune system

○ Nettle, as an antihistamine

It's important to remember that herbal remedies are medicines and can have harmful side effects if used incorrectly. Remember, too, that some plants are poisonous to animals (see Appendix C), so do careful research or work with a veterinary herbalist. You can learn more about herbal remedies from the Veterinary Botanical Medicine Association at vbma.org.

Flower remedies: Also called essences, flower remedies are homeopathic remedies made from flowers or parts of flowering plants formulated to treat health and behavioral issues. Probably the most well known is Rescue Remedy, used to treat stress and anxiety. Developed by Dr. Edward Bach in the early twentieth century, each Bach Flower Remedy includes several flower essences formulated to treat imbalances in the body and spirit.

Rescue Remedy, for example, includes several flower essences, including these:

○ Star of Bethlehem

○ Clematis

○ Impatiens

○ Rock rose

○ Cherry plum

The remedies were developed for use in people, but many are also used for dogs and administered with an eyedropper, either directly into the dog's mouth or added to his water or food. Because they're homeopathic, they're highly diluted, so you just give your dog a few drops.

Essential oils: Also from the plant kingdom, essential oils are made from roots, leaves, flowers, or seeds and used to heal wounds, repel insects, and treat skin problems. Unlike other remedies, these aren't taken internally; they're applied to your dog's skin or fur. One of the most well known is citronella, which is made from lemongrass and repels mosquitoes. Tea tree oil (from the melaluca tree) is another popular oil known for its antiseptic, antibacterial, and antifungal properties. Some essential oils formulated specifically for animals treat skin irritation and repel ticks and fleas.

TIPS AND TAILS

Investigate essential oils carefully because many are safe for people but not for dogs. Also, some oils that are safe for dogs are harmful for use on cats.

Pheromones: As mentioned earlier, pheromones are naturally produced chemicals dogs can sense in other animals, usually of the same species. Synthetic dog appeasing pheromones (DAPs), similar to the pheromones a mother dog releases to calm her newborn puppies, are recommended for fearful or anxious dogs or dogs with aggression issues. DAPs are widely available as sprays, misters, or collars.

NUTRITION

Dog food can influence your puppy's behavior, as mentioned earlier in this chapter, so it's important you know what you're feeding your Lab and serve him the best food possible.

The Links Between Food and Behavior

Puppies who are fed diets high in cereal-grain carbohydrates sometimes have signs of hyperactivity, are unable to concentrate, don't retain what they've been taught, and just can't seem to hold still. Although a teenage Lab certainly exhibits all these symptoms regardless of what you feed him, you might see a noticeable improvement in his behavior simply by changing his food.

Protein contributes to the *serotonin* levels in your dog's body. Just like in people, serotonin affects his mood, sensitivity, and sleep cycle. Serotonin is produced by tryptophan, an amino acid often found in proteins, like meat, that makes you sleepy after you eat a big turkey dinner on Thanksgiving. If too many carbohydrates replace the protein in his diet, it can cause a shortage of serotonin in his body, which results in hyperactivity, aggression, and restless sleep.

The types of carbohydrates in his food also play a role in his behavior. Carbs with a high *glycemic index* raise his blood sugar rapidly and cause a "sugar high," a sudden increase in energy followed by a dramatic letdown and sleepiness. Rice and corn are two carbohydrates with a high glycemic index, and both are common dog food ingredients because they're inexpensive.

DOG TALK

Serotonin is a neurotransmitter involved in the transmission of impulses between nerve cells. It's found in the brain, blood platelets, and intestinal tract. The **glycemic index** is a scale that measures the speed at which the body converts carbohydrates into sugars.

Carbohydrates with a lower glycemic index digest slowly and are easier to digest. This provides a balanced blood sugar level, which evens out your dog's behavior. Oatmeal, apples, barley, and beans are all low–glycemic index foods.

The Debate Over Foods

You want to give your puppy the best care possible, and feeding a quality food is part of that mission. But it's not easy to know if you're feeding the right food. The choices are endless, and marketing claims and pretty packaging don't always tell the entire story.

If you've chosen to feed your Lab commercially made dog food, which is how most people feed their dogs, it's important that you educate yourself about the food yet be skeptical. Don't believe everything you hear or read. Many passionate people fervently believe they know how your dog should be fed. However, most aren't scientists and might not have facts to back up their claims. Consider the source, and make your own decision.

Until the early twentieth century, dogs were fed table scraps or horsemeat from the local butcher. The first canned dog food, Ken-L Ration, was introduced in the 1920s, yet quality wasn't much of an issue in these early time-saving and convenient foods, and pet food companies didn't invest in much research. Easily available, inexpensive ingredients—like wheat and surplus horse and mule meat—were the basis of most dog foods. Things soon changed as horses became scarcer and cars filled the roads. During World War II, tin was scarce, so canned dog foods were less available. By the 1950s, kibble was on the market. Convenient and sold as "better than table scraps," it soon took over the pet food industry.

Today's dog food manufacturers spend millions of dollars researching ingredients as well as canine health. They've developed unique protein sources like duck and lamb plus veterinary diets that address particular health problems such as allergies and kidney disease.

Modern manufacturing methods are a mixed blessing. Although you get a food with quality ingredients, the process used to make that food destroys some of the nutrients. Most foods today are cooked under pressure at such a high temperature that it kills some minerals, enzymes, and vitamins. Then the manufacturer has to add ingredients like fat and other nutrients back to the food, along with preservatives to prevent rancidity. Often synthetic chemicals, artificial flavors, and coloring are used, which are harder for your dog to digest.

Cost is a huge factor in dog food manufacturing. Some companies use less-expensive ingredients like cereal grains, by-products, and meat that aren't fit for human consumption. Leftover ingredients from processing human foods, from slaughterhouses, or imported from overseas where countries have less-stringent regulations are also sometimes included.

Although there had been dog food recalls over the years, the 2007 recalls involving Menu Foods brought pet food safety to the public's attention. At that time, the FDA forced a recall of more than 100 different brand-name products. More than 6,000 pets became ill, and more than 3,000 died because wheat gluten imported from China was contaminated with melamine. Soon after, contaminated corn and rice gluten were also discovered.

TIPS AND TAILS
Since 2007, recalls have affected many brands of pet food—dry, wet, and treats. The FDA maintains a database of all recalls at fda.gov, where you can search for dog food recalls to find a complete list sorted by brand name.

Commercial food manufacturers aren't trying to kill our pets with tainted ingredients. Although not all food is made with high-quality ingredients, remember that dog foods must reach minimum nutritional standards set by the Association of American Feed Control Officials (AAFCO) and other federal and state agencies. Price is one factor you can look at, but the quality of the ingredients is the key factor.

Grocery store and generic (private-label) brands are usually the least expensive and include grains and by-products as their main protein sources. Artificial colors, flavors, and preservatives are often used, too. Many dogs are just fine on these foods, but some develop skin or digestive issues.

Premium foods contain a wide variety of ingredients, and some are better than others. They might still contain synthetic preservatives or other chemicals, and the price is higher. Most of these foods are found in pet supply or feed stores.

Super-premium foods fall into this category because they're usually made with the best ingredients. You might still find some artificial additives, but on the whole, these brands strive to use healthy ingredients. Many varieties and mixtures of ingredients are available in this category.

Natural foods cannot claim to be natural if any synthetic chemicals or additives are used during processing. The FDA doesn't regulate the use of the word *natural* but states: "natural can be construed as equivalent to a lack of artificial flavors, artificial colors, or artificial preservatives in the product." AAFCO regulates the use of the term, but its regulations allow a lot of leeway. If a label says, for instance, "Natural, with added vitamins," the vitamins could be synthetic.

Organic foods earn this designation based on the way the plant and animal ingredients are raised. Although the U.S. Department of Agriculture doesn't specifically certify organic dog food at this time, most companies follow the guidelines for human organic foods. To be labeled organic, the food must contain at least 95 percent organic ingredients. The other 5 percent must consist of approved ingredients. Organic foods must be raised with no fertilizers, pesticides, growth hormones, antibiotics, or genetically modified sources.

HAPPY PUPPY

Feed your Lab twice a day. A dog who eats just once a day can suffer from low blood sugar and hunger, which can contribute to stress, irritability, and aggression.

With all these choices and factors to consider, choose a food based on your budget and your dog's overall health.

GROOMING

In addition to your regular grooming routine, which includes brushing his coat, cleaning his teeth, and trimming his toenails, pay attention to your dog's seasonal grooming needs this month. It's easy to forget that your heavy-duty Labrador needs extra TLC during different times of the year, so let's take a look at what he needs each season.

Spring Grooming Needs

Spring is the heavy shedding season for Labs. You might need to brush him every day to keep his fur from taking over your house.

After outings in spring and summer, check your Lab puppy carefully for foxtails, especially if he's been in unmown grassy areas. One blade of grass lets loose hundreds of tiny barbed seedlings, and dried foxtails are the most dangerous because they're sharp and can easily penetrate the skin. Foxtails are so small they're often hard to see, and unfortunately, shorthaired dogs like Labs seem to get just as many as longhaired dogs do. The best prevention is to inspect your dog's entire body every day, including his ears, his rear end, between his toes, in the folds around his face, and his armpits. A foxtail can penetrate his skin easily and migrate into his bloodstream, causing an abscess.

If your Lab puppy suddenly develops an explosive sneeze, suspect a foxtail or other foreign body in his nasal passage. He also might rub or paw at his nose, have a nasal discharge, or get a nosebleed. During heavy exercise, the vocal folds that protect your dog's windpipe won't close completely when he exhales, which increases the chances he could inhale foxtails or other foreign bodies. An inhaled foxtail can lodge in his lungs and cause serious illness. Schedule a vet visit to have the foxtail removed before it causes serious problems.

If your dog has seasonal allergies, he might show signs during the spring when plants and grasses are in bloom. Rinsing him off with cool or distilled water can ease his irritation. His eyes are vulnerable to seasonal pollens and debris, too.

If you see a discharge from his eye, or if it appears excessively watery, inspect it to be sure he doesn't have something under his eyelid. A bit of grass can severely irritate his eye, scratch his cornea, or cause other eye injuries. An affected dog will rub at his eye, blink, or squint continuously. You might be able to remove the offending matter by pulling out his lower eyelid and sweeping it with your finger or a wet cotton swab. Be careful not to scratch his eye as you work.

You also can use an eye rinse or artificial tears (saline solution) to wash out your puppy's eye to remove small irritants. This washes the surface of his eye as well as the surrounding tissue. Also wipe the skin around his eye with a towel to remove any discharge. If his eye is still irritated, use a cool, wet compress on it. (If both eyes are irritated, apply the compress on one eye at at time.) If this doesn't clear up the problem, have your vet examine him to rule out an injury. Eye irritation also could be a symptom of allergies, and your vet can help you determine what the problem is.

TIPS AND TAILS

Your vet may prescribe an antibiotic ointment to heal your puppy's injured eye. To administer the ointment, pull down on your puppy's lower eyelid and apply the ointment on the inner surface of his eyelid, not on his eyeball. Rub his eyelid gently over his eye to spread the medication.

Fleas and ticks are coming out about now, too, so if you discontinued preventatives during the winter, restart them now.

Summer Grooming Needs

Your Lab is probably quite active during summer months, so he'll need more baths or rinsings to keep him clean and smelling nice. Always rinse him off after he swims in a pool, ocean, or lake. Chlorine and salt water are both extremely drying to his coat, and fresh water carries bacteria and parasites that can make him sick.

During his weekly grooming sessions, check your Lab's mouth to be sure no bits of sticks, seeds, or other debris are stuck between his teeth or lodged in his mouth.

A dog's fur usually protects him from direct skin contact with poison oak or poison ivy, two summertime hazards. Still, learn what these plants look like, and keep your Lab away from them because the oil in the leaves and branches causes an allergic reaction. If he runs through the woods and gets it on his coat and you touch him later, you can be infected, too. Wear gloves and thoroughly bathe your puppy if you think he's been exposed.

If he does get the oil on his skin, he could get an itchy rash just like you would. Especially vulnerable are areas where his hair isn't as thick, such as his tummy, inner legs, and muzzle. If he ingests some of the plant, he can suffer from vomiting or diarrhea, or his airway could swell. If this happens, take him to the vet immediately.

HAPPY PUPPY

Your Lab might love riding with his head out the car window, but that's not a safe idea. With his head outside the safety of the car, he's at increased risk for injury from flying debris. His eyes are especially susceptible.

Fall Grooming Needs

Your Labs sheds his summer coat in the fall and grows in his heavier winter coat, so he'll need extra brushing for several weeks during this time to remove the loose hair. His coat will pick up more debris during the fall, too, like fallen leaves and dead flowers. You're lucky you have a Lab; these bits and pieces brush off their shorter hair easily.

Fall outings also mean he'll track in mud and dirt. It's easier to brush out of his coat when he's dry, if you can stand to wait. You can remove what doesn't easily brush out with a dry shampoo.

Winter Grooming Needs

If you live where the white stuff falls, your Lab will love romping in the snow. Clean his feet after these chilly outings to remove ice from between his toes and road salt from his paw pads. Don't leave your Lab wet, especially if he's gotten soaked to the skin. Dry him well with towels, and use a hair dryer to finish the job. Set the dryer on low so you don't burn his skin.

Your Lab might get a dry coat from being in a heated house all day. Regular brushing helps distribute the oils in his skin and coat, and a humidifier could ease his dry skin. You also could add 1 teaspoon flaxseed oil to his food. This nutritious oil helps keep his coat healthy.

SOCIAL SKILLS

Your puppy doesn't look so much like a puppy anymore. Strangers often don't react to an adult dog like they do a puppy, so your Lab needs to learn how to interact with people differently now that he's growing up. Pay attention to how other people greet your dog, and ensure his safety and theirs.

When People Don't Like Your Dog

How could anyone not love a Lab? Yellows and chocolates are usually recognized immediately, but black dogs have a public relations problem. It even has a name: black dog syndrome. Shelter workers across the country will tell you they have a much harder time placing black dogs, especially large dogs, because people are afraid of them. Movies portraying black dogs like Dobermans and Rottweilers as aggressive monsters are no help.

Many people won't recognize that your dog is a Lab, especially if he's a heavy-boned dog with a larger, blocky head. They'll ask you if he's a Mastiff or Pit Bull. Reassure them he's a Lab, and he's not aggressive. You can help alleviate their fears by putting a bright pink collar on your female or adding a flower to her leash. For a male, tie a bright bandanna around his neck, use a fun cartoon-style collar, or even have him wear a bright cape. You'll break down barriers just by having a friendly looking dog.

TIPS AND TAILS

Some people are afraid of dogs of any color, especially big dogs. A lunging, barking Lab isn't a good canine ambassador. Help put others at ease by having a well-behaved and polite Lab when he's out in public.

Respect the feelings of others, and don't force your dog on anyone. If someone appears afraid, don't try to talk her out of it; you don't know her history or her reasons. Instead, avoid her and keep your dog at a distance. Let her approach you when and if she chooses to do so.

Meeting New People

So many people, especially children, want to rush up and pet or hug dogs, whether they know the dog or not. Protect your Lab from their ill-informed enthusiasm by introducing him to new people so both parties are comfortable—because even the nicest dog likes to take his time to get acquainted. Shield your pup from the onslaught and say, "Let me introduce you" to those who want to meet your Labrador Retriever.

Always allow your dog to approach the person rather than the other way around. A large human looming over a dog is scary. (Remember the socialization process in Months 1 and 2 and 3?) Think of how you'd feel if someone much bigger than you got in your personal space. You'd probably immediately back up until you were comfortable.

A dog interprets someone coming straight at him as confrontational and someone looking straight into his eyes and holding his gaze as challenging him. Your Lab might even see it as an attack on you and try to protect you. This is all very noble, but it's still inconvenient if he defends you from the wrong person.

You might find that your Lab purposely stands between you and the person you're talking to. He's being protective of you, and you need to alleviate his fears. If you stand face to face with a person, he might see it as a threat, so walk side by side so your dog understands you're friends.

A person meeting a new dog should never put her face right in the dog's face—which is exactly what a child does when she hugs a dog. As she throws her arms around your dog, he'll feel trapped and unable to leave. Most Labs love the attention and wiggle and kiss their new friend right back, but why take a chance? He might someday decide he doesn't care for the stranger who's smothering him with affection. Or when he doesn't feel well, or the person steps on his toes, pulls his sore ear, or otherwise accidentally hurts him, he might not remember his manners when responding.

When you meet someone who isn't comfortable with the attention of an overly assertive dog, have her stand sideways to your dog, which makes her seem smaller and less threatening, and tell her not to make eye contact. To encourage a shy dog to approach someone, have the person crouch on the ground while still facing sideways.

Invite new people to scratch your Lab's chest rather than pat him on the head. Patting is annoying, and stroking is much more pleasant for your pup. And a hand coming at your dog from below is less threatening than a hand approaching his face.

Every outing is an opportunity to practice your Lab's social skills. Continue to incorporate obedience commands into your walks so he'll respond to you when he has the chance to show off for someone new.

Out and About in Nature

A well-socialized city dog might be terrified during his first hike in the woods, or he might love it. The safest way to hike is with your Lab puppy on leash until he knows his way around the area and you're sure no predators are nearby. Wild animals move silently in their natural environment, and you might never realize they're close. Your dog can sense them, though. Snakes, bears, crocodiles, mountain lions, poisonous toads, and even raccoons can seriously hurt you or your Lab. If he appears anxious or reluctant to go on, listen to him and turn back.

Many parks require that dogs be kept on leash to protect both you and the wildlife. Early in the morning, the scent from all the nocturnal creatures who were out and about the night before will be heavy, and your dog will love absorbing all the new smells … until he encounters a deer. He might react fearfully and bark, or he might get excited and chase. Either way, if he takes off running, he could easily get lost. Always keep him on leash until you're sure he's well-enough trained to stay with you.

If he's never seen one, an encounter with something as harmless as a tree stump can cause your dog to approach cautiously until he's familiar with his surroundings. Teach him to climb over logs and cross streams, and accustom him to carrying a backpack. Soon he'll be an eager companion for days outdoors.

BEHAVIOR

As your teenager develops, he'll undoubtedly test your patience and misbehave. If you continue to work to establish a good relationship with your Labrador and pair that with calm and consistent leadership and discipline (not necessarily punishment), your Lab will trust you and look to you for cues on how to behave.

How Adult Dogs Show Leadership

Adult dogs earn a puppy's respect and compliance by using gentle but firm discipline. They chastise unruly puppies with just enough aggression to make their point, and no more. A mother plunks a paw on a pup to stop him from harassing her, puts her mouth over the puppy's muzzle, or gets up and leaves when a puppy bites on her teats too hard. A puppy who oversteps his bounds with other adult dogs receives a snap and a roar that sends him packing. The adult settles back into her nap, and the pup minds his manners from then on.

When a dog rolls another dog over or pins him to the ground, she's either playing or putting a pushy offender in his place. A submissive dog rolls over voluntarily and shows his tummy to appease the aggressor; he isn't forced. That's usually the end of the discussion. Pinning a dog to the ground and holding him there or grabbing his neck is likely to start a fight.

We'd do well to follow the example of our canine friends. Discipline misbehavior with the minimum amount of force needed to stop the behavior, and no more.

Is *Dominance* a Dirty Word?

Dog behavior is often compared to that of wolves in a pack. The example given is usually one of a dominant wolf who rules the pack and forces the others to submit to him in order to retain his position. In recent years, however, wolf-pack theory, especially as it relates to dogs, has been disproßved. The concept of an alpha wolf who is *dominant*, with the rest of the pack deferring to him, was based on observation of unrelated wolves living in captivity. These wolves were thrown together in an artificial situation and had to establish a social order of some sort to get along.

In the wild, wolves live in family groups with a dynamic entirely different from that of captive wolves. Their relationship is one of cooperation and respect, not aggression and violence. A breeding pair of wolves leads the pack, and youngsters are born, grow, and leave the pack to form their own family units. Oftentimes the pack includes a very young litter of infants and older adolescents who haven't struck out on their own yet. Leadership shifts among members of the pack all the time, depending on what they're doing. The females are in charge when it comes to caring for the pups, and the males are in charge when it's time to forage for food.

Dominance has become a controversial term in dog training and behavior, and experts debate the meaning and how it applies to our relationship with our pets. You might have been told you have an "alpha," or dominant, dog so you must be the dominant one or he'll take over the household and become aggressive. You might think you have a problem that can't be fixed. Not necessarily. What you probably have is a silly adolescent Lab.

Being a Kind and Fair Leader

Rather than think of yourself as having to be dominant over your dog, think of yourself as his leader, much like parents act toward their children. A parent leads the family and provides resources: food, clothes, money, and shelter. The child looks to her parents for care, education, and protection, and he respects their authority. That's really what we do for our dogs, too.

What is a leader, and why does your dog need one? A good leader is respected. His followers listen to him and go along with his example. A leader sets limits, establishes rules, and enforces them consistently and fairly. When your leadership is well established, your dog feels secure and happy because he knows what's expected of him. Your puppy has had rules since he was in the litter with his mother and siblings, and he learned what he could and couldn't do.

A dog without a leader feels he has to make decisions for both of you, and his will be doggy decisions, not necessarily what you'd choose. Your Lab puppy needs you to step in when you see him taking over a situation. This reassures him that you'll protect him and he doesn't have to respond to every little thing.

Dogs thrive on consistency. Your Lab learns how to earn what he wants through good behavior. You probably aren't thinking about a being a leader all day, but your dog is watching you 24/7, taking mental notes. What do changes in your behavior mean for him? Should he test the boundaries to see if the rules have changed? What should he do?

You love your dog, and it's tempting to spoil him, or at least be lenient when he's misbehaving. After all, he's still a puppy. But spoiled dogs are like spoiled children; they want more and more. The more you cater to your dog, the more he'll demand to be petted, fed, entertained constantly, etc. And he'll throw a tantrum or act out when he doesn't get his way.

Leaders love their dogs. They aren't overly harsh or dominant. Being a leader doesn't mean you can't pet your Lab or hug him. When you have a problem with a rude, hyper, or misbehaving dog, that's when you have to tighten the rules and reestablish your authority. Leadership and respect are earned, not a gift.

TIPS AND TAILS

Your household is not a dictatorship. Every member of the family should be a leader in your Lab's eyes, and he should respect the children as well as Mom and Dad. He'll quickly learn who he can manipulate, so avoid conflict by having a family agreement that everyone enforces the rules the same way.

Think of a reestablishing your leadership program as "no free lunch"—a concept introduced by canine behaviorist William E. Campbell decades ago to help owners deal with doggy dictators. Dole out your attention and resources. If he sticks his head under your hand to be petted, ask him to sit first. When he wants to come indoors, have him do a down. Before you put down his food dish, have him perform a trick. Ask for something meaningful so he has to make some effort to respond. Sometimes a sit is just too easy and he'll impatiently offer 20 sits in a row just to say "Get *on* with it already!" Take this opportunity to sharpen his skills. Be sure his elbows touch the ground during the down or his rear stays on the floor for more than a nanosecond during the sit.

Be clear when you respond to his behavior. Say "Yes" or "No," and don't ignore him or avoid an issue. Use your body language to show him you're confident and in control. Don't beg him to comply, and don't repeat yourself. Tell him; don't ask him. Practice dozens of downs, sits, stays, leave its, and waits—all commands you've been working on and he should know. Two minutes once a day and scattered moments throughout make a big difference in how he responds to you.

Don't get angry at your Lab; it just confuses him and makes him think you're unpredictable. Any kind of aggression—hitting, yelling, grabbing, or throwing him down on the floor—is likely to be met with aggression from your dog. He sees it as protecting himself from an irrational attacker. A good leader does not throw his dog on the ground in an *alpha rollover* to prove he's dominant and that the dog must submit. How would you feel if your boss threw you against the wall when you disagreed with him? That's an exaggeration, of course, but a good example of how your Lab feels if his beloved owner is suddenly aggressive and cruel. There are better ways to earn your puppy's respect.

DOG TALK

An **alpha rollover** is a punishment that's supposed to mimic how wolves establish their dominance over each other. A person forces his dog to the ground and holds him on his side or back until the puppy "submits" and stops fighting the handler. Don't try this at home, and don't let a "trainer" do this to your dog. Trainers who years ago advocated the alpha rollover now have retracted their endorsement. If you try it, you're more likely to get bitten than earn your puppy's respect.

Dealing with a Rude Dog

Does your teenage Lab block your path as you try to walk? Does he crash through doors ahead of you? Lean on you? Charge out of his crate? Counter surf? Grab food? If so, he's rude, and he needs to know who the leader is at your house.

When your space invader crowds you, do it right back to him. Lean toward him. Don't bend over; just push slightly with your body, and he'll back off. Don't move out of his way or go around him if he blocks you. Shuffle your feet and keep moving forward in short steps to push him out of your way. Don't use your hands either. He sees hands as the human version of mouthing and playing. He understands a body block because that's what he does. Remember, he reads your body language before he hears what you say.

TIPS AND TAILS

Horse trainers have perfected the art of using their bodies to move a horse. By moving toward the horse's back hip, they can move the horse forward. By putting on pressure, or leaning forward toward the horse, they make him back up. The same type of movement works with your Labrador Retriever.

When you see a total body block coming at you full speed, do the same thing to him. Take a couple quick steps toward him, and aggressively push your hands toward him in a "Stop!" motion. This should startle him and make him veer away. You don't want to turn it into a game, so don't reward him or praise him a great deal. Just say "Good dog" and move on to another activity, like asking for a sit. When he's pestering you for attention, stand with your arms folded and ignore him. Tilt your chin up, and turn your body away.

Doorways are a big issue for dogs. Fights often start between dogs as they jostle with each other, trying to crowd through the door at the same time. Your puppy's excited to go out or in, and he doesn't want to be left behind. He's impolite and impatient, and as soon as he sees you head for the door, he leaps up and gets there before you.

Teach your Lab puppy that calm behavior gets him what he wants. As soon as he starts to rush the door, stop and walk away. When he comes back in and settles, start again. After a few tries, he'll be watching you carefully. If he runs up behind you, block his way to the door. Without saying anything, herd him back into the room with your body, not your hands or the leash. If you drag him by the leash, he's not learning anything except that you'll do the work. And don't say anything to him. He must figure out that he has to wait behind you. It's not an instant process, but eventually he'll understand.

Here's another exercise you can try with your Lab on leash. Open the door, and as he dashes out, shut the door behind him with you still on the inside holding the leash. Whoops! That isn't the result he had in mind! In a few seconds, he'll whimper or scratch at the door. He can't leave because he's still attached to you, but he's not actually with you, either. Let him in and try again. After a few tries, he'll hesitate and look at you. Praise him, walk through the door, and let him follow you. Remember that you taught your Lab to wait in Month 7. This is the perfect place to use that command.

If he charges out of his crate the second you open the door, that's the next behavior to address. Never open the crate door for a dog who's whining, scratching, or otherwise demanding to be released. Ignore him because if he sees he has your attention, he'll continue fussing much longer. Wait until he's quiet. Then, when you open the door, don't let him come crashing out. Quickly shut it in his face if he tries to charge. Do this as many times as you need to until he hangs back. Then quietly let him out and calmly go about your business.

Continuing Use of the Crate

Adolescence is the age of mischief for your puppy, and the crate is an important tool for preventing trouble during this time. Your puppy looks grown up, and he sleeps through the night without incident, so you might be tempted to leave him loose at night or during the day. Don't.

A 9-month-old Lab isn't mature enough to handle the responsibility of entertaining himself for long periods of solitude. By putting him in his crate, he'll feel secure, and he won't feel like he has to investigate every sound. When he's excited in anticipation of your return, he won't be able to act out by tearing up a pillow or blanket that smells like you. If he gets hungry, he can't raid the trash. When he realizes he can't act on his adolescent impulses, he gives up and takes a nap. He also learns self-control in the process.

TRAINING

Continue to develop your Labrador's skills this month with more advanced challenges. Because his attention span is no longer that of a little puppy, he's capable of learning more complex concepts. He can remember his new lessons much better for the same reason.

Solving Problems with Leash Walking

By 9 months old, your Lab puppy is really strong. You can't drag him or hold him back when he's distracted, and at this age, *everything* distracts him. Walking quietly at your side isn't a natural canine behavior. When you don't let him rush off every time he sees something that interests him, he's likely to mutiny and try all kinds of different maneuvers to get out of walking at your side. Solving this problem requires your full attention. This isn't the time to be pushing a baby stroller or talking on your cell phone.

First, use a 4-foot leash, or take up the slack in your 6-foot leash so he doesn't have as much length available for his antics. The clip on the leash should hang down, and the rest of the leash should form a U shape. Don't let too much length hang down, or he'll walk over it and become tangled. Hold your hands at waist level, where you'll have more control.

If you continually hold the leash tight, you're doing his thinking for him. He assumes the leash is supposed to be that way, and he doesn't have to pay attention to you because he knows right where you are. When he's on a loose leash, he makes mistakes and learns from them, and in the process, he learns self-control. When he's walking at your left side, you're tempted to pull tighter if you hold the leash in your left hand. Take your left hand off the leash, and hold it in your *right* hand at your waist.

When he balks, stands up on his rear legs, or refuses to go forward, start walking in the opposite direction. Turn around, walk right past him, and keep going. If he still doesn't follow you, walk in a circle around him. If he continues to dance around at the end of the leash, stop and work with him until he'll sit. When you start walking again, stop after just a few steps and ask him to sit again. Reward him when he does what you ask.

When your pup cuts in front of or behind you, block him with your leg, calmly turn into him, and start walking in another direction. If he runs behind you from the left, pull the leash in front of you to the right so he can't get all the way around you and then do an about-turn and walk into him. This also works if he tangles himself in the leash or wraps it around your legs.

TIPS AND TAILS

When walking your Lab, start calm and end calm. He must sit quietly while you put on the leash and walk politely out the door. If he starts acting wild, you must stay calm or his behavior will escalate. When you get home, he must sit politely while you remove the leash.

Your Lab might take the leash in his mouth because he knows you're going to give him a correction and he wants to avoid it. Have you jerked on the leash too often? Are you nagging him? The simplest solution is sometimes the best. Let him carry his bumper or other toy in his mouth while you walk. If that doesn't work, spray the leash with pepper spray or chewing repellent before your walk. Spritz a little in his mouth, too, so he recognizes the taste and smell.

If you try to jerk the leash out of his mouth, he'll quickly turn it into tug-of-war. To combat this, you might want to switch to a chain leash, which hurts his teeth when he bites it. Chain leashes are chew-proof, but they're also uncomfortable on your hands, so you might want to wear garden gloves. Horse-supply stores have chains for horse leads (called stud chains) that are 12 to 18 inches long. You can attach one to his collar and then attach the leash to it.

Does your pup bump into you as you walk? You might think he doesn't realize he's bumping into you, and sometimes he's certainly oblivious to his own body. But most of the time, he knows exactly what he's doing. Bump him back, but overexaggerate the move. Don't be subtle, either. Bump him to the left or make a hard turn or about-face to the left. Don't lean into him, or that will throw you both off balance. His motivation is similar to pulling on the leash—he keeps track of where you are, but he doesn't have to pay attention. He's also being very pushy and rude!

Your puppy might lean against you when you're standing still. Again, by doing so, he knows right where you are so he doesn't need to pay attention. He's also invading your space. Step away quickly so he loses his balance. He won't fall all the way to the ground, but he will pay closer attention to you.

Maybe you've seen other Labs dragging their people down the street, or maybe your pup has done this to you. This is the most common problem—and the toughest to fix. While you work on this, and practice sits, downs, and short stays, your walks might not take you very far from home. Do plenty of U-turns so he has to pay attention and see what you're going to do next. As you turn, talk and joke with your Lab, saying "Hey, you missed it! Where'd you go?" Make it a game. Every once in a while, when you do a sudden turn, pull out his favorite toy or treat and reward him with it.

To prevent pulling, you need to be more interesting than his surroundings. You get to decide when it's time to stop and sniff, not him. If you see something you know will make him pull, turn his attention to you and reward him before he starts pulling. If you need to, lure him with a treat right in front of his nose as you walk past the tempting distraction. You can reward him for his good behavior with "Go sniff!"

If one method isn't working for you, there are other ways to teach your dog to walk nicely. For example, stand still and don't move a muscle when he hits the end of the leash. Hold the leash at your waist, and don't pull back against him. Make no eye contact, and ignore him until he looks at you to see what you're doing. Then calmly praise him. If he immediately lunges ahead, stop again.

Or if he's pulling ahead, stop and back up slowly. Instead of reaching his goal, he's moving farther away. When he stops pulling, you can start walking forward again.

HAPPY PUPPY

If your wild child just can't settle down for a walk, take the edge off his energy by playing a game of fetch out before you set out. A walk by itself doesn't provide adequate exercise for a young, energetic Labrador. He'll love both the game and the walk, and you'll benefit from a slightly worn-out pup.

If you're using a no-pull harness or a prong collar, you and your Lab might become dependent on these tools. Practice with a trainer so you both can learn to walk without them. If you have to use severe equipment to control your Lab, you'll never get to the point where you can let him off the leash because he isn't listening to you.

Teaching "Watch Me"

When your Lab is distracted, the "Watch me" command helps him focus on you. Labs don't take much of anything seriously, so this is an entertaining way for him to learn to pay attention. You can teach this command in several ways.

Place treats or kibble in both of your hands, let your dog see them, and then hold your arms out sideways at shoulder level. He'll probably sit in front of you or leap at your hands to get the goodies. Wait him out. When he stops focusing on the goodies and looks at you, praise him and deliver a treat immediately. After a few tries, he'll be staring at your face to get those treats, ignoring your hands completely. Now you can use the words "Watch me" just before he makes eye contact and then praise him for looking at you.

You also could hold a treat right in front of his eyes, bring it up to your face, and say "Watch me." When his eyes shift from the treat to your eyes, praise him and give him the treat. If he looks away before you can give him the treat, don't give it to him. He only gets a treat when he maintains eye contact. Do this just a few times and then quit. You don't want him to fill up on treats or get bored.

When he's paying attention, back up while moving the treat to your nose. This helps him focus on you while you're moving. Then you can add zigzags, circles, and other variations.

You also can teach him to watch while he's sitting at your side so he doesn't have to swing in front of you. Then he'll know how to keep his eyes on you when you're out on a walk and you ask for his attention.

Teaching "Stand" and "Stand-Stay"

When your veterinarian is examining your Lab, wouldn't it be nice if your dog would stand quietly while being handled? Beginning obedience competition requires a stand for exam exercise, where your dog must stand still while the judge runs her hands over him. Advanced competition requires a moving stand, where the dog stops while walking and remains in a stand-stay as you continue moving forward.

To teach your Lab to stand, kneel facing his side while he's sitting. Tweak his skin where his rear leg meets his belly, and lightly poke him up into a standing position while saying "Stand." He'll quickly learn to stand when you touch that spot.

You also can lure your dog from a sit into a stand. Stand facing him as he sits. Take one step back while holding a treat just out of reach, putting pressure on the leash and telling him to stand. When he knows the command, turn the motion of luring him with a treat into a hand signal.

YOU AND YOUR PUPPY

Earlier in this chapter, you learned about your Lab's incredible nose and talent for scentwork. In this section, you learn how to use that talent by developing his brainpower and putting those scenting skills to good use—all while having some fun together.

Challenging Your Lab's Mind

Scientists have shown that dogs can learn up to 300 words. With that potential, your Lab's brain is full of opportunity. Think about what a hunting dog is capable of doing: marking the fall of three different birds, remembering where he saw them, figuring out how to pick them up in the order they fell, and returning the birds to his master. Assistance dogs must learn to turn on lights, pick up keys, alert their owners to the doorbell, and perform many more specialized skills. Future service dogs already know at least 30 commands by the time they leave their puppy-raiser to go into training. Your Lab is capable of great things and, like a child, he must practice using his brain to develop these skills.

Challenge your Lab with puzzle games, and he'll figure out how to slide open a compartment to find a treat. Teach him the names of different objects during scenting and retrieving games as well as the names of specific locations in the house. Surely he recognizes the words *walk* and *dinner* by now. Teach him to go to his bed or crate, to ring a bell hanging from a doorknob to go outside, or to fetch the morning paper.

Challenging Your Lab's Nose

You might not be interested in, or ready for, competitive sports, but there are many other ways you can have fun with a young Lab.

Nosework: An activity you can enjoy together at home, out in public, or in classes and workshops, nosework is a way for you both to learn search dog skills in a fun, stress-free environment. You don't need a lot of equipment or training; all you need is a motivated puppy and his favorite reward, whether it's food or a toy. The goal of nosework is pure fun.

Nosework starts out easy, with your Lab searching for his toy that's hidden under or in one of a group of cardboard boxes. The challenges get progressively harder as your dog builds his skills and learns the game.

If you're interested, you can check out training workshops and trials where your dog can earn nosework titles while searching for a specific scent such as birch. The first step is an odor recognition test (ORT), during which he demonstrates he knows how to search for a scent. Then your Lab can earn titles beginning with Nosework 1 (NW1), where he identifies one target odor, up to NW3, where he identifies three target odors under increasingly difficult conditions. Dogs can continue to get elite titles for multiple qualifying rounds as well as titles for identifying different elements like anise and clove. For more information, visit the National Association of Canine Scent Work's website at nacsw.net.

HAPPY PUPPY

Nosework, tracking, and barn hunts are sports your Labrador Retriever can begin as young as 6 or 7 months old. He's too young to do a lot of strenuous jumping or running at this age, so scentwork is a perfect outlet for his energy. He gets to use his mind, build his confidence, and spend time with you, and you learn to read his subtle communication signals and recognize when he realizes he's on the scent. If you decide to move on to search-and-rescue work, this is a great way to get started.

Tracking: Tracking was one of the first performance events introduced by the American Kennel Club (AKC), back in 1936. Originally part of what were called Obedience Test Field Trials, tracking became a separate event in 1947. Today's rules remain similar to the original tests: your Lab demonstrates his scenting ability by following human scent and finding "lost" articles, such as gloves, dropped by the tracklayer along the way. The handler (you) has no idea where the track goes, so it's completely up to your dog to find and follow the trail.

Before your Lab participates in an actual test, he must earn a certification to compete. He completes a basic Tracking Dog (TD) track while being observed by an AKC judge. If he completes it successfully, he's eligible to compete in official AKC tracking competitions. Unlike the other canine sports that require several outings and qualifying scores, a dog earns his AKC title after one successful track. The levels are

Tracking Dog (TD), Tracking Dog Excellent (TDX), and Variable Surface Tracking (VST).

For a TD, the dog must follow a track in an open field that's 30 minutes to 2 hours old and 440 to 500 yards long. A flag marks the beginning of the track, and a second flag marks direction of the first leg. The track includes three to five legs, or changes in direction. At the beginning of the test, the dog is presented with an article such as a piece of cloth containing the scent he's supposed to track. At the end of the test, the dog finds an additional article (a glove or wallet) that was left there when the tracklayer laid the track.

When he moves up to TDX level, your Lab must follow a longer and older track: 800 to 1,000 yards long and 3 to 5 hours old. A TDX test includes five to seven changes of direction and two crosstracks made by humans. No flag indicates the direction of the first leg of the track, and four articles are placed throughout: one at the starting flag, one at the end, and two more along the track itself. A TD is conducted on an open field, but a TDX might include natural and manmade obstacles along the route, such as gullies, plowed land, woods, vegetation, streams, fences, bridges, or lightly traveled roads.

In the VST, dogs face a much more difficult challenge. The track is 600 to 800 yards long and presents a varied tracking environment. The dog trails a scent 3 to 5 hours old in an urban setting rather than in the wilderness over at least three types of surfaces, such as concrete, asphalt, gravel, sand, or mulch. Tracks can be laid along the sides of buildings and fences, through buildings with two or more openings, breezeways, shelters, or roofed parking garages. There are no obstacles, as on a TDX track, and a VST track includes four articles along the way—one each of leather, plastic (rigid or semirigid), metal, and fabric.

A dog who has earned all three titles becomes a Champion Tracker (CT).

The AKC also offers an optional tracking title, the Tracking Dog Urban (TDU), in which the track is plotted on surfaces such as roads, pavement, and parking lots. This test is less difficult than the VST in that the track is shorter (400 to 500 yards) and only aged $1\frac{1}{2}$ to 2 hours. The TDU does not count toward the Champion Tracker title.

TIPS AND TAILS

You can get started in tracking by taking classes offered by local obedience clubs. Your breeder may know of a tracking group in your area, and the AKC website also lists tracking clubs by state.

Search and rescue: Labrador Retrievers make excellent search-and-rescue dogs, can work with professionals as arson or drug dogs, and can serve in many other capacities. If you've enjoyed tracking and want to volunteer with your dog, this is an excellent way to give back to your community. Rescue teams work with law enforcement agencies and must be available to join a search at a moment's notice, day or night. Search dogs must be able to concentrate on a single scent that might be days old while blocking out distractions such as traffic, crowds, food, and other animals.

To qualify, you and your Lab must undergo extensive training, and you must be certified in various skills such as CPR, canine and human first aid, radio communication, map reading, and crime scene preservation. You can participate in urban and wilderness searches or human remains searches or serve as a first responder in case of a national disaster. The National Association for Search and Rescue offers more information on how you can get involved at nasar.org.

Barn hunts: Barn hunts are an exciting dog sport for all breeds, not just terriers. Both the Barn Hunt Association and United Kennel Club offer barn hunt titles to all breeds. (The AKC recognizes titles but doesn't offer barn hunt.)

A barn hunt tests the hunting and teamwork of dog and handler. The dog follows a scent through a maze of straw bales to find a rat (who's safe in a protected, aerated tube) at the end within a set amount of time. Dogs who complete the challenge are awarded a leg toward their title. Dogs can start by taking the Barn Hunt Instinct Test (RATI). Judged on a pass/fail basis, the dog has 1 minute to get to three tubes laid out side by side and to correctly identify the one tube containing the rat.

For the Novice Barn Hunt (RATN), the dog must qualify at three different hunts. In each, the dog must enter an official tunnel, climb over bales of hay, and indicate the correct tube containing the rat, all within 2 minutes. Besides earning a qualifying leg toward a title, first through fourth place ribbons are awarded based on the fastest times.

For the Open Barn Hunt (RATO), the time increases to 2 minutes, 30 seconds; the tunnels are more complicated; and there are two rats to find.

At each level the difficulty increases, and your Labrador Retriever can earn additional titles: Novice Barn Hunt (RATN), Open Barn Hunt (RATO), Senior Barn Hunt (RATS), Master Barn Hunt (RATM), Barn Hunt Champion (RATCh), and Master Champion (RATChX). To learn more about barn hunts, visit the Barn Hunt Association at barnhunt.com.

	SOCIAL	BEHAVIOR	TRAINING	PHYSICAL	HEALTH
MONTH 1			Littermates and mother teach appropriate canine behavior	Rapid growth	
MONTH 2	Breeder starts socialization				
MONTH 3	Socialization at home with new owner and other pets	Fear-imprint period	Begin house- and crate training		1st DHPP vaccine
MONTH 4		Teething begins—heavy chewing period	Enroll in puppy class		2nd DHPP vaccine
MONTH 5	Socialization in public		Ready for basic commands	Switch to adult food	3rd DHPP and rabies vaccines
MONTH 6					
MONTH 7		Adult teeth are in—chewing continues	Enroll in basic obedience class	Moderate growth	Sexual maturity
MONTH 8					
MONTH 9			Ready for more advanced training		
MONTH 10					
MONTH 11				Slow growth—reaches adult size	
MONTH 12 AND BEYOND					Annual vaccinations and checkup

MONTH
10

In Transition

Although your Lab isn't quite full size between 9 and 10 months old, at this age, you can get a better idea of what she'll look like as an adult. It's hard to realize she's still a puppy, but she hasn't lost her sense of fun and teenage mischief. As she participates in more activities, she's prone to injuries, so we introduce some basic first aid in this chapter.

You should be able to control her exuberance better now as she learns more advanced obedience skills and starts to listen to you more consistently. Labs aren't pushovers, though, so in this chapter, we continue to work on discipline and preparation for off-leash privileges.

At this age, she can start preparing for her Canine Good Citizen certificate, so we share information on that and also take a look at some activities your Lab and your children can participate in together.

PHYSICAL DEVELOPMENT

Variation exists from dog to dog, but there are reasons why Labrador Retrievers look the way they do. The breed has been developed over 150 years to produce the characteristics we see today in our own beloved puppies. The originators of the breed put a lot of thought into what would, in their minds, make the perfect retrieving gundog.

Looking at the Breed Standard

Breed standards are written descriptions for breeders to follow that define the function, ideal structure, size, proportions, coat characteristics, and temperament for a specific breed of dog and how those features relate to the function of the breed.

In 1916, the English Labrador Retriever Club approved the first written breed standard for Labradors. The American Kennel Club (AKC) recognized the breed in 1917, but the American Labrador Retriever Club wasn't formed until 1931. The club submitted a breed standard to the AKC that same year. Minor changes have been made to the Standard over the years (the latest version has been in effect since 1994), but the basic description remains the same. As a result, when you purchase a purebred Labrador Retriever, you have a good idea of what kind of dog you're getting. After more than 25 years as the dog with the largest number of annual AKC registrations in the United States, it appears the founders of the breed did a pretty good job. As both a pet and a hunting companion, the Lab reigns supreme.

The Standard describes the features that make a Labrador Retriever look like a Labrador Retriever. If the dog had a curly tail or upright ears, she wouldn't resemble the Labrador described in the Standard. If she weighed 25 pounds or was white with black spots, she wouldn't look like a Lab, either.

TIPS AND TAILS
To read the complete Labrador Retriever breed standard, visit The Labrador Retriever Club's website at thelabradorclub.com.

At dog shows, dogs are judged on how well they conform to the Standard physically and temperamentally. There's no such thing as a perfect Lab (or a perfect dog of any breed), so the dog who wins on a particular day is the one who, in the eyes of the judge, appears the closest to the description of the ideal Labrador Retriever.

Some parts of the breed standard are purposely vague. There can be acceptable variations in the characteristics that define a Labrador Retriever, so the breed standard has to allow for those differences. Although conformation judges look at the total dog, judges might differ in their priorities regarding the importance of specific characteristics. For instance, when evaluating two good examples of Labradors and trying to decide between them, the judge might see that one moves better than the other, so the better mover gets the top award that day. Another judge might put more emphasis on head and coat character.

You might have heard breeders say "form follows function." When a judge looks at a Labrador, he evaluates features like the dog's stride, the length of her forearm, and the angle of her shoulder. Is this Labrador built to work all day over rough terrain? Will her coat protect and insulate her from cold water? Are her jaws strong enough to carry a duck or pheasant? Does she have the correct number of teeth? Is her temperament correct, meaning does she appear to be kind, outgoing, and friendly? The breed standard defines all these characteristics.

Comparing Your Puppy to the Standard

Although your Labrador hasn't yet reached maturity, you can have fun comparing her to the breed standard. Ask your puppy's breeder for a conformation evaluation. Even as puppies go through their awkward growth stages, you can learn about general conformation characteristics such as how tall your dog will be and what she'll look like when she's fully grown. Ask if you should consider entering a dog show. Puppies can be shown in AKC-approved conformation events at 6 months old.

Even if your puppy doesn't look like a show prospect, to you and your family she'll be just as beautiful as any award-winning dog. In the long run, it won't matter much to you if she's too tall or is missing a tooth. In fact, some quirks make your own pet that much more endearing.

Let's explain some of the terms used in the breed standard and what to look for in your Labrador. This is the first paragraph of the Standard:

General appearance:

> *The Labrador Retriever is a strongly built, medium-sized, short-coupled, dog possessing a sound, athletic, well-balanced conformation ...*

Short-coupled refers to the area between her last rib and the point of her hip. Why is this important? A short loin, or short coupling, provides a strong connection between the front and rear parts of her skeleton and uses less energy for movement, helping increase her stamina (an important characteristic for a retrieving gundog).

> *... The typical Labrador possesses style and quality without over refinement, and substance without lumber or cloddiness.*

When the Standard states "substance without lumber," remember that a Labrador Retriever is supposed to be an athletic dog. Although she should have strong, substantial bones that can support her frame, she shouldn't be so big and heavy that she fatigues easily.

Size:

> *The height at the withers for a dog is 22½ to 24½ inches; for a bitch is 21½ to 23½ inches. Any variance greater than ½ inch above or below these heights is a disqualification. Approximate weight of dogs and bitches in working condition: dogs 65 to 80 pounds; bitches 55 to 70 pounds.*

Although males can be 24 inches tall at the shoulders, you rarely see one that tall in the show ring. You won't often see a pet Lab who's undersize, but many grow overly tall. Labs are intended to be a medium-size dog. A 100-pound Lab who's 26 inches at the *withers* is extremely large for the breed and would be too heavy to sit comfortably in a duck hunter's boat.

DOG TALK
Withers are the highest point of a dog's shoulders, behind the neck.

Skull:

The skull should be wide; well developed but without exaggeration.

This is a good example of beauty being in the eye of the beholder. It's one of those statements open to interpretation by different judges because most experienced judges have formed a picture of what the skull should look like.

The skull and foreface should be on parallel planes and of approximately equal length. There should be a moderate stop—the brow slightly pronounced so that the skull is not absolutely in a straight line with the nose.

Using a profile picture of a Labrador head, if you draw a line from the back of the skull to the dog's nose, you'll see a definite "break" in the line at the eyes at roughly the center point. This is the Labrador's eyebrow, or stop, a transition from the back skull to the foreface. It should be a moderate angle, not a flat, continuous line, and it also shouldn't be an abrupt angle that moves the eyes forward on the skull.

Nose:

The nose should be black on black or yellow dogs, and brown on chocolates. Nose color fading to a lighter shade is not a fault.

A black nose on a yellow Labrador might fade during the winter. Some noses turn back to a deep black in summer, but some don't. Many Labs have some pink on their noses. A pink nose with no black or brown at all is a disqualification.

Teeth:

The teeth should be strong and regular with a scissors bite, the lower teeth just behind, but touching the inner side of the upper incisors.

This explains how the teeth meet in the mouth. A scissors bite is when the top teeth are in front of the bottom ones, which is correct in the Labrador. If the teeth meet evenly, this is called a level bite, and causes the teeth to wear faster as the dog ages. An underbite, where the bottom teeth are in front of the top teeth, impairs a Labrador's ability to carry game.

Ears:

> *Ears should not be large and heavy, but in proportion with the skull and reach to the inside of the eye when pulled forward.*

Labrador ears have a distinct triangular shape. Heredity plays a part in size and ear placement, and some Labradors appear to have longer, droopy ears, which can be the result of how and where the ears are located on the skull. Correct ear set keeps water out of the ears while the dog swims, an important characteristic for a retriever. If the ears are set too low, water could get in and cause ear infections.

HAPPY PUPPY

Just for fun, test your Lab's ears to see if they reach or go past the inside corner of her eyes. Make it a peek-a-boo game!

Tail:

> *It should be very thick at the base, gradually tapering toward the tip, … clothed thickly all around with the Labrador's short, dense coat, thus having that peculiar rounded appearance that has been described as the "otter" tail.*

A Labrador's "otter" tail is a unique characteristic of the breed. It's your Labrador's rudder in the water. When carried straight off the back, it's in a perfect position for swimming. The tail should be broad at the base and covered with the same thick coat as on the rest of the body but without feathering. When your Lab puppy is excited, you'll likely see a happy tail carried up, higher than her body. But when she's moving naturally, a correct Labrador tail should be carried straight off her rear.

Hindquarters:

> *Viewed from the side, the angulation of the rear legs is in balance with the front.*

When viewing a Labrador in profile, *angulation* refers to the angles of both the front and back limb bones. When viewed from the front, it refers to the angles where the shoulder bone (scapula) meets the upper arm bone (humerus), and to the bones that meet at the front point of the chest from the shoulder and elbow. If both the front and back are nicely balanced with similar angles, the dog moves gracefully and has more stamina. It takes a practiced eye and hands-on examination to recognize correct angulation.

Coat:

> *The coat is a distinctive feature of the Labrador Retriever … [It] should have a soft, weather-resistant undercoat that provides protection from water, cold and all types of ground cover.*

A Lab's thick, water-resistant coat should be heavier over the shoulders and can have a slight wave to it. The proper coat is made of coarse guard hairs and a finer, wooly textured undercoat that insulates your pup.

Temperament:

> *True Labrador Retriever temperament is as much a hallmark of the breed as the "otter" tail.*

This one sentence describes why we all love this breed so much. As wild as your dog might be when she's a teenager, the Labrador Retriever is a fabulous family dog and companion. We've never met a Lab who doesn't make us laugh at least once a day—they should have added her sense of humor to the Standard.

The Conformation Certificate Program

The Labrador Retriever Club (LRC) offers a Conformation Certificate evaluation any Labrador, even one who's spayed or neutered, may earn. It's noncompetitive, and Labs over 1 year old are eligible to be evaluated. To be considered for the certificate, your dog is judged to determine if she possesses the "basic attributes" of a Labrador Retriever. The evaluators aren't looking for a perfect dog; they just want to raise awareness and provide education on correct *breed type*. As the LRC website states:

> It is an opportunity for owners of Labrador Retrievers who are not interested and/or familiar with competitive conformation events to have their dogs evaluated and recognized as having basic Labrador Retriever conformation characteristics.

DOG TALK

Breed type refers to the qualities that define a Lab and make her different from other dog breeds, as set forth in the breed standard.

Many dogs who wouldn't win in the show ring still have correct Labrador characteristics, and the Conformation Certificate recognizes that. For example, many field trial/hunting dogs have lighter-weight coats than conformation dogs do. But they still have *correct* coats and, therefore, would pass that portion of the evaluation.

The evaluation contains nine conformation and temperament categories a judge scores from 1 to 3 points each. A dog is required to have a total score of 18 or better and demonstrate, in the judge's mind, a 65 percent likelihood of conforming to the characteristic as described in the Standard. The judge also looks at the following:

- Does the dog possess the basic attributes of a Labrador Retriever?
- Does the dog exhibit a majority of breed characteristics?
- Would the dog be excused (from the show ring) for lack of merit?
- Does the dog possess any disqualifying characteristics according to the breed standard?

General disqualifications apply, such as lameness, blindness, deafness, or change by artificial means (such as surgery to correct an eye problem). Dogs noted to possess a disqualifying fault would not receive a Conformation Certificate.

Conformation Certificate evaluations are held in conjunction with events such as hunt tests, field trials, agility or obedience trials and also during National Specialty Event Week every October. Learn more at thelabradorclub.com.

HEALTH

We covered CPR and life-threatening emergencies in Month 6. Now let's look at some other injuries and health problems your Lab might encounter and how to administer first aid or treat them.

Treating Injuries

When your Lab puppy is injured, it can be easy to panic. But your cool-headedness is important to ensure her safety. Here's what to do:

Bleeding: If a wound is deep or spurting bright red blood, apply direct pressure and take your dog to the vet immediately. This is an emergency. She could have a severed artery, which quickly causes major blood loss. Don't wash the wound because that could prevent clotting. Less-drastic wounds bleed slowly, ooze dark red blood, and stop bleeding within 5 minutes.

If possible, elevate the bleeding area above her heart to reduce blood flow. Apply direct pressure with a clean cloth, sanitary pad, nonstick gauze bandage, or paper towels. When the bleeding stops, don't remove the cloth because it could cause the bleeding to resume. If one bandage becomes soaked through, add another bandage on top of it rather than remove the first. If the bleeding doesn't stop, have a second person apply pressure just above the wound. Secure the bandage by wrapping it against your dog's body, and get her to the veterinarian.

Bleeding ear: A cut on the ear bleeds a lot, and your Lab might make it worse by shaking her head. The good news is that ear wounds usually look worse than they really are. Place a gauze bandage or small sanitary pad on either side of her ear, and apply pressure for several minutes to stop the bleeding. Without removing the bandage, fold her ear against her head and secure it by wrapping a length of gauze or panty hose over her head and ear and under her chin. Don't wrap it too tightly, or it could interfere with your Lab's breathing. You should be able to slip two fingers between the bandage and her chin.

Within 24 hours, check the wound, clean it, and apply antibiotic ointment. Be careful when doing so because ear injuries can reopen easily. Take your dog to the vet if you feel it needs more attention or may get infected.

Bleeding tail: If her tail is bleeding at the tip, your puppy might have whacked it against a wall or fence repeatedly. This is a common injury for Labs, and it can make an awful mess. Elevate her tail to minimize blood flow, and apply pressure to the underside of her tail at the base, near her anus. This is a pressure point that helps slow the bleeding.

The hardest part of treating a tail wound is keeping it bandaged so she doesn't break it open again every time she wags her tail. Clip away fur from the open wound, and wash the area with saline solution or antiseptic soap.

TIPS AND TAILS
To make saline solution, add 1 teaspoon salt to 1 quart warm water.

You want to bandage her tail, but not too tightly because you could cut off blood circulation and cause severe injury. Put one long strip of adhesive tape against each side of her tail, extending several inches below the wound and above the wound off the end of her tail. Wrap her tail and the tape with gauze, starting well below the wound and ending just past the end of her tail. Fold the tape back over the bandage, and twist the tape so the sticky side adheres to the bandage and past it, adhering to her hair, too. Sticking the tape to her hair helps anchor the bandage so it won't slide off the end of her tail. Place an elastic bandage (like VetRap) over the gauze wrapping, ensuring the wrap sticks to plenty of hair. To keep your dog from chewing off the bandage, you might have to put an Elizabethan collar on her.

If the injury is severe or isn't healing, take her to the vet. Most Labs with tail injuries end up at the vet anyway because it's so hard to keep their tails bandaged.

Bleeding paw pad: The most common foot injury in Labs is stepping on a sharp object like glass. Your puppy's paw pads contain many blood vessels, and they bleed profusely when cut.

Be sure you remove all the glass or other material from the bottom of your puppy's foot (see "Object imbedded in body," later in this section), flush her foot with running water to wash out any remaining debris, wash the area with saline solution or warm water, and dry her foot. Bandage her foot to keep dirt and debris out of the wound, using a similar technique as for bandaging a tail injury. Put one strip of adhesive tape against each side of her foot, extending several inches above and below her foot. Wrap her foot and the tape with gauze, starting at her toes and ending just above her ankle. Fold the tape over the bandage and twist it so the sticky side adheres to the bandage. Place an elastic bandage (like VetRap) over the gauze, wrapping from her toes to her ankle, tight enough to stick but not so tight that it cuts off circulation. Check after a few minutes to be sure your pup's toes aren't swollen; if they are, the bandage is too tight. Take your Lab to the vet because she might need antibiotics or further treatment.

Broken limbs: A fracture might mean one or more broken bones, usually to a leg. Suspect a broken bone if your Lab is holding her leg in an abnormal position, she appears to be in extreme pain, or she's unable to put weight on the limb.

Before you transport your Lab puppy to the vet, put her in a crate or immobilize the break with a splint. The splint must cover the joints above and below the break to safely protect the limb. If your dog struggles too much, she risks worsening the injury. In that case, forego the splint and transport her to the vet as soon as possible.

When splinting a broken limb, do not reposition the bones. Place a rolled magazine, a rolled newspaper, or a yardstick on either side of or around the limb to prevent movement. Keep the splint in place using multiple pieces of tape wrapped around the splint and leg, but don't wrap too tightly. If you can't find any splinting material, use the opposite leg to stabilize the fracture, putting a piece of cloth or other pad between her legs and wrapping them together.

If a bone is protruding from the skin, you'll need to take additional precautions. Don't move the bone, or you could cause internal damage or bleeding. Wash the area with saline solution, and cover it with a sterile nonstick gauze pad. Secure the pad with a covering of cloth or gauze, and tape it a few inches above and below the exposed bone. Immediately transport your dog to the veterinarian because a broken bone requires professional treatment.

TIPS AND TAILS

When she's hurt, you might need to muzzle your dog so she doesn't bite out of fear or pain. If you don't have a muzzle, wrap a long length of gauze (or a piece of panty hose) around her mouth and tie it behind her ears. Double the gauze for added strength. Make a loop in the center of the length of gauze, slip it over her nose, and tie a knot on the top of the muzzle. Wrap the gauze under her jaw, and tie again. Then pull the ends behind her ears and tie. Don't cover her nose, or she won't be able to breathe.

Burns: Cooking accidents or caustic chemicals can cause painful burns and permanent scars. Your dog's fur might mask the seriousness of a burn, so take her to a vet after you've performed first aid, even if the burn seems minor. First-degree burns are the least serious and usually just cause redness and pain. Second-degree burns cause blisters and swelling. Third-degree burns, the most serious, damage the skin, hair, blood vessels, and deeper tissue.

To treat a burn from fire, steam, or hot water, flush the burned area for 5 to 10 minutes with cool water. This reduces the temperature of your Lab's skin and prevents further tissue damage. Don't submerge your dog's entire body in water, or you risk sending her into shock. Cover the burned area with a nonstick bandage or torn, clean cloth. Don't use any type of material that might stick to the burn, and don't apply any ointments or creams. If the burn is near your dog's neck or head, remove her collar so it won't restrict her breathing if the skin swells. Seek immediate veterinary attention.

To administer first aid for chemical burns from products like bleach, pool chemicals, battery acid, or weed killers, first protect yourself with rubber gloves, a face mask, safety glasses, and protective clothing before you treat your dog because if she tries to shake off the chemical and you're not protected, you could be burned, too. Then restrain your dog and muzzle her so she won't try to lick off the chemical. If the burn is near her neck, remove her collar.

A chemical burn will continue to burn into the tissue long after it makes contact with her skin so flush the burned area with cool water for at least 20 minutes. If the chemical is oily, add mild dish soap to the rinse. For powder burns, attempt to brush off as much as you can before rinsing. With either kind of burn, take your dog to the vet immediately.

TIPS AND TAILS

To prevent burn injuries, keep your Lab out from underfoot when you're cooking, whether you're in the kitchen or outdoors. The smells entice her to investigate, but you might not see her when you're carrying hot pans. She also might try to stick her nose in an open oven to see what's cooking.

Electrical cord/shock: Even though you puppy-proofed your house, your teenage Lab might have found an unprotected electrical cord. If she bites it, she could get electrocuted and collapse, have a seizure, or experience other severe symptoms as a result, so consider it a life-threatening emergency. If she stops breathing, perform CPR (see Month 6), and take her to the vet immediately.

Most electrical injuries are less severe and consist of a mild burn on her lips, tongue, or mouth, for example.

If your dog is still touching the cord, put on rubber gloves and disconnect the power before you touch her, move her away from the cord with a broom or wooden chair, or trip the main circuit breaker. Avoid stepping in water, which conducts electricity.

Make your dog as calm as possible to keep her breathing normally and prevent her from going into shock. Flush burns in her mouth with cool water, and apply an ice pack to burned lips. Then take her to the veterinarian immediately. She could have internal damage that isn't immediately apparent.

Insect bites or stings: When a curious puppy approaches something buzzing that's new to her, like a bee, wasp, or hornet, the result is often a sting on her face or nose. Unless she has an allergic reaction or multiple stings, these usually aren't life-threatening.

To treat minor stings, remove the stinger as quickly as possible if it's still embedded in your Lab's skin. Pull it out with tweezers, or scrape it with a credit card (you'll squeeze less venom into the wound this way). Soothe her skin with a paste made of baking soda and water, hydrocortisone cream, aloe vera gel, or cold compresses.

TIPS AND TAILS

When you travel, carry a bottle of meat tenderizer in your first-aid kit. You can mix the tenderizer with water to make a paste to apply to bug bites or stings. (This remedy works great on people, too.)

If the sting is on or near her face and starts to swell dramatically, your puppy could be having an allergic reaction that might interfere with her breathing. Take her to the vet immediately.

Object imbedded in body: If your Lab puppy comes running up to you with a stick protruding from her side, do not pull it out. Muzzle your Lab because she's in pain and could attempt to bite you. Then wrap cloth around the base of the object without repositioning it, and tape the cloth into place to stabilize it. Keep your dog calm and as immobile as possible, and take her directly to the vet.

You can remove smaller objects like splinters, thorns, or porcupine quills with tweezers, a needle, or pliers. If a splinter is completely under her skin, sterilize the tweezers or needle before using them by dipping them in alcohol or running them through a flame. Grasp the object as close to the skin as possible, and slowly pull it out. After you remove the object, soak the area with a mixture of warm water and Epsom salt for 15 minutes. The Epsom salt, which is made of magnesium and sulfate, absorbs into the skin and reduces inflammation. Repeat daily until completely healed.

Glass or small sticks might break if you try to remove them, and you'll need to have her examined by a vet to be sure no pieces remain in the wound. If your dog has more than a few porcupine quills, she'll need to go to the vet to have them removed and her wounds thoroughly cleaned.

Fishhook in the skin: A Lab can get a fishhook imbedded in her face or lips while tasting bait or fish. If this happens, push the hook farther through the skin so the barb is exposed, cut off the barb with wire cutters, and pull out the hook the way it went into the body. If there's no exit wound, take your pup to the vet for removal. She'll probably need antibiotics to prevent infection.

TIPS AND TAILS
Removing a fishhook deserves special attention because pulling out a hook incorrectly can do a lot of damage to your puppy's skin.

Torn dewclaw or toenail: If your dog's nails grow too long, they risk being snagged and torn; her front toenails seem to be more at risk for this injury. Dewclaws are loosely attached, so her entire toe is in danger of tearing. Because the nail quick is comprised of living tissue, a torn nail can be very painful. Your dog might need to be muzzled and restrained while you treat the injury.

Stop the bleeding by applying pressure with a cloth or your finger. The dead portion of the nail might be split or torn, so trim it off if you can. Then apply styptic powder, cornstarch, or flour to help the blood clot.

If the dewclaw is injured, wash the area, dry completely, apply antibiotic ointment, and tape or wrap it against her leg to keep the wound from reopening.

Wrap her foot and take her to the vet for treatment if the tear is deep or involves the flesh on the dewclaw. She might need antibiotics to prevent infection or stitches to repair the tear. If the dewclaw is badly injured, it might need to be surgically removed.

Treating Symptoms of Illness

When you realize your puppy is not well, you can take steps to treat the problem while you evaluate how serious it is. Some issues, like diarrhea and vomiting, could be minor and respond to treatment quickly. If these conditions don't resolve, or if they accompany other troublesome symptoms, a vet will need to investigate further. Others symptoms, like seizures, might be indicators of a much more serious problem and require immediate veterinary treatment.

Diarrhea: If your puppy is vomiting at the same time she has diarrhea, she could be seriously ill. If there's blood in her stool, either fresh (bright red) or digested (dark red or black), take her to the vet immediately. Take a stool sample with you for the vet to examine.

At the first onset of diarrhea, you can give your puppy antidiarrheal medication. Check with your vet to find out what brand to use and the proper dosage. To prevent dehydration, be sure your Lab has plenty of water available. A pediatric oral electrolyte solution can replace some of the nutrients and moisture she's lost. You'll find this product in the children's section at your grocery store or pharmacy.

Also, temporarily switch her to a high-fiber or bland diet. You can purchase a prescription diet from your vet or make your own by combining cooked white rice with boneless boiled meat with the fat drained off. If the diarrhea subsides, slowly switch your puppy back to her regular food. If the diarrhea lasts longer than 48 hours, see the veterinarian for further care.

Seizure: Witnessing your Labrador have a seizure is frightening. Before a seizure, she might seem dazed or anxious. During an active seizure, she might twitch and fall over, lose control of her bowels or bladder, and not recognize you. Afterward, she may appear dazed and disoriented, or she might seem just fine. The length of the seizure can vary dramatically. A seizure lasting longer than 2 minutes is an emergency and can cause high fever or brain damage.

To protect your dog from injury during a seizure, move her away from stairs or furniture so she won't fall or hit anything. Don't disturb or restrain her during the seizure. She won't swallow her tongue, contrary to popular belief, so don't put your hand in her mouth; she could accidentally bite you. If this is your dog's first seizure, have her examined by a vet immediately. Make a note of how long the seizure lasts, the time of day, the date, and when she last ate a meal.

Possible causes of seizures in dogs include poisoning, a tumor, a bacterial infection in the brain, organ failure, diabetes, and epilepsy. If your vet can identify the cause, he might be able to treat the condition and your dog might never have another episode. The cause is often hard to identify, though, as is the case with epilepsy. Some animals need antiseizure medication for the rest of their lives.

Vomiting: When your Lab eats something yucky (as they so often do), she might vomit to get it out of her system before it makes her sick. She could have a simple gastrointestinal upset, or she might have eaten an inedible object like a toy. If she doesn't pass the object in her stool, she'll get increasingly ill. Serious infections like pancreatitis also cause vomiting. If your puppy is lethargic or has a fever, take her to the vet immediately.

Rapid dehydration is the biggest risk when your dog is vomiting over a period of hours. Withhold food, but offer small amounts of water or ice chips if she'll take them. If your Lab seems otherwise healthy, after 12 hours, reintroduce food in small amounts—about ½ cup at a time. If she continues to vomit, she might need to visit the vet for antinausea drugs and fluids.

NUTRITION

We've talked about dog food before, but it's such a vast topic, it warrants further discussion. From ingredients to nutrients to calorie count, it might seem like there are a hundred different ways to evaluate dog foods and figure out what's best for your Labrador Retriever. Try to balance out the information you gather from each source without relying too much on any single one. As always, the best way to decide if you're feeding correctly is to look at your Lab, not the label on the dog food bag.

Counting Calories

As you learned in Month 7, dog food manufacturers are required to include information about ingredients, nutrient percentages, serving sizes, etc. on the label. They aren't required to list the calorie count, but many companies do. That's how many people keep track of their own diets, so it makes sense to look at your dog's caloric requirements.

There's no one correct calorie amount your dog should consume each day. Quality of ingredients, premium or generic brands, your Lab's activity level, and her health all play a part in determining her recommended daily amount. Recommended calorie counts are based on the measurement—for example, 1 cup = 400 calories. A healthy Lab who weighs 50 pounds and maintains an average activity level needs about 1,000 to 1,400 calories a day. A 70-pound dog needs about 1,400 to 1,800 calories.

In general, most adult or large dog formulas have between 350 and 400 calories per cup. Premium brands have a higher calorie count than other foods, so you should feed less of these. "Light" or weight-loss formulas vary dramatically. Some have as little as 50 calories fewer than the regular formula, and some have more than 100 calories fewer per cup. Nutrient percentages vary, too, with some containing less fat and more fiber. (For more about treating obesity in Labrador Retrievers, see Month 12.)

You need to know the exact calorie count of the specific formula you're planning to feed. If it's not listed on the bag, call the company or visit its website to find the information you need.

Choosing Training Treats

For training sessions, most Labs are happy with bits of their regular dry food. But to really motivate your puppy, choose a high-value treat that's especially tasty to her. Look for treats with the highest meat content available and human-grade ingredients.

Dehydrated and freeze-dried treats are convenient and don't make a mess in your pocket. You should be able to cut up the treats so you can feed tiny amounts during training sessions. Remember, treats should make up no more than 5 to 10 percent of your dog's total daily calories. To keep her from gaining weight, use part of her daily food ration for training mixed in with special goodies.

HAPPY PUPPY

Your Lab needs to respond even when you don't have food, so mix up her training rewards with toys and games. The latter are sometimes more valuable to her.

GROOMING

Labs aren't dainty dogs who never get their feet muddy. In fact, your puppy probably loves nothing better than a good digging session or a roll in a pungent garbage pile. So although Labs are a wash-and-wear breed, sometimes a good rinsing just isn't enough.

Determining When Your Lab Needs a Bath

You might go more than a year before you feel like you need to do more than just rinse off your Lab. You might see a dirty spot developing on her favorite chair or couch cushion, but that could be surface dirt from her outer coat. If she's been out in the fields or swimming in a river, you might see a buildup of dirt in her coat when you separate her fur down to her skin. This is obvious even in black Labs because the brownish dirt dulls her coat.

Labs don't get doggy odor from the oils in their skin or coat like a Basset Hound will. During humid weather in the summer, more crud may stick to her coat and she might not smell as clean as usual. If she's had fleas, you definitely want to wash out all the flea dirt. (Don't be alarmed when you see the bath water run red from the blood in the flea droppings.)

Taking all this into consideration, it's really up to you whether your dog needs regular baths or not. Just be aware that bathing her too often—like more than once a month—will dry out her coat and cause problems rather than solve them. Most owners bathe their Labs once or twice a year with some thorough rinses in between.

Employing Professional Groomers and Dog Washes

You're probably thinking there's no reason anyone would ever need to take a Lab to the groomer, but people do. When your Lab is shedding snowdrifts of hair in the spring, you might consider taking her for a professional bath. Groomers have powerful dryers that blow out more hair than you can do at home. Their specialized grooming tools can remove mountains of undercoat, too. If your Lab is unruly and hard to groom, a groomer uses a table and harnesses to restrain her while he works, which might be easier—and cleaner—than you trying to wrestle your pup in the bathtub at home.

Groomers also have shampoos and conditioners that soothe her dry skin and coat. If your dog gets skunked, your groomer might be able to remove the odor with a powerful enzymatic cleaner. If your dog gets into something especially disgusting in the middle of winter and you don't want it all over your bathroom, take her to a groomer. If you don't like to or are unable to trim your dog's toenails, a groomer can do the job for you. They usually trim nails à la carte, without requiring a full bath and brush. Some groomers even offer toothbrushing.

HAPPY PUPPY
When it's bath time, also wash your Lab's bedding and clean her crate to remove fleas and odor.

Many communities have mobile dog-washing companies that come to your door and bathe your dog in their van. They supply everything, even the water. This is less time-consuming and more convenient for you—and less stressful for your Lab—than spending half a day at a grooming shop.

Do-it-yourself dog washes are another option for stress-free grooming. They supply a wide variety of shampoos, conditioners, and towels, and you have access to the facility's high-powered sprayers, raised tubs, power dryers, and grooming tables to make the job easier.

If you take your dog to the beach, check to see if a DIY dog wash is located nearby so you can clean your Lab before you take her home. If not a bath, she'll need a thorough rinsing at least.

SOCIAL SKILLS

We each have our own ideas about what makes a well-behaved dog and how we'd like our pet to act in public. As more and more laws are enacted restricting dogs' access to public places, we all have a duty to be sure our dogs aren't part of the problem, but part of the solution. To that end, the AKC has created a program to help owners reach their goals for a well-socialized and welcome canine member of the community.

The Canine Good Citizen Program

The AKC Canine Good Citizen (CGC) program was developed to encourage responsible dog ownership and acknowledge owners for their training efforts. It also recognizes dogs who have good manners at home and in the community. For families just starting out with a new puppy, the program provides a clear definition of what makes a well-behaved dog and offers goals for you to strive for when you begin training.

While learning the exercises for the CGC, you enjoy time with your Lab, exercise her mind, and forge a deeper bond. The best benefit is that a dog who has passed the CGC exam is a joy to live with.

The CGC is accepted throughout the United States (34 states now have CGC resolutions on the books) and the world as evidence that your dog is well behaved and you are a responsible owner. Carry the certificate with you when you travel to present to hotels and other public facilities. Many landlords now require it as a condition of allowing a dog in a rental home. Therapy dogs often must pass the CGC test as part of their certification for visits, and animal-control agencies might require owners and their dogs to earn a CGC certificate when issues arise with the dog's behavior in public.

Many obedience instructors use the CGC program as the basis for their classes and incorporate the test into graduation. Check with local trainers to find classes for the CGC test. The AKC website lists evaluators you can contact for more information and posts a schedule of upcoming tests in various areas.

The Canine Good Citizen Test

There are two versions of the Canine Good Citizen (CGC) test, the original CGC and the newly added Canine Good Citizen Urban (CGCU), which is formatted for city dwellers and the unique challenges their dogs face. To earn a Canine Good Citizen Certificate, your Lab must demonstrate her training and good manners during a 10-step evaluation by an AKC examiner. At the same time, you sign a pledge to be a responsible dog owner.

As you'll see from the following exercises, the test is challenging and requires practice before you both are ready. When the two of you complete the test successfully, you receive a CGC certificate from the AKC. Passing is an achievement you and your Lab should be very proud of.

The CGC test is made up of 10 challenges:

1. Your Lab accepts a friendly stranger who approaches and speaks to you. The evaluator ignores your dog while greeting you in a friendly manner, shaking hands, and engaging in conversation.

2. Your dog sits politely for petting by a stranger. She sits at your side and shows no aggression or resentment while a stranger pets her on her head and body.

3. Your dog accepts grooming and handling by a stranger and is presented in clean, healthy, and well-groomed condition. Your puppy must permit a veterinarian, groomer, or other person to groom or examine her. This also demonstrates that you provide good care for your Lab.

4. Your dog walks nicely on a leash at your side. This shows you can control your dog. She must be attentive to you and respond to your changes in direction during a left turn, a right turn, a halt, and an about-turn.

5. You can walk your dog through a crowd and keep her under control without her showing excessive shyness or resentment around strangers. Your Lab demonstrates that she's under control and polite in public places. She shouldn't jump on anyone or strain on the leash.

6. Your dog sits and downs on command and stays in place while you walk 20 feet away and return. This exercise demonstrates that your Lab has been trained and will remain in position. You first demonstrate that she'll do both a sit and a down. Next, you replace her leash with a 20-foot line and ask her to do either a sit or a down (your choice). Your puppy must stay in position until the evaluator instructs you to release her.

7. Your dog comes when called. She's still on a long line, and you walk 10 feet away, turn to face her, and call her to you.

8. Your Lab demonstrates a polite reaction to another dog while owners greet each other and walk together. Two handlers and their dogs approach each other from about 20 feet away, stop, shake hands, and speak to each other. Both then continue on another 10 feet.

9. The dog demonstrates confidence when faced with a distraction she might normally encounter, such as someone dropping a chair or rolling a cart past her. Your Lab can express interest or be startled, but she shouldn't panic, try to run away, bark, or show aggression.

10. Your Lab tolerates separation from you without becoming overanxious while someone else holds her leash. This test shows your dog can be left in someone else's care and will maintain her training and good manners. The evaluator takes hold of your dog's leash while you leave and go out of sight for 3 minutes.

If you successfully complete the test, congratulations! You have a well-trained Labrador Retriever.

The CGCU recognizes that city dogs sometimes need extra skills to be a truly canine good citizen. Here are the 10 tests your urban dog must pass:

1. Your dog exits/enters doorways with no pulling.

2. She walks through a crowd on a busy urban sidewalk.

3. She reacts appropriately to city distractions such as horns and sirens.

4. Your dog waits on leash and crosses the street under control.

5. She ignores food and food containers on the sidewalk.

6. She allows a person to approach her on the sidewalk and pet her.

7. She performs a 3-minute down-stay in the lobby of a dog-friendly building.

8. She safely negotiates stairs and elevators.

9. You can confirm she's housetrained.

10. She can enter and exit or ride in dog-friendly transportation (e.g. cars, cabs).

After she's earned her CGC certificate, the most advanced level, the AKC Community Canine (CGCA), tests her real-world skills out in the community. To pass this test, she must walk past distractions without pulling, come when called through distractions, "leave it" when passing food, and pass other exercises that demonstrate her self-control and good manners.

Think about all the work you've put into raising your Labrador puppy. You deserve recognition for the care and training you provide. The Responsible Dog Owner's Pledge represents the promise you made to your puppy when you added her to your family:

AKC CGC Responsible Dog Owner's Pledge

I understand that to truly be a Canine Good Citizen, my dog needs a responsible owner. I agree to maintain my dog's health, safety, and quality of life. By participating in the Canine Good Citizen test, I agree that ...

I will be responsible for my dog's health needs:

○ Veterinary care, including check-ups and vaccines

○ Adequate nutrition through proper diet and clean water at all times

○ Daily exercise and regular bathing and grooming

I will be responsible for my dog's safety:

○ I will properly control my dog by providing fencing where appropriate, not letting my dog run loose, and using a leash in public.

○ I will ensure that my dog has some form of identification, be it collar tags, tattoos, or microchip ID.

I will not allow my dog to infringe on the rights of others:

○ I will not allow my dog to run loose in the neighborhood.

○ I will not allow my dog to be a nuisance to others by barking while in the yard, in a hotel room, etc.

○ I will pick up and properly dispose of my dog's waste in all public areas, such as on the grounds of hotels, on sidewalks, in parks, etc.

○ I will pick up and properly dispose of my dog's waste in wilderness areas, on hiking trails, at campgrounds, and in off-leash parks.

I will be responsible for my dog's quality of life:

○ I understand that basic training is beneficial to all dogs.

○ I will give my dog attention and playtime.

○ I understand that owning a dog is a commitment in time and caring.

BEHAVIOR

Your Lab's behavior improves every day, but you'll still suffer through moments of regression, when she reminds you she's still an adolescent. As much as you want to use positive methods to train your dog, Labs can be pretty obnoxious and sometimes need a firmer hand to deal with their behavior.

Barking Barking Barking Barking Barking

Problem barking often begins during the teenage months. Your Lab goes through periods of uncertainty, and one way she expresses that concern is to bark. The more socialization she's had up to this point, the less fearful she'll be.

Barking is a natural behavior you can never entirely eliminate, but if you can get it under control now, you'll prevent her from becoming a chronic barker later, when she matures and becomes more territorial and protective.

Manage your puppy's surroundings and figure out what makes her bark so you can discourage and prevent excess barking. For example, if she barks out in the yard, limit her view. Put up a solid fence instead of chain link. Don't let her out on the upper deck where she can see the neighbor kids playing. Bring her in when kids are walking home from school. If she barks out the living room window, don't let her in the living room, or close the drapes.

TIPS AND TAILS

You want your Lab to bark occasionally. When she does, check out what she's barking at and then quiet her and redirect her to another activity. She's done her job, and now you've taken over.

Does she bark every time the doorbell rings? Think about how she sees it: you jump up and head for the door, so she does, too. She could be excited or frightened, but either way, it's a big deal in her eyes. Teach her to sit quietly when the doorbell rings or to go to her crate. (This lesson might require a helper.) Put a leash on her before you open the door, and practice her sit-to-greet. Give her a toy if you need to. After all, when she has a toy in her mouth, she can't bark!

Does she bark aggressively at the neighbor through the fence or at someone at the front door? If she does, she's most likely afraid of the person. She's too young to be overprotective (something that happens closer to 18 months old), but this type of barking can turn into an ugly habit. Have the person offer her a treat. After a few treat sessions, she'll be happy to see the person and engage in an entirely different type of barking.

Maybe you have a bossy barker. She wants in, so she barks. She knows it's close to dinnertime, so she barks. She wants to play fetch, so she drops a toy at your feet and barks. It's time to wake up, so she stands by the bed and barks. Are you seeing a pattern here?

You might inadvertently teach your dog to bark by responding to her every request. Make her earn your attention instead. Ask for a sit or a down before you give her what she wants. Down is a subordinate position, and most dogs don't bark while lying down. She might not want to lie down when she's excited and wants something, but that's all the more reason to insist on compliance. Don't reward her or let her up until she calms down; put her on a leash if you have to. Give her a 5-minute time-out in her crate if she's barking at you to do something. If bossy barking is really getting to be a problem, have her do many 1-minute down-stays throughout the day.

Another tactic is simply to ignore her barking. This is hard to do, but if you can hold out, she'll give up eventually. The barking will get worse before it gets better, though, as she gives it one last over-the-top burst of effort right before she stops. This is when many people cave in and respond. If you do, she'll bark much longer next time. Reward her when she stops barking, even for a few seconds.

Some people yell at their dog to be quiet, but she has no idea what that means. She figures you're just barking with her. The more excited you are, the more excited she gets, so stay calm.

Teach her to bark on command. Catch her when she's barking and praise her, saying "Good bark!" or whatever word you want to use (*speak* or *talk,* for example). As soon as she breaks off, say "Good quiet" and reward her. She'll learn to respond to "Bark" and "Quiet."

Try to head off barking binges before they get started. If you see something you know is going to make her bark, call her and get her attention on you. Practice when there are no distractions by rattling a treat shaker (a small container of kibble) and calling her. Once she learns that something good happens and she gets treats, you'll be able to call her away from that exciting thing before she starts barking.

TIPS AND TAILS

Labrador Retriever rescue groups report that behavior problems are the main reason Labs are given up for adoption—usually between 1 and 2 years old. The time you spend training and resolving behavior issues while your dog is still young helps ensure you have a well-behaved family member throughout her life. If you've adopted a rescued Lab, it's never too late, but training will take a little more time and patience on your part. Labs are especially resilient and forgiving, and they adapt quickly to their new environment and new rules.

Disciplining Your Lab

Most people agree that physical punishment can destroy your relationship with your dog, but what are you supposed to do when positive methods don't work and you need to discipline your dog?

When your Lab was a puppy, it was enough to stop her and redirect her to an acceptable activity. You can still do this, but you'll have to use a lot more conviction. Stop her by saying, "No!" or "Ack!" Your tone of voice conveys your displeasure, and for some Labs, that's enough.

Be sure your dog realizes why she's being disciplined. You must catch her in the act or she won't understand what she did wrong. Dogs live in the moment. She won't understand why she's being punished for something she did 2 hours ago, or even 5 minutes ago. If you come home and find she's destroyed the couch, she'll look guilty because she knows you're mad, not because she knows she did something wrong. To effectively discipline your Lab, use the same methods you use in obedience training. Praise her while she's doing it right so she understands exactly what action earned the praise. Punish her *during* the misbehavior, not after, so she knows what caused your anger.

Give your Lab an opportunity to earn praise right after you discipline her, and she'll forgive you instantly. Give her a few obedience commands she can easily perform.

Consider this example: you're walking with your Lab, and she rudely jumps up on a woman in dressy clothes, frightening and angering her. A voice correction ("Off!" or "No!") is appropriate, but that might not be enough. You might have to give a firm pop on the leash to force your puppy to drop to the ground. Then immediately have her do a down-stay. After everyone has calmed down, release her and ask for a few sits and downs so you can praise her for listening. Once she puts her brain back in obedience mode, she'll listen to you better and you can stop misbehavior before it happens.

One good strong correction is better than nagging. "Puppy, no, honey, come here, sit down, good girl … no …" isn't even going to get your Lab's attention, and it contains so many contradictions, any dog would be confused. Repeated nagging corrections teach your Lab to ignore you until you get really mad. Then she knows you mean it, and she complies. A correction should last 1 or 2 seconds and no longer. Make it as firm as it needs to be for the situation, quickly said, done, and over with.

TIPS AND TAILS
When you need to discipline your Lab, use the *minimum* amount of force necessary to stop the behavior.

Never hit your Labrador Retriever. Hitting your puppy only makes you look unpredictable, and you don't want a relationship based on fear. Even the best-trained dog may at some point decide she has to defend herself, and you don't want her to ever feel she has to bite you or anyone else. When you lose your temper, give yourself a time-out from your dog so you can cool down.

Environmental corrections discipline your dog when you aren't around so she doesn't associate the correction with you. For example, if she puts her paws up on the counter, booby trap it with cans full of pennies. When she hits one, it will fall off the counter and startle her. Other environmental correction devices include ultrasonic buzzers that make an unpleasant noise when she barks, a battery-operated mat that gives her a mild shock when she jumps on the couch, and a bitter spray that tastes terrible when she chews something she shouldn't.

TRAINING

Teaching your Labrador Retriever self-control continues this month, and although you probably don't dare let her off-leash yet, you'll enjoy teaching her the basic principles so she'll be ready when her brain catches up to her body.

Teaching the Emergency Drop

If your Lab dashes into the street, she could be hit by a car and killed. If she breaks her collar and takes off, you need tools to catch her. When she decides to chase a cyclist down the road or bound into the woods after a bear, your dog needs to respond to you instantly.

A life-saving command, the emergency down is a lightning-fast version of down. When you give this command, sometimes called *drop*, she'll probably be running away from you, so it takes some practice for her to understand it.

Start by speeding up the "Down" exercise. If she can't drop quickly in front of you, she won't be able to drop from a distance. Practice the down when you're in different positions—at her side, in back of her, with her in back of you (use a hand mirror so you can see her comply). Release her with "okay" when she drops. Once she understands the concept, you can use the word "Drop," which has a popping sound at the end that helps get her attention. When she gets confused—and she will—go to her and put her in the down. Then release her by tossing her a treat.

She won't have time to look back at you in an emergency, so she can't read your body language to figure out what to do next. Practice while you're standing and sitting so she doesn't learn to look at you for cues. Always toss a treat behind her to release her. You don't want her to automatically think she's supposed to come to you unless you call her. In an emergency, you'll either call her or go to her, so she needs to learn both scenarios.

Now you're ready to add movement. While walking alongside her, suddenly point to the ground, yell "Drop!" and pivot in front of her to stop her forward movement. Use an urgent tone of voice; this is an emergency. Release her by saying "Okay," tossing a treat away, and letting her run to get it. Practice just a few times. For the next step, attach a long line, and as she's wandering around a few feet from you, give the drop command again.

This exercise is very stressful for your Lab, so don't train for more than a few minutes per session. She'll build up a lot of excitement as you work; take advantage of her energy and make it a game. Toss treats, let her chase them, and come back to you. Occasionally, on her way back, give the drop command and rush toward her a few steps to encourage her to stop and drop. Then toss a treat behind her and let her go.

Once she can drop coming toward you, she needs to learn to drop from any position. As she's running around chasing treats, occasionally throw in a drop command. Give her a jackpot once in a while: pull her favorite toy out of your pocket or feed her a full handful of treats when she complies.

The emergency drop takes hundreds of repetitions and regular practice for your Lab to be reliable with it. Use the command often during play sessions and walks to be sure she understands it.

Preparing for Off-Leash Control

A 10-month-old Lab is not ready for the responsibility of being allowed off leash. Reliable off-leash control takes a long time to develop. Your goal is that when she's mature enough to handle it, she's had the training that makes it possible.

Answer these questions before deciding if your Lab is ready for off-leash freedom:

- Is her recall ("Come") always perfect and immediate? Does she consider it a positive command?
- Does she know and reliably perform the emergency drop?
- Is her obedience reliable on-leash? Can she ignore distractions and respond when you ask her to?
- Do you have off-leash control in the house? In the backyard?

If the answer to any of these questions is "No," or "Most of the time," polish her skills until you can answer "Yes" to all of them.

When your Lab is off leash, you must pay attention and be ready to intervene before she does something impolite or dangerous. If your Lab is defiant and sometimes purposely ignores your commands, that could have fatal results.

TIPS AND TAILS

Many trainers offer a beyond-the-basics course that starts teaching owners and their dogs off-leash control. It's a course you can take several times just for the fun of training with your Lab.

You'll need two training tools: a 15- to 20-foot light line and a 6- to 8-inch short leash or line. The 15- or 20-foot line is for outdoor training. The short line is a handle you can use to quickly grab your dog when you're close to her. It should be so light she doesn't feel the weight. You want her to forget it's there.

You've been working on indoor off-leash control since the day you got her, but now she needs to perfect her responses in anticipation of new and bigger responsibilities. You can let her drag a shorter line, maybe 6 to 8 feet long, indoors. If there's no loop at the end, it's less likely to tangle in furniture.

TIPS AND TAILS
For her safety, never leave any kind of training line, collar, or leash on your Lab when you can't supervise her.

Tie her loosely with the long line to a tree or fence post in the backyard, walk about 10 feet away, and give her an easy command like "Sit." At first, she'll be confused. She's not used to responding to you from a distance. If she doesn't respond, move closer and try again. When she sits, praise her and try something else, like "Down." Once she gets the idea, you can try commands at different distances and positions, like you did when teaching the emergency drop.

Next, untie the line and let your puppy drag it. Walk around the yard and give an occasional command from a distance. Include come and the emergency drop. Use the line to reel her in or detain her if she stops paying attention to you.

Teach her to check in with you, similar to when you practiced the recall. Drop the line and let her wander. When she's in the midst of something, call her to you and enforce the command. Her reward for coming is that you let her go back to what she was doing. Find fenced areas away from home where you can practice this.

When you're comfortable that she no longer needs the long line, attach the 8-foot light line and work with her close to you. You can hold the light line and she won't feel the weight of a leash, so she might try to take off, thinking you can't control her. She'll soon learn.

YOU AND YOUR PUPPY

Your children are a big part of family life, and there are many ways yours can enjoy spending time with your Lab puppy. Organized activities introduce them to dog sports and pet care. At the same time, your kids learn how to be good pet parents and discover the many facets of dog ownership. They can even explore careers with dogs.

Boy Scouts, Girl Scouts, and 4-H

Children of all ages can participate in activities with their Labs. Besides organized activities like scouting and 4-H, many animal shelters offer day-camp programs and workshops for groups of kids working on badges and awards.

Boy Scouts can earn several different badges while learning about their pets. To earn the Pets merit badge, a child must care for his dog for 4 months, write a report about it, keep records, and read a book about their breed or other aspect of pet care. He also must participate in an activity like a dog show with his Lab or teach his dog tricks. The Dog Care merit badge introduces boys to responsible dog ownership. They explore different breeds and track the care and health of their dogs. They also teach obedience commands and learn how to perform pet first aid. The Boy Scout must also visit a shelter or veterinary hospital. To earn the Veterinary Medicine merit badge, the Boy Scout learns about veterinary care for many different species, observes at an animal hospital, and explores other aspects of veterinary care and careers.

Girl Scouts can earn animal-related badges at each level. Brownies can earn a Pets merit badge by learning about and practicing pet care skills. Juniors earn the Animal Habitats badge by researching wild animals and ways to protect their habitats. Cadettes earn the Animal Helpers merit badge by studying how dogs and other animals help people in fields like search and rescue, therapy visits, and as service animals. Senior scouts earn the Voice for Animals badge, for which they learn about volunteering and animal welfare.

Your local Cooperative Extension generally offers dog 4-H programs for your county. Kids can participate in Grooming and Handling, Obedience, Rally, and Agility. Some counties offer additional classes such as freestyle, or dancing with your dog. 4-H'ers learn to keep records about their dog's care and training, develop public presentations, and compete at county and state fairs.

Junior Showmanship

Children between 9 and 18 years old can participate in Junior Showmanship at AKC conformation and performance events, showing their own or a relative's Lab. Kids have the opportunity to explore more about dogs and dog shows, develop handling skills, and learn about good sportsmanship while enjoying time with their dogs. In conformation, beginners compete in Novice classes. Once a child has received three first-place ribbons in novice, he or she can move up to Open competition.

Children are judged on their ability to present their dogs in a similar fashion as dogs in the breed ring at a conformation show. The quality of their presentation is judged, not the quality of the dog. Juniors learn to groom their dogs and present them to a judge, conduct themselves properly, and dress appropriately for judging. Top-winning juniors from around the country travel to the Westminster Kennel Club Show and the AKC/Eukanuba National Championship to compete for honors.

Attend some dog shows with your family and watch the junior showmanship competition to learn more about it.

In addition to conformation, the AKC has recently introduced recognition programs for children who compete in performance events like obedience, agility, and tracking. The AKC also offers other activities for juniors, along with extensive educational materials and scholarship programs. Learn more at akc.org/kids_juniors.

MONTH	SOCIAL	BEHAVIOR	TRAINING	PHYSICAL	HEALTH
1			Littermates and mother teach appropriate canine behavior	Rapid growth	
2	Breeder starts socialization				
3	Socialization at home with new owner and other pets	Fear-imprint period	Begin house- and crate training		1st DHPP vaccine
4		Teething begins—heavy chewing period	Enroll in puppy class		2nd DHPP vaccine
5	Socialization in public		Ready for basic commands	Switch to adult food	3rd DHPP and rabies vaccines
6					
7		Adult teeth are in—chewing continues	Enroll in basic obedience class	Moderate growth	Sexual maturity
8					
9					
10			Ready for more advanced training		
11				Slow growth—reaches adult size	Annual vaccinations and checkup
12 AND BEYOND					

MONTH
11

Putting Your Lab to Work

When your puppy reaches 10 or 11 months, he's ready to start practicing canine sports like hunting, agility, and obedience. Labs are incredibly smart and willing to do almost anything you could ask of them, so you can choose activities you both will enjoy. He'll relish having a job to do, exercising his mind and body while building his skills, and love spending time with you.

Meanwhile, prepare yourself for his adventures by establishing a pet disaster preparedness plan, considering pet health insurance, and beginning to take him traveling with you.

PHYSICAL DEVELOPMENT

Your Lab puppy might reach his full height this month, but his bones are still growing, so they aren't strong and fully developed yet. Continue to limit his running on hard surfaces, and don't let him jump much for a few more months.

His teeth are almost fully erupted and not as painful as they have been. They'll continue to develop strength until he's 3 years old, and he'll continue chewing as well.

Now that your Lab is almost full size, so is his tail, and he has no idea what it's doing back there. That means it's time to clear the coffee table and protect your valuables. His tail is always wagging, so when you hear strange thumping sounds in the night, look for the tail.

Your teenager will start looking more coordinated this month, as his proportions even out and he gets comfortable using his adult height and body. He'll dive into activities with great enthusiasm. In fact, he'll be hard to hold back!

HEALTH

In this section, we show you how to plan ahead for your puppy's care in case of natural disasters, and we investigate pet health insurance to cover major illness or accidents. We also look at inherited health challenges that could affect your Labrador Retriever.

Planning for Disasters

Your family's emergency plans should include provisions for your Lab's health and safety. When disaster hits and you have to evacuate, you might not be allowed back into your neighborhood for days, so always take your dog with you. *Always.* Leaving him in the house or turning him loose could be a death sentence.

Some Red Cross evacuation shelters allow dogs, but most don't. During a crisis, hotels might relax their pet policies, and places that do allow pets will require them to be crated. Before a disaster strikes, make a list of pet-friendly hotels, boarding kennels, and veterinarians within 100 miles of your home. You don't know how far you'll have to travel when you're forced to leave, and it's best to be prepared with locations you know you can go to with your pup. Also line up friends who can take your dog in an emergency. And make arrangements with a neighbor to evacuate your dog if disaster strikes while you aren't at home.

HAPPY PUPPY
Your Labrador will adjust better to the stress of emergencies or travel if he's already used to spending time in his crate.

If you live in an area at risk for floods or hurricanes, purchase a neon-colored life vest made especially for dogs. If you get separated from your Lab in a disaster, he'll be easier for rescuers to spot if he's wearing a bright vest. If you have a two-story home, buy a canine evacuation harness similar to the ones used by search-and-rescue organizations. Keep it under your bed so if a fire breaks out downstairs, you can lower your dog out the window. Practice putting these devices on your Lab when everything is calm. In a disaster, you'll be fumbling and in a hurry and will appreciate the practice. Be sure the vest and harness fit and can support his weight.

If you can't evacuate, plan a safe area within your house. If it's a basement or similar room, be sure no hazardous materials are nearby that can harm your dog. As soon as you know a storm is coming, find your Lab, be sure he's wearing his leash and collar, and keep him indoors with you. Frightened animals will often wander away during the commotion and become disoriented. Then, after the storm has passed, nothing looks or smells the same, and your dog might not be able to find his way home.

During disasters, keep a leash on your Lab, even when he's in the car, and keep him crated as much as possible. He'll be as anxious as you are, he'll feel safer in his crate, and you won't have to worry about keeping track of him. After the crisis passes, keep your dog leashed and with you until you're home and safe.

When planning your disaster kit, include the following:

○ Your Lab's microchip and license information, your contact info, emergency caretaker phone numbers, your dog's medical records, a photo of your Lab, and feeding and care instructions, all inside a waterproof bag or container

○ Extra leash, trash bags, poop scoop supplies, and towels

○ Food and water bowls

○ Food and water for 3 days

○ His crate, marked with your cell phone number and emergency contact info

○ Calming medication or herbal/flower formula, like Rescue Remedy or chamomile tea bags to add to your dog's water

○ First-aid kit

○ Medications, including heartworm and flea control products

Store your kit in an outdoor shed, near an exit door where it's easily accessible, or in your car.

Considering Pet Health Insurance

Should you purchase health insurance for your puppy? If so, should you buy it now or wait until he's older and more likely to get sick? You have many considerations when deciding whether to purchase pet insurance. No one wants to be faced with the horrible decision of euthanizing their dog because they can't afford a procedure that could save his life. Lesser expenses add up, too, and you might decide the expense of coverage is worth it for your peace of mind. By removing financial pressure from the equation, it frees you to make better decisions about your Lab's care.

Insurance companies offer many different types of pet coverage. Depending on what you're willing to pay, almost any type of coverage is available. The most inexpensive is usually a major medical plan that only covers accidents and major illnesses like cancer or heart disease. More comprehensive plans include hereditary diseases and routine care like vaccines, spay/neuter, and teeth cleaning. Most plans don't cover preexisting conditions, or they have a waiting period before a previously cured disease is covered. Behavioral problems, parasites (like heartworm), and special veterinary food are also excluded from most policies. In one policy we examined, hip and elbow dysplasia and anterior cruciate ligament injury—conditions common in Labs—are specifically *not* covered.

TIPS AND TAILS

Examine pet insurance plans carefully to be sure you completely understand what is and isn't covered.

The following is a sampling of claims filed by Labrador Retriever owners over the past several years with a national pet health insurance company (all these Labs survived with no lasting effects):

- Tiki, a black male, swallowed 62 hair bands, 8 pairs of underwear, and a bandage. Surgery was required to save his life.

- Bones, a yellow male and hunting dog, got a 6-inch tree branch embedded deep in his throat.

- Lola, a chocolate female, suffered severe burns on her mouth when she chewed through an electrical cord.

- Major, a chocolate male, ran into a large rock while retrieving, broke several teeth, and suffered a concussion.

- Stella, a black female, got an open can of green beans stuck on her lower jaw. She had to be anesthetized to remove it.

- Gus, a yellow male, ate more than 5 pounds of Christmas cookies and fudge, including the plastic wrap and boxes.

- Tobey, a yellow male, drank so much water while playing in the sprinklers he became swollen and ill. His owners were afraid he would bloat.

- Ellie, a yellow female, ate a hive's worth of dead bees after an exterminator killed them at her home. She had a major stomach upset but no ill effects from the pesticide or the bees themselves.

- Rock, a black male, ate 23 packages of instant breakfast powder, wrapping and all.

- Quincy, a yellow male, imbedded a fishhook with two barbs in his nose.

- Marley, a yellow male, retrieved a poisonous sea urchin at the beach.

Virtually all these emergencies involved a Lab and something in his or her mouth, and many could have been prevented with better supervision and management. And note that color doesn't seem to be a factor in Labrador mishaps—more proof that chocolates aren't necessarily more mischievous.

TIPS AND TAILS

Although not mentioned on this list, the insurance company reported that ingested socks are the most common emergency requiring surgery. More reason to train your Lab to leave your socks alone—and for you to pick them up!

When researching pet insurance policies, here are some good questions to ask:

- Is there a deductible?
- Will the price increase as my dog ages?
- Will the price increase if he's diagnosed with a chronic disease?
- What illnesses or injuries are *not* covered? What *is* covered?
- Are hereditary conditions covered, even if my dog shows no symptoms now?
- Is there a waiting period before some chronic, hereditary, or preexisting conditions are covered?
- May I choose my own vet?
- Are diagnostic tests covered?

With most pet insurance policies, you, the owner, pay the bill, submit a claim and receipts, and are reimbursed by the insurance company. The veterinarian doesn't get involved in billing or receiving payment. Some plans have a set amount they reimburse for each type of illness or injury, so that's something to keep in mind, too.

Handling Inherited Lab Health Challenges

In recent years, researchers have made great strides identifying the genetic components of inherited diseases in Labrador Retrievers. You may have received copies of health clearances for the parents of your puppy from your breeder (see Months 1 and 2), so you know your own Lab has a lower risk of developing some of these conditions. If you didn't get clearances, here are the diseases, their symptoms, and their treatments.

Hip and elbow dysplasia: Research has shown that overly rapid growth and obesity, in addition to genetics, play a role in whether your dog will develop these diseases. Dogs suffering from hip or elbow dysplasia develop arthritis, sometimes at a very young age. Puppies don't exercise as hard as adults and don't carry a lot of weight, so symptoms in a severely affected dog might not show up until he reaches his full adult size. Some dogs with dysplasia never show symptoms, like gait abnormalities or holding their elbows at unusual angles, but most develop arthritis in their middle years, between 5 and 8 years old.

Hip dysplasia: Widespread in Labradors, hip dysplasia develops as the dog matures and the head of the femur (ball) no longer fits properly into the hip socket. Symptoms can appear as early as 6 months of age, when a dog may show lameness in his hind legs, possibly caused by overactive play. When a vet manipulates the rear legs, the dog shows evidence of joint pain, and x-rays are used to confirm the diagnosis. The vet will prescribe crate rest and analgesic drugs, but the pain and lameness will reoccur as soon as the dog is active again.

Hip dysplasia ranges from mild to severe. Some dogs never show symptoms, even though they're mildly affected. Others develop symptoms as they age because the hip joints develop osteoarthritis.

In a young dog 8 to 14 months old, surgery might be an option. A triple pelvic osteotomy (TPO) is a procedure in which the surgeon cuts the hipbone in three places and rotates it so it will heal in a better position, supporting the ball of the femur. As long as arthritis hasn't already developed, most dogs can return to normal activity afterward. But this is major surgery, and the recovery time is several months. Your dog must remain inactive for long periods, working back up to normal exercise slowly.

For an older dog, total hip replacement surgery is an option. The ball and socket are removed and replaced with metal and plastic, similar to the same procedure in humans. This option also involves a long recovery period.

HAPPY PUPPY
Arthritis, hip dysplasia, and other ailments can be prevented or at least improved by keeping your Lab slim and trim.

For dogs who aren't candidates for surgery, owners can take steps to make their Labs more comfortable, like avoiding high-impact activities such as jogging or anything else painful for the dog. Low-impact exercise like walking and swimming help build muscle mass, and anti-inflammatory drugs can ease the pain. These dogs shouldn't be allowed to carry extra weight because obesity is hard on their joints.

Many people give their dogs supplements like glucosamine and chondroitin to lubricate joints and ease arthritic symptoms.

A responsible breeder waits to breed her dogs until they're 2 years old and have been x-rayed and cleared to minimize the possibility of producing puppies with hip dysplasia. However, there's a slight chance two parents who are clear can still produce hip dysplasia.

Elbow dysplasia: This inherited disease is caused by abnormal development of the three bones that make up the elbow joint, which leads to formation of bone chips and areas of loose cartilage. You won't know your dog has elbow dysplasia until you notice front lameness, usually after exercise. He also might move with an unusual gait in front, throwing his elbows slightly out.

Treatment of elbow dysplasia is similar to that for hip dysplasia. Walking, swimming, and other non-weight-bearing exercise, and keeping your Lab at a lean weight reduce pressure on his joints and help build his muscle strength. Anti-inflammatory medications can ease the pain, and joint supplements might also help. Arthroscopic surgery can remove the bone chips in his elbows to make your Lab more comfortable.

As with hip dysplasia, breeding dogs should be x-rayed at 2 years of age and not bred if they show signs of the disease.

Exercise-induced collapse (EIC): Young adult Labs of field breeding seem to be the most common victims of EIC, but it has been seen in show-bred Labs, too. Although it can happen as young as 4 months, most dogs are at least 1 year old when the first episode occurs. This often coincides with the beginning of intense hunting training.

An affected Lab in the midst of exercise will suddenly have an uneven gait or appear uncoordinated and eventually completely collapse. The dog will still be conscious and may try to get up and continue running but will appear confused and disoriented. Symptoms worsen for 3 to 5 minutes. The dog does not appear to be in pain, and he usually recovers within 5 to 25 minutes. Some dogs have died during an episode when they were allowed to continue exercising, so don't let your pup get up. Dogs seem to be more likely to suffer an episode during hot and humid weather. With EIC, some people think their Lab is suffering from heatstroke, but the symptoms are different. (See Month 8 to learn about recognizing and treating heatstroke.)

Labs with intense drive and excitable personalities seem to be more likely to be affected by EIC. If they're prevented from excessive exercise and excitement, they can live an otherwise normal life. There's no cure for EIC, but a genetic test is available, and potential breeding dogs should be screened for this disease.

Progressive retinal atrophy (PRA): This retinal disease affects many breeds of dogs and is especially prevalent in Labs. The cells of the retina die and eventually cause blindness. First, night vision decreases and then daytime vision diminishes, and ultimately the dog's eyesight fails completely. Labs don't usually show symptoms until they're middle-aged, at about 5 to 8 years old. Dogs adapt well to blindness, and you might not notice your dog is affected until you move the furniture or take him somewhere where he's unfamiliar with the room layout.

An ophthalmologist can diagnose PRA in a puppy or adult, but there is no treatment. Fortunately, the genes causing PRA have recently been discovered and a test is available to identify dogs who carry or are affected with the disease long before they show any symptoms. These dogs can be removed from a breeding program before they produce affected puppies.

Retinal dysplasia: Another genetically inherited eye disorder, retinal dysplasia is caused by abnormal development of the retina. There is no treatment or cure, nor is there a genetic test, so breeders must have their dogs checked annually for signs of the disease. Responsible breeders also take their litter of puppies to be checked by an ophthalmologist at 7 or 8 weeks old. Puppies who are at risk for retinal dysplasia may have retinal folds visible at this age.

Mildly affected dogs may never show obvious symptoms, while other dogs will be completely blind if the retina is totally detached. Affected dogs may also suffer from cataracts or glaucoma.

Tricuspid valve dysplasia (TVD): A defect on the right side of the heart, TVD is the most common type of heart disease in Labrador Retrievers. This malformation causes blood to leak back into the right atrium and forces the heart to work harder. TVD varies in severity, and a mildly affected dog can live a long, normal life. In severe cases, it causes congestive heart failure and death. Symptoms include excess fluid buildup in the abdomen, which might make you think your dog is getting fat. An affected dog also tires easily and isn't as active. Symptoms can develop when your Lab is a puppy or not until years later when signs of heart failure develop. To diagnose, your veterinarian may first listen for a heart murmur. Chest x-rays and heart ultrasound provide confirmation of the disease.

Treatment includes limiting your dog's exercise and feeding him a low-salt diet. Occasionally, it may be necessary to remove excess fluid from his abdominal cavity. Some dogs respond to cardiac medications, too.

A genetic test is not yet available to identify TVD, but responsible breeders have their dogs examined by a cardiologist to be sure they're clear of the disease.

TIPS AND TAILS

This list of genetically inherited conditions sounds scary, but don't panic. Labs are generally healthy. However, by learning about these diseases, you'll recognize any symptoms that show up in your puppy and be able to get an affected dog treated before he becomes seriously ill.

NUTRITION

Your Lab might be perfectly healthy on a diet of dry food, but other options and supplements are available. As you ponder the multitude of choices at the pet store, you might worry you aren't doing enough for your beloved Lab.

The best advice is, if it works, don't try to "fix" it. If your Lab has a healthy and shiny coat, clear eyes, and healthy skin; if he's the appropriate weight; and if he enjoys good health, he probably doesn't need anything added to his diet. As he ages, this might change, but most Labs live long, healthy lives by eating a diet based on a quality dry dog food.

Feeding Beyond Dry Food

Should you add canned or semimoist foods to your Lab's meals? Or should you feed wet food exclusively? Or maybe you'd like to give him a daily bowl of wet food as a treat. Dogs certainly seem to love it.

Canned dog food contains up to 78 percent water, which helps fill up your dog. It usually includes more protein, fat, and animal-based ingredients than dry dog food and less grain. So overall, the ingredients are usually better quality than you'll find in most dry foods, but read the ingredients on the label to be sure, and look for named meats and minimal grain. The nuggets, chunks, and other shapes aren't actually meat. They're formed from textured plant proteins or sometimes (although rarely) natural meat tissues. Some foods also contain "vegetables" like carrots and peas. These might be real or artificially colored and shaped.

There are advantages to feeding canned food. If your Lab has kidney problems or is constipated, the extra moisture will be beneficial. If he's ill or dehydrated, he'll need extra moisture, and canned food is one way to provide it. Canned food contains fewer preservatives because the can is an oxygen-free environment, which, when properly sealed, does not allow bacteria to grow. (Be sure to refrigerate leftovers to avoid spoilage.) Canned food is more expensive, however, so you probably won't want to feed him an exclusively canned diet.

Semimoist foods, usually packaged in foil packets, contain lots of additives, particularly sugar, for taste and to solidify the food. These are generally the least-healthy diets you can feed your pup. Although semimoist foods contain more moisture than dry food—about 25 to 30 percent—they're extremely expensive in comparison. Reserve semimoist food for treats, if you use it at all.

What About Nutritional Supplements?

If your Lab puppy is eating a quality dog food and in good health, you don't need to add supplements to his diet. In fact, too much supplementation can throw his system out of balance and actually cause health problems. And too much of a nutrient is just as bad as too little.

But once in a while, supplements can be beneficial to your dog's health. For example, owners who feed raw or home-cooked diets need to give their dogs supplements to be sure they're getting all the essential vitamins, minerals, and nutrients.

Work with your vet or consult a nutritionist to determine when and how to add supplements to your dog's diet, because some can interfere with other medications your dog is taking. And be sure you use products specifically meant for dogs because a dog's nutritional needs are different from a human's.

Nutritional supplements are not subject to evaluation by the Food and Drug Administration for their purity, safety, or ability to improve your dog's health, and not all supplements are necessarily equal or risk free. Do some research, and purchase only brands you trust. The National Animal Supplement Council (nasc.cc) certifies manufacturers' products and awards a seal to those that meet their standards of safety, quality, and accuracy.

TIPS AND TAILS

If you feel your Lab needs supplements with his food, consider switching to a different or better-quality food rather than oversupplement. Most of the supplements discussed in this section are already included in commercial dog foods.

Probiotics: Probiotics contain beneficial bacteria that can bolster your Lab's immune response to harmful bacteria in his intestinal tract. Probiotics are an important contributor to your puppy's overall health because 70 percent of his immune system is found in his digestive tract. When added to your dog's diet, probiotics help return his system to a normal state by restoring the balance of good and bad bacteria.

Many things can affect your dog's gastrointestinal health. Eating a poor-quality diet, consuming unclean water, eating feces or grass, or ingesting fertilizers or pesticides all can introduce bacteria to the gut that throw it off balance and cause problems like diarrhea and incomplete food absorption. Stress caused by a change in routine, such as travel or boarding, can be a factor, too. Inflammatory bowel disease, colitis, or kidney disease also can affect the balance of bacteria in his body. Antibiotics and cortisone can kill good bacteria as well as bad bacteria. For this reason, some veterinarians prescribe probiotics for your Lab if he's on antibiotics.

Antioxidants: Antioxidants such as vitamins A, C, and E; beta-carotene; and other compounds help support your puppy's immune system and protect him from disease. Antioxidants protect his cells against the effects of free radicals, which cause cellular damage and are produced when his body breaks down food or is exposed to pollution, cigarette smoke, or other environmental toxins. You might want to add antioxidants to your dog's diet if he's suffering from cancer or heart disease. Always check with your veterinarian first because too much of some items, such as vitamin A, can be toxic.

Digestive enzymes: These are sometimes packaged with probiotics because both affect your dog's gastrointestinal health. Digestive enzymes break down nutrients in food so his body can absorb them. When commercial dog foods are cooked at high temperatures, these enzymes are killed and must be added back into the food. Dogs also produce their own digestive enzymes in their saliva glands, pancreas, and stomach. Yogurt is an excellent source of digestive enzymes; purchase one with live, active cultures. A dog's production of digestive enzymes is affected by aging, and sometimes older dogs benefit from their addition to his diet. A young, healthy Lab shouldn't need these.

Bone meal: Bone meal adds calcium to the diet, which is something young Labs don't need. In fact, breeders recommend you *not* feed him puppy food or any dog food high in calcium because it can cause orthopedic problems later in life.

Vitamin and mineral supplements: These are necessary for dogs eating home-cooked or raw food, but they're usually unnecessary for Labs eating a commercially made food. If you feel you need to give your dog additional vitamins and minerals, choose those made especially for dogs. And don't oversupplement any vitamins or minerals because they can have toxic effects.

Fatty acids: Fatty acids must be added back to dry dog food after cooking. If your Lab has a dry, dull coat, a supplement in the form of fish oil or cod liver oil can provide essential fatty acids (linoleic acid) and vitamins A and D. Flaxseed is high in beneficial fatty acids, too. Some fatty acids are high in calories, so be careful not to give your Lab too much.

Whole foods: If you give your Lab fresh whole foods to supplement his diet, you're less likely to overdose him on any specific nutrient because his body expels the excess as it digests the food. Carrots, cottage cheese, apples, bananas, blueberries, green beans, dandelions, and kelp all provide extra nutrition. Be sure the foods you choose are beneficial and not toxic to dogs (see Appendix C). Prepackaged whole-food supplements are available. Missing Link is an established, well-known brand. When in doubt, consult your veterinarian and research different product lines before adding a supplement to your Lab's diet.

Glucosamine and chondroitin: Both of these exist naturally in the body, but when a dog has arthritis, his body might not make enough of these substances. Glucosamine helps build connective tissue and stimulates the growth of healthy new cartilage, and chondroitin protects joints and slows the breakdown of existing cartilage. The two supplements are usually taken together and are often added to senior formula dog foods. It takes several weeks to see the effects, but many dogs enjoy greater mobility and less pain when on these supplements.

GROOMING

Most dog owners are a bit more tolerant of the smells and messes their dogs make than people who don't have dogs. By keeping your Lab and his bedding clean, a guest shouldn't be able to smell a dog in your house. And because your teenager is pretty inquisitive, we help you prepare for the most obnoxious grooming chore ever in this section: bathing a skunked dog. Finally, a Lab's coat can collect anything from burrs to bubblegum, so we also look at how to remove the goo without ruining his good looks.

Dealing with Doggie Odor

Some of us are more sensitive to doggie odor than others, but Labs shouldn't smell bad by anyone's standards. If you do detect strong odors, they could be caused by health problems such as ear infections, tooth decay, gum disease, skin disease, or kidney problems, so your pup might need a vet visit.

If your puppy rolls in something disgusting, swims in foul water, or just generally makes a stinky mess of himself, add vinegar to the rinse water when you bathe him, or purchase an enzymatic odor-removing shampoo, like Nature's Miracle. The skunk bath described in the following section also works very well.

Skunked!

Is there anything worse than the smell of a freshly skunked dog? You let him out for a last pee of the night, and when he comes back in … ack! Run for the tomato juice! But wait. There are more effective ways to remove the skunk smell than tomato juice. Instead, bathe your dog in a mixture of the following:

1 quart 3 percent hydrogen peroxide

¼ cup baking soda

2 teaspoons Dawn dish detergent

Mix the ingredients just before using, and lather your Lab's *dry* coat thoroughly, down to the skin, and rinse well. Be sure to keep the mixture out of his eyes because the hydrogen peroxide will burn. Use a washcloth around his head, and rinse his face carefully. You'll know immediately if the smell is dissipating. You might have to repeat this treatment several times, so be prepared to make more of the mixture. And because the solution doesn't keep, always make a fresh batch.

Removing Sticky Stuff

Just like children get chewing gum in their hair, puppies get tree sap, tar, and other sticky things in their fur. Home remedies such as vegetable oil, peanut butter, and mayonnaise all contain enough oil to break down the gummy texture so you can scrape or comb out the gunk, and they won't irritate his skin. Commercial products like Simple Green and some orange oil cleaners are nontoxic for use on pet fur.

If your Lab has gum in his fur, put an ice cube on the gum to harden it enough that you can chip it off. Tar and tree sap or pitch might be tough to remove, so apply vegetable oil and let it soak on the area for 24 hours. You might want to put a T-shirt or Elizabethan collar on your Lab so he won't lick it while it works. Paint is easier to remove if you let it dry and harden and then clip it off.

Sometimes you just can't lubricate, wash, or soak the crud out of your Lab's coat, and you'll have to cut out the offending substance. Use blunt-tip scissors or grooming clippers, and be very careful. Don't use regular, pointed scissors because they could too easily cut his skin.

TIPS AND TAILS
Never use gasoline, kerosene, turpentine, or solvents on your Lab. These products can severely burn his skin and are toxic if he ingests them.

SOCIAL SKILLS

Your Lab puppy is a member of the family, too, and he'd love to tag along when your family goes on vacation. With a little preparation and planning, your best friend can get away from the hustle and bustle of everyday life with you. While on vacation, no one has to go to work or school or other activities, and you all have more time to relax with each other and with your puppy. Most buses and trains won't accept dogs, so to travel with your pup, cars and airplanes are your best bets.

Traveling by Car

Although you might like to let your pup run from open window to open window while you drive, restrain him when he's in the car. A dog who leaps around in the car can cause an accident, hit you in the face with his tail, or knock the gear shift out of gear. And as much as he might love it, don't let him hang his head out the car window. Bugs or flying debris could hit him in the eyes and injure them. If the window is down far enough, he could jump out and be badly injured.

If you have room for it, the safest place for him is in a crate. Prevent the crate from tipping over when you go around corners by either tying it down or wedging it between your luggage. If your car isn't large enough for a crate, use a seat-belt harness. Special car harnesses are available for pets, or you can make one with a harness and short leash. And always put him in the backseat so he won't be injured by the front seat airbag if you're in an accident.

HAPPY PUPPY

It gets hot in the back of an SUV or van, even while the car is running. As you travel, be sure your Lab is shielded from direct sun and has plenty of air circulation if he's back there. (You can purchase small battery-operated camping fans to provide extra ventilation.) Stop often to give him water and be sure he isn't overheated.

Flying with Your Labrador Retriever

Transporting a large dog is expensive, and his plane ticket may cost as much as yours. Most airlines don't allow online reservations for pets, so call the airline directly to schedule your Lab's flight. Make your reservations early because spots for pets are limited, and reconfirm your reservation with the airline 24 to 48 hours before you leave. Your Lab is too large to travel in the cabin, so he'll have to be shipped in the cargo hold. If you're taking an international flight, research the regulations at your destination because there might be a long quarantine period. Hawaii also has strict guidelines when it comes to bringing animals to the islands.

Also be aware of the weather when you plan to fly. When the ground temperature is too high or too low, some airlines refuse to fly with animals (more on this coming up). Try to schedule an overnight or late-night flight if you're traveling in the summer so you don't fly during extreme heat and humidity. Avoid traveling on holidays or weekends, and try to book a nonstop or direct flight so your dog doesn't have to switch planes.

Your Lab's shipping crate must conform to the airline's regulations and to the standards developed by the International Air Transport Association. The crate must be sturdy plastic (not wire); properly ventilated; and large enough that he can stand, turn around, and lie down. Many airlines require metal doors rather than plastic to prevent the dog from chewing and escaping from the crate. In addition to including your name and address on your dog's kennel, you must use arrows or stickers to indicate the top.

TIPS AND TAILS

Airline policies for traveling with pets vary, so check with your carrier for its specific requirements. To view the pet policies for specific airlines, visit pettravel.com/airline_rules.cfm.

Fasten empty food and water dishes inside the crate door so they're accessible from outside. Attach a food and water schedule, and tape a bag of food to the outside of the kennel. The crate must not be locked in case someone needs to remove your Lab in an emergency, but it must close securely with a latch that can be opened without tools. You cannot leave a leash with the kennel, but be sure to take one with you so you can take your dog out of the crate for a walk. Airline security will inspect your Lab and his belongings like any other passenger's.

Most veterinarians and airlines recommend you do *not* tranquilize your dog before flying. Tranquilizers and sedatives can affect your dog's equilibrium, breathing, and ability to regulate his body temperature. He also might be more likely to have a bad reaction due to the altitude and change in air pressure. A fully awake dog is usually safer.

If you're not traveling with your Lab, he'll ship as cargo. You'll deliver him to the freight terminal, which is in a different part of the airport from where passengers go.

Because you won't be at the airport to claim him when he arrives, mark the crate with the phone number of a person at your destination who can be contacted about your Lab.

Find out where the freight terminal is at the destination airport so you know where he must be picked up. Get the direct phone number at your departure site and any connecting airports so you can confirm your Lab has made all his connections and arrived safely. Most airlines have complete instructions for shipping pets posted on their websites.

Staying at Pet-Friendly Accommodations

Plan in advance to stay at pet-friendly hotels and campgrounds. Most major chains accept dogs, but call ahead to be sure. Pet-friendly hotels might have a limited number of rooms available, so it's important to make advance reservations. Others designate their smoking rooms as dog friendly. Some hotels charge an extra fee for dogs, require a deposit against damage, or don't accept dogs above a certain size. Many facilities offer extra amenities for dog owners, like dog day care, play yards, dog walkers, and treats.

Some hotels don't allow guests to leave their dogs alone in their room. Housekeeping personnel might be frightened if a big black dog greets them at the door, and your Lab could escape. If you are allowed to leave your dog in the room, crate him while you're not there to watch him, and don't leave him alone for too long, especially if he might bark in the crate and disturb other guests. Leave the TV on to keep him company when you go out. Don't allow your Lab to relieve himself right outside the door, where the stains and smell might offend other guests. Take him away from the building instead. Some hotels have designated pet areas or may be able to guide you to nearby dog parks or walking trails. Always pick up after him, too.

TIPS AND TAILS
Feed your dog in the bathroom of your hotel room so he doesn't damage or dirty the carpets while he eats.

When investigating dog-friendly campgrounds and RV parks, ask if there are any size restrictions on the dogs allowed or if you have to pay extra fees to bring your pooch. Clarify if your dog is allowed in all parts of the park or if he must stay at your site. Dogs are allowed in most national parks, but they must be kept in your car, on the roadway, or in parking lots, and they aren't allowed on hiking trails at all. National forests do allow on-leash dogs to hike on the trails. The rules vary at various facilities, so contact each one to confirm that you can bring your Lab with you.

Research dog-friendly accommodations at petfriendlytravel.com, petswelcome .com, and dogfriendly.com. While you research hotels and campgrounds, you also can find lists of dog-friendly beaches, dog parks, and other activities. Local dog day cares might allow you to leave your Lab temporarily while you spend the day at an amusement park, and some large parks, such as Disney, provide kennels for your dog to stay in while you enjoy the park.

Preparing Your Dog for Travel

You must ensure your dog is healthy and safe for his vacation, and review his doggie manners before you leave. Also, there are some requirements and precautions you should take before you hit the road or fly.

Health certificate: If you take your dog across state lines or fly him anywhere, you must carry a health certificate, a veterinarian-signed document that certifies your dog is healthy enough to travel and is current on your state's required vaccines. (All 50 states require a rabies vaccine.) Some airlines also require an acclimation certificate, which states the dog is allowed to travel when the temperature is below 45°F. Both certificates must be signed by a federally accredited veterinarian. No acclimation certificate is available pertaining to hot weather, although airlines usually don't accept pets for transport in the cargo hold when the temperature is above 84°F.

Identification: Be sure your puppy's tags are securely fastened and that the lettering is legible. Consider adding a tag with your cell phone number and emergency contact information on it, too. If he isn't already microchipped, do so now before you travel, and be sure he has a tag that states he's microchipped so anyone who finds him will know to scan him. Dogs traveling internationally should have a chip that meets International Organization for Standardization (ISO) standards, an internationally recognized frequency. Check with your microchip registry to be sure your contact information as well as your backup information is up to date before you travel.

Heartworm preventative: If your Lab isn't already on heartworm preventative, have him tested and on medication before you leave. In almost any area of the country, he'll be exposed to heartworm, especially in the summer, when mosquitoes are common.

Training: You've probably already taught your dog to eliminate on different surfaces, but if he needs more work, do so before your trip. If he's used to going on grass only, he might not want to go in a strange place or on a new surface. Many dogs who stay in kennels don't like to relieve themselves on concrete nor where they sleep.

Review his other obedience and manners, too. Practice skills like sitting to greet people, leave it, and walking nicely on leash. Refresh his memory so he'll wait to jump out of the car or go through a door. He could be lost if he rushes off when you're someplace new. Also review his crate training if you haven't been using it much. He might have to spend more time in the crate while you're on vacation—in the car, in a hotel room, on a plane, or at your host's home. He should feel comfortable and safe when crated.

TIPS AND TAILS
Teach your pup to eliminate on cue. Give it a name, like "Go potty" or "Hurry." Praise and give him a treat when he goes, and he'll soon associate the word with the action, making your rest stops much shorter.

It's inconvenient, if not impossible, to leave food down for your Lab while traveling. Most owners don't free-feed their Labs, or leave food down all day for him (there would be a lot of 200-pound dogs!), so teach him to eat within 10 minutes. If he doesn't eat, pick up the food and put it away until the next meal. He'll quickly learn to eat when it's put in front of him.

If you'll be using fold-up travel bowls or giving him water from a bottle, teach him to use them before you leave home. Many dogs refuse to stick their noses in a canvas bowl or other tight spot. Drinking from a water bottle is an acquired skill, and it might take a few days for him to get the hang of it.

Packing for Your Pup

Pack a suitcase for your Lab when you're packing for yourself. If you're traveling by car, you'll be able to bring more supplies with you. Here's what to pack:

Health certificate: If you're flying or crossing state lines, this is required.

Microchip information: Bring the chip number, brand name, and registry contact information.

Photo of your Lab: If your dog gets lost, you'll need a photo to identify him and make posters.

Food and treats: You might not be able to find the same brands, and a diet change could cause a stomach upset.

Water: Water from an unfamiliar place can cause diarrhea. If you can, take some of your own from home.

Leash: Always leash your Lab in public. Bring a regular leash rather than a retractable leash, because in most places, the latter is impractical and dangerous.

Crate: If you're traveling by air, be sure the crate is airline approved. Familiarize your Lab with the crate before you travel, if he isn't already comfortable with it.

Bedding and toys: Things that smell like home will make your Lab more comfortable in strange places.

First-aid kit: Include medication to treat carsickness. Over-the-counter medication for humans that contains the active ingredient meclizine is safe for dogs, but check with your veterinarian to find out brand names and dosage amounts. Ginger (as in gingersnap cookies) also helps prevent motion sickness.

Clean-up supplies: Bring disposable bags and paper towels.

Travel Tips

You and your Lab must mind your manners in pubic places. If you don't see signs prohibiting dogs, that doesn't necessarily mean they're welcome. Keep him under control at all times, and prevent him from jumping on or sniffing strangers. Don't leave him tied up outside a building either; he could be stolen, or someone might accuse him of biting.

Being left in a hot car can kill a dog, so eat at drive-thru restaurants while traveling with your Lab. Stop at public rest areas to use the restroom, too. Terry once walked two Labs, a Collie, and a Sheltie into a restroom with her because it was too hot to leave them in the car. They all crowded into the handicapped stall.

Highway rest areas often designate doggie relief areas. Keep your Lab on leash, and clean up after him, even in designated doggie zones. If there's a fenced dog area, patrol the field for scattered food, wrappers, trash, broken glass, and waste left by other dogs before you turn your dog loose. Wild animals often scavenge at rest areas, so be on the lookout for raccoons, possums, rats, mice, and coyotes. Rattlesnakes nap under picnic tables, in the restrooms, or under nearby bushes.

Wherever you go, and however you get there, always be a good citizen so dogs continue to be welcome in public places.

When Your Lab Must Stay Home

If your pup can't travel with you, you have several options for dog care while you're gone. You can board him in a kennel, hire a pet sitter, or have family or friends care for him. Wherever you leave him, it will be a stressful time for your puppy, especially if he goes to a place he's never been before.

A young, active Labrador Retriever should probably be boarded in a kennel for his own safety. If you leave him at home and have someone come in to see him twice a day, that still leaves him with more than 20 hours a day to entertain himself, and by now you know what that entails. After a few days of isolation, a lonely Lab will do things he'd never do when you're home. Although you might leave him alone while you're at work through the week, that's much different from leaving him to his own devices for a full weekend or more.

Kennels provide safety and a choice of amenities for your Lab. He'll be confined or supervised at all times, and you may be able to add extra activities to his daily routine like exercise, walks, doggie playgroups, or swimming. Some facilities offer deluxe suites for your Lab that mimic a home environment with a couch, TV, and real walls instead of chain-link or plastic panels. Although there's usually an extra charge for these services, your Lab will adjust better and suffer from less stress if he can get out of the confined kennel each day. Although Labs are adaptable and happy dogs who adjust well to almost any situation, kennels are noisy and stressful places, no matter how well they're operated. Your Lab may come home extremely tired.

A boarding facility requires proof of vaccines: DHPP, rabies, and bordetella (kennel cough). The kennel cough vaccine should be given at least 1 week, and not more than 6 months, before you board your Lab. By giving the vaccine a week in advance, your dog has time to absorb the protection of the vaccine into his system.

You'll be asked to sign a contract and a liability release in case your Lab bites someone or injures another dog. Provide your veterinarian's contact information, too. Be honest about any behavioral problems your Lab has, like separation anxiety or fear of men. Kennel staff are trained professionals and can take precautions to prevent injuries or extreme stress.

TIPS AND TAILS
Alert your veterinarian that you'll be away, and authorize them to treat your dog or give information to the kennel, caregiver, or another clinic should the need arise.

Request a tour of the facility when you visit so you can see where your Lab will stay. Ask some questions as you look around:

- Will he be housed with another dog in the same kennel?
- Can I bring his food or a bed that smells like home?
- Is someone on-site 24 hours a day?
- What veterinarian is used in case of an emergency or illness?
- Are there extra charges for administering medication or feeding my own food?

Boarding your Lab with friends or family puts a lot of responsibility on people who might not be able to handle a big, goofy Lab. If your dog knows them well, if they have another dog he knows, or if he's spent time at their house with you, the arrangement might work out.

Think carefully before you impose on your acquaintances. If something happens to your Lab, it could ruin your relationship. Dogs often escape from private homes—they're in a strange place, anxious, and want to go home. A dog who never digs at home could dig out of a stranger's yard or jump the fence. Your friends don't know your dog or his habits, and their children could inadvertently leave a gate open.

A pet sitter is a good option for an adult Lab who has matured and settled down. Remaining at home is less stressful for your Lab, as long as you trust him to behave. If you have multiple pets, this is also a less-expensive option than boarding. You might already have a sitter who walks your Lab while you're at work.

With a professional pet sitter, you'll sign a contract and liability release. Because she'll be providing more than just a daily walk, ask some in-depth questions:

- How much experience do you have caring for Labs? How do you deal with their activity level and strength?
- Do you have liability and property damage insurance?
- Do you do each visit yourself? Do you have employees?
- How long do you stay each visit?
- Are there any extra charges I should know about? Any extra services you provide?
- Do you provide references? Could I call other Lab owners whose dogs you care for?
- Do you know pet first aid? Have you completed a pet first-aid course?
- Are you a member of any professional associations?
- How would you handle a personal emergency? Do you have backup help?

Some pet sitters also board dogs in their home. In this situation, your dog is in a cage-free environment and treated like a member of the family. In-home or cage-free boarding services vary. Some operators take only a few dogs, while others operate more like a doggie day care and crate or kennel all the dogs at night.

A house sitter is another option for vacation dog care. When interviewing a house sitter, ask many of the same questions you'd ask a potential pet sitter, with extra attention given to the house sitter's personal routine while in your home. Some sitters only stay overnight and go to another job during the day. Some guarantee they'll stay in your home a certain number of hours each day. Be sure to clarify these details.

Also be clear about sleeping arrangements, food, cleaning, and whether the house sitter can have guests over. Some house sitters treat their time at your house as a personal vacation. Be sure they understand they're there to care for your Lab and spend time with him.

BEHAVIOR

Even a well-adjusted, happy-go-lucky Lab will sometimes be anxious or afraid. He might react to new situations and people or something that has frightened him in the past, possibly during one of the fear-imprint periods in his youth. The situation may be temporary and easy to deal with, or it could have catastrophic results.

Respect your puppy's stress or fear. Protect him from real danger, and acclimate him to safe situations where he's reacting poorly. Use the socialization methods you've practiced in previous months. In rare situations, medical help or behavior counseling might be necessary to cure symptoms of an emotional nature.

Recognizing Signs of Stress

Stress can be good or bad. Trying to hold a sit-stay could be stressful for your dog. Your arrival at the end of the day is even stressful, but in a good way. Although a short burst of stress causes an adrenaline rush (a flood of stress hormones) that results in a temporary but sometimes extreme reaction, low-level chronic stress can cause serious health problems in your dog.

Your Lab puppy might exhibit subtle signs of stress that you won't recognize unless you learn to read his behavior:

Ears pinned back: This is a classic sign your Lab is worried. Watch how his ears perk up when he's interested in something, how they appear when he's resting, and how they fall down and back when he's unsure.

Yawning: He's not sleepy; yawning is a stress-relieving mechanism.

Licking his nose: He might be gathering scent and pheromones so he can further evaluate the situation.

Teeth chattering: This can be a sign of excitement.

Turning his head away: He refuses to look at the thing that bothers him. Dogs often avoid eye contact to deflect a confrontation with another dog.

Panting: This isn't his normal panting in hot weather or after exercise. You'll see rapid stress-related panting even in cool weather.

Drooling: He might lick his lips or his feet, have sweaty paws, or whine.

Wide, round eyes: The white haw in the corner of his eye will show (referred to as whale eye), or he'll have dilated pupils.

A dog subjected to chronic stress with no relief will develop physical symptoms:

Stomach upset: He might vomit or have chronic diarrhea.

Hyperactivity: He might suffer from an inability to settle down or listen to you, be constantly vigilant, and overreact to everything around him.

Obsessive-compulsive behaviors: Symptoms include chronic licking or chewing on himself to the point of leaving permanent, open sores; tail chasing; barking; or pacing.

Separation anxiety: He might be destructive when left alone, or he might howl or bark the entire time you're gone.

The Fearful Lab

A frightened or extremely anxious dog responds in one of three ways: freeze, flight, or fight. He freezes to evaluate what's happening, maybe lying down and refusing to move or appearing not to recognize you. Next, he flees by either running away or frantically struggling to escape. If he runs away, he's not paying attention to where he's going or what hazards are in his way. He fights if he's cornered and feels he has no other options, starting with a warning snap or growl. If that doesn't work, a full-on bite is his next line of defense.

The signs of stress listed in the previous section will tell you he's worried. Don't comfort him if you see him exhibiting these symptoms. For example, if his hackles go up and he starts barking as you approach a mailbox he's sure contains something scary, don't pet him and tell him not to be afraid. He could interpret your tone of voice as confirming there really is something to worry about. By petting him, you're also inadvertently praising him for his fearful reaction.

Keep the leash slack so your Lab never feels trapped by a scary thing. Let him observe from a distance and approach only if he wants to. Don't bribe him; he'll endure his terror just to get the treat. Instead, use your jolly routine and get his attention on you. When he sees you think that scary thing is no big deal, he'll learn to look to you for your reaction before he decides to be afraid.

HAPPY PUPPY
Got a tense puppy? Herbal or flower remedies like Rescue
Remedy might help calm him.

If your dog is chronically afraid, work with a behaviorist to develop a program to
improve the situation. Counterconditioning and desensitization are two treatment
options. You can't force him to face his fears, and he'll only become more and more
terrified. You might not think they're rational, but they are very real to your Lab.

TRAINING

Labrador Retrievers are willing to work hard and learn complex tasks. If you enjoy
training your dog and would like to try more challenging things together, competitive
obedience and hunting tests make use of your Lab's natural abilities while honing his
skills and yours. You'll enjoy training as much as competing and make many like-
minded friends along the way.

Participating in Rally and Obedience Competition

The American Kennel Club (AKC) offers two types of competitive obedience for dog
owners in which Labs do very well. The sports require dog/handler teamwork and
performance skills and use similar obedience exercises in different ways. Rally and
obedience both offer novice classes for beginning handlers who have never entered
trials or earned titles with their dog.

You can take classes just for the fun of working with your Labrador, and you're
not required to enter trials. Although first through fourth places are awarded in each
trial class, you and your dog really compete against a perfect score. If you qualify,
you earn a leg toward a title. You can earn a title without the need to compete against
another team in a class. At each level, you must achieve three legs—a qualifying
score—to earn a title.

Rally and obedience trials are usually held in conjunction with conformation
events. Labrador *specialty shows,* in which only Labs compete, often offer an
obedience or a rally trial at the same time. To start training or learn more about rally
and obedience, find a local obedience club or dog trainer who teaches competition
classes.

DOG TALK

A **specialty show** is a conformation dog show for a single breed of dog held by a breed club. In a Labrador Retriever Specialty, the breed club often also conducts obedience, rally, hunting tests, and agility trials.

Rally is a good place for a newcomer to start in competitive obedience because it's less structured than traditional obedience, yet it's a step up from the Canine Good Citizen test you read about in Month 10. You and your Lab move through the course at your own pace, completing challenges at individual stations. Each station has a sign with instructions regarding the skill you are to perform. Scoring isn't as precise and rigorous as in regular obedience, and you're encouraged to talk to your dog and have fun while you're going through the course.

A rally course includes 10 to 20 stations, depending on the level of competition, with both stationary and moving exercises. Stationary exercises include halting and sitting your dog, and moving exercises include executing an about-turn and heeling at a face pace.

The levels in rally are Novice, Advanced, and Excellent. In Rally Novice, there are no more than five stationary exercises, and all are performed on-leash. Dogs earn the Rally Novice (RN) title after three qualifying scores. In Rally Advanced (RA), all exercises are done off-leash, and there are no more than seven stationary exercises. The exercises are more difficult, and one jump is included. Rally Excellent (RE) exercises include challenges like backing up three steps while the dog stays in the heel position and a moving stand while the handler walks around the dog. Rally Excellent includes 15 to 20 stations and no more than 7 stationary exercises. An added challenge in the Excellent class is the honor exercise, where your dog must remain in a sit or down-stay while another competitor navigates the entire course with their dog. This exercise is done on leash and you are 6 feet away from your Lab.

HAPPY PUPPY

Both rally and obedience trials test your teamwork as you and your Lab perform obedience exercises together. Rally is less formal, and you can talk to your dog and praise him in the ring. Obedience is more precise and structured, with rules that restrict touching or talking to your dog.

Once you've conquered rally, the Novice class in traditional obedience will seem easy. Rally was officially accepted as an AKC event in 2005, but obedience competition has been part of the AKC for decades. In fact, the first AKC obedience test in 1933 had only eight entries, and two of them were Labrador Retrievers.

AKC clubs hold all-breed obedience trials and specialty trials, which are usually held in conjunction with conformation events. When compared to rally, obedience competition requires a more structured and precise performance and much less interaction between dog and handler while in the ring.

The exercises in obedience are the same at each trial, whereas courses can vary quite a bit in rally. In the Novice class, handlers and their dogs perform on- and off-leash heeling, figure-eight heeling, stand for examination, recall, 1-minute sit-stay, and 3-minute down-stay. When you and your Lab have completed three qualifying rounds, he earns the Companion Dog (CD) title.

In the Open class, all the exercises are performed off-leash: heeling, figure eight, retrieve a dumbbell, go over a jump and retrieve a dumbbell, drop on recall (a formal version of the emergency drop you taught your Lab in Month 10), broad jump, 3-minute sit-stay, and 5-minute down-stay. Both stays are performed with the handler out of sight. After three qualifying scores, your dog earns the Companion Dog Excellent (CDX) title.

The Utility class is the most difficult. Your dog must respond to hand signals for the stand, stay, down, sit, and come. He also must demonstrate scent discrimination by finding an article with his handler's scent on it from a pile of identical articles. In the directed retrieve, he must retrieve a glove indicated by the handler. The directed jumping exercise consists of the dog going away from the handler and returning over a specified jump. In the moving stand and examination, the handler moves forward while the dog halts and stays standing. A judge walks up to the dog and runs her hand over him, and the dog then must return to the handler on command.

As you see, the Utility class requires a high level of teamwork between you and your dog, and it usually takes much longer to earn a title than at the other two levels. The Utility Dog (UD) title is given to teams who successfully qualify in three trials. Dogs can continue to compete and earn a Utility Dog Excellent (UDX) title after qualifying in both Utility and Open classes at 10 trials.

In addition to regular classes, obedience clubs and breed clubs often offer nonregular classes at their trials. Nonregular classes don't count toward titles, but they are enjoyable for you and your dog. You can enter them for fun or while training for the next level of competition. There also are optional titling classes: Beginner Novice (BN), Grad Novice (GN), Grad Open (GO), and Versatility (VER).

HAPPY PUPPY

One nonregular class in particular is fun for Labrador Retriever owners: team obedience. Often offered at specialty shows, a team of four Labs and their handlers perform the novice exercises together in the ring, like a drill team.

Competing in Hunting Tests and Field Trials

Plenty of opportunities are available for you to practice hunting skills and compete with your dog, even if you don't want to hunt. The AKC conducts hunting tests and field trials, and the United Kennel Club (UKC) also has a hunting division that conducts tests. Learn about the UKC Hunting Retriever Club and its levels at huntingretrieverclub.org. The North American Hunting Retriever Association also holds competitions (nahra.org). The competitions profiled here are AKC, but all the organizations have similar levels and procedures. To get involved in hunting tests, contact local clubs for a referral to trainers and group practices.

For beginners, The Labrador Retriever Club, Inc. (thelabradorclub.com), the AKC Labrador Retriever parent breed club, offers a Working Certificate (WC) to test a Lab's natural working ability and retrieving instinct. This gives owners the opportunity to enjoy and experience the work Labs were bred for without having to spend months training for competition. It's a great way to see if you're interested in pursuing the sport. Your dog only needs to pass the test once to earn his WC. Labs who have earned their conformation championship are encouraged to earn a Working Certificate before they use the champion title.

To earn a Working Certificate, the Lab must do the following:

○ A single retrieve of 50 yards on land in light cover (Pheasant and ducks are used, or sometimes pigeons and ducks.)

○ Back-to-back single retrieves in water to prove he's willing to reenter the water

○ Drop the bird within the boundaries designated by the judge (The dog does not have to deliver the bird "to hand"; it can be dropped on the ground.)

○ Not be gun shy

Local and regional Labrador Retriever clubs hold the tests in conjunction with AKC Hunting Tests or separately if they have enough people entered. You don't have to be a member of a club to enter.

Hunting tests are the next step for you and your Lab. In these noncompetitive events, if your dog completes the retrieves according to the rules, he qualifies and earns a leg toward his title. The purpose of the tests is to evaluate a retriever's ability as a hunting companion. Natural situations are set up on land and water, and dogs must retrieve any type of game bird. There are three levels of hunting tests: Junior, Senior, and Master Hunter.

In the Junior tests, your Lab is judged on his ability to mark where the bird falls and remember it, along with his style, perseverance, and hunting ability. He must retrieve four single *marks*—two on land and two in the water. Each retrieve is completed one at a time. When he returns one bird, he turns and another bird is thrown. He must stay quietly at his handler's side until he's sent to retrieve the bird, return it to the handler, and release it to hand when asked. The handler doesn't have to actually shoot a bird (throwers out in the field throw or shoot for them), but your dog must have a soft mouth and not damage the bird. After your Labrador qualifies in four tests, he earns the Junior Hunter (JH) title.

DOG TALK

In a hunting test, a bird is thrown or shot and the dog **marks** it by visually recognizing where it fell and remembering the location.

After the Junior Hunter, dogs and handlers can work toward entering Senior Hunter (SH) and Master Hunter (MH) tests, which include "blind" retrieves, where the dog doesn't see the bird fall. The handler must guide his Lab using signals to find and retrieve the bird. The handler isn't allowed to touch his dog, and the dog must remain steady—that is, not leave until sent. Advanced tests also include "doubles" and "triples," in which the dog must visually mark multiple falls, remember where each bird is, and retrieve them in the same sequence they fell. Dogs also must "honor" by sitting quietly while another dog retrieves.

Top trainers and serious sportsmen compete in field trials, which are more competitive and difficult. At a field trial, dogs compete for placements, and only dogs finishing in the top four placements receive points toward their Field Trial Championship. While Hunt Tests strive to mirror realistic hunting situations, dogs in field trials typically retrieve birds shot several hundred yards out in the field—much farther than a hunter could normally shoot a bird.

Once a dog achieves a certain number of points in field trials, he earns a Field Champion (FC) or Amateur Field Champion (AFC) title. The highest honor a Labrador can achieve is Dual Champion, or both a Field Championship and a Conformation Championship.

YOU AND YOUR PUPPY

Finding a job for your puppy means finding something you'll enjoy, too. From dancing to therapy visits, you and your Lab can share many activities together.

Enjoying Competitive Dog Sports

You don't have to be a super athlete to compete in most canine sports. In fact, people with disabilities perform in a number of AKC-approved activities. You also can train just for fun and never actually enter a competition.

Some of the sports listed in this section offer AKC competitions, others are put on by the sport's parent organization, and some have several groups that sponsor events, which gives you access to more trials and training.

For AKC sports (referred to by the AKC as "companion events"), your Lab must either have registration papers or get a Purebred Alternative Listing (PAL) number, which is available to unregistered dogs and mixed breeds. The PAL used to be called Indefinite Listing Privilege (ILP), so you might hear both terms used. Along with the PAL application and registration fee, you must submit two recent and clear color photographs of your Labrador Retriever, one full front view showing his facial characteristics, and one view showing the full side profile of him standing on a flat surface. Once you've received your PAL number from the AKC, you use that number on the entry forms for events.

Agility: Agility classes are fun and help your Lab develop his coordination. Similar to jumping competitions in the equestrian world, dogs run an obstacle course and must complete it within a preestablished time frame and without any faults, such as knocking over a jump pole or failing to hit a required contact point on an obstacle.

Although your puppy shouldn't start jumping until his growth plates have closed, he can learn many aspects of agility at this age. Weave poles, the A frame, seesaw, pause table, dog walk, and tunnel are all safe for a young dog's growing bones if you don't overdo it. When he starts jumping, instructors usually set the jumps low while your dog learns. When he's fully grown and able to compete, in the AKC, jumps for Labs are designated by height in one of two classes: 20-inch Class for dogs between 18 and 22 inches at the withers (shoulder) or 24-inch Class for dogs over 22 inches at the withers.

Contact obstacles have painted zones at the ends that your dog must touch with at least one paw in order to qualify. This keeps the dogs from leaping off the top of an obstacle and being injured. Contact obstacles include A frame, dog walk, and seesaw.

Seven organizations in the United States offer agility trials, and your dog can earn dozens of titles. The titles can't be mixed and matched with each other, but your Lab can build an impressive list of initials at the end of his name. Here are the groups:

○ American Kennel Club (AKC): akc.org/events/agility

○ United States Dog Agility Association, Inc. (USDAA): USDAA.com

○ United Kennel Club (UKC): ukcdogs.com/WebSite.nsf/WebPages/DogAgility

○ North American Dog Agility Council (NADAC): nadac.com

○ Australian Shepherd Club of America (ASCA; accepts all breeds for competition): asca.org/programs/agility

○ Canine Performance Events (CPE): k9cpe.com

○ Dogs on Course in North America (DOCNA): docna.com

The organizations have similar obstacles, levels of competition, and awards. As an example, the AKC offers three levels: Novice, Open, and Excellent. The maximum time allowed and the number of obstacles to complete increase as the level of difficulty increases. Novice dogs compete on 14 to 16 obstacles, and judging focuses on the owner's handling technique while scoring any faults. Open agility consists of 16 to 18 obstacles. They're more difficult than novice and require the handler to use more advanced skills. Excellent, the highest level for AKC agility, consists of 18 to 20 obstacles. The handler and dog must work as a team and have advanced skills to complete the course. In Masters (for dogs who have completed titles), a dog must qualify 10 times in their class. The ultimate title is the Master Agility Champion (MACH) title, which requires multiple qualifying scores tallied on a point system.

The AKC divides the classes into Standard, Jumpers With Weaves (JWW; no contact obstacles), Fifteen and Send Time (FAST), and Time to Beat (T2B). FAST classes include additional challenges so dog and owner can demonstrate speed, handling skill, accuracy, and distance handling. T2B uses obstacles from JWW, with the option of having one or two contacts included on the course. Each owner has the chance to set the "Time to Beat" for each jump height division.

In addition, trials offer the Preferred Class, which offers longer course times and lower jump heights for the regular classes.

Canine freestyle: Freestyle, or dancing with dogs, is fun and increasingly popular. You don't have to be a great dancer to participate. Based on basic obedience training and dressage, musical freestyle adds music, timing, costuming, and showmanship as you and your Lab perform heelwork or dance moves to music. Your Lab dances both at your side and away from you. Both men and women enjoy the sport, and you can see the dogs are having fun and enjoying the crowd's approval.

You select the music and develop your own choreography, and once you've developed your routine, you can do demos or compete in freestyle events. For more information about canine freestyle, visit the World Canine Freestyle Organization at worldcaninefreestyle.org or the Canine Freestyle Federation at canine-freestyle.org.

Dock dogs: This sport must have been invented for Labs, because they *love* it. You might have seen dock dogs at the fair or on television. It's exciting to participate in and easy for a beginner to get started. If your Lab loves to chase a retrieving toy and enjoys swimming, you're ready. All you need is a floating toy he loves, a leash, plenty of towels, and a place to practice. There are clubs all over the United States where you can practice and compete.

Dock dogs compete in three types of games:

Big air, a long jump for dogs, is the event you see on TV. Handlers throw a floating toy in the pool, and their dog retrieves it, running the length of a 40-foot dock and jumping into the water to get his toy. His jump length is measured where the base of his tail enters the water. The goal is jump length; he doesn't have to return the toy to earn a score.

Extreme vertical tests a dog's jumping ability. A toy is suspended 8 feet out and $4\frac{1}{2}$ feet up from the edge of the dock, and dogs have two chances to jump and grab the bumper. If they make it, the bumper is raised in 2-inch increments until all the other dogs are eliminated.

Speed retriever is a timed event. You hold your Lab 20 feet back from the edge of the dock, behind an infrared beam that serves as the starting line, and a foam duck toy is suspended at the far end of the pool. When you get the green light, you release your Lab and he leaps off the end of the dock and swims to the duck. The dog is timed, and when he grabs the duck, the timer stops. He doesn't have to bring the duck back to you. The challenge is finished when the timer stops.

Iron Dog is a point system that ranks dogs participating in all three disciplines. To learn about dock dogs and to find local clubs, visit dockdogs.com.

Flyball: Another exciting sport based on speed and retrieving, flyball races consist of two teams of four dogs who compete against each other in relay races. The course is 51 feet long with 4 jumps. Each dog jumps low hurdles, steps on a tennis-ball launcher at the end of the line to release the ball, and returns with the ball. When he crosses the finish line, the next dog is released to do the same thing. Both teams run at the same time, side by side, so competition is fierce as the audience cheers their team on to the finish line. Teams are divided into divisions so they can compete against teams with similar levels of ability.

The hurdle heights are determined by the height of the shortest dog on the team, so you'll often see an odd combo of breeds, such as three tall dogs like Labs and a short Yorkie. The start line and timing are measured electronically, and the winning team might win by a thousandth of a second—important when four experienced dogs can finish a run in less than 20 seconds. The North American Flyball Association has more information available at flyball.org/aboutflyball.html.

Conformation: When you watch a televised dog show, like the AKC/Eukanuba National Championship or the Westminster Kennel Club show, that's a conformation event. In these events, dogs are judged against the breed standard, which we talked about in Month 10. For each breed, the judge evaluates dogs in classes separated by male and female and further divisions within each sex. The first place dogs of each class compete against each other in the Winners class, and the winning male and female in that class both go on to compete against dogs who have their championship for the Best of Breed award.

Dogs earn points based on how many dogs they're shown against, and when they've won a certain number of points against a representative number of dogs for the particular breed, they earn their championship. Champion dogs are considered excellent candidates for breeding because they've proven they have the correct structure and temperament representative of the breed. After they have their health clearances, these dogs can go on to produce sound, healthy puppies and improve the breed overall.

Breeds are divided into seven groups in AKC competition. Labrador Retrievers are part of the Sporting Group, and the Best of Breed Lab competes against other retrievers, spaniels, pointers, and setters for the Best in Group award. The other breed groups (and some representative breeds) are the Working Group (Rottweilers, Boxers), Herding (Collies, German Shepherds), Toy (Maltese, Chihuahua), Non-Sporting (Standard Poodle, Keeshound), Terrier (Scottish Terrier, Airedale Terrier), and Hound (Bloodhound, Dachshund). The winner of each group then proceeds to the Best In Show ring, where a judge chooses a winner among the seven top dogs from that day's competition.

If you're interested in conformation, talk to your breeder. Your Labrador Retriever may or may not be a "show-quality" dog, and an expert will need to go over him to confirm whether he should be shown. Conformation dogs must be intact (not spayed or neutered). Also, you'll need to learn about handling your dog in the ring, grooming, nutrition, conditioning, and pedigrees so you can be competitive. Many breed clubs have fun matches in which you can practice or offer classes, and some breeders will mentor people who are new to the sport.

Therapy Dogs

Accompanied by their owners, therapy dogs make visits to schools, nursing homes, rehabilitation hospitals, libraries, and other facilities to cheer the patients, residents, and staff. Labrador Retrievers are naturally suited for this kind of work.

Therapy dogs must be immaculately groomed for their visits. For example, their toenails must be cut short so they don't tear the skin of fragile or elderly patients. They also must be healthy and free of parasites because they'll be around patients with compromised immune systems.

Most facilities require that you and your dog be trained and certified through a recognized therapy dog organization, and local and national groups offer training and testing. Therapy Dogs International (tdi-dog.org) and Pet Partners (petpartners .org) both have local chapters all over the United States that train and certify animal-assisted therapy dogs. Pet Partners also offers a home-study course to prepare you and your dog for visits.

Many therapy groups use the Canine Good Citizen test as the basis for certification and expand it to include exposure to wheelchairs and hospital situations. Dogs with more advanced training can participate in animal-assisted therapy, attending actual physical or psychological therapy sessions. For example, a patient in a rehab hospital could relearn to use her hands by brushing your Lab, throwing a ball for him, or opening a can of dog food. Or your dog might sit next to a child who's undergoing a frightening procedure to calm him. In schools, a child could read to your dog while working on her reading skills.

To find a therapy dog group near you, ask local obedience trainers or hospitals to refer you to a group. Or contact the national organizations to see if there's a chapter in your area.

	SOCIAL	BEHAVIOR	TRAINING	PHYSICAL	HEALTH
MONTH 1			Littermates and mother teach appropriate canine behavior	Rapid growth	
MONTH 2	Breeder starts socialization				
MONTH 3	Socialization at home with new owner and other pets	Fear-imprint period	Begin house- and crate training		1st DHPP vaccine
MONTH 4		Teething begins—heavy chewing period	Enroll in puppy class		2nd DHPP vaccine
MONTH 5	Socialization in public		Ready for basic commands	Switch to adult food	3rd DHPP and rabies vaccines
MONTH 6					
MONTH 7			Enroll in basic obedience class		
MONTH 8				Moderate growth	Sexual maturity
MONTH 9		Adult teeth are in—chewing continues			
MONTH 10			Ready for more advanced training		
MONTH 11				Slow growth—reaches adult size	
MONTH 12 AND BEYOND					Annual vaccinations and checkup

12

AND BEYOND

Your Lab Grows Up

Labrador Retrievers have an extended puppyhood, and yours won't settle down much until she's 2½ to 3 years old. Some Labs are quiet and mellow, but most keep their happy-puppy attitude well into old age. You have many years of laughter to look forward to as your pup matures.

PHYSICAL DEVELOPMENT

Over the next 2 years, your teenager will continue to physically mature, although the changes won't be nearly as dramatic as those you've seen during her first year.

Changes from 1 Year to Adulthood

Your Lab will continue to look like a teenager until she's about 18 months old. Then she'll fill out and look fully mature and balanced at 2½ to 3 years old. The growth plates in her limbs will close between 10 and 18 months, and her height will stabilize. Her legs will grow stronger and sturdier, too. With males, characteristics like a broader head and chest will develop if he's not yet neutered. Females won't look a lot different when they reach maturity, but they, too, will stop growing and fill out a little.

Right now, your Lab has the maturity of a 15-year-old child. She's still very much a puppy, with a teenager's exuberance and energy level, and she might not have much common sense yet. By the time she's 18 months old, she'll have matured a bit. She'll be less frantic, but still very active.

Adult Sizes and Weights

Your adolescent probably won't grow more than another inch between now and full maturity. She'll add on a few pounds, and she'll eat like a horse, but don't excuse weight gain as "filling out." Continue to check her body condition (see Appendix B), and adjust her food accordingly.

Remember that an adult male should weigh between 65 and 80 pounds when he's 3 years old, so depending on his height and build, he should be less than his expected weight now. A female should be 55 to 70 pounds at 3 years old. When in doubt, keep your Labrador lean rather than heavy.

HEALTH

With a little attention, your dog should be healthy and active for many years to come. Schedule regular wellness exams and vaccines, and watch for signs of health problems so you can catch them before they get serious.

When Are the Next Vaccinations Due?

Assuming your Lab puppy had her rabies vaccine and final DHPP booster at 4 months, she should need her next inoculations at 16 months, or 1 year later. Consider waiting a week between the DHPP and rabies vaccines to avoid overloading her immune system. Once this round of vaccines is completed, you shouldn't have to revaccinate your dog for 3 years.

TIPS AND TAILS

In 2003, the American Animal Hospital Association (AAHA) changed its vaccine guidelines, recommending veterinarians vaccinate dogs only every 3 years. Research has shown that yearly vaccines are unnecessary because most animals retain the immunity from the initial vaccines for many years. There are also indications that overvaccination is potentially harmful. Adverse long-term effects are still being studied, but researchers suspect excessive vaccination could contribute to anaphylaxis, immunosuppression, autoimmune disorders, infections, and other disorders.

You may have given your Lab other noncore vaccines such as those for Lyme disease, coronavirus, or leptospirosis. Discuss optional vaccines and the risk of contracting the diseases in your area with your veterinarian.

If you'll be boarding your dog, the bordetella vaccine is required and must be given on a 6-month or yearly basis, depending on the kennel's requirements.

If you take your dog to the veterinarian for a suspected illness and her vaccines are ready to be updated, wait until she's recovered from whatever ails her. Her immune system is compromised when she's ill, and the vaccine might not create the protective immunity it's supposed to provide. Likewise, as your Lab ages, consider her health status before administering vaccines. It's possible that older dogs with diabetes, hypothyroidism, glaucoma, or any other chronic medical condition should no longer be vaccinated. Explore this option with your veterinarian when the time comes.

Titers

A *titer*, an alternative to booster vaccines, is a blood test that confirms if a dog has responded to a specific vaccine and still has that immunity. If she does, no further vaccination is necessary. Veterinarians usually test for parvovirus and distemper because if the dog is protected from these two, it's fairly certain her immunological status is in good shape. Titers should be repeated yearly to detect when or if your Lab loses her immunity.

DOG TALK
A **titer** measures the amount of antibodies to a particular disease your Lab is carrying in her body.

Vaccines cost less than running a titer test, but the benefit is that you don't expose your dog to unnecessary vaccines.

The Annual Checkup

Even if you don't vaccinate your dog every year, she still needs an annual wellness exam. Dogs age faster than humans, and your Labrador Retriever changes dramatically between vet visits. Dogs also hide pain well, and your vet might discover something you haven't noticed yet.

The annual exam establishes a history so that when your Lab does have a problem, the veterinarian has a record of her past health status to compare to. This helps him decide if further tests are needed and aids his diagnosis.

Before you take your Labrador to the vet, make a list of questions about her health, behavior, nutrition, and anything else on your mind. Review her health record so you know the date of her last vaccines and any other treatments she's had. Bring her treats with you to the appointment so you can make the visit a positive experience for your dog. Also bring in a stool sample to be checked for worms and other parasites, along with any medications or supplements you're giving her.

During your visit, the veterinarian will examine your dog. He will …

○ Check her weight and assess if it's normal or if she's overweight.

○ Conduct a nose-to-tail examination, listening to her heart, lungs, and digestive sounds and feeling for any abnormalities, lumps, or signs of pain.

○ Test your dog's reflexes to be sure they're normal.

○ Examine her teeth to see if they're clean and the gums are a healthy color.

○ Draw blood for heartworm test and any other tests indicated, such as those for tick-borne diseases.

○ Administer annual bordetella (kennel cough) vaccine if needed, and update any other inoculations as needed.

○ Examine her ears to see if they're healthy (pink and free of infection) and contain no foreign bodies.

○ Renew her prescriptions for flea control, heartworm preventative, and any other necessary medications.

If the vet finds a problem, he may order further bloodwork, x-rays, or other testing.

Common Lab Ailments

Like all dogs, Labs are vulnerable to disease as they mature. Some ailments strike young dogs for no apparent reason. Others are preventable if you take sensible precautions.

Allergies: Many Labs suffer from allergies. If yours is licking her paws, scratching for no obvious reason, chewing the base of her tail, or has dander or flaky skin, she might be reacting to an allergen. A Lab's allergies could be caused by food sensitivities, flea allergy, or environmental allergies. Just as people do, she might suffer more during certain times of the year.

We've talked about food, noting your Lab could be sensitive to a particular grain or protein source. Food allergies are actually uncommon in dogs. Careful experimentation with elimination diets might solve this problem, and your vet might prescribe a hypoallergenic food. It can take up to 12 weeks to see a difference in your dog's health if a food allergy is the issue.

Your pup also can be allergic to flea saliva, and it only takes one flea to cause an intense, itchy reaction. Check her coat for flea dirt, and bathe her if you see evidence of infestation. Keep her on a regular flea preventative, too. Some preventatives lose their effectiveness because your dog builds up immunity to them, so switch brands if your dog is still suffering from fleas. If your Lab is clean and in excellent health, she won't be as attractive to fleas.

Environmental allergies are harder to treat because you usually can't eliminate the allergen. Such allergies, called atopic dermatitis, often start slowly, with just one or two sensitivities. Over time, your dog might start reacting to additional substances. Many things can affect her, including pollen, grasses, dust mites, feathers, and mold. As your dog continues to suffer, she might develop thick, greasy-looking skin.

Your veterinarian or a veterinary dermatologist can perform skin sensitivity testing and develop injections to desensitize your dog to the offending substances. Unless the allergies are extreme, your best bet is probably to just take measures to keep her comfortable. Your veterinarian can prescribe antihistamines, antibiotics, and steroids to control her symptoms. Be aware that, as your puppy scratches, she might also get secondary yeast and staph infections, which also need treatment.

HAPPY PUPPY

If your Lab has allergies or hot spots, a cool, medicated bath will soothe her skin. Don't use oatmeal shampoo. Although it soothes the itching, it's a grain, and dogs with grain sensitivities may have an additional allergic reaction.

If you think your Lab has environmental allergies, keep her indoors with the windows closed when the pollen count is high. (Check your daily paper or online for that information.) Also keep her indoors during the peak hay fever times of day— early morning and evening. When you bring her in from outdoors, rinse her feet and wipe her down with a damp towel.

Even if they don't have a food allergy, some dogs with atopic dermatitis improve when switched to a higher-quality dog food. If your Lab is allergic to house dust mites, they often react with grain mites. In that case, your puppy will benefit from a grain-free canned food or kibble.

Keep in mind that not all itching is caused by allergies. Parasites like sarcoptic mange (scabies) cause intense itching. If your dog gets wet and isn't dried thoroughly, she can get hot spots (see Month 8) or yeast infections. Your vet can rule out all the possibilities before diagnosing allergies.

Arthritis: Manage your Lab's exercise for life so she won't be crippled by arthritis as she ages. Whenever possible, have her run and play on soft ground because hard pounding jars her bones and joints. Although arthritis is sometimes caused by hip dysplasia, otherwise healthy dogs also can get it due to a previous injury, tick-borne disease, autoimmune disorder, obesity, or cartilage problems caused by poor diet.

If your veterinarian diagnoses arthritis …

- Manage your Lab's weight, and provide gentle exercise such as swimming and walking to maintain her muscle tone.
- Give her glucosamine and chondroitin supplements that lubricate her joints and may relieve her pain.
- Consider getting her acupuncture to help relieve symptoms.
- Be sure she has a soft bed that cushions her sore joints.
- Allow your Lab to stay indoors on cold, damp days.
- Raise her food bowl if she has a stiff neck.
- Help her climb stairs, and provide a ramp to help her get in and out of the car.
- Ask your vet about pain-relieving medications.
- Put carpet runners on hard floors so she can walk more easily.

Bloat: Gastric dilatation volvulus, or bloat, most often occurs in large, deep-chested dog breeds. Although Labs are vulnerable, it's not common in the breed. The risk increases as your dog ages. With bloat, the stomach fills with gas and fluid and swells because the dog cannot expel it (gastric dilatation). As a result, the stomach twists (volvulus). Symptoms include drooling, unproductive retching, restlessness, biting at her side, a distended abdomen, and signs of shock. Emergency surgery to relieve the twisting could save your dog's life. If your dog's stomach doesn't twist, your veterinarian can relieve the gas by passing a tube into the dog's stomach.

Dogs who have suffered from bloat are very likely to have another occurrence. To prevent bloat …

- Restrict access to water for 1 hour before and after meals.
- Avoid strenuous exercise 1 hour before and after meals.
- Divide her food into three small meals, spaced well apart.
- Do not feed your Lab from a raised food bowl. For many years, it was thought that feeding large dogs from raised bowls helped prevent bloat. A 2000 study conducted by Purdue University found that feeding from elevated bowls actually increased the likelihood of bloat.
- Avoid feeding dry food that lists fat among the first four ingredients.
- Never let her gulp a large amount of water all at once so she doesn't take in too much air. If she's very thirsty, let her have a quick drink and then wait a minute or so for another one. Repeat as needed to quell her thirst.

> **TIPS AND TAILS**
> Bloat is a life-threatening situation, so if your dog shows symptoms, take her to the vet immediately.

Cold tail: Also called "limber tail," cold tail is a painful condition that can affect a Labrador of any age. It occurs most often in hunting dogs, and it also shows up in some other sporting breeds. When moving, a Lab normally carries her tail straight out or at least up off her back legs. An affected dog holds her tail down limply against her rear. The condition has been blamed on hard workouts, heavy hunting, and swimming or bathing in water that's too cold. The tail isn't broken; rather, the condition may be associated with muscle or nerve damage to the tail. It most often occurs in male Labs.

Dogs usually recover within a few days, but sometimes it takes as long as a week. Warm packs at the base of the tail and analgesics will help ease your Lab's pain.

Gum disease: Caring for your Lab's teeth and gums is crucial to ensuring her lifelong health. By the time your dog is 3 years old, she might need a teeth cleaning to remove tartar and plaque on her teeth and beneath the gum line where the toothbrush can't reach. Without diligent dental care, she could get a serious infection that could spread through her system and shorten her life. Your veterinarian can determine if your Lab needs her teeth cleaned and can show you where plaque has built up or gum disease has started.

Although her teeth are beautiful and white now, chewing on sticks and tennis balls can wear them down significantly over time. She might also break a tooth that will need to be removed.

Impacted anal glands: These are two tiny glands (also called anal sacs) just inside the anus. When a dog defecates, the firm stool presses against the glands and expels fluid. If you see your dog scooting her butt on the ground, sitting in an odd position, or in obvious discomfort, suspect impacted anal glands. Your veterinarian can express them during an office visit, and no sedation is needed.

There could be several causes. When a dog has soft stool or diarrhea, the glands aren't forced to empty naturally. Other problems that cause impacted anal glands include inflammation in the intestinal tract, allergies that cause your Lab to scratch or chew at her anus, or an infection. A small minority of dogs has improperly placed anal glands. In some cases surgical removal is the only option.

A healthy dog doesn't need to have her anal glands emptied for her. In fact, emptying the sacs too often causes trauma to the duct. The anal glands close and can no longer expel fluid on their own. Don't have the procedure done unless your dog actually needs it.

Occasionally, in a highly stressful situation, a dog will suddenly expel the anal sac fluid. You'll know, because the smell is extremely offensive.

Laryngeal paralysis: A disease that affects primarily older Labrador Retrievers, laryngeal paralysis occurs when a dog's vocal folds, which usually open when the dog inhales, don't open at all or open out of sync with the dog's natural breathing rhythm. Part of a neurological disease process that develops over a long period of time, it can affect one or both vocal folds. A dog who has laryngeal paralysis pants excessively, is overly sensitive to heat, and is easily fatigued. Often her breathing won't return to normal until hours after exercise.

A surgeon can tie back the vocal fold (or folds) to the outer sides of the larynx so her airway will remain open. Although the dog's breathing improves, she's susceptible to aspirating (inhaling) her food. When she eats, she might get food or water in her lungs, which can cause pneumonia.

Lumps: As Labs age, they often get an assortment of lumps on their bodies. This is perfectly normal, but you'll want your vet to take a look at them to be sure they're not something serious. Sometimes he can tell what a lump is by how it's attached to your dog's body. Or he might withdraw some fluid or cells from the lump and examine it microscopically to confirm it's harmless. If the lump is benign, there's no need to remove it except for cosmetic reasons, and you can wait until your dog has to go under anesthesia for another procedure, like teeth cleaning, if you want it removed. If a lump starts to grow or drains fluid, take your dog to the vet for further testing.

TIPS AND TAILS

Select a permanent guardian for your Lab to ensure she won't end up in a shelter if something happens to you. In fact, get three people to agree to care for your Lab. If someone's situation changes and he's unable to fulfill your wishes, someone else can.

NUTRITION

In the previous section, we touched on food allergies. There are other ways your Lab's diet can affect her health, and we look at those here. We also explore raw and home-cooked diets, along with their benefits and drawbacks.

The Relationship Between Food and Health

Poor-quality food can cause nutritional deficiencies in your pup and lead to major illness. Now that the pet food industry does a much better job of manufacturing complete and balanced dog foods, there's a much lower incidence of diseases caused by nutrient imbalances. But even a food label that states "complete and balanced" might not provide the best nutrition for your dog's particular needs.

Here are some examples of what happens when certain nutrients are out of balance:

- Vitamin A toxicity can occur when too much liver, cod liver oil, or vitamin A is added to the diet. It causes lethargy, loss of appetite, and bone and joint pain.

- Vitamin B_{12} deficiency causes anemia.

- Vitamin D toxicity causes excess levels of calcium in the blood and can lead to kidney stones and organ failure.

- Fatty-acid deficiency causes skin and hair disorders, such as a dry, brittle coat and hair loss. It also causes slow healing from injury or illness.

- Zinc deficiency sometimes occurs in dogs fed poor-quality or generic foods, or those who have been oversupplemented with other minerals like iron, calcium, and copper. A deficiency causes poor growth in puppies. Too much zinc causes calcium and copper deficiencies.

- Protein deficiency causes infections, weakened immune system, slow healing, hormone deficiencies, and skin problems.

TIPS AND TAILS

If you're feeding your Labrador Retriever a raw or home-cooked diet, you must ensure she's getting the proper balance of the nutrients she needs.

Dealing with Obesity

Labs gain weight very easily. They're active, but they also love to eat and don't seem to know when to stop. If your Lab is 20 percent or more over her ideal weight, she's not just plump, she's obese. That means an 84-pound dog who should weigh 70 pounds has to lose 14 pounds—that's a lot of dog biscuits. Spayed females are the most likely to gain weight, but all Labs are susceptible. If your pup is overweight, you're risking serious future health problems, such as arthritis, heart and respiratory disease, hip dysplasia, cruciate ligament injury, kidney disease, cancer, pancreatitis, and a decreased life expectancy—up to 2 years less.

Once you've established that your Labrador Retriever is too heavy, work with your veterinarian to put together a realistic weight-loss plan. Before you start anything, have your vet do a complete physical exam. Health conditions like thyroid disease can cause weight gain.

Helping your dog lose weight is similar to going on a diet yourself. To say "less food and more exercise" is simple, but you need to do more. Let's look at productive ways to help your Lab maintain a healthy weight:

- Cut back on her food gradually so she isn't suddenly starving. If you cut back too fast, her metabolism will slow down to compensate for the decrease in food.

- Add beans, pumpkin, and other high-fiber veggies to her meal to help her feel full.

- Switch to a "light" commercial dog food or a low-calorie, high-fiber prescription diet food. The bulk is the same so she doesn't feel deprived.

- Feed her twice a day, and pick up her food between meals.

- Soak her food in water before feeding her so it expands in the bowl and makes her feel full as soon as she eats.

- Eliminate coat supplements that might be high in fat and calories.

- Cut back on treats. A big dog doesn't need giant dog biscuits; a little snack will do just fine. Choose less-fattening treats like carrots, rice cakes, or popcorn (if she isn't sensitive to rice or corn). Give her air-popped popcorn, and don't add butter or salt.

- Avoid table scraps. Those calories add up fast.

- Put her meal in a treat-dispensing toy so she'll be entertained and less focused on scarfing down her food.

Last but never least, begin an exercise program with your Lab. Assuming she's healthy enough to exercise, start with walks and work up to more energetic games of fetch or other activities when her fitness begins to improve. Daily exercise builds muscle tone, and muscle tone decreases the amount of fat she carries around. Muscle mass also increases metabolism, which helps burn calories.

HAPPY PUPPY
Swimming is excellent exercise, and most Labs enjoy it.

Home-Prepared Food

Today you have more options than ever when choosing food for your dog. Instead of commercially manufactured dog foods, some people opt to feed their dogs raw or home-cooked diets. Many of these owners want to provide their puppy optimum nutrition and have control over the quality and ingredients they're feeding, without added dyes, fillers, or preservatives. Others might have lost faith in commercial foods due to food recalls. And some might want to try a home-prepared diet to see if they can resolve a health problem their Labrador suffers from, like allergies or digestive issues.

There are advantages and disadvantages to home-prepared foods, and you'll find plenty of advice in books and online. When you're researching diets, take into consideration the source. This is a subject people get very passionate about, but they're sometimes long on opinions and short on facts.

A poorly prepared, imbalanced diet can cause more health problems than it solves, as you saw in the previous section about the links between health and nutrition. Consider working with a veterinary nutritionist to be sure you're providing the healthiest possible diet for your Lab. Remember that dogs are carnivores, so whatever type of diet you choose, it should contain about 75 percent meat. No more than 10 percent should consist of grains, and 15 percent can be vegetables and fruits.

TIPS AND TAILS

Feeding home-prepared foods is not an all-or-nothing proposition. You can feed a quality commercial food to be sure your Lab is getting sufficient vitamins and minerals and supplement it with raw or home-cooked ingredients.

Monitor your dog's health to be sure the diet is working for her. Her teeth should be cleaner, her gums healthier, her skin should be healthy, and her coat should be thick and shiny. Overall, she should appear healthy and happy, with clear eyes and ears and plenty of energy. Her stools should be smaller because her body is making better use of the nutrients she consumes and she isn't eating too many grains and fillers that are hard to digest efficiently. If you find bits of bone in her stool, she's not chewing them completely so grind them smaller or discontinue feeding bones. If your Lab suddenly develops diarrhea, vomiting, or gas or has a decrease in appetite, discontinue feeding the diet and consult with your veterinarian. It could be due to a single ingredient, or something else might be wrong.

Raw diets are often referred to as BARF (Bones And Raw Food, or Biologically Appropriate Raw Food). The BARF diet was popularized by Dr. Ian Billinghurst, an Australian veterinarian who believes dogs should eat the way their ancestors ate. But considering that dogs have been domesticated for more than 10,000 years, this might not be an appropriate comparison. Plus, wolves still eat this way in the wild. Wolves are much different from dogs, and dogs have changed dramatically since they were first domesticated. Wolves don't necessarily get the nutrients they need for good health, and ancient dogs quickly became dependent on humankind for food.

So although the reasoning may be flawed, there are some advantages to feeding raw, whole foods. You have complete control over the ingredients, for one. Also, you can purchase fresh, whole foods and avoid pesticide-treated, processed foods and meat raised with antibiotics or growth hormones. Finally, you can experiment with different ingredients and take advantage of seasonal produce.

Now for the disadvantages. It's hard to know whether you're feeding a proper balance of nutrients, especially vitamins and minerals. For example, a dog needs a good balance of calcium and phosphorus in her diet. Raw meat provides phosphorus, and raw bones provide calcium, but getting a correct balance is often the biggest problem with a raw diet. You also run a risk of feeding too much fat, which can cause pancreatitis, a potentially fatal disease. And because it isn't cooked to kill bacteria, raw meat must be from healthy animals and handled carefully during processing to prevent spoilage or contamination. If you aren't careful, ingesting raw meat can give you or your dog E. coli or salmonella. Also, large, raw bones can break a dog's teeth or perforate her stomach or intestinal tract. Small, softer raw bones, like chicken or turkey necks, are safer. You also can grind raw bones to minimize the risks. Finally, raw foods are more expensive than commercial dog food and take a lot of planning and preparation time.

TIPS AND TAILS
As with any change in your dog's food, make the transition to a new diet gradually to avoid major stomach upsets.

Home-cooked diets are usually a stew made of meat, grains, and vegetables. Your dog gets many of the benefits of a raw diet without as much risk of contamination, although safe handling practices are still necessary on your part.

Table scraps don't provide adequate nutrition for your Lab and usually contain excessive amounts of fat. Cooked bones should be removed and discarded after cooking or ground into small, safe pieces.

GROOMING

You've taught your puppy to enjoy handling and grooming, and now it's time to make good use of those skills and not let her forget them.

Maintaining a Regular Grooming Schedule

Every Sunday night, as she relaxes in front of the television, Terry gets down on the floor with her Lab and has a good grooming session. Her dog is tired after an active weekend and willing to sit still, and he looks forward to their time together—and the multitude of treats he gets when she trims his toenails.

A weekly grooming is all your Lab should need on a regular basis, except when she's blowing coat twice a year. You can break up grooming chores into several sessions during the week if you want to. Toothbrushing Tuesdays, Friday fur-fights—the idea is to be able to look forward to spending this time with your dog while keeping her clean and healthy.

The more time you spend grooming, the more cooperative she'll be. If you slack off for a couple months, maybe in the winter, you'll find she gets a case of the wiggle-butts come springtime when you want her to sit still for grooming.

TIPS AND TAILS

Trim your dog's toenails weekly (see Month 3) as part of your grooming routine; otherwise, the long nails cause her feet to splay, which affects her balance and ability to stand and walk correctly. Overly long nails also contribute to the development of arthritis as her legs take on added stress. And don't forget the dewclaws while you're trimming. If they get too long, they can easily snag when she's scratching or digging.

Performing Weekly Health Checks

Don't forget to perform a weekly health check (see Month 4) during your grooming sessions. Go over your Lab's entire body—her skin, feet, mouth, eyes, and ears—to identify grooming needs and health issues before they cause serious problems. As your Lab ages, you'll also want to look for lumps and signs of soreness due to arthritis or other conditions.

SOCIAL SKILLS

You've spent a lot of time and effort raising a well-behaved Labrador, and now it's time to enjoy the fruits of your labor. A backyard dog quickly forgets her manners and social skills, and she also develops the behavioral problems you've worked to avoid. So continue socializing her and enjoying her company.

Enjoying Daily Walks

No matter how old she is, your Labrador Retriever needs some daily activity, both for companionship with you and exercise. A daily walk helps you unwind and gives her some much-needed exposure to the outside world, and you'll enjoy some nice time together. Once around the block won't be enough to wear her out, though. She needs at least a half hour of active exercise and a long walk. A nightly trip to the dog park or a visit to the neighbor dog for a play date takes care of both.

If you don't keep up with walks and exercise, your Lab will gradually get harder to handle and her training will deteriorate. The more trouble she is, the less time you'll want to spend with her, and next thing you know, she's spending way too much time alone or in the crate.

HAPPY PUPPY

Remember, your Lab is still young and needs a lot of exercise, guidance, discipline—and time with you.

Keeping Up with Socialization

As we've mentioned before, dogs quickly become desocialized if they don't get out regularly. Plus, at 12 months, males are reaching an age when they might become more territorial and protective, so they still need diligent socialization.

Include your dog in activities when company comes to your house so she continues to welcome people into your home. Be sure she spends time with children if you don't have any of your own. She also needs to continue meeting other friendly dogs of all sizes on a regular basis. With a little work on your part, her social skills will continue to improve, and she'll remain the friendly, outgoing dog a Lab is supposed to be.

BEHAVIOR

She might look like an adult, but your Labrador Retriever isn't quite there yet. Give her leeway as she earns it, but don't be afraid to continue with crating and discipline when she needs it. If her behavior deteriorates, back up a few steps and put her on a puppy boot-camp program around the house. When her skills have been reviewed, try again to offer her some adult privileges.

Changes as Adulthood Approaches

As your Labrador Retriever encounters adulthood, she'll still be your happy-go-lucky puppy, but she'll grow bigger, stronger, and more protective of her territory. Although Labs aren't particularly good defenders, you might find her sounding the alarm well before your doorbell rings. You shouldn't see any aggression like might appear at this age in other breeds, however, because a typical Labrador is universally friendly to one and all.

You'll find that her attention span has improved and she concentrates better. She's not as distracted and impulsive as she once was, and she obeys you more readily and accepts your leadership. In other words, although she's still a rambunctious youngster, your pup should be developing into a sociable, well-mannered member of society.

If you haven't spayed or neutered your Lab yet, be sure to plan this in the next few months.

Continuing Crating

A 12-month-old Labrador isn't mature enough to have full run of the house when you're not there to supervise her. It's just too much responsibility. Continue crating her at night and when you're unable to watch her. She can't resist temptation yet, and like most teenagers, she always needs to be doing something. She might need to be crated at night until she's past 2 years old.

You'll also find her spending time in her crate by her own choice, so don't worry that you're being cruel.

TRAINING

She's still an adolescent, and she will be for many months, so your Lab puppy may suddenly test the rules when you least expect it. Continue practicing, taking her to classes, and adding new skills to her repertoire. Socialization and training go hand in hand, and the more time you invest in both—while having fun with your Lab—the better companion and pet she'll become.

Lifetime Training

When you finished basic obedience class, your work wasn't done. A Lab puppy still has a lot of maturing to do, and her skills need reinforcement on a regular basis. Here are some reminders of how to use training throughout her life and keep her skills fresh:

- Always ask her to sit when you put on the leash and wait for you before going through doors.
- Have her sit to greet people.
- Ask her to do a down-stay while you eat dinner or are out in public.
- Incorporate sits, downs, and stays into your daily walks.
- Have her sit or do a down before you give her her food bowl.
- Ask her to earn privileges—to play or go for a walk—by sitting first. Don't allow her to boss you around.
- Practice self-control exercises. You don't want her to be rambunctious and out of control when you most need her to behave.
- Keep the recall a fresh and happy command so you can always rely on her to come when you call her.
- Enforce commands like give, off, and sit, even when you're playing a game. She'll enjoy the challenge.

Training an Adult Labrador Retriever

If you've adopted a teenage or adult Labrador Retriever, chances are she didn't get much training in her former home. You *can* teach an old dog new tricks, and Labs in particular are eager to learn and work hard to earn your approval, no matter their age.

Positive reinforcement training is very effective with rescued dogs. Start training on the day you bring home your new dog, when she's trying to figure out her new surroundings. She's paying close attention to what you say and do, what pleases you, and what earns treats or discipline. The more you can find to praise in her behavior, the quicker she'll adapt to her new home.

Enroll in a beginning obedience class, even if she appears to have had some training. This helps you get better acquainted and gives you a structure for training and measuring her progress. You'll soon realize if she lacks social skills or is fearful, and you can begin working on these issues right away.

YOU AND YOUR PUPPY

Your Labrador Retriever puppy's first year presented a lot of challenges, and now she is almost grown. All the time you've invested has built a good foundation for your next decade or more together.

Your Changing Relationship

Your relationship with your puppy will gradually change from one of constant supervision and training to one of friendship and understanding. You've spent a lot of time getting to know each other, and your Lab can read your moods so well, sometimes you'll think she's human. And of course, you'll learn to read her, too, especially when she's about to take off with your shoe.

Check in with your breeder at least once a year, and give her an update on your puppy. She'll want to know if your Lab has any health issues you're concerned about, and she'll be thrilled to catch up on your pup's activities.

Enjoying Social and Fitness Activities

Hiking with your Lab is fun and challenging. When she's matured, work up slowly to more challenging hikes so she doesn't get overly tired, heated, or injured. Also research hiking trails before you go to be sure dogs are welcome.

Don't head out empty-handed. Here are some things you should take along with you:

- 1 quart of water for each of you
- A portable water bowl for her
- Snacks for energy (Peanut butter on dog biscuits gives her a quick energy boost.)
- Waste bags (Be a responsible hiker, and pick up the poop.)
- First-aid kit that includes Benadryl, eyewash, tweezers, antibiotic ointment, a large bandana for bandaging, gauze pads, insect repellent, and meat tenderizer to put on insect bites

○ Her leash

○ A doggie backpack (Be sure you've tested it beforehand and it fits her without rubbing.)

Sometimes it's hard to get yourself off the couch to exercise, but your Lab can help you get out the door. You two can participate in a multitude of doggy fitness classes. Walking groups, exercise classes, and even doga—yoga for you and your dog!—offer the opportunity to strengthen the bond between you and your Lab while reaping health benefits for both of you.

Meetup groups offer get-togethers for like-minded folks in any number of hobbies and activities, including dogs, and you're sure to find a special Labrador meetup group in your area. Go to meetup.com, put in your zip code, and see what's happening near you. Lab owners schedule play dates at local dog parks, beach walks, costume contests, and even "yappy" hours.

Labrador Retriever rescue groups always need more volunteers, and members share a common love for their breed. Even if you can't bear to visit a shelter, you can help out with adoption fairs, transportation, fund-raising, and other events. Members often bring their own Labs along, so be sure to take yours, too, if she's well socialized.

You also could join the local or national Labrador Retriever breed club, especially if you're interested in obedience, conformation, hunting tests, tracking, or agility. You'll find plenty of fellow Lab owners to train with, and you'll stay up-to-date on upcoming events and activities.

Outfitting Your Lab

Owning an active Lab means outfitting her with her own gear for your adventures together. These products make it easier to take your dog along and ensure her safety.

Your Lab might be more comfortable on your adventures if she's wearing boots. Protective boots come in everyday lightweight styles that provide air circulation while protecting her paw pads from hot pavement. For snowy, cold weather, tall, insulated boots keep snow out while a textured sole prevents her from slipping on ice. Traction sole boots also help her navigate rocky terrain and slippery boat decks.

Carrying a backpack gives your Lab a job to do and helps you out, too. She can carry her own gear in the pack, or you can get a special water pack that has two compartments for water—one for yours and one for hers. Start with light loads and get her used to carrying the pack before you take her on a longer trip. She should never carry more than 25 percent of her body weight. For a 70-pound dog, that's 17½ pounds.

If you're boating, kayaking, or hunting from a boat with your Lab, a life vest helps keep her safe. Most life vests are reflective so you can easily see your dog, and they have a handle you can use to lift her out of the water. For larger boats, you can buy boat ladders made especially for dogs.

Hauling a wet dog in the back of your SUV is no fun, but bench seat covers make it a little easier. Removable and washable, they fasten around the seat with straps so they'll stay in place and protect the upright part of the seat as well as the bench.

Some other smaller convenience items for Labrador activities you might want to check out include the following:

- Reflective waterproof collars
- Safety reflectors to hang from her leash or collar
- Bungee leashes you can attach to your waist and to your dog for use while jogging or hiking
- Folding canvas food and water bowls with waterproof inserts
- Crate-cooling fans
- Heated dog beds
- Canvas and rubber bumpers for retrieving

Enjoying Your Best Friend

The loving companion you envisioned sleeping at your feet in front of the fireplace is well on her way to growing up.

During this first year, she's probably given you lots of laughs, made you want to tear out your hair, eaten your prize rosebush, and vomited at the foot of your bed. She's also probably snuggled with the kids and dried your tears with her big, sloppy tongue while knocking over your favorite lamp with her tail. Maybe it's her sense of humor that's made you love her so much, but you can't imagine life without her now, and why would you want to?

We hope you'll enjoy your Labrador Retriever's youth and exuberance, her maturity and loyal companionship, and her devoted old age. She'll be your best friend through thick and thin, always ready to play, always happy to see you come home. Include her in your life, and allow her to love you. There's something about a Lab that's made the breed the most popular dog in the United States year after year, and you are lucky enough to find out why.

APPENDIX

A

Glossary

alpha rollover   A punishment that's supposed to mimic how wolves establish their dominance over each other. A person forces his dog to the ground and holds him on his side or back until the dog "submits" and stops fighting the handler. Don't try this at home, and don't let a "trainer" do this to your dog.

bitch   A female dog.

bite inhibition   A lesson a puppy's mother and littermates teach him that helps him control his bite. He soon learns to bite hard enough to communicate but not so hard as to injure.

breed type   The qualities that define a Lab and make him different from other dog breeds as set forth in the breed standard.

bumper   A rubber or canvas retrieving toy. Used for training hunting dogs, bumpers are long and narrow enough that they stick out of either side of the dog's mouth so you can take them easily.

"come"   The command that means "Quit what you are doing and come here, to me, right now."

dam   The mother of the litter.

displacement behavior   A behavior that occurs out of context in response to an internal emotional conflict.

dog   A term that can mean any dog or specifically refer to a male.

dominance   A relationship between two or more dogs that's established by force and submission to gain power over resources.

"down"   The command that means "Lie down, roll on one hip, and don't move." The hand signal is to sweep your flat hand, palm down, toward the ground.

"give"   The command that means "Release that item into my hand." The hand signal is to hold your hand open, palm upward, in front of his face.

glycemic index   A scale that measures the speed at which the body converts carbohydrates into sugars.

growth plates   Discs at the end of each long bone (of the leg, for example) that are composed of soft cartilage. The cartilage is eventually replaced by bone.

holistic veterinarian   A practitioner who addresses the whole dog, including mental and social factors, instead of limiting treatment to the symptoms of disease.

homeopathy   The practice of using herbs, minerals, and natural compounds to strengthen the body's natural defenses and cure disease.

intact   An unneutered male or unspayed female dog.

learning plateau   A period when a puppy suddenly seems to have forgotten everything he's learned. This may last a few days or a week or more.

"leave it"   The command that means "Turn away from what you're looking at and look at me."

"let's go" or "walk"   The command that means "Pay attention. We're going for a walk." The signal is to step off on your left foot (when he's at your left side).

malabsorption   The body's inability to process and use nutrients in food.

mark   In a hunting test, a bird is thrown or shot and the dog "marks" it by recognizing where it fell and remembering the location.

marking   When a mature dog deposits urine so other dogs can identify him or her and determine the dog's age or readiness to breed. Marking also establishes territorial boundaries.

microflora   Microorganisms that live in the digestive tract and perform various functions, such as training the immune system, producing vitamins, and preventing growth of harmful bacteria.

neonatal period   The first 2 weeks of a puppy's life, when the puppy sleeps and eats and not much else.

"off"   The command that means "Put all four feet on the floor." The hand signal is to push your flat palm, with your fingers spread, toward the dog.

"okay"   The command that releases your dog from whatever he's doing. Okay signifies "You're finished; relax," or "At ease." The hand signal is both hands palms up.

pheromone   A chemical secreted by an animal that another animal, usually of the same species, can interpret.

serotonin   A neurotransmitter involved in the transmission of impulses between nerve cells. It's found in the brain, blood platelets, and intestinal tract.

sire   The father of a litter of puppies.

"sit"   The command that means "Put your rear end on the floor and don't move." The hand signal is to scoop one hand upward, palm up.

socialization period   The period between 3 and- 12 weeks of age when your puppy starts to explore his world. During this time, positive or negative experiences impact his behavior for the rest of his life.

specialty show   A conformation dog show for a single breed of dog, held by a breed club. In a Labrador Retriever Specialty, the breed club often also conducts obedience, rally, hunting tests, and agility trials.

"stay"   The command that means "Do not move a muscle until I come back and touch you." The hand signal is your flat palm in front of the puppy's nose as you step off on your right foot.

"take it"   The command that means "Take this item" as you present it to him, like a toy.

titer   A test that measures the amount of antibodies to a particular disease your Lab is carrying in his body.

transition period   The time between 2 and 3 weeks of age when your puppy starts to be more aware of his environment.

weaning   The process of gradually changing a puppy's diet from mother's milk to solid food.

whelping box   A large nest where the mother gives birth to her puppies. There's often a ledge around the sides, so the mother won't accidentally crush a puppy against the wall.

withers   The highest point of a dog's shoulders, behind the neck.

zoonotic disease   A disease that's transmissible from one species to another, for example, from dogs to humans.

APPENDIX

B

Body Condition Assessment

It's difficult to predict exactly what a Lab's size and weight should be at any given month during her first year. The most dramatic growth period is from birth to 6 months, when your dog grows to roughly 75 percent of her adult height. After that, growth slows dramatically until she reaches her full height at 10 to 12 months. Although the breed standard states that an adult male Lab should be 22½ to 24½ inches at the shoulders (females 1 inch smaller), in reality, some Labs are taller. Labs from field breeding will be taller and leaner than their show-dog brethren.

So when you read the following estimates, take your own Lab's build into consideration. There will be clear differences, even between two 12-week-old puppies. Even within a litter, puppies grow at different rates.

AGE, HEIGHT, AND WEIGHT ESTIMATES

The following numbers are estimates you can compare to, taken from the growth records of Lab puppies:

Birth: 12 to 20 ounces

8 weeks: 10 to 12 pounds

12 weeks (3 months): 20 to 25 pounds

16 weeks (4 months): 32 to 35 pounds; 14 inches at the shoulder

20 weeks (5 months): 44 to 48 pounds; 18 to 20 inches at the shoulder

6 to 12 months: 55 to 70 pounds

Maturity (2 to 2½ years): for males: 65 to 80 pounds and 22½ to 24½ inches at the shoulder; for females: 55 to 70 pounds and 21½ to 23½ inches at the shoulder.

All the heights and weights are approximate. It might be better to look at the percent of increase. For example, weight doubles between 8 and 12 weeks.

IS MY PUPPY FAT?

Obesity is a common problem in Labs. Your dog loves to eat, and many Labs don't do the energy-intense work they were bred to do. A family pet doesn't need as many calories as a hunting dog. Even puppies can overeat, and this predisposes them to grow into heavy adults.

Being overweight puts extra stress on her bones and joints. And because Labs are prone to arthritis and other joint problems as they mature, a little light is better than a little heavy in this breed.

Don't feed your puppy according to the instructions on a food bag; feed her according to her current size, weight, condition, and overall health.

BODY CONDITION ASSESSMENT

Regardless of any charts and estimates, the best way to know if your dog is obese, ideal weight, or too thin, is to do a body condition assessment. At any age, use the following guidelines to check your dog. If you have any doubts about your puppy's weight, consult with your veterinarian or your puppy's breeder for advice.

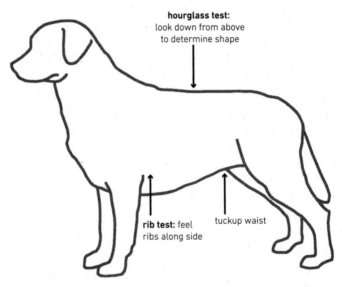

Use this illustration to help determine if your puppy is ideal, too heavy, or too thin.

Have someone help you by holding your puppy in a standing position and keeping her relatively still. Look down on your puppy from above and note where her rib cage ends. See if she is ...

- ○ **Ideal:** There's a slight narrowing behind her rib cage that continues to her rear. She's shaped like an hourglass.
- ○ **Too heavy:** Your puppy is wider or rounder in the back half.
- ○ **Too thin:** She appears dramatically narrower; you also might be able to see her ribs.

The size of her rib cage won't change, but the padding on it will. Run your hands down each side of her rib cage. See if she is ...

- ○ **Ideal:** You can find her ribs with little effort. You might barely see them when she's in sunlight.
- ○ **Too heavy:** There's a layer of fat that makes it hard to find her ribs.
- ○ **Too thin:** You can see her ribs without feeling for them. You also might easily see her spine.

The bottom outline of your Lab puppy's body should start at her front elbows and tuck up slightly behind her rib cage. See if she is ...

- ○ **Ideal:** You can see or feel a slight rise after her rib cage. This varies between show and field Labs, with field-bred dogs sometimes having a more prominent tuckup.
- ○ **Too heavy:** There's no tuckup; her abdomen protrudes or sags.
- ○ **Too thin:** There's a noticeable waist; you can probably see her hipbones.

If you feel your pup is too heavy, cut back *slightly* on the amount you feed her—a drastic cut will leave her hungry. Supplement her meals with some vegetables (like beans or carrots) to help her feel full. And consider switching to a higher-fiber food.

If your puppy has a potbelly, have a stool sample checked for worms.

If your Labrador is too thin, see your veterinarian. She might just need more food, or she might not be digesting her food properly.

Check your puppy's body condition regularly every 2 weeks during the first 18 months. As she grows, her calorie needs will vary. For the first 6 months of dramatic growth, you need to feed her increasing amounts of food. When she reaches her full height, you can gradually reduce her daily amount to a normal adult quantity based on her size.

APPENDIX

C

Household and Yard Hazards

Puppies have no concept of what's good to eat or play with and what's dangerous. Never assume your puppy won't touch something. If it's different, out of the ordinary, has a smell, or is within reach, he'll probably investigate it.

PROBLEM FOODS

Many foods can be a problem for your dog. Some may cause mild gastrointestinal upset while others are poisonous and potentially toxic. If your puppy consumes any of the following, call your veterinarian or emergency veterinary clinic right away:

- Alcoholic drinks (of any kind)
- Caffeine
- Chocolate (milk chocolate is the least toxic; dark and baking chocolate are the most toxic)
- Coffee
- Grapes and raisins
- Macadamia nuts
- Onions and onion powder
- Xylitol (including baked goods, gums, or candies that contain it)
- Yeast dough

As a general rule, don't allow your puppy to eat any spicy foods, fatty foods, leftover grease, or spoiled or moldy foods to avoid gastrointestinal upset.

HAZARDOUS MATERIALS

A wide variety of potentially hazardous materials are around your house:

○ Bug sprays, traps, and repellents

○ Cigarettes, cigars, pipes, and tobaccos

○ Cleaners and cleansers (floor, kitchen, bathroom, shower, countertop, toilet cleaners)

○ Craft supplies (beads, small pieces, paints and glues)

○ Holiday decorations (Christmas tree decorations, Halloween, electrical cords, ribbons, tinsel, batteries, plants)

○ Laundry products (detergents, bleach, fabric softener sheets)

○ Makeup, hair-care products, nail polish, and polish remover

○ Mothballs

○ Houseplant fertilizers and insecticides

MEDICINES

Almost all medications can have a detrimental effect on your puppy. Keep these items secure and away from your dog:

○ Cold remedies

○ Pain medications

○ Prescription medications (especially antidepressants and anticancer drugs)

○ Vitamins

If you believe your puppy has ingested a medication, call your veterinarian or emergency veterinary clinic immediately. Do not wait for a reaction to begin.

IN THE GARAGE AND YARD

To keep up your home and yard, you often use a number of potentially dangerous substances. Keep these away from your pup:

○ Automobile care and maintenance products (gas, oil, antifreeze, cleaning products, waxes)

- Paint
- Pest traps and poisons
- Yard maintenance products (fertilizers, insecticides, herbicides, fungicides)

In the yard, be aware of frogs and toads, insects (ants, spiders, scorpions, and others), and snakes that will pique your puppy's curiosity.

POISONOUS PLANTS

Many common plants (landscaping, decorative, and houseplants) are potentially hazardous to your dog. Some may cause a contact allergy, such as poison sumac or ivy; others can be potentially fatal. For example, when ingested, the following can kill a dog:

- Castor bean
- English ivy
- Oleander
- Hemlock

If you have any of these plants in your house or yard, either remove them or be sure your dog doesn't have access to them:

- Flowering plants:

  - Amaryllis
  - Anemone
  - Azalea
  - Bird of paradise
  - Buttercup
  - Christmas cactus
  - Crocus
  - Cyclamen
  - Foxglove
  - Impatiens

  - Jasmine
  - Lantana
  - Larkspur
  - Lilies
  - Lily of the valley
  - Morning glory
  - Oleander
  - Snapdragon
  - Sweet pea
  - Verbena

- Bulbs, tubers, and fungi
  - Amaryllis
  - Calla lily
  - Daffodil
  - Gladiola
  - Hyacinth
  - Iris
  - Jonquil
  - Mushrooms and toadstools
  - Tulip
- Trees, decorative plants, and shrubs
  - Asparagus fern
  - Bottlebrush
  - Boxwood
  - Caladium
  - Creeping charlie
  - Croton
  - Dieffenbachia
  - Dogwood
  - Dracaena
  - Elephant ear
  - Emerald feather fern
  - English ivy
  - Heavenly bamboo
  - Hemlock
  - Holly
  - Horse chestnut
  - Hydrangea
  - Ivy
  - Kalanchoe
  - Mistletoe
  - Nightshade
  - Pennyroyal
  - Philodendron
  - Privet
  - Rhododendron
  - Sago palm
  - Wisteria
  - Yew
- Vegetables, fruits, and nuts:
  - Avocado (leaves, stems, pit)
  - Eggplant
  - Grapes (fruit)
  - Macadamia nut (nut)
  - Peach and other stone fruit (seeds/pits)
  - Potato (foliage)
  - Rhubarb
  - Tomato (foliage)

TIPS AND TAILS

The vegetables, fruits, and nuts section lists a variety of plants that contain different parts dangerous to dogs. If one specific part is dangerous, that's noted. If nothing is noted, the entire plant should be avoided.

- Herbs, weeds, and miscellaneous plants
    - Belladonna
    - Castor bean
    - Jimson weed
    - Locoweed
    - Marijuana
    - Milkweed
    - Pokeweed
    - Poison ivy
    - Poison oak
    - Poison sumac
    - Pokeweed
    - Sage

SEASONAL HAZARDS

Some potential problems are only apparent during certain seasons. Because these products or hazards are around only occasionally, they can be more attractive to a curious puppy:

- Antifreeze
- Blue-green algae in ponds (especially during hot weather)
- Candles (lit or unlit)
- Cocoa mulch
- Compost piles
- Ice-melting products
- Potpourri
- Swimming-pool supplies

APPENDIX

D

Resources

When you need in-depth information or are searching for professionals to help you care for your Lab puppy, this list can help. It includes resources for registration information, dog clubs, first aid, health care, veterinarians, trainers, dog sports and activities, microchip registries, pet sitters, and more.

CLUBS

American Kennel Club (AKC): akc.org

Canadian Kennel Club (CKC): ckc.ca

Labrador Retriever Club, Inc. (AKC Parent Club for the Labrador Retriever): thelabradorclub.com

National Disaster Search Dog Foundation (SDF): searchdogfoundation.org

North American Hunting Retriever Association (NAHRA): nahra.org

United Kennel Club (UKC): ukcdogs.com

FIRST AID AND POISON CONTROL

American Red Cross Pet First Aid app: redcross.org/mobile-apps/pet-first-aid-app

Animal Poison Hotline (provided by North Shore Animal League and PROSAR International Animal Poison Center): 888-232-8870

ASPCA Poison Control Center: aspca.org/pet-care/poison-control; 1-888-426-4435 (North America; fees apply)

Pet Poison Helpline: 1-800-858-6680 (United States and Canada; fees apply)

PetMD Dog First Aid app: petmd.com

PetTech PetSaver First Aid app: pettech.net/app/index.php

FOOD AND SUPPLEMENTS

American Association of Feed Control Officials: aafco.org

Food and Drug Administration Pet Food Recalls: fda.gov/Safety/Recalls/default
.htm

National Animal Supplement Council: nasc.cc

MICROCHIP REGISTRIES

**American Animal Hospital Association (AAHA) Universal Pet Microchip
Lookup:** petmicrochiplookup.org

American Kennel Club (AKC) Reunite: akcreunite.org

AVID (American Veterinary Identification Devices): avidid.com

HomeAgain: public.homeagain.com

PERFORMANCE SPORTS

AKC Kids and Juniors: akc.org/kids_juniors

Barn Hunt Association: barnhunt.com

Canine Freestyle Federation: canine-freestyle.org

DockDogs: dockdogs.com

Dogs On Course in North America (DOCNA): docna.com

National Association for Search and Rescue: nasar.org

National Association of Canine Scent Work: nacsw.net

North American Dog Agility Council (NADAC): nadac.com

North American Flyball Association (NAFA): flyball.org

United States Dog Agility Association (USDAA): usdaa.com

World Canine Freestyle Organization (WCFO): worldcaninefreestyle.org

PET INSURANCE

AKC Pet Insurance: akcpetinsurance.com

ASPCA Pet Health Insurance: aspcapetinsurance.com

Embrace Pet Insurance: embracepetinsurance.com

Nationwide Pet Insurance: petinsurance.com

Pets Best Insurance: petsbest.com

PET SITTERS

National Association of Professional Pet Sitters (NAPPS): petsitters.org

Pet Sitters Associates, LLC: petsitllc.com

Pet Sitters International (PSI): petsit.com

THERAPY DOG TRAINING AND CERTIFICATION

Alliance of Therapy Dogs: therapydogs.com

Love on a Leash: loveonaleash.org

Pet Partners (formerly Delta Society): petpartners.org

Therapy Dogs, International (TDI): tdi-dog.org

TRAINING AND BEHAVIOR ASSOCIATIONS

American College of Veterinary Behaviorists: dacvb.org

Association of Companion Animal Behavior Counselors:
animalbehaviorcounselors.org/acabc_members

Association of Professional Dog Trainers (APDT): apdt.com

Certified Applied Animal Behaviorists (CAAB): certifiedanimalbehaviorist.com

International Association of Animal Behavior Consultants (IAABC): iaabc.org

International Association of Canine Professionals (IACP): canineprofessionals.com

National Association of Dog Obedience Instructors (NADOI): nadoi.org

Tellington Touch: ttouch.com

VETERINARY AND RELATED ORGANIZATIONS

Academy of Veterinary Homeopathy: theavh.org

AKC Canine Health Foundation: akcchf.org

American Academy of Veterinary Acupuncture: aava.org

American Animal Hospital Association (AAHA): aaha.org/pet_owner

American College of Veterinary Ophthalmologists (ACVO): acvo.org

American Holistic Veterinary Medical Association: ahvma.org

American Veterinary Chiropractic Association: avcadoctors.com

American Veterinary Medical Association (AVMA): avma.org

Morris Animal Foundation: morrisanimalfoundation.org

Orthopedic Foundation for Animals (OFA): offa.org

PennHIP: info.antechimagingservices.com/pennhip

Veterinary Botanical Medical Association: vbma.org

INDEX

A

AAFCO (Association of American Feed Control Officials), 40, 165, 227
AAHA (American Animal Hospital Association), 33
ACLs (anterior cruciate ligaments), torn, 219
activity levels, changes, 64
acupressure, 221
acupuncture, 221
adjustable martingale collars, 27
administering pills, 96-97
adolescent Labrador Retrievers
7 months, 155
  behavior, 176-179
  grooming, 168-171
  health, 157-170
  nutrition, 164-168
  physical development, 155-157
  socialization, 171-175
  training, 179-184
8 months, 187
  behavior, 203-205
  grooming, 197-199
  health, 189, 193
  nutrition, 195-197
  physical development, 187-189
  play, 200
  socialization, 199-203
  training, 205-212
9 months, 213-215
  behavior, 234-239
  grooming, 228-231
  health, 216-225
  nutrition, 225-228
  physical development, 215-216
  socialization, 231-234
  training, 239-246
10 months, 249
  behavior, 269-272
  grooming, 263-265
  health, 255
  nutrition, 262-263
  physical development, 249-254
  socialization, 265-269
  training, 273-275
11 months, 279
  behavior, 300-302
  grooming, 290-291
  health, 280-287
  nutrition, 287-290
  physical development, 279
  socialization, 292-300
  training, 302-306
12 months, 313
  behavior, 327
  grooming, 325
  health, 314-320
  nutrition, 320-324
  physical development, 313
  socialization, 326
  training, 327-329
seasonal safety hazards, 189-194
adopting juvenile or adult dogs, 26-27
adulthood, 313
aggression, dog-to-dog, 199-203
agility classes, 307-308
air travel, 292-294
airbags, disabling, 97
AKC (American Kennel Club), 23, 25, 250
  CGC (Canine Good Citizen) program, 265-266
  pledge, 268-269
  test, 266-268, 311
  Junior Showmanship, 276-277
  Reunite, 118
allergies, 316-317
alpha rollover, 237
alternative medicine, 220-223
American Animal Hospital Association (AAHA), 33
American Association of Feed Control Officials (AAFCO), 165
American Holistic Veterinary Medical Association, 221
American Kennel Club (AKC). See AKC (American Kennel Club)
American Society for the Prevention of Cruelty to Animals (ASPCA) Animal Poison Control Hotline, 132
American Veterinary Identification Devices, 118
American-style Labrador Retrievers, 22
anal glands, impacted, 319-320
annual checkups, 315-316
anterior cruciate ligaments (ACLs), torn, 219
antibodies, 14
antioxidants, 289
APDT (Association of Pet Dog Trainers), 34
arthritis, 284, 317-318
ASPCA (American Society for the Prevention of Cruelty to Animals) Animal Poison Control Hotline, 132
Association of American Feed Control Officials (AAFCO), 40, 227
Association of Pet Dog Trainers (APDT), 34
automatic sit, 150
automobiles
  airbags, disabling, 97
  carsickness, 97-98
  seat covers, 331
  travel, 292
autumn safety hazards, 193

B

backpacks, 330
bad breath, 64
balls, 30
BARF (Bones And Raw Food) diet, 324
  raw diet, 40, 69
barking, 269-271
  vocal discovery, 76
barn hunts, 244-246
baths, 136-138, 264

bedding, 30
  travel, 297
behavior
  3 months, 51
    biting, 52
    curiosity, 52
    night sleeping, 51
  4 months, 73
    mouthing, 75
    overexcitement, 75
    separation anxiety, 74-75
    vocal discovery, 76
  5 months, 105-106
    chewing, 106-107
    corrections, 107
    keeping on leash, 106
    outgrowing bad, 107-108
  6 months, 143
    digging, 143-144
    distractions, 143
    soft biting, 144-146
  7 months, 175
    adolescent fear period,
      176-177
    chewing, 177-178
    marking, 178-179
    regression, 175-176
    rough play, 174-175
  8 months, 203
    being proactive, 203-204
    exercise, 205
    mounting, 204-205
  9 months, 234
    crate, 239
    dominance, 234-235
    leadership, 234-237
    rudeness, 237-238
  10 months, 269
    barking, 269-271
    discipline, 271-272
  11 months, 300
    signs of fear, 301-302
    signs of stress, 300-301
  12 months, 327
    adulthood, 327
    crating, 327
  consultations, 212
  displacement, 204
  nutritional links, 225-226
  socialization period, 19
belly rubs, 213

big air games (dock dogs), 309
Biologically Appropriate Raw
  Food (BARF), 324. See
  also Bones And Raw Food
  (BARF) diet
    raw diet, 40, 69
birth weight, 3
birthing process, 4
bitches, 10
  adolescent femininity, 216
  marking, 178-179
  mounting, 204-205
  sexual maturity, 155-156
  spaying, 157-161
bites, insect, treating, 259-260
biting, 52
  bite inhibition, 7
  teaching soft, 144-146
black Labrador Retrievers, 22
bladder problems, 64
bleeding
  excessive, 128
  treating, 255-257
bloat, 128, 318-319
boarding, 299
body language, 147
bolo marks, 93
bone meal, 289
bones, broken, 128, 257
bones, feeding
  cooked, 87
  dangers, 69
Bones And Raw Food (BARF)
  diet, 324
    raw diet, 40, 69
booster vaccinations, 65
boots, protective, 330
bordetella (kennel cough), 94
bowls, 27
Boy Scouts, merit badges, 276
breathing difficulties, 64, 128
breed club, 330
breed standard, 92, 249-255
  coat, 254
  comparing, 251-254
  ears, 253
  general appearance, 251
  hindquarters, 253
  nose, 252
  size, 251
  skull, 252
  tails, 253

teeth, 252
  temperament, 254
breeders
  interviewing, 24-25
  supplies provided, 36
breeding, heat, 155-156
broken bones, 128, 257
brucellosis, pretesting, 9
brushing, 44, 100-101
  curry brushes, 29
  rubber curry brushes, 29
  slicker brushes, 29
brushing teeth, 168-170
  toothpaste, 29
bully sticks, 87
bumpers, 146
burns, 128
  preventing, 259
  treating, 258

C

CAAB (Certified Applied
  Animal Behaviorists), 212
call names, choosing, 57
calories, counting, 262-263
canine communication, 88-89
canine freestyle, 308
Canine Good Citizen (CGC)
  program. See CGC (Canine
  Good Citizen) program
canine hepatitis, 37
canine scabies, 162
canned dog food, 287-288
carbohydrates, 40
carrying puppies, 8
cars
  airbags, disabling, 97
  carsickness, 97-98
  seat covers, 331
  travel, 292
cat feces, consumption, 196
catching a loose puppy, 116-117
cavalettis exercise, 189
cavities, nose, 219
Center for Veterinary Medicine
  (CVM), 165
centronuclear myopathy
  (CNM), 10, 65
Certified Applied Animal
  Behaviorists (CAAB), 212

CGC (Canine Good Citizen)
program, 265-266
pledge, 268-269
test, 266-268, 311
chain collars, 210
chattering teeth, 300
checkups, annual, 315-316
chewies, 86
chewing, 7, 28, 106-107, 177-178
bite inhibition, 7
cheyletiellosis, 162
children
developing friendships, 121-122
socialization, 49, 103-104
chiropractic therapy, 221
chocolate Labrador Retrievers, 22
choking, 128
chondroitin, 223, 290
choosing juvenile or adult dogs, 26-27
choosing puppies, 21-23
characteristics, 21-22
contracts, 23
interviewing breeders, 24-25
littermates, 23
personalities, 25-26
registration papers, 23-24
Christmas trees, screening off, 32
cleaning supplies, 29
clicker training, 208-209
clippers, toenail, 29
clipping toenails, 15
CNM (centronuclear myopathy), 10, 65
coat
breed standard, 254
brushing, 100-101
grooming, 99-100
problems, 197-199
removing sticky substances, 291
shedding, 100, 138, 197
coccidia, 39, 164
cold tail, 319
coldness, newborn puppies, 12
collars
chain, 210
choosing, 27-28

handling, 84-85
prong, 210-211
shock, 211
come command, 56, 147
commands
come, 56, 147
down, 79-81, 139, 147
down-stay, 113-114
drop, 273-274
give, 146-147
leave it, 150-151
name, 109
nicely, 145-146
off, 139-141, 147
okay, 78-79, 147
roll over, 183-184
shake, 183-184
sit, 78-79, 147
sit-stay, 111-113
sit-to-greet, 141
softly, 145-146
speak, 271
stand, 242-243
stay, 111-112, 147
take it, 147
wait, 173
walk, 147
watch me, 242
communication, canine, 88-89
competitive dog sports, 307
agility classes, 307-308
canine freestyle, 308
conformation, 310-311
dock dogs, 309
flyball, 309-310
complete and balanced, dog food labels, 166
conformation, 310-311
Conformation Certificate Program, 254-255
constipation, 64
contracts, 23
control devices, 209-211
cooked bones, 87
cooking, home-prepared dog food, 323-324
coordination, 188-189
coronavirus vaccination, 94
corrections, 107
counter surfing, preventing, 140
CPR (cardiopulmonary resuscitation), performing, 128-131

crates, 239
adulthood, 327
choosing, 28
purchasing two, 28
training, 3 months, 55
travel, 297
curry brushes, 29
CVM (Center for Veterinary Medicine), 165

D

daily walks, 326
dams, 10, 19
dandruff, 197
DAPs (dog appeasing pheromones), 225
day care, 171-173
deep cuts, 128
dehydration
from vomiting, 262
recognizing, 63
demodetic mange, 161
dental plaque, 168-169
desocialization, preventing, 199
dewclaws, 4
torn, 260-261
diarrhea, 63, 134
treating, 261
diet. See dog food; nutrition
digestive enzymes, 289
digging, 143-144
disaster planning, 280-281
discipline, 271-272
diseases
arthritis, 284
bloat, 318
bordetella, 94
brucellosis, 9
canine hepatitis, 37
centronuclear myopathy, 65
CNM (centronuclear myopathy), 10
cold tail, 319
coronavirus, 94
distemper, 36
EIC (exercise-induced collapse), 285
elbow dysplasia, 9, 284-285
exercise-induced collapse, 10
giardia, 95

gum disease, 319
hip dysplasia, 9, 284-285
leptospirosis, 95
Lyme disease, 95
parainfluenza virus, 37
parvovirus, 37
PRA (progressive retinal atrophy), 9, 286
retinal dysplasia, 9, 286
tetanus, 95
tricuspid valve dysplasia (TVD), 9, 286
zoonotic, 95
displacement behavior, 204
distemper, 36
dock dogs, 309
dog appeasing pheromones (DAPs), 225
dog food. *See also* nutrition
  canned, 287-288
  generic brands, 228
  governmental regulations, 165
  ingredients, 167-168
  labels, 40, 165-167
  natural, 228
  organic, 228
  premium brands, 228
  semimoist, 288
  storage, 41
  super-premium brands, 228
  transitioning, 99
  travel, 296
dog parks, socialization, 105
dog sitters, 299
dog-to-dog aggression, 199-203
doggie odor, 290
dominance, 234-235
down command, 79-81, 139, 147
down-stay command, 113-114
drooling, 301
drop command, 273-274

E

ears
  bleeding, treating, 256
  breed standard, 253
  cleaning, 101-102
  examining, 70
mites, 162
  pinned back, 300
  unusual odors, 64
Easter hazards, 190
easy command, 145-146
EIC (exercise-induced collapse), 285
  pretesting, 10
elbow dysplasia, 284-285
  pretesting, 9
electrical cords, protecting, 31
electrical shock, treating, 259
emergencies, 127-128
emergency drop, teaching, 273-274
English Labrador Retriever Club, 250
English-style Labrador Retrievers, 22
essential oils, 225
excessive bleeding, 128
exercise
  importance, 205
  pens, 29
exercise-induced collapse (EIC), 285
  pretesting, 10
expiration date, dog food, 167
external parasites, 66-68, 161-162
extreme vertical games (dock dogs), 309
eyes
  discharge, 64
  examining, 70
  wide, round, 301

F

4-H programs, 276
fading puppy syndrome, 12
fading treats, 150
fat, 41
fatty acids, 289
  deficiency, 321
FDA (Food and Drug Administration), 165
fear, signs, 301-302
fear-imprint stage, 46-47, 176-177
feces
  consumption, 195-196
  monitoring, 99
feet
  care, 170-171
  examining, 70
  protective boots, 330
  treating bleeding, 257
females
  adolescent femininity, 216
  marking, 178-179
  mounting, 204-205
  sexual maturity, 155-156
  spaying, 157-161
fetch, playing, 241
fever, 64
field trials, 306
fighting, play, 7
fireplaces, screening off, 32
fireworks, dangers, 192-193
first-aid
  classes, 133
  kits, 131-132, 297
fishhooks, imbedded, treating, 260
fleas, 198
  controlling, 39, 67-68
  preventing, 66-67
flower remedies, 224
flyball, 309-310
food. *See also* nutrition
  dispensing toys, 120-121, 144
  guarding, preventing, 134-135
Food and Drug Administration (FDA), 165
Fourth of July hazards, 192-193
freestyle, canine, 308

G

Galileo Bones, 86
garages, puppy-proofing, 33
gas, 134
gates, 29
general appearance, breed standard, 251
generic dog food, 228
genetic diseases, 283-287
gently command, 145-146
giardia, 39, 163-164
  vaccination, 95
Girl Scouts, merit badges, 276
give command, 146-147

global positioning systems
(GPSs), 119
glucosamine, 223, 290
gluten, 167
glycemic index, 226
golden Labrador Retrievers, 22
Golden Retrievers, 22
GPSs (global positioning
systems), 119
grass, consumption, 196-197
Greater Newfoundland, 93
grocery store dog food, 228
groomers, 264-265
grooming, 290
  3 months, 43
    brushing, 44
    massage, 43-44
    trimming toenails, 44-45
  4 months, 69
    weekly routine, 69-71
  5 months, 99
    brushing, 100-101
    cleaning ears, 101-102
    coat, 99-100
  6 months, 136
    bathing, 136-138
    shedding, 138
  7 months, 168
    brushing teeth, 168-170
    paw care, 170-171
  8 months, 197
    coat/skin problems,
    197-199
  9 months, 228
  10 months, 263
    determining when to
    bathe, 264
    employing professionals,
    264-265
  11 months, 290-291
    doggie odor, 290
    removing sticky
    substances, 291
    skunk odor, 291
  12 months, 325
    regular schedule, 325
    weekly health checks, 325
  autumn, 231
  initial, 15-16
  spring, 229-230
  summer, 230
  winter, 231

growth plates, 160, 218
growth spurts, 68
guaranteed analysis, dog food
labels, 166
guarding food, preventing,
134-135
gum disease, 319

H

Halloween hazards, 193
hand signals, 147
harnesses, no-pull, 209-210
hazards, 189-194
  autumn, 193
  Christmas trees, 32
  Easter, 190
  Fourth of July, 192-193
  Halloween, 193
  spring, 189-191
  summer, 191-193
  winter, 193-194
head halters, 209
health
  3 months, 35
    diseases, 36-38
    first veterinary
    appointment, 38
    parasites, 38-39
    records, 35-36
    vaccinations, 36-38
  4 months, 63
    booster vaccinations, 65
    centronuclear myopathy,
    65
    external parasites, 66-68
    veterinary visits, 63-65
  5 months, 94
    administering pills, 96-97
    carsickness, 97-98
    heartworm preventative,
    96
    vaccinations, 94-95
  6 months, 126
    checking vitals, 127
    emergencies, 127-128
    first-aid classes, 133
    first-aid kits, 131-132
    performing CPR, 128-131
  7 months, 157
    external parasites, 161-163
    internal parasites, 163-164

neutering, 157-161
spaying, 157-161
8 months, 189
  autumn safety hazards, 193
  spring safety hazards,
  189-191
  summer safety hazards,
  191-193
  winter safety hazards,
  193-194
9 months, 216
  lack of energy, 216-217
  limping, 217-219
  nose, 219-220
10 months, 255
  treating illnesses, 261-262
  treating injuries, 255-261
11 months, 280
  disaster planning, 280-281
  pet insurance, 281-283
12 months, 314
  allergies, 316-317
  annual checkups, 315-316
  arthritis, 317-318
  bloat, 318-319
  cold tail, 319
  gum disease, 319
  impacted anal glands,
  319-320
  laryngeal paralysis, 320
  lumps, 320
  vaccinations, 314-315
alternative medicine, 220-223
breeder tasks, 11-13
certificates, 295-296
mother dog's care, 10-11
natural remedies, 223-225
nutrition, 321
pretesting for inheritable
defects, 8-10
health records, 35-36
heartworm, 39
  preventative, 96, 295
heat, 155-156
  calming male dogs, 157
heat exhaustion, 191-192
heat stroke, 128, 191-192
hepatitis, 37
herbal remedies, 223-224
hernias, newborn puppies, 13
hiking, 329-330
hindquarters, breed standard,
253

hip dysplasia, 284-285
  pretesting, 9
holiday hazards
  Christmas, 32
  Easter, 190
  Fourth of July, 192-193
  Halloween, 193
holistic veterinarians, 220-223
home-prepared food, 323-324
HomeAgain national registry, 118
homeopathy, 222-223
homes, puppy-proofing, 31-32
hookworm, 38
hormones, adolescence, 188
hot cars, dangers, 191
hot spots, treating, 198-199
hotels, pet-friendly, 294-295
house sitters, 299-300
houseplants, poisonous, 32
houses, puppy-proofing, 31-32
housetraining, 54, 84
  crates, 28
  marking, 179
hunting tests, 305-306
hydration
  dehydration, 63
  importance, 43
  refusal of water, 63
  summer, 191
hyperactivity, 206, 301
  carbohydrates, 41
hypothermia, 193

I

IAABC (International Association of Animal Behavior Consultants), 212
identification tags, 117-119, 295
illnesses, symptoms, treating, 261-262
  diarrhea, 261
  seizures, 261-262
  vomiting, 262
imbedded objects, treating, 260
immunizations. *See* vaccinations
impacted anal glands, 319-320
ingredients, dog food, 167-168
ingredients list, dog food, 167
inheritable defects, pretesting, 8-10

inherited diseases, 283-287
injuries, treating, 255-261
  bleeding, 255-257
    bleeding ears, 256
    bleeding paws, 257
    bleeding tails, 256
  broken limbs, 257
  burns, 258
  electrical shock, 259
  hot spots, 198-199
  imbedded fishhooks, 260
  insect bites/stings, 259-260
  limping, 217-219
  torn dewclaws, 260-261
  torn toenails, 260-261
insect bites/stings, treating, 259-260
insurance, health, 281-283
intact dogs, 155-156
  calming male dogs, 157
internal parasites, 163-164
International Association of Animal Behavior Consultants (IAABC), 212
interviewing breeders, 24-25
intestinal microflora, 196
itchy skin, relieving, 198

J

Jacobson's organ (vomeronasal organ), 220
jolly routine, 102-103
Junior hunting tests, 306
Junior Showmanship (AKC), 276-277
juvenile Labrador Retrievers, 91, 125
  3 months
    behavior, 51-52
    grooming, 43-45
    health, 35-39
    nutrition, 39-43
    physical development, 35
    socialization, 45-51
    training, 52-55
  4 months
    behavior, 73-75
    grooming, 69-71
    health, 63-68
    nutrition, 68-69

    physical development, 61-62
    socialization, 71-73
    training, 76-85
  5 months
    behavior, 105-108, 143-146
    grooming, 99-102
    health, 94-98
    nutrition, 98-99
    physical development, 91-93
    socialization, 102-105, 121-122
    training, 108-117
  6 months
    behavior, 143-146
    grooming, 136-138
    health, 126-133
    nutrition, 133-136
    physical development, 125-126
    socialization, 138-142
    training, 146-151
adopting, 26-27
canine communication, 88-89
diseases, 36-38
early expectations, 57-58
first veterinary appointment, 38
food-dispensing toys, 120-121
frustration, avoiding, 119-120
health records, 35-36
identification tags, 117-119
mental development, 35
overprotection, 87
parasites, 38-39
play time, 89
practicing patience, 58
routines, 59
safe toys, 85-87
vaccinations, 36-38

K

kennel cough (bordetella), 94
kennels, 297-298
kitty litter, consumption, 196
knotted rope toys, 30, 86
KONG toys, 30

L

labels, dog food, 165-167
Labrador Retriever Club of
America, 25
Labrador Retriever Club of
Canada, 25
Labrador Retrievers, 21
adolescent. *See* adolescent
Labrador Retrievers
American style, 22
black, 22
chocolate, 22
English style, 22
golden, 22
juvenile. *See* juvenile
Labrador Retrievers
littermates, 23
sexes, 23
yellow, 21
lack of energy, 216-217
ladder walk exercise, 188
laryngeal paralysis, 320
leadership, 234-237
learning plateau, 148
leashes, 27, 106
choosing, 27-28
off-leash control, 274-275
retractable, 142
travel, 296
walking, 81-84, 239-242
leave it command, 150-151
leptospirosis vaccination, 95
Lesser Newfoundland, 93
lethargy, 216-217
let's go command, 147
levels, rally competitions, 303
licking noses, 300
life stages, dog food labels, 166
limber tail, 319
limbs, broken, treating, 257
limited registration, 24
limping, treating, 217-219
litter size, 3
littermates
choosing multiple, 23
influence, 19
loose puppy, catching, 116-117
lumps, 320
Lyme disease vaccination, 95

M

malabsorption, 163
males
adolescent masculinity,
215-216
marking, 158, 178-179
mounting, 204-205
neutering, 157-161
sexual maturity, 156-157
marking, 158, 178-179
marks, hunting tests, 306
martingale collars, 27
massage, 43-44, 222
Master Hunter (MH) tests, 306
medicine
administering pills, 96-97
alternative medicine, 220-223
mental development, 3 months,
35
microchips, 118-119, 295-296
microflora, 196
mineral supplements, 289
minerals, 41
mites, 161-162
motels, pet-friendly, 294-295
motherly influence, 19
motor skills, 188-189
mounting, 204-205
minimizing, 75
mouth
examining, 70
unusual odors, 64

N

name
choosing, 57
using, 109
natural dog food, 228
natural remedies, 223-225
nature hikes, 233-234
navel infection, 12
neonatal period, 3-5
birth weight, average, 3
dewclaws, 4
ears and eyes open, 5
litter size, average, 3
nutrition, 13-14
supplementation, 14
weaning, 15
whelping boxes, 4

neutering, 157-161
nicely command, 145-146
no-pull harnesses, 209-210
nose
breed standard, 252
challenging, 243-246
discharge, 64
health, 219-220
licking, 300
nosework, 243-244
nutrition, 133, 320. *See also* dog
food
3 months, 39-42
feeding practices, 42
hydration, 43
portion size, 42
transitioning to kibble, 42
4 months, 68
appetite, 68
feedings, 68-69
growth spurts, 68
5 months, 98
monitoring feces, 99
monitoring weight, 98
transitioning to dog food,
99
6 months
food guarding, 134-135
speed eating, 133-134
treats, 135-136
7 months, 164
8 months, 195
grass eating, 196-197
portion sizes, 195
stool eating, 195-196
9 months, 225
10 months, 262
counting calories, 262-263
training treats, 263
11 months, 287-290
semimoist food, 287-288
supplements, 288-290
12 months, 320
health benefits, 321
home-prepared food,
323-324
obesity, 321-322
behavioral links, 225-226
carbohydrates, 40
fat, 41
governmental regulations,
165

ingredients, 167-168
labels, 165-167
malabsorption, 163
minerals, 41
neonatal period, 13-15
protein, 40
quality, 226-228
vitamins, 41
Nylabones, 86

O

obedience classes, 149-150, 211
obedience commands
    come, 56, 147
    down, 79-81, 139, 147
    down-stay, 113-114
    drop, 273-274
    give, 146-147
    leave it, 150-151
    names, 109
    nicely, 145-146
    off, 139-141, 147
    okay, 78-79, 147
    sit, 78-79, 147
    sit-stay, 111-113
    sit-to-greet, 141
    softly, 145-146
    speak, 271
    stand, 242-243
    stay, 111-112, 147
    take it, 147
    wait, 173
    walk, 147
    watch me, 242
obedience competitions,
    302-305
obesity, 321-322
obsessive-compulsive behaviors,
    301
OCD (osteochondritis
    dissecans), 218
odor recognition test (ORT),
    244
OFA (Orthopedic Foundation
    for Animals), 9, 36
off command, 139-141, 147
off-leash control, 274-275
okay command, 78-79, 147
organic dog food, 228
ORT (odor recognition test),
    244

Orthopedic Foundation for
    Animals (OFA), 9, 36
osteochondritis dissecans
    (OCD), 218
Otodectes cynotis, 162
overexcitement, minimizing, 75
overprotecting puppies, 87

P–Q

packing for travel, 296-297
panosteitis, 218
panting, 301
parainfluenza virus, 37
parasites, 38
    coccidia, 39
    external, 66-68, 161-162
    fleas, 39
    giardia, 39
    heartworm, 39
    hookworm, 38
    internal, 163-164
    roundworm, 38
    whipworm, 38
parvovirus, 37
passive immunity, 14
paws
    care, 170-171
    examining, 70
    protective boots, 330
    treating bleeding, 257
PennHIP, 9
permanent guardians, selecting,
    320
personalities, puppies, assessing,
    25-26
Pet Food Institute (PFI), 165
pet gates, 29
pet insurance, 281-283
Pet Partners, 311
pet sitters, 299
PFI (Pet Food Institute), 165
pheromones, 220, 225
physical development
    3 months, 35
    4 months, 61
        size and weight, 61
        teething, 62
    5 months, 91
        characteristics, 92-93
        paws and legs, 91-92
        teething, 92

    6 months, 125-126
    7 months, 155
        female sexual maturity,
            155-156
        male sexual maturity,
            156-157
    8 months, 187-188
        coordination, 188-189
        fearlessness, 189
        hormones, 188
    9 months, 215-216
        females, 216
        males, 215-216
    10 months, 249-255
        breed standard, 249-254
        Conformation Certificate
            Program, 254-255
    11 months, 279
    12 months, 313-314
        adult sizes and weights,
            313-314
        physical changes, 313
    growth plates, 160, 218
    neonatal period, 3-4
        average birth weight, 3
        dewclaws, 4
        ears and eyes open, 5
        whelping boxes, 4
    socialization period, 6, 35
        carrying, 8
        chewing, 7
        play-fighting, 7
        potty training, 7
        teething, 6
        vision, 7-8
    transitional period, 5-6
pig snouts, 87
pills, administering, 96-97
pinned-back ears, 300
Planet Dog Orbee-Tuff toys, 86
plastic water bottles, 30
platform exercise, 189
play-fighting, 7
playing, 89, 183
    adolescence, 200
    fetch, 241
    importance, 89
    play-fighting, 7
    rough, 174-175
    swimming pools, 151-152
playpens, 29

poison, 128
American Society for the Prevention of Cruelty to Animals (ASPCA) Animal Poison Control Hotline, 132
poisonous plants, 32
potty training. *See* housetraining
PRA (progressive retinal atrophy), 286
pretesting, 9
premium dog food, 228
pretesting for inheritable defects, 8-10
preventatives, heartworm, 96
probiotics, 288-289
product name, dog food labels, 165
professional groomers, 264-265
professional pet sitters, 299
progressive retinal atrophy (PRA), pretesting, 9, 286
prong collars, 210-211
protective boots, 330
protein, 40
deficiency, 321
puppies
classes, enrolling, 76-78
naming, 57
personalities, 25-26
socialization, 51
puppy food, 39. *See also* dog food; nutrition
choosing, 40
feeding practices, 42
governmental regulations, 165
ingredients, 167-168
labels, 40, 165-167
portion size, 42
refusal, 63
storage, 41
transitioning, 42
puppy testing, 18
puppy-proofing
garages, 33
homes, 31-32
yards, 32-33

R

rally competitions, 302-305
rattlesnake venom vaccination, 95
raw diet
3 months, 40
Bones And Raw Food (BARF) diet, 324
grinding bones, 69
rawhide toys, 30, 86
records, health, 35-36
rectal thermometers, 64
Red Cross first-aid classes, 133
refusal of water, 63
registration papers, 23-24
rescue groups, 330
adoptions, 26
Rescue Remedy, 302
retinal dysplasia, 286
testing, 9
retractable leashes, 142
Retrievers. *See* Labrador Retrievers
retrieving, training, 181-182
roll over command, 183-184
roundworm, 38
routines, establishing, 59
rubber curry brushes, 29
Rule of Sevens, 17
rules, reinforcing, 109-110

S

safety hazards, 189-194
autumn, 193
Christmas trees, 32
Easter, 190
Fourth of July, 192-193
Halloween, 193
spring, 189-191
summer, 191-193
winter, 193-194
saline solution, creating, 256
sarcoptic mange, 198
scabies, 162
Schaap, Pat, 17
schedules, establishing, 59
search-and-rescue dogs, 246

seasonal grooming needs
autumn, 231
spring, 229-230
summer, 230
winter, 231
seasonal hazards, 189-194
autumn, 193
holidays
Christmas, 32
Easter, 190
Fourth of July, 192-193
Halloween, 193
spring, 189-191
summer, 191-193
winter, 193-194
seat covers, automobile, 331
seizures, 128
treating, 261-262
self-control, teaching, 206-208
semimoist dog food, 288
Senior Hunter (SH) tests, 306
separation anxiety, 301
preventing, 74-75
serotonin, 225-226
shake command, 183-184
shedding, 100, 138, 197
shedding blades, 29
shock collars, 211
short coupling (short loin), 251
silver Labradors, 22
sires, 10
sit command, 78-79, 147
sit-stay command, 111-113
sit-to-greet command, 141
skin
checking, 70
problems, 197-199
skull, breed standard, 252
skunk odor, 291
sleep
6 months, 126
night, 51
slicker brushes, 29
snakes
avoidance training, 190
bites, 128
rattlesnake venom vaccination, 95
socialization, 292
3 months, 45-46
children, 49
fear-imprint stage, 46-47

other pets, 50-51
other puppies, 51
temperament, 45-46
4 months, 71
calming adult dogs, 71-72
new things, 72-73
people, 72-73
5 months, 102
children, 103-104
dog parks, 105
routines, 102-103
strangers, 103
walks, 104-105
6 months, 138
off command, 139-141
sit-to-greet command, 141
visiting different places,
142
7 months, 171
doggie day care, 171-173
introducing new animals,
173-174
rough play, 174-175
wait command, 173
8 months, 199
dog-to-dog aggression,
199-203
preventing desocialization,
199
9 months, 231
nature hikes, 233-234
strangers, 231-233
10 months, 265
CGC (Canine Good
Citizen), 265-269
11 months, 300
12 months, 326
socialization period, 17
puppy testing, 18
Rule of Sevens, 17
transitional period, 16
travel, 297
air, 292-294
automobile, 292
boarding, 299
house sitters, 299-300
kenneling, 297-298
packing, 296-297
pet sitters, 299

pet-friendly
accommodations,
294-295
preparing for travel,
295-296
socialization, puppies, 6, 17
behavior, 19
carrying, 8
chewing, 7
play-fighting, 7
potty training, 7
puppy testing, 18
Rule of Sevens, 17
teething, 6
vision, 7-8
soft biting, teaching, 144-146
softly command, 145-146
spaying, 157-161
speak command, 271
specialty shows, 302-303
speed retriever games (dock
dogs), 309
splashes, 93
spring
grooming needs, 229-230
safety hazards, 189-191
squirt bottles, 140
stainless-steel bowls, 27
stairs, introducing, 114-115
stand command, 242-243
stay command, 111-112, 147
sticky substances, removing,
291
stings, insect, treating, 259-260
stool eating, 195-196
storage, dog food, 41
strangers, meeting and
socialization, 103
stress, signs, 300-301
stuffed bones, 87
stuffed toys, 30
summer
grooming needs, 230
safety hazards, 191-193
super-premium dog food, 228
supplementation
antioxidants, 289
bone meal, 289
chondroitin, 290
digestive enzymes, 289
fatty acids, 289
glucosamine, 290

neonatal period, 14
nutritional, 288
probiotics, 288-289
vitamin and mineral, 289
whole foods, 290
swimmer puppies, 13
swimming, 322
pools, 151-152

T

table scraps, feeding, 69
tails
bleeding, treating, 256
breed standard, 253
take it command, 147
talk command, 271
teeth
breed standard, 252
brushing, 168-170
chattering, 300
teething, 6
5 months, 92
juvenile period, 62
temperament
breed standard, 254
juvenile period, 45-46
temperature, taking, 64
tennis balls, 86, 146
testing
inheritance defects, 8-10
puppy testing, 18
toys, 30
tests
CGC (Canine Good Citizen),
266-268
hunting, 305-306
tetanus vaccination, 95
therapy dogs, 311
Therapy Dogs International,
311
ticks
controlling, 67-68
preventing, 66-67
titers, 315
toenail clippers, 29
toenails
clipping, 15
treating torn, 260-261
trimming, 44, 45
toothbrushes, 29
toothpaste, 29

torn ACLs (anterior cruciate ligaments), 219

torn dewclaws, treating, 260-261

torn toenails, treating, 260-261

toys, 30
- balls, 30
- bumpers, 146
- creating interest, 30
- food-dispensing, 120-121, 144
- grabbing, 145
- knotted ropes, 30
- KONGs, 30
- plastic water bottles, 30
- rawhide, 30
- safe, 85-87
- stuffed animals, 30
- tennis balls, 146
- testing, 30
- toy boxes, 30
- travel, 297

tracking, 244-245

trainers, choosing, 34

training. *See also* obedience commands
- 3 months, 52
  - come command, 56
  - crate, 55
  - family rules, 53-54
  - housetraining, 54
  - kindness, 53
  - limitations, 55
- 4 months, 76
  - down command, 79-81
  - family participation, 80
  - handling collar, 84-85
  - housetraining, 84
  - leash walking, 81-84
  - puppy class enrollment, 76-78
  - sit command, 78-79
- 5 months, 108
  - catching, 116-117
  - decreasing treats, 110-111
  - down-stay command, 113-114
  - introducing stairs, 114-115
  - name usage, 109
  - recall, 115-116
  - reinforcing rules, 109-110
  - sit-stay command, 111-113
  - stay command, 111-112
- 6 months, 146
  - automatic sit, 150
  - come command, 147
  - down command, 147
  - give command, 147
  - leave it command, 150-151
  - obedience classes, 149-150
  - off command, 147
  - okay command, 147
  - problems, 147-149
  - sit command, 147
  - stay command, 147
  - take it command, 147
  - walk command, 147
- 7 months, 179
  - cooperation, 181
  - easy tricks, 183-184
  - practice, 179-181
  - retrieving, 181-182
  - wait command, 173
- 8 months, 205
  - clicker, 208-209
  - control devices, 209-211
  - hyperactivity, 206
  - professional, 211-212
  - self-control, 206-208
- 9 months, 239
  - leash walking, 239-242
  - stand command, 242-243
  - watch me command, 242
- 10 months, 273
  - emergency drop, 273-274
  - off-leash control, 274-275
- 11 months, 302
  - field trials, 306
  - hunting tests, 305-306
  - rally and obedience competition, 302-305
- 12 months, 327-329
  - challenging mind, 243
  - challenging nose, 243-246
  - choosing treats, 263
  - housetraining, marking, 179
  - learning plateau, 148
  - repetitions, 148
  - snake avoidance, 190
  - travel, 295

transitional period, 5
- hygiene, 6
- response to light, 6
- socialization, 16
- weaning, 5

trauma, 128

travel, 297
- air, 292-294
- automobile, 292
- boarding, 299
- house sitters, 299-300
- kenneling, 297-298
- packing, 296-297
- pet sitters, 299
- pet-friendly accommodations, 294-295
- preparations, 295-296

treating injuries and illnesses, 255-262
- bleeding, 255-257
  - ears, 256
  - paws, 257
  - tails, 256
- broken limbs, 257
- burns, 258
- diarrhea, 261
- electrical shock, 259
- hot spots, 198-199
- imbedded fishhooks, 260
- insect bites/stings, 259-260
- limping, 217-219
- seizures, 261-262
- torn dewclaws, 260-261
- torn toenails, 260-261
- vomiting, 262

treats
- choosing, 135-136
- decreasing, 110-111
- fading, 150
- grabbing, 145
- training, 263

tricks, teaching, 183-184

tricuspid valve dysplasia (TVD), 9, 286
- testing, 9

trimming toenails, 44-45

TVD (tricuspid valve dysplasia), 9, 286

twizzles, 92-93

U

UKC (United Kennel Club), 305

upset stomach, 301

urine
   marking, 158, 178-179
   problems, 64
Utility class, 304

V

vaccinations
   3 months, 36-38
   12 months, 314-315
   AAHA guidelines, 314
   boosters, 65
   bordetella, 94
   coronavirus, 94
   final puppy, 94
   giardia, 95
   leptospirosis, 95
   Lyme disease, 95
   rattlesnake venom, 95
   tetanus, 95
   titers, 315
   waiting for reactions, 38
veterinarians. *See also* health
   annual checkups, 315-316
   choosing, 33
   first appointment, 38
   health certificates, 295
   health records, 35-36
   holistic, 220-223
   licensing, 221
   reasons to visit, 63-65
   vaccination reactions, 38
veterinary behaviorists, 212
vitamins, 41
   supplements, 289
   toxicity, 321
vocal discovery, 76. *See also*
   barking
vomeronasal organ (Jacobson's
   organ), 220
vomiting, 63
   treating, 262

W-X

wait command, 173
walk command, 147
walks
   daily, 326
   leash, 81-84, 239-242
   socialization, 104-105

watch me command, 242
water bottles, toys, 30
WCs (Working Certificates),
   305
weaning, 5, 15
weight
   6 months, 125
   at birth, 3
   monitoring, 98
Weimaraners, mixes, 22
whelping boxes, 4
whipworm, 38
white spots, chest, 93
whole foods, 290
whole grains, 40
winter
   grooming needs, 231
   safety hazards, 193-194
withers, 252
wood-burning stoves, screening
   off, 32
Working Certificates (WCs),
   305

Y

yards, puppy-proofing, 32-33
yawning, 126, 300
yellow Labrador Retrievers, 21

Z

zinc deficiency, 321
zippers, 93
zoonotic diseases, 95